German-English Translation
Texts on Politics and Economics

Deutsch-englische Übersetzungsübungen
Lehrbuch mit Texten über Politik und Wirtschaft

Von

John Desmond Gallagher
Lehrbeauftragter
an der
Universität Münster

Vierte Auflage

R. Oldenbourg Verlag München Wien

Die Deutsche Bibliothek - CIP-Einheitsaufnahme

Gallagher, John Desmond:
German-English translation : texts on politics and economics =
Deutsch-englische Übersetzungsübungen / von John Desmond
Gallagher. - 4. Aufl. - München ; Wien : Oldenbourg, 1996

ISBN 3-486-23729-2

© 1996 R. Oldenbourg Verlag GmbH, München

Das Werk einschließlich aller Abbildungen ist urheberrechtlich geschützt. Jede Verwertung außerhalb der Grenzen des Urheberrechtsgesetzes ist ohne Zustimmung des Verlages unzulässig und strafbar. Das gilt insbesondere für Vervielfältigungen, Übersetzungen, Mikroverfilmungen und die Einspeicherung und Bearbeitung in elektronischen Systemen.

Gesamtherstellung: R. Oldenbourg Graphische Betriebe GmbH, München

ISBN 3-486-23729-2

Was man auch von der Unzulänglichkeit des Übersetzens sagen mag, so ist und bleibt es doch eins der wichtigsten und würdigsten Geschäfte in dem allgemeinen Weltwesen.

                                      Goethe to Carlyle, 20 July 1827

Contents

Foreword 7

Translation Problems and Processes 12
Text I: Vor seinem Amtsantritt 34
Text II: Sie gelten als intelligent. 48
Text III: Weiter an der kurzen Leine 94
Text IV: Konjunkturprognosen 114
Text V: Das (. . .) Währungssystem 144
Text VI: Antizyklische Haushaltspolitik 160
Text VII: Beschäftigung 178
Text VIII: Europa-Parlament lehnt EG-Haushalt ab 198

Bibliography 240

Glossary of Technical Terms 253

German Word Index 260

English Word Index 263

Subject Index 271

FOREWORD

> To see what is general in what is particular and what is permanent in what is transitory is the aim of scientific thought.
>
> (A.N. Whitehead, *An Introduction to Mathematics*)

In recent years there has been a welcome move towards multidisciplinary studies and away from excessive specialization. The present volume is thus intended for the benefit of a large public comprising German students of English and English students of German, economists and sociologists, publicists and diplomats, political scientists and specialists in contemporary history, prospective interpreters and translators, professional linguists engaged in comparative research, and last but not least, general readers who may wish to study contemporary texts in order to keep abreast of the latest trends in German and English prose.

Two varieties of modern German are represented in this book: the language of newspaper reporting, and the language of economic science. The passages deal with topical subjects such as the politicoeconomic problems of the Third World, the legitimacy of strike campaigns, banks and credit, economic forecasting, the international monetary system, cyclical budgeting, the labour situation, and the internecine conflicts that have wreaked havoc within the European Economic Community. Texts I, II, III and IV were originally set by the Chamber of Commerce in Dortmund in examinations for interpreters and translators; texts V, VI and VII are from well-known textbooks for students of economics; and text VIII is from the *Frankfurter Allgemeine Zeitung*. As far as possible, the extracts have been arranged in approximate order of difficulty. Master translations have been printed opposite the original texts, and each translation is followed by a detailed commentary in the target language.

It is exceptionally interesting and instructive to translate newspaper articles, for modern languages are in constant flux, and it is especially in the press that they are renovated as in a perennial Fountain of Youth. Odd words and phrases keep cropping up in the columns of our newspapers: colloquialisms and vulgarisms, learned and foreign words, racy provincialisms and musty archaisms, together with a sprinkling of barbarisms that are sometimes amusing and often perplexing. The language of journalism is the language of the future, for new words and turns of phrase currently used in the press eventually pass into common use. Vast numbers of journalistic coinages are incorporated in the literary language, so that after a few years or a few decades lexicographers have no choice but to accord them official status in standard reference books.

Academic prose has certain features in common with the language of journalism. Both scholars and journalists exert a decisive formative influence on language; they are wont to use neologisms; and they have a natural proclivity to subordinate aesthetic considerations to the diffusion and appraisal of factual knowledge. They are often faulted for crossing the dividing-line between legitimate abstraction and pompous inflation, but in many cases they manage to reach a commendably high standard of acceptability in their writings.

It is no light task to make a perfect translation of a newspaper article or a piece of academic prose. As late as 1963, German-English lexicography was in a truly parlous state, and even today researchers have much leeway to make up, despite the epoch-making publication of *Langenscheidt's Encyclopedic Dictionary of the English and*

German Languages and the first three volumes of the *Oxford-Harrap Standard German-English Dictionary,* to say nothing of the countless smaller works of reference which have been brought out in recent years in order to meet the ever-increasing need for up-to-date lexicographical literature in this field of knowledge.

In many cases the translator finds little help from the dictionaries, grammars and stylistic reference books at present on the market. Owing to the constantly changing nature of language, even the best works of reference are always inevitably somewhat out of date; and the compilation of such books is fraught with such formidable difficulties that even the most efficient computers are often of little avail.

Thus, whether he likes it or not, the translator must often carry out gruelling, time-consuming comparative researches into the literature on the subject matter of his source texts; time and again, the exhausted translator is obliged to waste hours cudgelling his brains in an attempt to solve one of those knotty problems that the compilers of reference books are wont to fudge or slur over.

My chief aim in writing this book has been to remedy some of the aforementioned deficiencies by filling in gaps in the dictionaries, grammars and stylistic reference books that are in current use. The notes are not exhaustive, but they should go some way to helping the reader to solve a good many thorny translation-problems and to make sense of at least part of the bewildering mosaic of contemporary linguistic phenomena. As far as possible, I have avoided needlessly detailed discussion of the esoteric ramifications of unconscionably recondite theories.

Linguists are apt to stress the subjective aspects of translation, and it is beyond doubt that intuition plays a large part in translation work, as in every kind of artistic creation, and indeed in every kind of scientific research. Strictly speaking, the meaning of a word is always contextual, and the context in which a word is used is both verbal and situational, both linguistic and extralinguistic. Logic may enable us to determine the meaning of a word with reference to its immediate verbal context, yet only intuition can enable us to interpret a word correctly with reference to the wider communicative situation in which it occurs. It is only through intuition that we can ascertain the relations between spoken or written signs and their referents in the physical world or the world of ideas, and it is only through intuition that we can discover exactly how a sentence is related to its 'deep structure'. Specialists in computational linguistics have come to realize the virtual impossibility of providing a computer with all the necessary operational instructions for the successful interpretation of the utterances in an unprocessed connected text; and it is doubtful whether anyone will succeed in working out a universally applicable algorithm for deciding how the surface structures of contextually restricted sentences are related to their deep structures. In view of these immense difficulties, it is hardly surprising that most research programmes concerned with mechanical translation have been acknowledged as nugatory and abandoned; and it would obviously be invidious to compare the human translator's customary function to the rôle commonly assigned to language translation computers.

Nevertheless, one should be wary of overestimating the importance of intuition in translation work. It would be a grievous mistake to imagine that there are virtually no bounds to the translator's freedom. As Louis Kelly puts it, 'intuition has to be rooted in knowledge, and knowledge guided by intuition'.[1] The choice of words, phrases and sentence structures is not simply a matter of individual taste. Non-artistic language is a 'code that stands outside and above the individual user, unalterable by individual

---

[1] L. G. Kelly, *The True Interpreter* (Blackwell, Oxford, 1979), p. 119.

volition'.[2] Research in the field of generative grammar has confirmed this truth and has shown that a great many linguistic phenomena are amenable to rigorous logical analysis and experimental manipulation; and specialists in applied linguistics have benefited enormously from the spin-offs of theoretical studies bearing on problems such as commutation or selectional restrictions.

In my commentaries I have therefore made a detailed analysis of the various processes by which I arrived at the solutions given in the master translations. In some sections I have attempted to establish rewriting rules and collocational rules. The reader will find that there is a certain amount of inevitable overlapping in the explanatory notes, and a number of entries have been cross-referenced to each other with a view to avoiding pointless repetition.

The variants given in the boxes have been italicized in order to obviate misunderstandings as far as possible. However, the reader will do well to keep the commentaries constantly before his attention when consulting the lists of alternatives. In order to avoid undue expenditure of space, I have sometimes omitted combinatory variants which the reader can reasonably be expected to work out on his own. Sentence 7 in text II is a case in point. Eight equivalents of the syntagma *ein Flugzeug benutzt* have been combined with the plural subjects *people* and *those who,* while only one equivalent of *ein Flugzeug benutzt* has been combined with the singular subjects *anyone* and *whoever.* It stands to reason that all eight equivalents of *ein Flugzeug benutzt* can be combined with *anyone* and *whoever.*

Broadly speaking, formal correspondence between German and English is much less common than is generally assumed. This means that literal translation is possible only on rare occasions. The translator often has to cope with formidable difficulties when he is obliged to render a neologism, recast a whole sentence or rearrange material within a processing unit comprising several closely interlocked complex statements. Such work is frequently beset with uncertainties which can be eliminated only by a meticulous and systematic comparison of source language texts and target language texts dealing with similar or identical subject matter. In my commentaries I have therefore endeavoured to clear up doubts by showing usage with authentic material drawn from a wide range of sources: newspapers, periodicals, and books on all kinds of subjects. Each quotation has been provided with a bibliographical reference. The illustrative contextual examples may be examined in conjunction with the master translations or studied separately as a guide to contemporary usage. The reader will observe that nowadays the dividing lines between the various types of literary and non-literary prose are no longer as clear-cut as they used to be.

In the section entitled 'Translation Problems and Processes' I have summarized the principal problems associated with German-English translation and suggested various ways of tackling such difficulties.

The bibliography is fairly comprehensive, yet far from exhaustive. A full bibliography of scholarly writings on the subject matter of this volume would demand a book in itself. To make reading as easy as possible, I have provided a glossary of linguistic terms at the end of the book. Technical terms that are adequately explained in the text have been omitted, and so have linguistic terms of general currency such as *noun, verb* or *adverb.* In many cases the definitions have been deliberately simplified.

---

[2] Graham Hough, in M. Bradbury/D. Palmer (edd.), *Contemporary Criticism* (Arnold, London, 1970), p. 39.

I have also compiled a subject index and two word indexes with a view to bringing together material that is dispersed throughout the volume. *German-English Translation* can therefore be used both as a workbook and as a supplement to general works of reference.

The relationship between linguistics and translation work calls for a few remarks, especially since I have made liberal use of linguistic terminology in my commentaries. If we are to believe Jörn Albrecht, it is by no means essential that the translator should be an expert in linguistics.[3] This is doubtless true, particularly since professional linguists tend to be over-fond of useless and protracted disputations, and since they sometimes turn out jejune lucubrations which are as devoid of practical interest as the metaphysical speculations of ulemas.

Nevertheless, generative grammar, as it was elaborated between 1960 and 1965 by Noam Chomsky and the linguists of the Massachusetts Institute of Technology, has given us fresh insights into the nature of human language, providing essential criteria for a redefinition of such concepts as grammaticality, acceptability or idiomaticity, and enabling us to determine more precisely the infinitely complex patterns in which words may be arranged.

Stratificational grammar, which is an offshoot of transformational-generative analysis, has also made a valuable contribution to applied linguistics.[4] Sydney Lamb and H. A. Gleason, Jr., the fuglemen of the stratificational approach, have shown how semantic and syntactic structures may be determined to a certain extent by phonological factors; and stratificational studies will no doubt prove to be highly germinative as theoretical principles spread out in ever-widening circles of practical application.

Several brilliant French linguists have applied Saussurean[5] principles to translation-problems, thereby bringing a myriad of basic concepts into sharper focus and laying the groundwork for the pragmatic study of translation-processes. The thought-provoking works of A. Malblanc[6], J. P. Vinay and J. Darbelnet[7] are considerably more readable than most works on applied linguistics, and their terminology is admirably clear and practical.

Books and articles on translation theory and practice have multiplied with remarkable fertility in recent years[8]. Some of the most notable work in this field has been accomplished by J. C. Catford and L. G. Kelly. Catford's very short but thoroughly stimulating volume entitled *A Linguistic Theory of Translation* (first published in 1965) is strongly influenced by the London school of J. R. Firth, while Kelly's elaborate book *The True Interpreter* (published in 1979) is an impressively erudite and ingenious attempt to synthesize in an historical perspective the various principles enunciated by Catford, Vinay, Darbelnet and many other eminent theorists in translation research. Most of the specialized words employed in the present work have been drawn from contemporary linguistic studies, but I have not found it necessary to break entirely with

---

[3] Cf. J. Albrecht, *Linguistik und Übersetzung* (Niemeyer, Tübingen, 1973), p. 92.

[4] For bibliographical information, see T. Lewandowski, *Linguistisches Wörterbuch* (Quelle & Meyer, Heidelberg, 1980), s. v. Stratifikationsgrammatik.

[5] The great Swiss linguist, Ferdinand de Saussure (1857–1913), pioneered linguistic structuralism and the separation of scientific language description from historical philological studies. His main ideas are expounded in his posthumous *Cours de linguistique générale* (Payot, Paris, 1980).

[6] A. Malblanc, *Stylistique comparée du français et de l'allemand* (Didier, Paris, 1968).

[7] J. P. Vinay/J. Darbelnet, *Stylistique comparée du français et de l'anglais* (Didier, Paris, 1971).

[8] For bibliographical details, the reader is referred to Volker Kapp (ed.), *Übersetzer und Dolmetscher* (Quelle & Meyer, Heidelberg, 1974) and Werner Koller, *Einführung in die Übersetzungswissenschaft* (Quelle & Meyer, Heidelberg, 1979).

the classical tradition, and I have used the terms of Graeco-Roman rhetoric wherever they seemed appropriate.

The aforementioned spate of publications on the science of translation has shown that there is unceasing cross-fertilization between theoretical and applied linguistics. This being so, I feel that the translator ought to have at least a nodding acquaintance with linguistics. The acquisition of such knowledge should not be considered as an end in itself, but rather as a means of developing a more rational and methodical approach to practical translation work. Linguistic science has dissipated a host of popular misconceptions about language, and it can act as a hone to sharpen the translator's traditional tools.

It only remains for me to express my appreciation to Mr Martin Weigert for his helpful advice on the choice of the texts and for his expert handling of my intricate printing problems. I hope that my book will afford the reader pleasure as well as profit.

John Desmond Gallagher

Translation Problems and Processes

As has already been pointed out in the foreword, German-English translation is beset by many pitfalls. In this introductory section, I wish to draw attention to some of the most troublesome problems and suggest various ways of solving them. In the brief space of a single chapter, it is of course materially impossible to deal with the issues fully. I can do no more than sketch the outlines of the problems, putting individual practical difficulties into a broader context and supplying a theoretical underpinning for the arguments and explanations advanced in the commentaries.

The most prolific sources of difficulty may be brought under four main heads:
I) divergences between the lexical encoding systems
II) divergences between the syntactical systems
III) divergences between the stylistic systems
IV) the lack of universally accepted standards

I) Divergences between the lexical encoding systems

Language and culture are mutually influential and mutually interdependent. It follows therefore that cultural differences between German- and English-speaking communities are generally reflected in their linguistic systems. German and English language communities have evolved separate systems for structuring their worlds conceptually. Single distinct expressions are used to classify discrete objective or subjective phenomena which the members of the speech community believe to be important; and a very little consideration shows that distinctions which are made in one speech community may appear culturally irrelevant to the members of another group. Thus the translator is often confronted with the problem of filling so-called semantic gaps in the vocabulary of the target language.

Good examples of this are provided by vocables relating to culture-specific institutions, e.g. *Konkurstabelle, Reptilienfonds, Studienprofessor, Habilitationsschrift, Büttenrede, official receiver, trustee in bankruptcy, coroner, honour school, Mods, Greats, tripos, wrangler* (at Cambridge University), *fellowship* (in an educational context), *sophomore, Serjeant-at-Arms, Private Members' Bill, Supply days, decasualization, closed shop,* or *"Little Neddies"*.

In such cases, the editors of bilingual dictionaries normally have no alternative to indicating approximate correspondences between German and English institutions or offering windy explanatory phrases which the translator cannot use in a continuous context.

There are also special cases where semantic gaps are due to taxonomical divergencies which cannot be accounted for by reference to institutional differences. The relationship between the generic terms *Gemüse* and *vegetables* is a case in point. *Gemüse* is often translated as *vegetables*, and vice versa. Strictly speaking, however, *Gemüse* and *vegetables* cannot be placed in one-to-one correspondence. In English, *potatoes* is a hyponym of *vegetables*, whereas in German *potatoes* are not included among *Gemüse*. Thus the phrase *Gemüse und Kartoffeln* sounds perfectly natural in German, while **vegetables and potatoes* sounds absurd in English.

The problems arising from divergencies between the lexical encoding systems of German and English cannot be blinked away, but some of them will probably disappear in the course of time. The German and English language communities frequently impinge on each other, and English has an exceptional capacity for assimilating foreign vocabulary in 'language contact' situations. It is therefore hardly surprising that many gaps in the lexical system of English are gradually being filled in through cultural borrowing as nationalistic barriers are torn down and Great Britain and other members of the European Community draw closer together. For example, until quite recently, the British had no word for *Teigwaren*. In the 1958 edition of *Cassell's German and English Dictionary*, *Teigwaren* is rendered as *farinaceous products*. This term has never been in common use since *farinaceous* is a learned word which is unfamiliar to the rank and file of the nation. Besides, *farinaceous foods* (or *products*) may include bread and potatoes as well as *Teigwaren*. In the 1961 supplement to *Harrap's Standard French and English Dictionary*, the French term *pâtes (d'Italie)* is glossed as 'noodles, spaghetti, etc.', and in Lew Moore's *Dictionary of Foreign Dining Terms* (published in 1958), the Italian term *pasta* is explained as 'paste or spread; specifically, products made from dough or flour, egg and water'. In the meantime, the British have acquired a taste for exotic foods hitherto little known in the U. K.; new words have been imported by the bushel along with the new products, and the English now refer to *Teigwaren* as *pasta* or *pasta products*. The former term has already been recorded in several dictionaries and is offered as a translation equivalent of *pasta asciutta* in the 1979 edition of the *Italian Phrase Book* published by Penguin Books Ltd. The more technical term (*pasta products*) has not yet found its way into the dictionaries, though it is used quite often in academic publications. Here is a typical example taken from Dennis Swann's *Competition and Consumer Protection* (p. 286):

This (. . .) specifies that various canned and bottled foods, oils, jams, jellies, coffee, beer, cereals, pastry mixes, dry pasta products, pet foods, paper products and detergents be clearly labelled, not only with the total sales price, but also with the price per measure.

It should also be noted that Italian terms for specific varieties of pasta have already become firmly established in the English language. One of the latest additions to the vocabulary is *tortellini: a plate of tortellini* (*Time*, 12. 11. 1979, p. 67).

Borrowings from other languages such as Spanish and Greek are also on the increase. The Spanish term *paella*, for instance, was put into currency in British English as early as 1929, but it did not become more generally known in the British Isles until the sixties; and with the greatly increased numbers of British visitors to Greece, culinary terms such as *avgolemono* are now gradually nosing their way into the English language. *Avgolemono* (σούπα αὐγολέμονο) has not yet been recorded in the dictionaries. It is a kind of egg and lemon soup. An example of this new word may be found in Iris Murdoch's novel *An Accidental Man* (first published in 1971), p. 404:

Guess who we saw down by the Piraeus tucking into their avgolemono?

For further information on the divergencies between the lexical encoding systems of English and German, the reader is referred to Ernst Leisi, *Der Wortinhalt*, and Wolf Friederich, *Technik des Übersetzens* (especially pp. 20−29 and pp. 41−42).

II) Divergences between the syntactical systems

We may distinguish two basic types of syntactical divergence between the languages under description:
1) German and English exhibit similar structural patterns, but these patterns are put to different uses in each language.
2) Certain structural patterns are peculiar to one of the languages under description.

Let us consider a few examples of type (1):

(a) main clause + sub clause introduced by a subordinator such as *daß/that* or *wenn/if:*
(i) (. . .) wir werden kämpfen, und wir hoffen, daß die Bevölkerung uns das honoriert, (J. F. Page (ed.), *Penguin German Reader,* p. 77.)
We'll put up a fight, and we hope that the people will pay tribute to us for our efforts.
(ii) Es kann sein, daß er schon heute kommt. (*LEW,* s.v. können.)
Maybe he will even come today. (*ibid.*)
(iii) *Dorle H.* (. . .) ist bereit, auf die Barrikaden zu gehen, wenn ihr jemand die persönliche Freiheit nehmen will. (J. F. Page (ed.), *Penguin German Reader,* p. 73.)
Dorle H. is prepared to mount the barricades if anyone tries to deprive her of her individual liberty.
(iv) Die Mutter hätte es lieber gesehen, wenn das aufgeweckte Mädchen in Modejournalen geblättert hätte, statt die Notstandsgesetze zu diskutieren. (J. F. Page (ed.), *Penguin German Reader,* p. 71.)
The mother would have preferred the quick-witted girl to browse among fashion magazines instead of discussing the emergency laws.

In sentences (i) and (iii) there is little likelihood of error on the part of the translator since similar structural patterns are here used in the same way in both languages. In the other sentences, however, the translator may encounter difficulties since there is a considerable degree of divergence between the corresponding structural patterns of German and English. Sentence (ii) shows that two German clauses (main clause + *daß*-clause) may sometimes be rendered as a single English clause, and (iv) shows that a German *wenn*-clause may correspond to an accusative with infinitive construction in English.

It may not be amiss to add that the anticipatory *es*-construction in (ii) might be rendered by an anticipatory *it*-construction, though this kind of quasi-verbatim rendering of the introductory clause would result in a sentence of debatable acceptability. In sentence (iv), of course, formal structural equivalence is quite impossible. Nonetheless, there are many borderline cases in which a *wenn*-clause may be rendered in an equally acceptable manner through formal or dynamic equivalence, e. g.

Es wäre gut, wenn der Deutschlehrer seine Schüler dazu anhielte, stenographieren zu lernen. (E. Essen, *Methodik des Deutschunterrichts,* p. 190.)
The German teacher would do well to[1] encourage his pupils to learn shorthand (*Var.*: It would be a good thing if the German teacher were to encourage his pupils to learn shorthand.)

(b) Existential sentences:

Existential and pseudo-existential sentences are common in both the languages under consideration, and in a great many cases *es gibt* may be rendered as *there is/are*. However, it would be a gross error to assume that there is a complete formal match between the two systems. *There is/are* is much more frequent in English than *es gibt* is in German. The English surface structure *there is (are, has been,* etc.) + [noun phrase] corresponds to a wide range of deep structures, and the translator is bound to make mistakes unless he is aware of these underlying structures. For reasons of space it is not possible to analyze all the German equivalents of the *there is* construction and all the English equivalents of *es gibt,* but the following batch of examples should give the reader some idea of the astonishing diversity of these equivalents:

---

[1] Cf. M. J. Moroney, *Facts from Figures* (p. 4): 'In reading what follows, the reader will do well to keep Fig. 1 constantly before his attention.'

Es gibt keine nationalen Schranken (...). (F. J. Raddatz, *ZEIT-Bibliothek der 100 Bücher*, p. 8.)	There are no national barriers.
Es gab und gibt britische Unterdrückung, Ausbeutung, die koloniale Situation (*Plus*, 1. 4. 1981, p. 20.)	There has been and still is British oppression and exploitation, and the colonial situation has been and still is a reality.
Die schönsten Fresken dieser Art gibt es in den Kirchen *Sainte Christine* von *Campoloro* (bei *Cervione*), *Saint Thomas* (bei *Castello di Rostino*) in *San Nicolao* und in der Friedhofskirche von *Sermano* (*Bozia*). (H. Lajta, *Korsika*, p. 11.)	The finest frescoes of this kind are to be found in the churches of *Sainte Christine* at *Campoloro* (near *Cervione*) and *Saint Thomas* (near *Castello di Rostino*) in *San Nicolao* as well as in the cemetery church at *Sermano* (*Bozia*).
Gestern gab es Nudeln und Rindfleisch. (E. Kästner, *Drei Männer im Schnee*, p. 1.)	Yesterday we had noodles and beef.
„Dann lügt eben die Zeitung", meinte Frau Kunkel. „Das soll es geben." (ibid., p. 5.)	"Then what the newspaper says is simply a lie", said Mrs. Kunkel. "Such things are said to happen."
So etwas gibt's wirklich. (*ibid.*, p. 90.)	There really are such things. (*Var.*: Such things really do exist.)
Aber das gibt's doch gar nicht. (*ibid.*, p. 76.)	But such a thing is simply impossible. (*Var.*: But such a thing simply isn't done.)
Was es so alles gibt! (*ibid.*, pp. 29, 57.)	Of all things! (*Var.*: What all doesn't a person come across in this world! *or* Well, I never!)
Es gibt dich nicht mehr. (H. Böll, *Erzählungen, Hörspiele, Aufsätze*, p. 260.)	You no longer exist.
Es waren noch ein anderes Paar da und zwei elegant gekleidete jüngere Männer, die mit dem Barkeeper redeten. (D. Wellershoff, *Die Sirene*, p. 204.)	There was another couple, and two smartly dressed youngish men who were engaged in conversation with the bartender.
(...) und da waren Türen mit Emailleschildchen (...). (H. Böll, *Wanderer, kommst du nach Spa...*, p. 35.)	(...) and there were doors with enamel nameplates (...).
Auf dem Tische standen Becher. (A. Döblin, *Hamlet*, p. 69.)	On the table there were some goblets.
Eine kalte Sonne stand über den Schneefeldern. (D. Wellershoff, *Die Sirene*, p. 122.)	There was a frosty sun above the snowfields.
Ein großer Strauß Seidenblumen steckte darin. (*ibid.*, p. 129.)	There was a big bunch of silk flowers in it.
Ein Spiegel hing an der Wand. (H. Böll, *Wanderer, kommst du nach Spa...*, p. 23.)	There was a mirror on the wall.

Nicht einmal ein Schrank ist da. (E. Kästner, *Drei Männer im Schnee*, p. 51.)	There isn't even a wardrobe.
Und für einen Ofen ist kein Platz. (*ibid.*, p. 39.)	And there's no room for a stove.
Und wieder steht eine alte Frau an einer Kirche. (A. Döblin, *Hamlet*, p. 121.)	And once more there is an old woman standing by a church.
Hier fehlt ein Knopf. (*GPB*, p. 126.)	There's a button missing.[2]
Noch immer fluten Menschen vorbei. (A. Döblin, *Hamlet*, p. 121.)	There are still people surging past.
Weiter ist nichts zu sehen. (*Plus*, 1. 4. 1981, p. 20.)	There is nothing else to be seen.
Die Strömung ist hier sehr stark. (*GPB*, p. 144.)	There's a strong current here.
Fährt ein Bus zum Strand? (*ibid.*, p. 143.)	Is there a bus to the beach?
Fährt ein Zug nach . . . durch?[3]	Is there a through train to . . .?
Hat der Zug einen Speisewagen? (*GPB*, p. 50.)	Is there a restaurant car on the train?
Ein Pfund hat zwanzig Schillinge. (*O-HSG-ED*, s.v. haben.)	There are twenty shillings in a pound.
Muß man Zuschlag bezahlen? (*GPB*, p. 49.)	Is there a supplementary charge?
Kann man unter Wasser fischen? (*GPB*, p. 145.)	Is there any underwater fishing?
Wir waren vier. (G. Benn, *Doppelleben*, p. 68.)	There were four of us.
Ich verliere Benzin/Öl. (*GPB*, p. 65.)	There's a petrol/an oil leak.
Hier stimmt doch etwas nicht. (E. Kästner, *Drei Männer im Schnee*, p. 141.)	There's something wrong here.
Da stimmt etwas nicht. (*ibid.*, p. 146.)	There's something wrong.
Ist etwas nicht in Ordnung mit dem Vertrag? (D. Wellershoff, *Die Bittgänger/Die Schatten*, p. 29.)	Is there something wrong with the contract?
Auf der ‚Todesstrecke' (. . .) reißt die Unglücksserie nicht ab. (*Die Welt am Sonntag*, 6. 7. 1958.)	There is no end to the chapter of accidents on the 'death circuit' (. . .).
Die Preise ziehen stark an. (*O-HSG-ED*, s.v. anziehen.)	There is a sharp advance in prices.
Es riecht bereits nach Kaffee. (T. Sternheim, *Sackgassen*, p. 192.)	There's already a smell of coffee.
Es klappert/quietscht. (*GPB*, p. 65.)	There's a rattle/squeak.
Im Lager seiner Gegner (. . .) kam es bald zu Kompetenzstreitigkeiten (. . .). Cicero, *Staatsreden* I, ed. H. Kasten.)	In his opponents' camp there were soon clashes of authority.

---

[2] Cf. R. Quirk et al., *GCE*, p. 961.

[3] The word-order in the example given in *GPB* (p. 51) is unusual.

An verschiedenen Orten kam es zu Tätlichkeiten zwischen arbeitswilligen Schaffnern und Streikposten. (*Die Welt am Sonntag*, 21. 7. 1957.)	In several places there was fighting (*or* fighting broke out) between blackleg bus conductors and pickets.
Dabei kam es zu Zwischenfällen (*ibid.*)	There were some ugly incidents.[4]
Derzeit wagt er sich kaum aus seinem Zimmer, besonders wenn geschossen wird. (*Plus*, 1. 4. 1981, p. 21.)	At present he hardly ever ventures out of his lodgings, especially when there is shooting.
Es ist ein Unglück passiert. (*Langenscheidts Sprachführer Neugriechisch*, p. 44.)	There has been an accident.
Es läuft ein Hochgebirgsfilm. (E. Kästner, *Drei Männer im Schnee*, pp. 11–12.)	There's a mountaineering film on (at the cinema).
Es fehlt jede Spur. (E. Kästner, *Die verschwundene Miniatur*, p. 19.)	There is not a trace.
Es herrsche Mangel an Personal, Medikamenten und sogar an Reinigungsmitteln. (*Süddeutsche Zeitung*, 9. 4. 1981, p. 9.)	There is a shortage of staff, medicine and even detergents.
Es meldet sich niemand. (*GPB*, p. 135.)	There's no reply.

Now let us consider a few examples of the second type of divergence referred to at the beginning of this section: structural patterns which are peculiar to one of the languages under description:

(a) German attributive constructions

Complex attributive phrases often have to be rendered as postqualifiers. Cf. the following examples from a legal text:

Den im Rahmen des § 1 Abs. 2 oder im Auftrag der dort genannten Personen oder Stellen bei der Datenverarbeitung beschäftigten Personen ist untersagt, geschützte, personenbezogene Daten unbefugt zu einem anderen als dem zur jeweiligen rechtmäßigen Aufgabenerfüllung gehörenden Zweck zu verarbeiten, bekanntzugeben, zugänglich zu machen oder sonst zu nutzen. (*Gesetz zum Schutz vor Mißbrauch personenbezogener Daten bei der Datenverarbeitung*, p. 20.)
Persons engaged in data processing and referred to in Section 1 (2) or acting on behalf of the persons or establishments referred to therein shall not, without authorization, process, communicate, grant access to or otherwise use protected personal data for any purpose other than that of the legitimate accomplishment of their task. (*ibid.*, p. 21.)

In this excerpt all the complex attributive phrases are based on participles (*genannten, beschäftigten, gehörenden*). It should, however, be noted that there are also complex attributive phrases based on adverbials. In the following example, the adverbial *bis dahin* has to be expanded into an English relative clause:

---

[4] In English the impersonal use of *come* is generally restricted to *if*-clauses. Cf. the following examples from A.T.Q. Stewart, *The Ulster Crisis*:
He knew that, if it came to a collision between the Army and Ulster, the U.V.F. would quickly be overwhelmed (. . .). (p. 166.)
He wished to make it perfectly clear that if rebellion came the Government would put it down, and if it came to civil war they would do their best to win the war. (pp. 214–215.)
There is also a fixed expression that belongs to this category: *if the worst comes to the worst* (= wenn alle Stricke reißen).

Das Bier verlor dadurch seinen bis dahin bitteren Geschmack.
Thanks to this, the beer lost the bitter taste it had had hitherto. (Cf. C.V.J. Russ (ed.), *Contrastive Aspects of English and German*, p. 25.)

For further information on the translation of German attributive phrases, the reader is referred to H. F. Eggeling, *A Dictionary of Modern German Prose Usage*, s.v. participle (past), and W. Friederich, *Technik des Übersetzens*, pp. 72–76.

(b) German impersonal constructions

The impersonal use of verbs has a much wider application in German than in English. There is a good example of the impersonal use of the verb *untersagen* in the legal text cited in the preceding section. The anticipatory *es* has been dropped because of the inverted word-order. Here are some other examples of German impersonal constructions which have no exact counterparts in English:

(i) Mir ist geraten worden, von meiner Forderung abzustehen. (H. F. Eggeling, *A Dictionary of Modern German Prose Usage*, s.v. impersonal verbs.)
I have been advised to waive my claim. (*ibid.*)
(ii) Die Schule erfuhr davon, und gleich hieß es im Lehrerzimmer: ‚Die haben schon wieder eine Schweinerei vor!' (J. F. Page (ed.), *Penguin German Reader*, pp. 103–104.)
This became known at the school, and immediately the word went round in the staff room: "Those kids are planning another piece of obscenity!"
(iii) In dem Tanzlokal ging es hoch her. (E. Kästner, *Die verschwundene Miniatur*, p. 84.)
In the dance hall everybody was having a great time.
(iv) An den Tischen, in den Logen und Nischen ging es immer lustiger zu. (E. Kästner, *Die verschwundene Miniatur*, p. 90.)
At the tables, and in the booths and alcoves the general gaiety was working up to a climax.
(v) In manchen Ecken ging es zärtlich zu. (E. Kästner, *Die verschwundene Miniatur*, p. 93.)
In some recesses couples became amorous.
(vi) Worauf kam es ihm bei seinem Artikel an? (E. Essen, *Methodik des Deutschunterrichts*, p. 191.)
What was his aim in writing[5] the article?
(vii) Es ist ein Bundesbeauftragter für den Datenschutz zu bestellen. (*Gesetz zum Schutz vor Mißbrauch personenbezogener Daten bei der Datenverarbeitung*, p. 40.)
A federal commissary for data protection shall be appointed (. . .). (*ibid.*, p. 41.)
(viii) Es wurde getanzt. (P. Grebe (ed.), *Duden Grammatik*, § 107.)
There was dancing.

For further details, see H. F. Eggeling, *A Dictionary of Modern German Prose Usage*, svv. impersonal verbs, es ist, es sind.

c) Negation

German does not always signal the scope of negation in the same way as English, so that the translator is sometimes obliged to shift the focus of negation in order to avoid misunderstandings. Shifting the focus of negation may entail (i) an intra-clausal transfer, (ii) an inter-clausal transfer, (iii) a shift from subordination to coordination or vice versa, (iv) the substitution of a positive expression for a negative one or vice versa (modulation).

---

[5] For a good example of this construction, cp. A. J. Hagger, *Inflation: Theory and Policy*, p. ix: 'My aim in writing this book has been to produce an undergraduate text that would be suitable both for specialist courses in the economics of inflation and for general courses in macroeconomics which emphasise inflation, as many now do.'

(i) Intra-clausal transfers

The focus of negation may be shifted from a noun object to the verb which governs it, e.g.

Ich dulde keinen Widerspruch. (G. Collier/B. Shields, *Guided German-English Translation*, p. 74.)
I won't stand for backchat. (*ibid.*)

This kind of transfer is particularly common in cases where a verb governs more than one object. German asyndetic constructions often have to be rendered syndetically. German uses two different negative words (*nicht* and *kein*), or simply repeats the negative determiner *kein* before each object. In English, however, such devices are rare except in highly rhetorical style. As a rule, the conjunction *or* is inserted to carry over the scope of negation from one word-group to another. Examples:

Er mag den Sommer nicht, überhaupt keinen Zustand der Gegenwärtigkeit (. . .). (M. Frisch, *Stiller*, p. 252.)
He does not like the summer, or any state of immediacy, for that matter (. . .). (G. Collier/B. Shields, *Guided German-English Translation*, p. 97.)
Ich sehe auch keine versteinerten Engel, es tut mir leid; auch keine Dämonen, ich sehe, was ich sehe (. . .). (M. Frisch, *Homo faber*, p. 28.)
And I can't see any petrified angels – I'm sorry – or demons; I can see what I can see.
Eugen Löbl hat nicht aufgemuckt gegen die Machtergreifung vom Februar 1948, hat sich nicht gerührt bei Jan Masaryks Fenstersturz. (K. Löw, *Warum fasziniert der Kommunismus?*, p. 306.)
Eugen Löbl did not jib at the seizure of power in February 1948 or say anything about the defenestration of Jan Masaryk.[6]

There are also special cases in which the focus of negation has to be shifted from the object to the subject. In German a subject such as *alles* is often followed by a negative construction, but in English a subject which contains one of the 'universal' items *all*, *any* or *every* tends to attract the negative element more strongly than the verb or the object[7]:

(. . .) Alles andere mache ihm keinen Eindruck (. . .). (M. Frisch, *Homo faber*, p. 10.)
(. . .) nothing else would make him sit up and take notice (. . .).

Expressions such as *once* also attract the focus of negation. In the following example, *once* (*ein einziges Mal*) has to be negated (*not once*) and moved from mid-position to front-position:

Kein Schriftsteller im Lande hat ein einziges Mal während der fünf Jahre seiner Diktatur etwas veröffentlichen können. (G. Collier/B. Shields, *Guided German-English Translation*, p. 74.)
Not once during the five years of his dictatorship was a writer able to publish anything.

(ii) Inter-clausal transfers

In English the negative is frequently transferred from a subordinate *that*-clause to the main clause. This kind of transferred negation is limited to verbs of belief or assumption such as *think, believe, suppose* or *expect*. Cf. R. Quirk et al., *GCE*, § 11.79. Examples:

Aber ich denke, sie können nicht ganz verloren sein. (R. Hinton Thomas, *Der Schriftsteller Dieter Wellershoff*, p. 167.)
But I don't think they can be quite lost.

---

[6] The periphrastic genitive is preferable to the inflected genitive in this case. Cf. E. M. Foster, *Aspects of the Novel*, p. 110: 'the defenestration of Noaks'.
[7] Cf. R. Quirk et al., *GCE*, § 7.51; O. Jespersen, *Essentials of English Grammar*, § 28.2_1.

Ich denke, wir werden nicht immer in der Stadt in einem schmutzigen Winkel in der Finsternis sitzen wollen. (A. Döblin, *Wallenstein*, p. 181.)
I don't think we'll always be prepared to sit in the dark in a filthy corner of the town.

(iii) Subordination and coordination

In English there is a special kind of negative sentence in which two infinitive phrases are governed by the periphrastic auxiliary *do,* and in which only the second infinitive phrase falls within the scope of negation. Consider the following example cited by J. T. M. Burnett in C. V. J. Russ, *Contrastive Aspects of English and German* (p. 184):

He doesn't wash the car and put it in the garage straightaway.

Both infinitive groups seem to lie within the scope of the negation, but in fact the negation applies only to the second group. The sentence may therefore be paraphrased as follows: 'He washes his car, but he does not put it in the garage immediately afterwards'. The type of syndetic coordination exemplified in the original English sentence cannot be reproduced in a German translation since in standard written German the use of the dummy operator *tun* is restricted to constructions of the type *Lieben tue ich ihn gerade nicht, aber . . . (Duden Grammatik,* § 1041). The translator has therefore no alternative but to render the English coordinate construction by means of subordination:

Wenn er seinen Wagen gewaschen hat, stellt er ihn nicht sofort in die Garage.

Now consider the following sentence:

He doesn't wrap it up and hand it to you over the counter.

This sentence seems to belong to the same type as the example we have just discussed. In this case, however, both infinitive groups lie outside the scope of the negation.[8] The negation applies to an idea which is implicit in the statement and which might be rendered by the adverbial *simply*. I should explicate the sentence as follows: 'He does not simply wrap up an article and hand it to the customer over the counter. He does much more than this. He has a chat with the customer and offers him advice, etc.' In German these ideas can be rendered by means of a main clause followed by a relative clause:

Er gehört nicht zu den Verkäufern, die einfach eine Ware einwickeln und über die Theke reichen.

(iv) The modulation of a negative statement to a positive one

One of the commonest focus-shifting processes is the substitution of a positive expression for a negative one or vice versa. In the following example the negative expression *Erreicht . . . nicht* has been rendered in positive terms (*is less than*):

Erreicht der Wert einer Sacheinlage im Zeitpunkt der Anmeldung der Gesellschaft zur Eintragung in das Handelsregister nicht den Betrag der dafür übernommenen Stammeinlage, hat der Gesellschafter in Höhe des Fehlbetrags eine Einlage in Geld zu leisten. (R. Mueller/B. W. Meister/M. H. Heidenhain, *The German GmbH-Law,* p. 56.)

---

[8] Mr Burnett believes that 'it is possible to take the domain of negation as covering the 1st and 2nd infinitive phrase' (C.V.J. Russ, *op. cit.*, p. 184). I think this is unlikely. The shop assistant or shopkeeper may serve his customers in a very friendly and informal manner, but he will no doubt wrap up the goods he sells, and he will certainly not refuse to hand them to the buyers. Mr Burnett has made no attempt to translate his example sentences into German. The translations given here are mine.

It may not be amiss to add that all the negative sentences belonging to the category under discussion are general statements about combinatorial aspects of various habitual actions. This remark may help linguists to identify the category in question more easily.

If, at the time of the application of the company for registration in the commercial register, the value of a non-cash contribution is less than the amount of the share capital contribution subscribed to in consideration thereof, then the shareholder shall pay a contribution in cash to the amount of the difference.[9]

d) Ellipsis

Certain forms of ellipsis are peculiar to German:

(i) Ellipsis of the subject

An impersonal passive construction of the type *Es wird gebaut* is transformed into a so-called 'plain-predicate clause'[10] when an adverbial occupies front-position. Thus *Es wird gebaut* becomes *Überall wird gebaut, Hier wird gebaut,* etc. Translation is relatively easy when the verb whose subject has been ellipted is a verb of saying or deciding. In such cases an anticipatory *it* is inserted and the sentence is realigned in accordance with the principles of English word-order:

In verantwortlichen Kreisen in Paris wird darauf hingewiesen, daß . . . (W. Friederich, *Technik des Übersetzens,* p. 97.)
It is pointed out in responsible quarters in Paris that . . . (*ibid.*)

However, the translator has to resort to augmentation and transposition when confronted with a clause such as the following:

(. .) in dem Bemühen, den britischen Nettobeitrag zum EG-Budget zu eliminieren, wurde gestümpert. (*Die Zeit,* 29. 2. 1980, p. 17.)
Gross blunders were made in the course of the negotiations conducted with a view to eliminating Britain's net contribution to the EEC-budget.

(ii) Ellipsis of the object

In German the direct object is frequently ellipted after verbs such as *anregen, verlocken* or *zwingen*. In a good many cases one can simply leave the preposition *zu* untranslated and render the German phrase almost verbatim. Thus *zur Diskussion anregen* is *to stimulate discussion,*[11] *zu Spekulationen verlocken* is *to encourage speculation,* and *zum Arbeitsplatzwechsel verlocken* is *to encourage job-hopping.* Examples:

Die angerissenen Problemkreise sind durchaus aktuell und regen zur Diskussion an. (K. E. Schuhmacher (ed.), *English—A World Language,* p. 3.)
The complexes of problems raised in this book are quite topical and should stimulate discussion.
Schon geringe Lohnunterschiede (. . .) verlocken zum Arbeitsplatzwechsel. (D. Hamblock/D. Wessels, *Englisch in Wirtschaft und Handel: Übersetzungstexte,* p. 21.)
Even minor wage differentials (. . .) encourage job-hopping.[12]

There are, however, special cases in which it may be advisable to resort to transposition, e.g.

---

[9] I have followed the translation proposed by Mueller, Meister and Heidenhain (*op. cit.*, p. 57), but I have changed *in the amount of the difference* to *to the amount of the difference*.

[10] Cf. H. J. Kufner, *The Grammatical Structures of English and German,* pp. 8, 12; W. Friederich, *Technik des Übersetzens,* pp. 97—99.

[11] For an example of this collocation, cp. T. Conway (ed.), *Ireland and its Problems,* p. 5: 'Further discussion on themes related to the text should be stimulated by these questions and provocative statements.'

[12] My translation is quite different from the solution given in D. Hamblock/D. Wessels, *Englisch in Wirtschaft und Handel: Übersetzungstexte — Lösungen* (p. 21).

Die Preise bleiben im Prinzip eingefroren, es sei denn, daß unvermeidliche Kostensteigerungen zu Erhöhungen zwingen. (D. Hamblock/D. Wessels, *Englisch in Wirtschaft und Handel: Übersetzungstexte*, p. 17.)
In principle, prices will remain frozen unless unavoidable cost increases render higher prices necessary.[13]

(iii) Ellipsis of the verb

In German, verbs of movement are often ellipted after modal auxiliaries, e.g.

Er will heute nach Frankfurt. (P. Grebe (ed.), *Duden Grammatik der deutschen Gegenwartssprache*, § 1170.)
He wants to go to Frankfurt today.

The ellipsis of *geschieht es* after *vielleicht* is a rather special case. German students of English should note that the subordinator *that* is never used after *perhaps* or *maybe*:

Vielleicht, daß er noch heute eintrifft. (P. Grebe, *op. cit.*, § 1170.)
Perhaps (*or* Maybe) he'll arrive today.

(iv) Ellipsis of an introductory head clause

In German it is possible to ellipt an introductory head clause before an interrogative or exclamatory sub clause:

[Ich frage mich,] Ob er glücklich ist. (P. Grebe, *op. cit.*, § 1170.)
I wonder if he's happy.
[Ich verlange,] Daß du mir die Wahrheit sagst! (*ibid.*)
Out with it!

In the first example, ellipsis is quite impossible in English. In the second example, however, ellipsis is used in both languages. In German, an entire clause is omitted, and in English the first element of the phrasal verb *come out with* (= utter, say, tell) is ellipted.

III) Divergences between the stylistic systems

Scholars who generalize about stylistic divergences between various languages are apt to end up floundering in a morass of contradictions. Nonetheless, divergences do exist, and some attempt must be made to define them.

The principal stylistic divergences may be brought under the following heads: (1) sentence movement; (2) levels of formality; (3) condensation.

1) Sentence movement

A very little consideration shows that German and English have fundamentally different ways of operating. German, like Latin or Greek, is a free-word-order language in which the 'comment' frequently precedes the 'topic'. English, like French, is a fixed-word-order language in which the 'topic' normally precedes the 'comment'. Examples:

Mit Springer und seinen Blättern legt man sich nicht gerne an. (J. F. Page (ed.), *Penguin German Reader*, p. 161.)
People don't like to get on the wrong side of Springer and his papers.
Automatisch wird das Jahressteuersoll errechnet (. . .). (*ibid.*, p. 198.)
The tax due for the year is calculated automatically (. . .).

---

[13] The solution proposed by Hamblock and Wessels (*op. cit.*, p. 17) is of doubtful acceptability.

Regiert wird der Inselstaat seit der Unabhängigkeit von einer Partei der Neger und Negermischlinge (. . .). (D. Hamblock/D. Wessels, *Englisch in Wirtschaft und Handel: Übersetzungstexte,* p. 17.)
Since its independence, the island state has been governed by a party of negroes and negroid half-castes (. . .).

In English it is occasionally possible to bring the direct object into prominence by moving it to the beginning of the sentence, as in the following example from Graham Green, *A Gun for Sale* (p. 8):
The suitcase and the automatic he was to leave behind.

In general, however, English offers relatively little scope for the spectacular types of dislocation and inversion that are characteristic of modern German. For statistical data, the reader is referred to O. Jespersen, *Growth and Structure of the English Language,* p. 10.

If one descends from the sentence level to the phrase level, the divergences between German and English are somewhat less apparent since in both languages the adjective nearly always stands before its noun. However, even in this domain there are important differences between English and German word-order. As we have already seen, lengthy German attributive phrases often have to be translated into English as postqualifiers; and the same is true for a considerable number of German compound adjectives which cannot be rendered as single words in English. The adjective *abschöpfungspflichtig* is a case in point:
die Einfuhr abschöpfungspflichtiger Gegenstände (J. Meyer-Landrut/F.G. Miller/G. F. Thoma, *Umsatzsteuergesetz 1980,* p. 120.)
the importation of objects subject to entry levies[14] (*ibid.,* p. 121.)

There are also significant divergences between the principles governing the order of attributive adjectives in English and German. In English, for example, adjectives of age generally precede adjectives of colour or material[15] (e.g. *an old red hat, an old wooden chair*), but they do not normally precede adjectives denoting other qualities (size, moral characteristics, prosperity, sartorial elegance, state of preservation, etc.). German usage often differs from English usage in this respect. Examples:
ein alter wohlgekleideter Mann (T. Storm, *Immensee,* p. 1.)
a well-dressed old man
junge, fröhliche, kunstbeflissene Burschen (J. Schillemeit (ed.), *Interpretationen: Deutsche Erzählungen von Wieland bis Kafka,* p. 317.)
cheerful young fellows who were keenly interested in art
in der alten verlassenen Gerberei (A. Andersch, *Sansibar oder der letzte Grund,* p. 27.)
in the derelict old tannery
einen alten, rostigen Schoner (*ibid.,* p. 39.)
a rusty old schooner

In both languages, however, the 'expected' order may be reversed for reasons of euphony, emphasis, or implied relationship between the adjectives and their head word:
an old lonely untidy man (G. Greene, *A Gun for Sale,* p. 8.)
ein alter, einsamer, unordentlicher Mann
eine vornehme alte Dame (T. Mann, *Sämtliche Erzählungen,* p. 162.)
a distinguished old lady

---

[14] The word-group 'subject to entry levies' is a reduced relative clause.
[15] Cf. D.Crystal, *Linguistics,* pp. 128–141; G. W. Turner, *Stylistics,* pp. 82–85.

eine hübsche junge Frau (A. Andersch, *Sansibar oder der letzte Grund*, p. 35.)
a good-looking young woman
ein hagerer junger Mann (U. Broich/J. Martin (edd.), *Deutsche Übersetzungstexte für englische Übungen*, p. 114.)
a rawboned young man

Both in English and in German, adjective order is often determined by the extent to which constructs such as *old man* or *junge Frau* are considered as lexical units. In this problem area the divergences between the languages under description are most evident when the head noun denotes an inanimate object.

Special attention must also be paid to the principles governing clause-arrangement in German and English. Embedding is very common in both languages, but the dominant patterns of clause interrelationship are quite different.

Let us consider two examples of complex sentences in which clauses have been combined in such a way as to build up a sense of anticipatory tension which is not resolved until the end of the statement:

Innumerable studies of young offenders have gone to show that whilst the mentally subnormal person is by no means predestined to be an offender, he is less fitted to stand up to strains. (W. Friederich, *Technik des Übersetzens*, p. 10.)
Unzählige Untersuchungen von Jugendlichen, die mit dem Gesetz in Konflikt geraten sind, haben hinreichend erwiesen, daß es für einen Minderbegabten zwar keineswegs vorbestimmt ist, daß er Gesetze übertritt; Belastungen zu widerstehen ist er aber weniger gut gerüstet. (*ibid.*).
Die Kreditinstitute haben, sofern hierfür nach anderen gesetzlichen Vorschriften nicht eine kürzere Frist vorgesehen ist, in den ersten drei Monaten des Geschäftsjahres für das vergangene Geschäftsjahr die Jahresbilanz und die Gewinn- und Verlustrechnung (Jahresabschluß) aufzustellen (. . .). (H. Schneider/H.-J. Hellwig/ D. J. Kingsman, *Das Bankwesen in Deutschland*, p. 108.)
Unless other statutory provisions prescribe a shorter period, banking institutions shall within the first three months of the business year prepare the annual balance sheet and profit and loss statement ("annual financial statements") for the preceding business year (. . .). (*ibid.*, p. 109.)

In English, as in Latin, two sub clauses are often combined in such a way that two subordinating conjunctions are juxtaposed, e. g. *that whilst, that if* or *that when*. This kind of embedding is acceptable in English but unacceptable in German.

In German, a sub clause is often inserted between an auxiliary (*haben* or *sein*) and a dependent infinitive group. This kind of embedding is acceptable in German but unacceptable in English.

Finally, it should be noted that English shows a marked predilection for 'push-down' clauses containing verbs of saying, thinking or knowing. Examples:

Jenny: Julian, is that you?
Julian: Who did you think it was? (C. H. Jaffé, *Englisch für alle Fälle*, p. 17.)
Jenny: Julian, bist du das?
Julian: Wer hätt's denn sonst sein sollen?
What do you think we ought to do?. (*ibid.*, p. 77.)
Was sollen wir tun?[16]

This type of clause is not unknown in German, but it is much less common than in English. Cf. the following example from a Volkswagen advertisement reprinted in J. F. Page (ed.), *Penguin German Reader* (pp. 143–144):

Was glauben Sie, warum seit neuestem auch der neue Porsche mit einer solchen Wahl-Automatic geliefert wird?

---

[16] Cf. Dürrenmatt/Andersch/von Doderer/Broch, *Erzählungen*, p. 48. Jaffé's translation (*Was, glauben Sie, sollen wir tun?*) is too literal.

Why do you think the new Porsche has also been quite recently made available with this kind of automatic gear selector?

2) Levels of formality

Two diametrically opposed tendencies may be observed in both the languages under description: a trend towards formality, and a trend towards informality.

In the German language community the trend towards formality is most apparent in academic publications and in quality papers such as the *Frankfurter Allgemeine Zeitung,* while the trend towards informality is most apparent in the popular press and in the controversial news magazine *Der Spiegel.*[17] The language of legal documents is still understandably ultraconservative (in the non-political sense), but it has already been modernised to such an extent that contemporary legal instruments drafted in German are often more readable than their English counterparts.[18] Commercial German has also been pruned and adapted to present-day needs, and most self-respecting business houses see to it that their letters are no longer couched in the dry and turgid formulae of nineteenth-century commercialese.[19]

In the English-speaking world the picture is rather different. Here, the trend towards overblown formality is most evident in legal and administrative documents and in erudite publications spawned by defence experts, technologists, scientists, sociologists and economists. There are, however, significant differences between the dominant trends in the U.S.A. and the United Kingdom. Broadly speaking, American jurists, administrators and academics tend to affect a more ponderous style than their British counterparts, and the baleful influence of American 'gobbledygook' has already come under attack on both sides of the Atlantic.[20]

In the English-speaking countries the trend towards informality is most pronounced in broadcasting, in newspaper reporting, and in academic publications written by scholars who have specialized in the more traditional branches of learning, or who have sufficient taste and intelligence to realize that good ideas are most effective when presented in a language untrammelled by verbiage.

An interesting article on the use of English in broadcasting recently appeared in *World and Press* (1st March issue 1981, p. 2). The author of the article admits that there is a growing trend towards informality in BBC broadcasts, but he reassures his readers that the resultant 'deterioration' is 'not enough to worry about'.

It is a remarkable fact that even highbrow newspapers and magazines such as *The Times,* the *Financial Times* and *The Economist* now extend a wide hospitality to words and expressions which were once confined to slang and familiar conversation: *wowser* (*The Times* of 9 April 1981, p. 14), *wampum* in the sense of *money* (*ibid.*), *rejigging* in the sense of *rearrangement* (*The Times* of 1 April 1981, p. 19), *to sell someone down the river* (*Financial Times* of 2 April 1981, p. 2), *to turf out* (*The Economist* of 4–10 April 1981, p. 13), *gung-ho* (*The Economist* of 15–21 August 1981, p. 21). One is constantly reminded of the colloquialisms that throng the columns of *Der Spiegel*: *Klitsche* (*Der*

---

[17] Cf. B. Carstensen, *Spiegel-Wörter, Spiegel-Worte.*
[18] For examples, see A. Lane/R. Catrice, *Internationales Formularbuch,* or R. Mueller/B. Meister/M. H. Heidenhain, *The German GmbH-Law.*
[19] For typical examples of modern commercial German, see W. Mannekeller, *So schreibt man Geschäftsbriefe!*
[20] Cf. E. Gowers, *The Complete Plain Words,* pp. 270–273; E. Newman, 'Language on the Skids', in *Reader's Digest* (December 1979), pp. 41–45.

Spiegel of 13 October 1980, p. 133), *vergrätzen* (6. 10. 1980, p. 22), *Mätzchen* (15. 9. 1980, p. 14), *Knast-Urlaub* (8. 9. 1980, p. 22), *Schnüffelei* (*ibid.*, p. 25).

This general trend towards greater informality is sometimes deplored by purists and *Kulturpessimisten,* but most people agree that the spread of everyday conversational language ought to be welcomed. Informality is not synonymous with vulgarity, nor is formality synonymous with gentility. Anyone who believes that culture is at a low ebb, or who has serious misgivings about the present trend towards informality in written prose, should read the books of contemporary authors such as Randolph Quirk, Brian Foster or John Ardagh. These writers have succeeded in producing a new kind of pellucid speech-based English in which the conflicting claims of informality and literary elegance have been reconciled. Their prose has some of the finest qualities of traditional oratory, yet it moves with the easy and unselfconscious flow of informal discussion. It is a pleasure to read.

3) Condensation

There is a curious similarity between latter-day technological advances and some recent linguistic trends in the 'new industrial state'. Just as the technologist endeavours to streamline industrial methods and products, so the language-user endeavours to streamline syntax. Never have appearances been so deceptive, for reality is now as complex as appearances are simple. Making all due allowance, we may liken many of our new syntactic forms to the chips that are used to store information in the brains of industrial robots.

Both in German and in English there is a marked tendency to condense information to the utmost, and this trend is particularly evident in scientific and journalistic publications. The miniaturization of complex linguistic structures is achieved by means of various devices: (i) the substitution of abstract nouns for verbs; (ii) long strings of compounds; (iii) convoluted syntax with internested assemblies of themes and rhemes.

(i) The substitution of abstract nouns for verbs

Consider the following examples:

The National Taxpayers Union, a feisty new citizens' lobby, took up the cause, and by April 1979 convention-call resolutions had been passed by 30 states. (*RD*, August 1979, pp. 95–96.)

Diese Ausbreitung der technischen Zivilisation und der mit ihr verbundenen Lebenseinstellung hat zugleich an lang tradierte Vorurteile gerührt, die aus dem Hochmut der Kulturen mit hoher Werkzeugbeherrschung den sogenannten primitiven oder barbarischen Völkern gegenüber herrühren. (*Universitas*, February 1981, p. 116.)

In the example sentence from *Reader's Digest,* the abstract compound *convention-call resolution* is a condensed form of the noun-verb phrase *resolution calling for a constitutional convention.* Cf. the following sentence taken from the same article (p. 95):

A few months later, Representative Halbrook got the Mississippi state legislature to pass a resolution calling for a constitutional convention[21].

In the example from *Universitas,* the abstract noun *Werkzeugbeherrschung* has a fairly complex underlying structure. The word sequence *Kulturen mit hoher Werkzeug-*

---

[21] A constitutional convention is a formal assembly at which amendments to the U. S. constitution may be proposed and discussed. Cf. Article V of the U.S. constitution. *Constitutional convention* has been rendered as *verfassunggebende Versammlung* in G. Haensch's *Wörterbuch der internationalen Beziehungen und der Politik.*

beherrschung could be expanded as follows: *Kulturen, die über gediegene Spezialkenntnisse und Erfahrungen technischer Art verfügen.* For further information on the use of abstract words, the reader is referred to E. Gowers, *The Complete Plain Words*, pp. 132−135, and A. Bach, *Geschichte der deutschen Sprache*, pp. 331−2, 343.

(ii) Long strings of compounds

Long strings of nominal compounds are particularly common in headlines. A very good example is quoted in G. W.Turner's *Stylistics* (p. 88):

Post Office Pay Dispute Inquiry Chairman Named (*The Times*, 25. 3. 1971.)

Owing to the paucity of inflexional endings in English, this type of sequence occurs somewhat more frequently in English than in German. In both languages, however, nominal condensation is often carried a stage further with the aid of acronyms (*Buchstabenwörter*) and clipped words (*Abkürzungswörter*) such as *BGB* (*Bürgerliches Gesetzbuch*), *L.D.C.* (*less developed country*), *Sozi* (*Sozialist*) or *divi* (*dividend*). Acronyms and clipped words are often combined with sequences of compounds, so that a headline may contain almost as much information as a medium-length paragraph written in a more relaxed and conventional style. Our newspaper headlines faithfully reflect the breathless haste and bustle of modern life.

(iii) Convoluted syntax

German academic and journalistic prose is often hard to read because sentences are stuffed with information until they burst at the seams. Consider the following example:

Wie kann man es sich erklären, daß ausgerechnet im freigebliebenen Teil Deutschlands, dessen Parteientradition mit so hohen Hypotheken belastet war, sich die, im Vergleich mit allen anderen westlichen Demokratien mit Einschluß der Vereinigten Staaten von Amerika wohl stabilste, krisenresistenteste, im Grunde problemfreieste Parteiendemokratie freiheitlichen Zuschnitts hat entwickeln können? (R. Rodenstock et al., *Freiheitsräume in der Industriegesellschaft*, p. 105.)

The Latinate arch construction of the *daß*-clause is a major obstacle to smooth reading; and a further impediment is constituted by the ponderous nominal groups: the adverbial group built up around the head word *Teil*, and the subject group built up around the head word *Parteiendemokratie*. Such constructions may be compatible with the inscrutable genius of the German language, but they are quite incompatible with the genius of contemporary English.

In general, the English prefer loosely-jointed, speech-based sentence-structures. The excessive latinity which so often mars German prose is comparatively rare in Britain [22], though a number of journalists and academics have recently manifested a disquieting tendency to replace post-modified nominal groups by heavily pre-modified ones [23].

IV) The lack of universally accepted standards

The lack of universally accepted standards is a common source of confusion in German-speaking countries as well as in the English-speaking world. Every German- or English-speaking country has its own linguistic peculiarities, and translators often find it hard to decide which forms they ought to use. Words, phrases and constructions that are in common use in Switzerland and Austria may be considered incorrect in central and north Germany, and similar problems arise in connection with the numerous varieties

---

[22] Cf. I. A. Gordon, *The Movement of English Prose*, pp. 153−167.

[23] Cf. R. Quirk, *The Use of English*, 172−174; G. W. Turner, *Stylistics*, pp. 87−88.

of English which are spoken outside England. In my translations and commentaries I have presented the two most important varieties — British and American English, but for practical reasons I have made no systematic attempt to analyse the countless divergences between them. A full discussion of this prickly issue would go beyond the scope of the present volume. For further information, the reader is referred to the following publications: H. F. Eggeling, *A Dictionary of Modern German Prose Usage*, pp. v–viii; A. Bach, *Geschichte der deutschen Sprache*, pp. 345–347; K. Wächtler, *Geographie und Stratifikation der englischen Sprache*; K. E. Schuhmacher (ed.), *English — A World Language*; T. Pyles, *The Origins and Development of the English Language*, pp. 229–274; R. Quirk et al., *A Grammar of Contemporary English*, pp. 16–19; R. Quirk, *The Use of English*, pp. 84–102; P. Hanks (ed.), *Collins English Dictionary*, pp. xxiii–xxx; B. Foster, *The Changing English Language*, pp. 17–75; H. Pilch, *Empirical Linguistics*, pp. 162–163; P. Strevens, *British and American English*; G. J. Forgue, *Les mots américains*; G. J. Forgue/Raven I. Mc David, Jr., *La langue des Américains*; H. W. Horwill, *Modern American Usage*; N. Moss, *What's the Difference?*

This chapter would be incomplete without a brief systematic survey of the principal processes involved in translation. These processes may be classified as follows:

I) Borrowing

Gaps in the resources of the target language are often filled by borrowing. Cf. the use of *Chip*[24] in German or *Prokurist* in English:

Menschenleere Montagestraßen: Die Arbeit verrichten von Chips gesteuerte Roboter (*Plus*, 1. 4. 1981, p. 10.)

The most far-reaching commercial employee-agency is that of the *Prokurist* (sections 48–53 *HGB*). (E. J. Cohn (ed.), *Manual of German Law*, Vol. II, p. 13.)

Sometimes the borrowing is accompanied by an explanatory phrase or an approximate target-language equivalent:

The year 1947 saw the adoption of what has become known as the *Kahlschlag* ('clean sweep') policy: a return to honesty of language, based on popular non-literary usage, and to honesty of theme, based on personal experience. (R. Newnham (ed.), *German Short Stories* I, p. 8.)

II) Calquing

Calquing is the adoption by the target language of a phrase or compound word whose components are literal translations of the components of a corresponding phrase or compound in the source language. *Jumbo-Rat, Killersatellit, Rüstungskontrollverhandlungen* and *Substitutionskonto* are recent calques (or 'loan translations') which have not yet found their way into the dictionaries. Examples:

Jumbo-Rat: jumbo council
„Jumbo-Ministerrat" ist in der EG das neue magische Stichwort, dessen Erwähnung vielen ausreichend scheint, den Einstieg in den Ausstieg aus den wirtschaftlichen Schwierigkeiten am Horizont auftauchen zu sehen. Die Bezeichnung „Jumbo-Rat" steht jetzt für eine gemeinsame Tagung der Wirtschafts-, Finanz- und Arbeitsminister der zehn Länder. (*HB*, 10./11. 4. 1981, p. 2.)

---

[24] In English the adjective *electronic* is often added in order to preclude gastronomical associations. Cf. the following quotation from *The Economist* (4–10 April 1981), p. 75: 'American chipmakers last year cried foul against Japan for subsidising research on electronic chips.'

(...) a "jumbo council meeting" will achieve little unless it agrees that the fundamentals of Community organisation should be tackled in order to make industry as important a subject in it as agriculture. (*Financial Times*, 2. 4. 1981, p. 15.)
They would surely form a fitting part of the agenda for this "jumbo council". (*ibid.*)

Killersatellit: killer satellite
Die Amerikaner sehen im Shuttle eine Gegenwaffe zu den 19 Killersatelliten der Sowjets, die so konstruiert sind, daß sie andere Raumflugkörper zerstören können. (*Süddeutsche Zeitung*, 9. 4. 1981, p. 3.)
Senior officers in the American air force's space programme gloomily list Russia's "firsts" in space: an unmanned satellite; a manned spacecraft; a manned space station; and an anti-satellite (or killer satellite). (*The Economist*, 4.–10. 4. 1981, p. 95.)

Rüstungskontrollverhandlungen: arms control negotiations
Mehr als vier Monate sind jetzt verstrichen, seit die amerikanisch-sowjetischen Gespräche über Rüstungskontrollverhandlungen und insbesondere das NATO-Angebot dazu vom Dezember 1979 in Genf aufgenommen wurden. (*HB*, 2. 4. 1981, p. 2.)
(...) there is (...) no question of delaying arms control negotiations on theatre nuclear forces while the new American proposals on strategic arms limitation (Salt) are being worked out. (*The Times*, 1. 4. 1981, p. 6.)

Substitutionskonto: substitution account
Einigung über das Substitutionskonto (*F.A.Z.*, 3. 10. 1979, p. 14.)
The International Monetary Fund tonight edged gingerly and imprecisely toward future adoption of a "substitution account" that might ultimately take some pressure off the U.S. dollar in foreign exchange markets. (*I.H.T.*, 2. 10. 1979, p. 9.)

Recent English idioms such as *to put someone into the picture* (= to bring someone up to date with the essential information) and *I wouldn't know* (= I don't really know) may also be regarded as loan translations. *To put someone into the picture* is presumably of German provenance, since the expression *jemanden ins Bild setzen* is used in exactly the same way[25]; and *I wouldn't know* is apparently modelled on *ich wüßte nicht* (a common example of the subjunctive of modest assertion)[26]. Such locutions often slip into English by way of third-rate translations[27].

III) Literal translation[28]

Some linguists make a distinction between *word-for-word translation* and *literal translation*[29]. Throughout my commentaries, however, I have used these terms interchangeably to denote exact word-word, group-group, clause-clause or full sentence-equivalence. In this particular section, the term *literal translation* is used to denote a form of translation in which it is unnecessary to resort to lexical or structural 'normalisations' in order to produce a grammatically and stylistically acceptable target text. This kind of translation is perforce rare. Here is an example from D. Stein, *Theoretische Grundlagen der Übersetzungswissenschaft* (p. 11):

Wilss (1977: 7) umschreibt die Situation treffend wie folgt (...).
Wilss (1977: 7) describes the situation pertinently as follows.

---

[25] Cf. B. Foster, *The Changing English Language*, p. 110.
[26] Cf. the following example from E. Kästner, *Georg und die Zwischenfälle*, p. 66: ‚Nun bin ich hier, und ich wüßte nicht, was ich Ihnen noch zu erzählen hätte.'
[27] Cf. B. Foster, *op. cit.*, p. 93.
[28] On the dispute about "free" versus "literal" translating, see W. Wilss (ed.), *Semiotik und Übersetzen*, p. 27.
[29] Cf. J. C. Catford, *A Linguistic Theory of Translation*, p. 26.

IV) Transposition

Transposition may be defined as a translation-process involving a shift of category or level. The following types may be distinguished:

1) Class-shifts

We may interchange various parts of speech without modifying their basic meaning. In the following example, the adjective *bedenklich* has been transposed to a noun (*worry*):

Was den Großstädten eitel Freude bereitet, stimmt die Landwirtschaft bedenklich (. . .). (J. F. Page (ed.), *Penguin German Reader*, p. 30.)
What brings sheer delight to the big cities is a source of worry to agriculture. (*ibid.*, p. 31.)

This kind of transposition may also be observed at the level of lexis. In the following example, the noun *Industrie* corresponds to the adjective *industrial*:

Industrieroboter: industrial robot
Zu der Teilrationalisierung des Fertigungsablaufes mit Hilfe dieses Sondermaschinenbaues kamen in jüngster Zeit Großaufträge für Industrieroboter aus dem Bereich der Automobilindustrie sowie der verstärkte Einsatz von verketteten Fertigungs- und Montagelinien. (*HB*, 1. 4. 1981, TL, p. V.)
The number of industrial robots in use in the United States has more than doubled in the past nine years, to 3500. (*RD*, May 1980, p. 156.)

There is also a special kind of class-shift known as *chassé-croisé*. In the following example, the verb *klettern* has been transposed to the adverb *upwards*, and the adverb *mit* has been transposed to the verb *follow*:

Die Löhne klettern mit.[30] (*Die Zeit*, 29. 2. 1980, p. 17.)

Wages are following it upwards.

2) Intra-system shifts

An intra-system shift is a translation operation involving a category-shift within a system, e.g. the substitution of a singular for a plural within the number system, the substitution of an active form for a passive form within the voice system, the substitution of a past tense for a present tense within the tense system, or the substitution of zero article for the definite article within the article system. Examples:

(. . .) die anderen Coupés dieses Wagens, wo man Zeitung las (. . .). (Dürrenmatt/Andersch/von Doderer/Broch, *Erzählungen*, p. 28.)
(. . .) the other compartments in the carriage where people were reading newspapers (. . .). (*ibid.*, p. 28.)

Gattungsware: generics
Kostensparenden Kauf von Gattungsware ("generics") möchte schon fast jeder zweite Konsument beim Shopping nicht mehr missen. (*Manager-Magazin*, Februar 1979, p. 56.)

---

[30] The last segment of the preceding sentence reads as follows: ‚(. . .) es gilt als sicher, daß die Rate sich noch etwas erhöhen wird, bevor sie wieder fällt.' Cp. J. D. Gallagher, *Cours de traduction allemand-français: textes politiques et économiques*, p. 134. For the English equivalent of *mitklettern*, cp. the following quotation from *The Times* (7 March 1980, p. 24): 'These tactics explain why minimum lending rate was in November 1979 raised above its anticipated value of 15–16 per cent, though not why market rates have subsequently followed it upwards'.

(...) unbesehen kann (...) nicht alles in den Papierkorb wandern. (D. Hamblock/D. Wessels, *Englisch in Wirtschaft und Handel: Übersetzungstexte*, p. 15)
not everything can be thrown into the waste-paper basket without inspection.
Der Generaldirektor der „Berolina" sprang entsetzt auf. „Was sagen Sie da?[31]. Erst seit einer halben Stunde? (...)" (E. Kästner, *Die verschwundene Miniatur*, p. 174.)
The managing director of the „Berolina" jumped up in horror. *"What* did you say?[32] Only for half an hour? (...)"
Was haben sie noch gesagt, als sie fortgingen?[33] (D. Wellershoff, *Die Bittgänger/Die Schatten*, p. 24.)
What else did they say when they were leaving?
Ziel des Bundesdatenschutzgesetzes ist der Schutz der Privatsphäre des Einzelnen. (*Gesetz zum Schutz vor Mißbrauch personenbezogener Daten bei der Datenverarbeitung*, p. 7.)
The aim of the West German Data Protection Law is to protect the privacy of individual persons.[34]

3) Structure-shifts

Structure shifts can be found at all ranks. For example, a structure-shift may occur at group rank when a German compound noun preceded by an adjective is rendered as [adjective] + [noun]. In such cases, a so-called 'bridge construction' may be used to separate the two adjectives. In the following example, *feelings of* has been inserted in order to separate two adjectives (*unadulterated* and *malicious*) which do not stand in the same relation to the head noun *glee*:
die reinste Schadenfreude: unadulterated feelings of malicious glee (cf. G. Collier/B. Shields, *Guided German-English Translation*, pp. 130, 141.)

Structure-shifts are particularly common at clause-rank. Examples:

Sie gingen, obschon die Tage kürzer zu werden begannen, noch regelmäßig jeden Abend in den Straßen ihres Viertels spazieren. (D. Clément/W. Thümmel, *Syntaxe de l'allemand standard*, p. 32.)
Although the days were beginning to draw in, they still strolled regularly through the streets of their district every evening.
What you don't understand is that (...). (H. M. Braem, *Übersetzer-Werkstatt*, p. 44.)
Bloß, Sie vergessen: (...). (*ibid.*, p. 45.)
Ich wüßte wohl, was zu tun wäre. (E. Kästner, *Georg und die Zwischenfälle*, p. 114.)
I think I know what to do.
(...) ich wüßte nicht, daß bis jetzt ihr architektonisches Bild durch die Unbilden des Luftkrieges irgendwelchen Schaden erlitten hätte (...). (T. Mann, *Doktor Faustus*, p. 50.)
As far as I know, its architectural profile has not as yet suffered any damage as a result of the ravages of air warfare.

---

[31] For another example of this tense usage, see T. Mann, *Buddenbrooks*, p. 407: ‚*Was* sagst du?'
[32] Cf. J. E. Mansion/R. P. L. Ledésert/M. Ledésert (edd.), *Harrap's New Standard French and English Dictionary*, Part 1, Vol. 1, p.v.: 'Our friends are no longer astonished to hear, "*What* did you say? I don't think we have that in our dictionary. Do you mind if I make a note of it in my little book?"'
[33] In the sub clause the preterite has evidently been used for reasons of euphony and aspect. Cf. J. Erben, *Abriß der deutschen Grammatik*, p. 55.
[34] The translation is mine. For the construction, cp. G. Bannock/R. E. Baxter/R. Rees, *The Penguin Dictionary of Economics*, p. 5: 'The general aim of this book is to provide a companion (...) to two sorts of users of economics.'

4) Inter-rank shifts[35]

An inter-rank shift is a translation operation involving a change of rank, i.e. the translation equivalent of a unit at one rank in the source language is a unit at a different rank in the target language. For example, a change in the sequence of elements in the structure of a German clause can fulfil the same function as the insertion of an adverbial in an English clause. Examples:

Petticoat Lane. It's certainly colourful. (C. H. Jaffé, *Englisch für alle Fälle*, p. 9.)
Petticoat Lane. Ja, bunt ist er.
He paid no less than twenty pounds. (O. Jespersen, *Essentials of English Grammar*, p. 301.)
Zwanzig Pfund hat er dafür gezahlt.

In the first example, inversion is used to render the adverb *certainly*, and in the second example inversion is used to render the phrase *no less than*, which expresses astonishment at the greatness of the amount paid.

5) Level-shifts

Level-shifts are shifts from grammar to lexis and vice versa. German bound morphemes (e.g. prefixes such as *er-*, *ent-* or *zer-*, or suffixes such as *-chen*) often correspond to complete words in English (prepositions, verbs or adjectives):

(Grenzen, *etc.*) *er*tasten: to grope *towards* (limits, *etc.*)
*ent*wesen: *to lose* essence, *become in*substantial
*zer*blättern: *to strip of* leaves
Däm*chen*: *little* lady

V) Modulation

A modulation is a translation mechanism involving a focus-shifting process. For example, a negative statement may be permuted to become a positive one, attention may be shifted from a cause to an effect, from the first person to the second person, from the abstract to the concrete, or from one image to another. Examples:

1) Positive/negative

Die Kletterei auf der Maschine war nicht ungefährlich. (Dürrenmatt/Andersch/von Doderer/ Broch, *Erzählungen*, p. 42.)
Climbing on to the engine like that was a pretty risky business. (*ibid.*, p. 43.)

2) Cause/effect

Rheinsalzvertrag: Rhine pollution treaty
In den Niederlanden herrscht Verärgerung darüber, daß Frankreich den Bonner „Rheinsalzvertrag" von 1972 nicht ratifiziert und auch keine Alternativmaßnahmen für die Senkung des Salzgehalts im Rheinwasser angeordnet hat. (*WN*, 12. 3. 1980.)
The Netherlands today recalled its ambassador to France in protest of the French government's decision to abandon the 1976 Rhine pollution treaty (. . .) (*IHT*, 5. 12. 1979, p. 4.)

3) 1st person/2nd person

But I don't hold out much hope. (C. H. Jaffé, *Englisch für alle Fälle*, p. 68.)
Aber versprechen Sie sich nicht zu viel davon.
„Sie wünschen?" fragte der Zugführer (. . .). (Dürrenmatt/Andersch/von Doderer/Broch, *Erzählungen*, p. 34.)
"Can I help you?" asked the guard (. . .). (*ibid.*, p. 35.)
Ich lasse von mir hören. (J. F. Page (ed.), *Penguin German Reader*, p. 133.)
You'll be hearing from me.

---

[35] I have coined this expression as a substitute for *unit-shift*, for *unit-shift*, as Catford himself admits (Catford, *op. cit.*, p. 79), is a very unsatisfactory term.

4) Abstract/concrete
Sein Vater läuft noch immer mit dem Bären herum, den wir ihm aufgebunden haben. (E. Kästner, *Georg und die Zwischenfälle*, p. 80.)
His father is still a victim of the hoax we played on him.

5) Shift of imagery
Wirtschaftskurs: general thrust of economic policy
Der Wirtschaftskurs ist zu schematisch (. . .). (*Die Zeit*, 29. 2. 1980, p. 17.)
The second point, the general thrust of economic policy, was at the centre of the dispute. (*The Times*, 9. 4. 1981, p. 1.)

VI) 'Equivalence'[36]
'Equivalence' is an extreme form of modulation involving the substitution of one institutionalized image for another. Most of these stock comparisons have been recorded in the dictionaries, e.g. *sie gleichen sich wie ein Ei dem anderen: they are as like as two peas*. For a detailed analysis of this type of fixed phrase, the reader is referred to K. D. Pilz, *Phraseologie*.

VII) Adaptation
Finally, there is an extreme form of 'equivalence' known as adaptation. The translator may have to resort to adaptation in order to render various forms of word-play. A good example may be found in *Der Spiegel* of 6 October 1980 (p. 150). The anti-Thatcher slogan *Ditch the bitch* has been rendered very freely as *Geht dem Flittchen ans Schlawittchen!*
The dividing lines between these various categories of translation shift are by no means clear-cut, and different kinds of translation operation are often combined within a word-group or sentence. Witness the following instance of modulated transposition (noun/verb, abstract/concrete):
Ein städtischer Bediensteter hatte an dem Deckenstück gerüttelt, um seine Haltbarkeit zu überprüfen. (*Süddeutsche Zeitung*, 9. 4. 1981, p. 1.)
A city official had prodded this part of the ceiling to see if it would hold.[37]

In this chapter, I have attempted to strike a balance between theory and practice, for theory and practice are mutually interdependent. The reader will do well to ponder Goethe's maxim: 'Das Höchste wäre zu begreifen, daß alles Faktische schon Theorie ist.'

---

[36] I have borrowed this term from Vinay and Darbelnet (*Stylistique comparée du français et de l'anglais*, p. 52.)

[37] Cf. *The Times* of 9 April 1981, p. 6: 'Later five policemen and a city official were badly injured when more of the ceiling, incautiously prodded by the official to see if it would hold, fell in on them.'

Text I*

Vor seinem Amtsantritt hatte Brasiliens neuer Präsident gelegentlich erklärt, er wolle das letzte militärische Staatsoberhaupt des Landes sein; wenn seine Amtszeit ablaufe, möchte er fünf oder sechs Parteien sehen, die das ganze Spektrum – „Kommunisten ausgenommen" – umfassen. In seiner Antrittsrede versprach er noch einmal die Rückkehr zur Demokratie.
Die Brasilianer, durch schlechte Erfahrungen gewitzt, haben ihre Zweifel. Denn diese Rückkehr zur Demokratie entspricht nicht einem Sinneswandel der Generäle, sondern der Einsicht, daß für den aufgestauten sozialen Unmut ein Ventil gefunden werden muß. Und da die finanziellen Forderungen der Arbeiter nicht erfüllt werden können, offeriert ihnen Brasilia einen „demokratischen" Ausgleich. Das brasilianische Modell, die verstärkte Industrialisierung des Landes mit Hilfe von Auslandskapital, erklärt seinen Konkurs in Raten.
Jahrelang mit Versprechen vertröstet, oft enttäuscht und ungeduldig geworden, steuert die Opposition nunmehr auf eine Machtprobe mit den Generälen zu, die zwar zähneknirschend mehr Freiheit gewähren, sich aber die Steuerung dieses „Öffnungs"-Prozesses nicht aus der Hand nehmen lassen wollen.

---

* Dolmetscher- und Übersetzerprüfung/22. 5. 1979/Industrie- und Handelskammer zu Dortmund.

Text I

Before taking office Brazil's new president had occasionally declared that it was his intention to be the country's last military head of state; at the end of his term of office, he said, he would like to see five or six parties comprising the whole political spectrum − "excepting Communists". In his inaugural address he again promised a return to democracy.

The Brazilians, who have learnt from bitter experience, have their doubts. For this return to democracy does not mean that the generals have experienced a change of heart; it merely means that they have realized that a safety valve will have to be found for pent-up social discontent. And since the financial demands of the workers cannot be met, Brasilia is offering them a "democratic" compromise. The Brazilian model − the increased industrialization of the country with the aid of foreign capital − is gradually going through the hoops.

Fed for years with empty promises, often disappointed, and now impatient, the Opposition is at present drifting towards a trial of strength with the generals; gnashing their teeth in rage, the generals are conceding a larger measure of freedom, but they are loath to surrender control of this "liberalization" process.

Annotations and Alternatives

> ① Vor seinem Amtsantritt hatte Brasiliens neuer Präsident gelegentlich erklärt, er wolle das letzte militärische Staatsoberhaupt des Landes sein; wenn seine Amtszeit ablaufe, möchte er fünf oder sechs Parteien sehen, die das ganze Spektrum − „Kommunisten ausgenommen" − umfassen.

a) Annotations

1. Vor seinem Amtsantritt: The noun *Amtsantritt* may be transposed to an *-ing* clause (e.g. *before taking office*), but a literal translation would be equally acceptable.

2. Brasiliens: Some precisians hold that the inflected genitive can be used only for people (cf. R. Flesch, *The ABC of Style*, s.v. −s), and contemporary authors are occasionally brought to book for not using the periphrastic genitive with inanimate nouns. Students of English must therefore be reminded that the use of the *-s* genitive with geographical names such as *China* or *the United States* is in no way contrary to established usage. Cf. R. Quirk et al., *GCE*, § 4.98.
The use of geographical names as adjectives is also quite common in contemporary English, especially in the language of newspaper reporting. For example, headline writers will often devise word sequences such as *City honors Bolivia chief* (cited by R. Flesch in *The ABC of Style*, s.v. adjectives). This form of functional shift is generally frowned upon because it is quite unnecessary: the noun adjective *Bolivia*, for instance, is in no way superior to the adjective *Bolivian*. However, the most cogent objection to this kind of conversion is that it produces word-groups which most language-users find artificial and pretentious. Phrases such as *Bolivia chief* or *Italy coalition* would sound preposterous in normal conversation.

3. er wolle: Several points need to be made here. To begin with, the omission of the subordinator *that* is grammatically possible since the dependent declarative clause is brief and uncomplicated. However, in this particular instance it seems advisable to insert the word *that* in order to add weight to the sub clause. This opening statement is the topic sentence of the paragraph, and it must therefore be constructed in such a way as to arrest the reader's attention. Zero *that*-clauses are generally less emphatic and less formal than their unshortened counterparts.
Secondly, the German present subjunctive *wolle* must be rendered as a past indicative since this is reported speech (back-shift).
Thirdly, the verb *wollen* need not be translated as *want*. It may often be rendered more aptly by means of the verb *intend* or the noun *intention*. The use of the noun *intention*, of course, is a common cause of uncertainty among foreign students of English. The *-ing* form is used in constructions of the type *to have no intention of doing* (+ object), while the infinitive is used in constructions such as *his intention was to do* (+ object). Here are a few typical specimens:

He has no intention of marrying her. (*DEWC*, s.v. intention.)
Nostromo's intention had been to sail right into the harbour. (. . .). (J. Conrad, *Nostromo*, p. 253.)
His intention was to walk the planks of the wharf till the steamer from Esmeralda turned up. (*ibid.*, p. 257.)

The problems posed by the use of the verb *intend* are somewhat similar, for *intend* occurs both with the infinitive and with the *-ing* form. The infinitive construction expresses the terminate aspect, while the *-ing* form expresses the durative aspect. A good example from a book by R. A. Close is quoted by Wolf Friederich in *Probleme der Semantik und Syntax des englischen Gerundiums* (p. 70):

"Where do you intend to hang this picture?" – "Nowhere yet, I intend keeping it hidden till Mother's gone."

The question asks for definite information about definite intentions, but the answer provides only vague and general information about a vague and general design. The infinitive would have been used in the reply if the second speaker's design had been unalterably fixed. This is a good illustration of the way in which the minutiae of consciousness can be mirrored in the subtly variegated forms of the English verb system. In the case under discussion, the *-ing* construction is precluded by the fact that except in causal clauses (e. g. *this being so*) the verb *to be* never occurs in the *-ing* form when it is used as a copula. The *-ing* form is, however, possible when *to be* takes on the meanings of verbs such as *feel* or *behave,* as in the following excerpt from Iris Murdoch's novel, *A Severed Head* (p. 193):

‚Martin', said Rosemary, 'you're not being angry, are you?' She spoke as to a sulky child.
'Of course I'm not being angry', I said. 'Why ever should I be angry?'

4. Staatsoberhaupt des Landes: Two points must be considered here. First, the noun *Staatsoberhaupt* must be translated as *head of state* in this context. *Head of a state* and *head of the state* would be unacceptable because the articles *a* and *the* are incompatible with a postmodifying prepositional phrase such as *of the country* or a premodifying noun phrase such as *the country's*.

Secondly, the translator will do well to render *des Landes* as *in the country* rather than *of the country* since the repetition of the preposition *of* is likely to grate on the sensibilities of fastidious language-users. The *-s* genitive is also possible.

5. wenn . . . ablaufe: A word for word translation would be grammatically acceptable, but somewhat cumbersome. The entire *wenn*-clause may be transposed to a prepositional phrase. The parenthetic speech tag *he said* should be inserted after the prepositional phrase in order to remind the reader that this is free indirect speech. The English speech tag fulfils the same function as the German subjunctive. The preterite (*he said*) sounds more natural than the pedantically correct past perfect (*he had said*). This looseness in tense usage is frequent in contemporary English.

6. die . . . umfassen: A literal translation would be rather ungainly. The simplest solution is to use an *-ing* form.

7. das ganze Spektrum: This scientific image can be reproduced in English. It is, however, advisable to add the adjective *political*. Cp. the following quotation from *World and Press* (2nd January issue 1980, p. 1):

Altogether there are said to be about ten rebel groups in action representing almost the whole political spectrum from ousted communist factions to right-wing monarchists.

b) Alternatives

Before *taking office*	Brazil's new president had *occasionally*	*declared*
assuming office	*on occasion*	*announced*
entering upon office	*at times*	*affirmed*
entering into office	*now and again*	
taking up his duties	*now and then*	
taking up his official duties		
taking up his functions		
taking up his official functions		
assuming his duties		
entering on his duties		
entering upon his duties		
beginning his duties		
his accession to office		
his entry to office		
his assumption of office		
his assumption of duties		
his commencement of duties		

that *it was his intention* to be *the country's last military head of state* ;
he intended *the last military head of state in the country;*

at the *end*	of his *term of office,*	he said, he would like to see
termination	*period of office,*	
expiration	*tenure of office,*	
expiry	*duration of office,*	
	presidential term,	
	presidency,	

five or six parties *comprising*	the *whole* political spectrum	– "*except-*
encompassing	*entire*	"*with*
embracing		
including		

ing	Communists".
the exception of	

② In seiner Antrittsrede versprach er noch einmal die Rückkehr zur Demokratie.

a) Annotations

1. Antrittsrede: Several equivalents have been listed in the dictionaries. *Maiden speech* would be wrong in this context because it denotes a new MP's first speech in Parliament. *Inaugural address* is the commonest expression for the first official speech made by a new president. Example:

Excerpts from Reagan's Inaugural Address (*World and Press,* 1st February issue 1981, p. 1.)

2. die Rückkehr: The definite article should be rendered as an indefinite article since the noun *return* has not become definite as a result of being mentioned a second time in the text. Moreover, it does not refer to a scheduled event: the 'return to democracy' is merely a pie in the sky.

3. zur Demokratie: The article must be omitted because in this word-group the abstract noun *Demokratie* is not used in a particular sense.

b) Alternatives

In his *inaugural address*	he *again*	*promised*	a return
inaugural speech	*once more*	*held out hopes of*	
inauguration address			
inaugural (U.S.)			
to democracy.			

③ Die Brasilianer, durch schlechte Erfahrungen gewitzt, haben ihre Zweifel.

a) Annotations

1. durch ... gewitzt: This postmodification should be expanded into a non-restrictive relative clause. A literal translation would sound jerky and unidiomatic.

b) Alternatives

The Brazilians, who	*have*	*learnt from bitter experience,*	have their doubts.
	"	*been made wise by experience,*	
	"	" *" wary "*	"
	"	" *taught by experience,*	

④ Denn diese Rückkehr zur Demokratie entspricht nicht einem Sinneswandel der Generäle, sondern der Einsicht, daß für den aufgestauten sozialen Unmut ein Ventil gefunden werden muß.

a) Annotations

1. entspricht: The dictionary equivalents of *entsprechen* would have an air of infelicity in this context, so the translator will do well to resort to modulation. The basic idea expressed by *entsprechen* is coincidence or correspondence, and the coincidence of certain occurrences normally provides a basis for inferential speculation about cause-and-effect relationships. It is therefore relatively easy to pass from the notion of coincidence to the notion of inference, which may be rendered in English by a verb such as *argue* or *mean*. Examples:

And this limitation of view argues inadequacy of penetrative imagination. (Shakespeare, *Macbeth,* ed. A. W. Verity, p. xxxii.)
A becoming deference argues deficiency in self-respect. (*WNDS,* s.v. indicate.)

His voice was muffled and argued a headache. (H. F. Eggeling, *A Dictionary of Modern German Prose Usage*, s.v. schließen.)
There was nothing to upset her mother's love of sameness in her daughter's slow response to her call. It merely meant that Elsie had come home in one of her moods. (T. Schumacher (ed.), *English Short Stories*, p. 52.)

2. Sinneswandel der Generäle: In this type of syntagma, the German genitive (*der Generäle*) may sometimes be rendered as *by*. Cf. the following quotation from the *International Herald Tribune* (3 December 1979, p. 5):

A change of heart by Labor could trigger a reaction against membership in Denmark (. . .).

If the German sentence ended with the word *Generäle*, we could translate as follows: *For this return to democracy does not argue a change of heart by the generals*. However, we have to add the sequence introduced by the words *sondern der Einsicht*, and this sharply reduces our room for manoeuvre. A quasi-literal rendering of the second half of the sentence would not be sufficiently clear, and it would sound more German than English. German authors tend to replace verbs by abstract nouns, thereby covering the most vapid utterances with a mist of vagueness. In this case, *Die Generäle haben eingesehen, daß* . . . has been converted into the cryptic word-group *der Einsicht, daß* . . ., and the identity of the persons who have 'realized' the need for a 'safety valve' has been concealed in a haze of abstraction. This kind of fuzziness must be avoided in English, so we have no choice but to reduce the surface structure to its deep structure, converting the noun into a verb and expanding the German noun phrase into a *that*-clause. This clause must be introduced by the verb *mean*, for *argue* (in the sense 'to give evidence of') is not normally followed by a *that*-clause; and we must use exactly the same construction in the first part of the statement in order to preserve the symmetry of the sentence: *For this return to democracy does not mean that the generals have experienced a change of heart*. For the collocation *experience + change*, cf. the following quotation from E. L. Stahl's edition of Goethe's *Torquato Tasso* (p. xxiii):

Now Tasso experiences a sudden change.

3. sondern der Einsicht: The need for a clause-structure shift has been explained in the preceding section. The subject of the verb *mean (this return to democracy)* should be repeated as a pronoun (*it*), and the adverb *merely* should be inserted in order to show the adversative relationship that obtains between the two main segments of the sentence. *Merely* fulfils more or less the same function as *sondern*.

4. daß . . . muß: In English the subject (*ein Ventil*) and the verb (*gefunden werden muß*) must be placed before the prepositional phrase *für. . . Unmut*. German word-order is predominantly impressionistic, while English word-order is predominantly analytical.

5. aufgestauten: In this kind of context *pent-up* and *bottled-up* are much commoner than *accumulated*. *Pent-up* often collocates with nouns such as *frustration*. Cf. the following example from *The Economist* (4–10 April 1981, p. 13):

Pent-up frustration at the delay is part of what caused Solidarity to blow the whistle after Bydgoszcz.

6. Unmut: The dictionary equivalents of *Unmut* would sound singularly out of place in this context. Words and expressions such as *displeasure, petulance, ill humour* or *bad temper* do not collocate with adjectives like *social*. The most acceptable equivalents are *discontent, unrest* and *dissatisfaction*. *Unrest* is a much stronger term than *discontent* or *dissatisfaction*, and it often suggests premonitions of revolt. It would be quite appropriate here since the generals evidently feel that the political mood has virtually reached flash point. Here are some illustrative contextual examples:

As the autumn advanced, and the Home Rule Bill went on its inexorable way through Parliament, dissatisfaction increased. (A.T.Q. Stewart, *The Ulster Crisis,* p. 103.)
Through its impact on the region's economies, the Sandinist victory over the Somoza regime has therefore worsened the living conditions of many poor and increased political discontent. (*IHT,* 11. 7. 1980, p. 1.)
We know (. . .) that tensions of everyday life cause public discontent. (*ibid.,* 18. 8. 1980, p. 1.)
The Communist Party clearly regards the independent union as a threat to its control, as an organization that could galvanize the general discontent and turn into political opposition. (*ibid.,* 1. 9. 1980, p. 2.)
Not all government officials were surprised at the depth of worker discontent (. . .). (*ibid.,* 25. 8. 1980, p. 1.)
Social unrest creates political problems that undermine economic confidence (. . .). (*ibid.,* 11. 7. 1980, p. 1.)
Mismanagement Held to Be Cause of Polish Unrest (*ibid.,* 21. 8. 1980, p. 2.)
In Honduras, the army has accepted a return to civilian rule in the hope of forestalling popular unrest. (*ibid.,* 10. 7. 1980, p. 1.)
Political unrest is also affecting the Guatemalan economy (. . .). (*ibid.,* 11. 7. 1980, p. 1.)

7. ein Ventil: The same metaphor can be used in English. In this type of context *safety valve* is much more common than *vent* or *outlet.* Examples:

From the Kremlin perspective, it has been necessary over the decades to permit the countries of Eastern Europe a form of latitude, a series of safety valves for the tensions that their submission to Moscow inevitably causes. (*IHT,* 23.–24. 8. 1980, p. 2.)
In Tim Healy's words, he needed 'a safety-valve for the Orangemen', and by the time of the Celtic Park riots it had already been found. (A.T.Q. Stewart, *The Ulster Crisis,* p. 61.)

8. muß: The back-shift rule is inapplicable here since the introductory verb in the reporting clause is in the present perfect (*have realized*) and the verb in the terminal noun clause refers to the present time. Cf. A. J. Thomson/A. V. Martinet, *A Practical English Grammar,* § 276.
The future may be substituted for the present tense (*a safety valve will have to be found*), but the use of the present tense is equally possible. If we use the present tense, we have to choose between *must* and *has to.* As a rule, *must* is more emphatic than the various *have to* forms, but there are other, more subtle differences which have to be taken into account here. The *have to* forms are often used to express external obligation imposed by circumstances as opposed to an obligation imposed by an individual speaker or writer. In this particular instance, the obligation is imposed by circumstances: the country seems to be on the brink of crisis. The use of *has to* would therefore be perfectly appropriate. Howver, the translator may substitute *must* for *has to* if he wishes to convey the impression that the author of the passage endorses the view adopted by the generals.
For further information on *must* and *have to,* the reader is referred to A. J. Thomson/A. V. Martinet, *A Practical English Grammar,* § 136. Some very useful example sentences have been listed in H. G. Hoffmann/F. Schmidt, *English Grammar Exercises,* pp. 84–85.

b) Alternatives

For this return to democracy does not mean that the generals		
have experienced a change of heart; it merely means that they have		
realized that a safety valve	*will have to be found* for	*pent-up*
	has to be found	*bottled-up*
	must be found	*the pent-up*
		„ *bottled-up*
social *discontent.*		
unrest.		
dissatisfaction.		

⑤ Und da die finanziellen Forderungen der Arbeiter nicht erfüllt werden können, offeriert ihnen Brasilia einen „demokratischen" Ausgleich.

a) Annotations

1. Arbeiter: A generic term such as *labour* would be quite appropriate here. *Labour* takes no article. Examples:

It was no theory, but the practical need to defend trade-union rights against judge-made law that brought labour into politics to form a party of its own. (G. M. Trevelyan, *English Social History,* p. 587.)

Although American labor was late in becoming organized, the beginnings go well back into pre-Civil War times. (P. A. Samuelson, *Economics,* p. 130.)

Wage-earning community would also be suitable. Cf. the following quotation from G. M. Trevelyan, *A Shortened History of England* (p. 526):

And cheap corn and meat was of great value to the wage-earning community.

The term *workers* could also be used in this context. It should, however, be noted that the noun *worker* covers a wider semantic field than *Arbeiter*. Both *Arbeiter* and *Angestellte* may be referred to as *workers* in English. Cf. the use of terms such as *post-office workers* (Postangestellte), *black-coated workers* (Büroangestellte), *white-collar workers* (Büroangestellte), *gray-collar workers* (Wartungskräfte) or *blue-collar workers* (Fabrikarbeiter). For further details, see J. Rudolph, *Langenscheidts Handbuch der englischen Wirtschaftssprache,* pp. 65–66.

The expression *working men* would be unsuitable here since it may simply denote persons who are obliged to earn their livelihood as opposed to people who live on their unearned income. Words such as *labourer, craftsman, tradesman* or *mechanic* would be too specific in the case under discussion. A labourer is a person engaged in physical work, especially of an unskilled kind; a craftsman is a member of a skilled trade; a tradesman may be a retail dealer; and a mechanic is a person skilled in maintaining or operating machinery.

2. erfüllt: In the bilingual dictionaries the expression *Forderungen erfüllen* has been rendered as *fulfil demands, satisfy claims* and *answer claims*. To these equivalents we may add *meet demands, respond to demands* and *agree to demands*. Examples:

They were content to meet those demands and to solve those problems of which the pressure was already felt. (G. M. Trevelyan, *English Social History*, p. 569.)
The Inter-Factory group said that the strikes in the 21 enterprises (. . .) would continue until all their demands had been met. (*IHT*, 18. 8. 1980, p. 2.)
But the Gdansk walkout was complicated by the demand for the dissolution of the official unions – a demand to which the government has not yet responded. (*ibid.*, 16.–17. 8. 1980, p. 2.)
But Mr. Schmidt's support for the loans was already coming under fire from the Christian Democratic candidate for chancellor, Franz Josef Strauss, who said that their guarantee by the government should only be granted if the Polish leaders agree to the workers' demands. (*ibid.*, 21. 8. 1980, p. 2.)

3. offeriert: The present progressive form may be used to denote a near future or an intention.

4. ihnen: If *Arbeiter* is rendered as *labour* or *the wage-earning community*, *ihnen* should be translated as a noun (*workers*) since the neuter pronoun *it* would sound rather odd in this context. If, on the other hand, *Arbeiter* is rendered as *workers*, then *ihnen* should be translated by the pronoun *them*. It is advisable to use the periphrastic genitive (*the demands of the workers*) in order to bring the noun *workers* closer to the anaphoric pronoun *them*.

b) Alternatives

And since the financial *demands* of	*the workers*	cannot be *met,*
claims	*labour*	*fulfilled,*
	the wage-earning	*satisfied,*
	community	*answered,*
		responded to,
		agreed to,

Brasilia is offering *them*	a "democratic" compromise.
the workers	

(6) Das brasilianische Modell, die verstärkte Industrialisierung des Landes mit Hilfe von Auslandskapital, erklärt seinen Konkurs in Raten.

a) Annotations

1. Modell: It seems advisable to replace the commas by dashes in order to mark more adequately the separation between the two units in apposition (the head noun phrase *das brasilianische Modell* and the explanatory appositive *die verstärkte . . . Auslandskapital*).

2. Landes: When *Land* is used in the sense of 'the territory of a state or nation' it is normally rendered as *country*. The word *land* is invariably tinged with emotion and is generally restricted to elevated diction. Examples:

It led, also, to greater interest in our own 'lands beyond the sea', the Imperialist movement of the nineties (. . .). (G. M. Trevelyan, *English Social History*, p. 570.)

The subject-matter of this book has been confined to the social history of England, and has not included the vast and varied expanse of lands beyond the ocean associated in the British Commonwealth of Nations and dependencies. (*ibid.*, p. 595.)

For further information on this point, the reader is referred to H. W. Klein/W. Friederich, *Englische Synonymik*, s.v. Land.

3. erklärt seinen Konkurs: The expression *erklärt seinen Konkurs* is here synonymous with *seinen Konkurs anmelden*. An insolvent debtor may file a bankruptcy petition against himself, and if the court to which the petition is presented finds sufficient proof of insolvency, the debtor is adjudged a bankrupt. The filing of a bankruptcy petition is referred to as *Konkursanmeldung,* and the adjudication order issued by the court in charge is technically called *Konkurserklärung*. The procedure followed in such cases varies from state to state. For information on the laws of bankruptcy in Germany, the United Kingdom and the U.S.A., the reader is referred to the following works: E. J. Cohn (ed.), *Manual of German Law*, Vol. II, pp. 261–275; J. Rudolph, *Langenscheidts Handbuch der englischen Wirtschaftssprache*, pp. 152–168; R. Sachs, *Commercial Correspondence*, p. 173.

Expressions such as *file a bankruptcy petition* or *file for bankruptcy* can hardly be used in a figurative sense; *to declare oneself bankrupt* would be somewhat better; but the most appropriate solution would be a racy metaphor such as *go through the hoops*. This locution means 'to be subjected to an ordeal or trial' and is often used in connection with bankruptcy. Cf. *Der kleine Eichborn*, s.v. hoops.

4. in Raten: This expression is normally translated as *in* (or *by*) *instalments*. In this case, however, we have to do with a sort of catachresis, a strained or forced figure of speech involving the application of a term to a thing which it does not properly denote. Cf. K. Beckson/A. Ganz, *A Reader's Guide to Literary Terms*, s.v. catachresis. For further references, see John D. Gallagher, *Cours de traduction allemand-français: textes politiques et économiques,* p. 23.

In its literal sense, *Rate* denotes any one of the parts of a payment spread over a period of time, but when used figuratively *Rate* can express a wide range of concepts which have nothing whatever to do with hire purchase. Thus, in *Die Zeit* of 29 February 1980 (p. 17), we read *Die erste Rate radikaler Maßnahmen* (= *Die erste Reihe radikaler Maßnahmen*). In such cases, the English prefer words such as *programme, package* or *series*. Examples:

President Carter has approved a program of diplomatic and economic measures over the next two weeks in a concerted effort to resolve the long-running Iran crisis without resorting to military action, official sources said last night. (*IHT,* 6. 12. 1979, p. 1.)

Federal Reserve Board Chairman Paul Volcker last night announced a package of measures including higher interest rates – aimed at bringing inflation under control and calming financial markets, (*ibid.*, 8. 10. 1979, p. 1.)

Friday's flight appeared to be the latest in a series of moves by the administration to make public its displeasure with the Soviet and Cuban governments over the presence of Soviet combat troops on the island and the refusal of Moscow to withdraw them. (*ibid.*, 8. 10. 1979, p. 1.)

In the sentence under discussion, it is as well to avoid undue linguistic impropriety by resorting to some form of dynamic equivalence. An adverbial such as *gradually* should be perfectly adequate here.

b) Alternatives

The Brazilian model – the	*increased*	industrialization of the country
	intensified	
	accelerated	
with the aid	of foreign	*capital* – is gradually going through the hoops.
by	" *help* "	*funds*
by means of		

(7) Jahrelang mit Versprechen vertröstet, oft enttäuscht und ungeduldig geworden, steuert die Opposition nunmehr auf eine Machtprobe mit den Generälen zu, die zwar zähneknirschend mehr Freiheit gewähren, sich aber die Steuerung dieses „Öffnungs"-Prozesses nicht aus der Hand nehmen lassen wollen.

a) Annotations

1. Jahrelang ... geworden: This is a good example of ternary enumeration, a device which serves to intensify the expression of the writer's thoughts. The rhythmical pattern of the German sentence should be preserved as far as possible.

2. jahrelang: The expression *for years on end* would be a shade too familiar in this context.

3. Versprechen: We may add the adjective *empty* in order to eke out the sense of *promises*, which by itself would scarcely render the full force of *Versprechen*.

4. oft: This passage is tinged with emotion, so the adverb *often* should be used in preference to *frequently* or *repeatedly*. Germanic words such as *often* tend to be stronger, more human, and more emotive than Romance words such as *frequently* or *repeatedly*. Cf. Thomas Weedon's pertinent remarks on the vocabulary of modern English im K. E. Schuhmacher (ed.), *English – A World Language*, pp. 26–27. *Frequently* and *repeatedly* belong to the practical language of fact. Examples:

It would be helpful to list the characters in question and indicate which of these he has used frequently and which are used only once or twice. (A. S. Maney/R. L. Smallwood (edd.), *MHRA Style Book*, p. 3.)

If we are self-conscious about it, we shall certainly not be at our best in using language, and that is why in this book it is being repeatedly stressed that the shibboleths of traditional 'correctness' handicap us rather than help us to move about confidently and pleasingly in our language. (R. Quirk, *The Use of English*, p. 230.)

The expression *time and time again* would be quite appropriate since it is highly emphatic, but *many times* and *many a time* would be out of place in the sentence under discussion. *Many times* would sound unduly pedestrian, and *many a time* would sound almost comically old-fashioned. When used in front-position and followed by inversion, *many a time* is decidedly literary or archaic, and even in end-position it is becoming increasingly rare, except in some urban dialects and in countrified speech. An example of *many a time* in end-position is cited in Hornby's *Oxford Advanced Learner's Dictionary of Current English*, s.v. many.

5. enttäuscht: The phrasal verb *let down* would be unduly informal in this context.

6. geworden: A quasi-literal rendering such as *having become* would be unduly cumbrous. The verb may be transposed to an adverb (*now*). Like the past participle of *werden, now* conveys the idea of the present viewed as the result of a development. Note the parallel between *often disappointed* and *now impatient*. This syntactic parallelism adds weight and drive to the sentence.

7. nunmehr: The word *now* is debarred by the proximity of *now* in the preceding syntagma. Repetition would be pointless here since there is no parallel between this main clause and the preceding word sequence.

The phrase *by this time* would be quite wrong in this context. *By this time* (or *by now*) means 'not later than the present moment'. Cf. the example cited by Hornby (*OALDCE*, s.v. by): *He ought to be here by this time.*

8. zwar: This particle can be safely left untranslated here.

9. zähneknirschend: The phrase *through clenched teeth* is sometimes used by British journalists, but it is apt to sound rather infelicitous in extended use on account of the kinetic implications of the preposition *through*. Cf. the following example from *The Times* (*World and Press*, 1st November issue 1980, p. 1):

He would have continued the eastern policy though somewhat through clenched teeth (. . .).

It is therefore preferable to use the phrase *gnash one's teeth*. The metaphor, however, requires expansion in English (*in rage* or *in fury*).

It would be technically possible to reproduce the syntactical pattern of the German sentence, but the resultant sequence would have an air of infelicity: the English equivalent of *zähneknirschend* would be stylistically disruptive if it were intercalated between the relative pronoun *who* and a verb phrase, and the subsequent use of *but who* would appear excessively cumbersome and unidiomatic. The translator will therefore do well to have recourse to a clause-structure shift. The participial phrase (*gnashing their teeth in rage*) can be positioned initially, and the coordinated relative clauses can be converted into main clauses.

10. mehr: The word *more* would appear rather insipid here. The phrase *a larger measure of* would be more consonant with the tone of the passage under discussion. The expression *a large(r) measure of* is normally followed by an abstract noun. Cf. the following example cited in the *Shorter Oxford English Dictionary* (s.v. measure): *Critias . . . begs that a larger measure of indulgence may be conceded to him.*

11. Freiheit: *Freedom* is an absolute word, while *liberty* is a relative word. *Freedom* is more concrete and human, while *liberty* is more abstract and sophisticated. One might argue that *liberty* is here preferable to *freedom* on the ground that the Brazilians have been enslaved by their rulers and that those who are redeemed from slavery enjoy liberty rather than freedom. Cf. the expression *set a slave at liberty* and the example from G. F. Graham cited by H. W. Klein and W. Friederich. However, this subtle distinction between *freedom* and *liberty* is somewhat specious and is rarely observed in ordinary, casual use. To all intents and purposes, *freedom* and *liberty* are interchangeable in the sentence under discussion. For further information on these terms, the reader is referred to H. W. Klein/W. Friederich, *Englische Synonymik*, s.v. Freiheit, and *Webster's New Dictionary of Synonyms*, s.v. freedom.

12. gewähren: The verbs *accord* and *concede* would be very appropriate in this context since they may imply reluctance on the part of a person in power. *Grant*, which is a term of very wide application, would also be quite acceptable here. For further information on the English equivalents of *gewähren*, see H. W. Klein/W. Friederich, *Englische Synonymik*, s.v. zugestehen, and *Webster's New Dictionary of Synonyms*, s.v. grant.

13. „Öffnungs"-Prozesses: This compound has not yet been recorded in any dictionary. The corresponding buzz phrase in English is *liberalization process*. Cf. the following example from the *International Herald Tribune* (3 September 1980, p. 2):

The news agency Tass charged that their recent statements were a part of Western efforts to advance the idea that "there ostensibly exist conditions [in Poland] for a so-called liberalization process."

14. sich . . . die Steuerung . . . aus der Hand nehmen lassen: This phrase is a variant of the idiom *das Heft aus der Hand geben*, which may be rendered as *surrender control* (*LEW*).

15. nicht . . . wollen: For a list of English expressions denoting various degrees of reluctance, see H. W. Klein/W. Friederich, *Englische Synonymik*, s.v. abgeneigt.

b) Alternatives

Fed for years	with empty promises,	*often disappointed,*
Consoled for many years		" *disabused,*
Put off		" *disillusioned,*
		disappointed time and time again,
and now *impatient,* the Opposition is at present	*drifting towards*	a *trial of strength*
restive,	*heading for*	*test of power*
restless,		
with the generals; *gnashing* their teeth in *rage,* the generals are		
grinding " " " *fury,*		
conceding a larger measure of *freedom,* but they are loath to surrender		
according *liberty,*		
granting		
control of this "liberalization" process.		

Text II*

Sie gelten als intelligent, die Fluglotsen, und wahrscheinlich sind sie es auch. Aber Intelligenz schützt vor Dummheit nicht. Wie auch einmal die deutschen Fluglotsen einen sogenannten Bummelstreik machten, so fingen ihre französischen Kollegen einen „Eiferstreik" an, das heißt: Um ihre Forderungen an die Fluggesellschaften und damit auch an den Staat durchzusetzen, tun sie das, was sie „Dienst nach Vorschrift" nennen und nicht einen Strich mehr. Da sie eigentlich nicht streiken dürfen, ist diese Form äußerster „Pflichterfüllung" ihr Ersatz für den Streik, zu dem sie sich, wie sie immer wieder betonen, genauso berechtigt glauben, wie andere Angestellte.

Bei solchen Unternehmungen ist der richtige Moment wichtig. Mit den Fluglotsen kommen gemeinhin weit weniger Menschen in Berührung als mit Zollbeamten. Wer ein Flugzeug benutzt, wird es sich leisten können, so heißt es. Die armen Leute fliegen nicht. Eine solche Maßnahme in normalen Zeiten macht also wenig Aufsehen. Aber zweimal im Jahr ist die Gelegenheit günstig: Anfang August, wenn die Urlauber ausfliegen, und Ende August, wenn sie heimfliegen wollen.

Dies erregt ganz besonderes Aufsehen. Wann meldeten Zeitungen, daß Verspätungen im Flugdienst bis zu acht Stunden und darüber hinaus dauerten? Wann sah man Szenen, in denen müde Frauen und hungrige Kinder auf nacktem Boden kauerten: das reinste Elend auf luxuriösen Flughäfen?

---

* Dolmetscher- und Übersetzerprüfung/27. 9. 1978/Industrie- und Handelskammer zu Dortmund.

Text II

They are reputed to be intelligent, these air traffic controllers, and so they probably are. Yet intelligence is no safeguard against folly.
Just as the German air controllers once staged a so-called go-slow strike, so their French counterparts have begun a *grève du zèle*; that is, in order to enforce their demands on the airline companies and thus on the Government, they are engaging in what they term a work-to-rule campaign, refusing to do a stroke of work more than is absolutely necessary. Since, strictly speaking, they are not allowed to strike, this form of over-punctilious adherence to rules and regulations is their substitute for the strike to which, they keep insisting, they believe they have exactly the same rights as other employees.
In such actions a great deal depends on timing. Generally speaking, far fewer people come into contact with air controllers than with customs officers. People who travel by plane will be able to afford it, or so they say. The poor do not go by air. In normal times therefore an action such as a work-to-rule does not attract much notice. Twice a year, however, an opportunity presents itself: at the beginning of August, when holiday-makers are going away, and at the end of August, when they are getting ready to fly home.
A work-to-rule at this time of year really does create a stir. When have newspapers ever carried reports of air service delays of up to eight hours and longer? When has one ever witnessed scenes with exhausted women and hungry children squatting on the bare floor? When has one ever witnessed abject misery at luxurious airports?

Annotations and Alternatives

① Sie gelten als intelligent, die Fluglotsen, und wahrscheinlich sind sie es auch.

a) Annotations

1. Sie gelten ... Fluglotsen: The word-order in this clause calls for a few remarks. The normal course of logical expression has been broken up through the duplication of the subject: the pronoun *sie* has been placed at the beginning of the clause, and the noun for which it stands (*Fluglotsen*) has been placed at the end. This dislocation of the elements of the sentence is a powerful means of bringing the subject into a strong position in which it may be given full vocal stress. Comma separation is mandatory since the amplificatory noun phrase tag constitutes a separate tone unit.

This type of construction is highly affective. Under the stress of emotion, utterance may begin before the speaker has had time to survey the whole field of the thought to which he wishes to give expression. Only at the end of the statement is the subject specified — more or less as an afterthought — for the benefit of the listener.

The German construction may be imitated in English. In *GCE* (§ 9.148), Professor Quirk and his colleagues point out that such double expression of the subject 'is restricted to informal spoken English, and is considered by some as substandard, though it is in fact very common'. There can be no doubt that the type of segmentation under discussion is particularly frequent in loose colloquial speech, and it seems to be on the increase in written English, too. A case in point is to be seen in the following snippet from Jean Stafford's short story "In the Zoo" (*Bad Characters*):

(. . .) they [*sc.* the monkeys] were husbands and fathers and brothers, these little, ugly, dark, secret men who minded their own business and let us mind ours.

In this example, the duplication of the subject fulfils a double function: (a) it imparts a somewhat familiar, emotional tone to the style, suggesting the writer's keen interest in the animals; (b) it enables the writer to enhance the balance of the clause: the lengthy noun subject would overweight the verb if it were placed in initial position.

The definite article *die* may be rendered as a demonstrative adjective (*these*). Cf. the examples cited in Quirk et al., *GCE*, §§ 9.148, 14.50. The affective use of the demonstrative adjective in modern English has been discussed at length in J. P. Vinay/ P. Darbelnet, *Stylistique comparée du français et de l'anglais*, § 239. In the case under discussion, the demonstrative adjective has a somewhat pejorative effect. The writer proceeds on the assumption that his readers already know something about the air traffic control staff. He is disgruntled, and he takes it that his readers share his feelings.

In lively colloquial style the amplificatory noun phrase may often be replaced by an amplificatory tag statement containing a repetitive operator or the substitute operator *do*:

That was a lark, that was! (Quirk et al, *GCE*, § 14.50.)
She has plenty of sense, has Joan. (Lamprecht, *GES*, § 29.)
He's a downy one, is old Joe. (F. T. Wood, *English Colloquial Idioms*, s.v. downy.)
He's a cultured all-round man, Bloom is. (James Joyce, quoted in Boris Ford (ed.), *The Pelican Guide to English Literature*, vol. 7, p. 305.)

Note that inversion is common, though not mandatory. The amplificatory tag statement has a fairly strong dialectal flavour and would therefore be inappropriate in the case under consideration.

2. Fluglotsen: So far only two equivalents have been recorded in the bilingual dictionaries: *air traffic controller* and *controller*. *Air controller*, however, is also in common use on both sides of the Atlantic:

But the two most important ones in the legal context are the recent strikes involving the nation's postal workers and the "sick-out" by American air controllers. (*The Times*, 6. 4. 1970, p. 23.)
Air Controllers Plan Slowdown in France. (*IHT*, 15–16. 12. 1979, p. 2.)

It should also be noted that *air traffic controller* and *controller* are not always interchangeable since *controller* is wider in application than *air traffic controller*. Translators should follow the sensible rule that they render *Fluglotse* as *air traffic controller* or *air controller* on its first appearance, abbreviating it subsequently as often as they please. A typical example of this procedure may be found in an article in the *International Herald Tribune* of 15–16 December 1979 (p. 2). *Air controller* is used in the headline, *air traffic controller* in the first paragraph, and *controller* in the second paragraph. Air controllers may also be referred to collectively as *the air-traffic control staff*:

Is it because of that go-slow by the air-traffic control staff? (H. G. Hoffmann, *Aufbaukurs Wirtschaft*, p. 6.)

3. wahrscheinlich: This adverb may be rendered in various ways: a) *probably*; b) *no doubt*; c) *likely*; d) *to be expected* + infinitive; e) *the odds* (or *chances*) *are that*; f) *apt*. Here are some examples:

She was taken prisoner in an Iroquois raid, which was probably the best lay she ever had. (Leonard Cohen, *Beautiful Losers*, p. 16.)
The situation is the same in most of the big towns in Britain, and it is probably the same in all the big cities of the world. (M. Knight, D. Whitling, P. Jonason, *All Right* I, p. 93.)
It would most probably turn out to our advantage if we included the Co-operative Society and also the voluntary chains. (D. Hamblock/D. Wessels, *Englisch in Wirtschaft und Handel*, vol. 1, p. 36.)
He meant to help, no doubt, but in fact he has been a hindrance. (Hornby, *OALDCE*, s.v. doubt.)
He is not likely to succeed. (*ibid.*, s.v. likely.)
It's highly likely that he will succeed. (*ibid.*).
(. . .) a psycho-analyst particularly would be likely to have guessed at it. (I. Murdoch, *A Severed Head*, p. 130.)
He is expected to arrive tomorrow. (*LGS*, s.v. voraussichtlich.)
The chances (*or* the odds) are that he will win. (*LEW*, s.v. wahrscheinlich.)
The incident is not apt to be followed by international complications. (H. W. Horwill, *Modern American Usage*, s.v. apt.)

These equivalents are not always interchangeable.
Probably is widest in application. It is in common use on both sides of the Atlantic. It may combine with any tense, and it can be inserted in sentences of the pattern *he is so* or *so he is*.
No doubt means 'very probably' and may also combine with any tense.
Likely is used more often of actions than of states. It generally combines with the present and the past tenses, but it sometimes combines with the conditional, too (cf. the example from *A Severed Head*).
To be expected + infinitive is used only with reference to the future considered from the vantage point of a person or persons not identical with the speaker or speakers. The speaker or speakers may or may not share the expectations of the person or persons implicitly referred to.
The odds (or *chances*) *are that* + sub-clause is generally used only in the present and the past tenses. This locution often has to be replaced by other constructions in order to avoid the repetition of the copula or the subordinator.

Apt is used in American English in cases where the British use *likely*. In British English, *apt* is used only to express a general or habitual tendency. Cf. the examples given in H. W. Horwill, *Modern American Usage*, s.v. apt.

4. sind sie es auch: In this type of construction, *es* should be left untranslated. The tonal particle *auch*, which expresses confirmation of the preceding statement, may be translated in three ways:

a) A stressed verb in terminal position is often enough to render the tonal particle. Italicization is unnecessary. In the following example, a native speaker will automatically place the stress on *am:*

I feel ill, and I am.

b) The adverb *too* may be placed at the end of the sentence. Comma separation is the rule here:

I feel ill, and I am, too.

c) The pro-form *so* may be placed before the subject:

I feel ill, and so I am.
He seems intelligent. So he is.

So and *that* may also occur in terminal position, but this usage is rejected by some native speakers. Cf. R. Quirk et al., *GCE*, § 10.54, Note (a). On other renderings of *auch*, see G. Collier/B. Shields, *Guided German-English Translation*, pp. 155–158.

b) Alternatives

They are	reputed to be intelligent,	these *air traffic controllers*, and
	supposed to be intelligent,	*air controllers*,
	thought to be intelligent,	
	reckoned to be intelligent,	
	reckoned as intelligent,	
	considered to be intelligent,	
	considered as intelligent,	
	said to be intelligent,	
	generally held to be intelligent,	
	regarded as intelligent,	
	looked upon as intelligent,	
	reputedly intelligent,	
	have the reputation of being intelligent,	

so they probably are.
they probably are, too.
they probably are.
so they are, no doubt.
no doubt they are, too.
no doubt they are.

② Aber Intelligenz schützt vor Dummheit nicht.

a) **Annotations**

1. **Intelligenz:** Abstract mass nouns such as *intelligence* take no article unless applied to a particular case. Cf. R. W. Zandvoort, *A Handbook of English Grammar,* § 328.

2. **schützt vor:** The most appropriate verbal equivalents are *guard, safeguard, preserve* and *protect*. *Guard* implies sustained watchfulness, *safeguard* implies taking precautionary measures against potential dangers, *preserve* (which has a somewhat literary flavour) emphasizes the idea of resistance to destructive agencies, and *protect* expresses the notion of shielding a person or thing from possible harm. *Protect* is occasionally employed without a direct object, as in the sentence: *Clothes protect from cold* (H. W. Klein/W. Friederich, *Englische Synonymik,* s.v. schützen), but *guard, safeguard* and *preserve* cannot be used absolutely. Thus, if, in the case under consideration, we wish to render *schützen* as *guard, safeguard* or *preserve,* we shall have to add a personal direct object such as *us*. It is, of course, possible to produce more elegant renderings by resorting to conversion, as in some of the example sentences given in *LEW,* s.v. schützen:

Warme Kleidung schützt vor Kälte: Warm clothing gives (*or* affords) protection from the cold.
Das Medikament schützt vor Grippe: The medicine is a safeguard (*or* protection) against influenza.

3. **Dummheit:** The antinomy referred to here is the contradiction existing between intelligence and lack of common sense or insight. It would therefore be quite wrong to render *Dummheit* by a term denoting an innate absence of intelligence or understanding. Such terms include *dullness, obtuseness, dumbness* (an American colloquialism), *denseness* and *unintelligence*. *Dullness, obtuseness* and *dumbness* suggest slowness of mind, *denseness* implies imperviousness to ideas, and *unintelligence* is the direct opposite of *intelligence*.
Stupidity is a borderline case. *Stupidity* does not always denote a lack of normal intelligence; it may merely denote a lack of common sense.
Folly, silliness and *foolishness* would be quite appropriate in the case under discussion, for they generally imply rashness, a lack of wisdom, a form of action devoid of reason or judgment. *Asininity* might also be considered acceptable since it implies obstinacy as well as utter failure to exercise normal intelligence, rationality, or perception. Yet another possible solution would be *imprudence,* which may denote a lack of good judgment, skill, shrewdness, caution or circumspection.

4. **nicht:** If the verb *schützen* is converted into a noun such as *safeguard,* then the negative particle *nicht* ought to be rendered as *no*.
The negator *no* may occur with all three noun classes:
a) mass nouns such as *money, lunch* or *milk*:
So far no money has been spent on repairs. (R. Quirk et al., *GCE,* § 7.29.)
We've had no lunch. (*ibid.,* § 7.44.)
No milk. (A. R. Tellier, *Cours de grammaire anglaise,* p. 277.)
b) singular count nouns denoting persons or things:

No person of that name lives here. (R. Quirk et al., *GCE*, § 7.29.)
No pen. (*ibid.*, § 4.15.)

c) Plural count nouns denoting persons or things:

No men. (R. A. Close, *RGSE*, § 6.2.)
No pens. (R. Quirk et al., *GCE*, § 4.15.)

No and *not a* are in a 'choice relation', i.e. they are mutually exclusive. However, *no* may combine with *more* or with a cardinal number. Cf. R. A. Close, *RGSE*, § 6.50; K. Schibsbye, *MEG*, § 11.1.1. Examples:

He had said no more at the time (. . .). (W. Thesiger, *Arabian Sands*, p. 301.)
No two business cycles are quite the same. (P. A. Samuelson, *Economics*, 237.)

Not a and *no* are often practically interchangeable, though *not a* tends to be commoner in colloquial English. Cp. R. W. Zandvoort, *HEG*, § 530; R. Quirk et al., *GCE*, § 7.44; A. Lamprecht, *GES*, § 315; T. Buck, *German into English*, Vol. I, p. 17. There are, however, three cases where the determiner *no* is equally common in spoken and written English:

a) *No* is used for unemphatic initial negation:

No man could remain more than a minute below. (J. Conrad, *Youth*, p. 44.)
No mind can comprehend a bundle of unrelated facts. (P. A. Samuelson, *Economics*, p. 7.)
No telephone message arrived (. . .). (F. Scott Fitzgerald, *The Great Gatsby*, p. 168.)

The corresponding emphatic form of initial negation is *not a*. This type of phrasal negation is never used in generalizations. Examples:

Not a soul came near to help us (. . .). (D. Newton, 'The Bad Eggs', in: *Short Stories*, p. 47.)
Not a word came from his lips. (R. Quirk et al., *GCE*, § 7.50.)
Not a sound was heard, (R. W. Zandvoort, *HEG*, § 533.)
Not a sound came from the crowd (G. Collier/B. Shields, *Guided German-English Translation*, p. 74.)

b) *No* is often used before abstract nouns. Examples:

But he knew that on this side of the water he ran no risk of discovery. (J. Conrad, *Nostromo*, p. 347.)
He had no doubt now. (*ibid.*, p. 350.)
There was no doubt that he had been waiting and listening outside (. . .). (I. Murdoch, *The Unicorn*, p. 225.)
They said there was no need for one. (*ibid.*, p. 232.)
However, the king had no time for me. (S. Bellow, *Henderson the Rain King*, p. 162.)
I see no reason why you shouldn't. (T. Buck, *German into English*, Vol. I, p. 17.)

In such cases it is possible to substitute *not a* or *not any* for *no*, but this inevitably results in a transfer of the focus of negation – a shift from noun-centred negation to verb-centred negation, and the difference of scope between the two types of negation reflects a difference of meaning often overlooked by foreign students of English. Cf. the following example cited by G. Collier and B. Shields in *Guided German-English Translation* (p. 74):

(i) I can find *no* cause for complaint.
(ii) I ca*n't* find *a* cause for complaint.

In sentence (i), negation is centred on the noun *cause*, while in sentence (ii) negation is centred on the verb *can*. It follows therefore that in sentence (i) stress is laid on absence of cause, while in sentence (ii) stress is laid on the speaker's inability to find a cause. However, if the verb is a copula, the shift from noun-centred negation to verb-centred negation does not necessarily entail a change of meaning. Hence, there is no semantic difference between *There would be no more fighting* and *There wouldn't be any more fighting*. It should also be noted that it is impossible to replace *no* by *not any* in an elliptical sentence of the type *No more putting back anywhere, if we all get roasted* (J. Conrad, *Youth*, p. 40.)

c) *No* is often used by way of litotes (the expression of an affirmative by the negative of its contrary). Examples:

No wonder she leaked. (J. Conrad, *Youth*, p. 34.)
At present the Rashid and the Duru were not at war, but there was no love lost between them. (W. Thesiger, *Arabian Sands*, p. 171.)
"Revenge may be wicked, but it's natural", answered Miss Rebecca. "I'm no angel". And, to say the truth, she certainly was not. (W. M. Thackeray, *Vanity Fair*, p. 10.)

No wonder she leaked means *It was natural that the ship should have leaked;* *There was no love lost between them* means *They detested each other*; and *I'm no angel* means *I'm anything but angelic*. By the same token, *Mr Smith is not an actor* means that Mr Smith is not an actor by profession, while *Mr Smith is no actor* means that Mr Smith is a very bad actor; *Mr Smith is not an Englishman* means that Mr Smith is not from England, while *Mr Smith is no Englishman* means that Mr Smith is an atypical or an unpatriotic Englishman. In short, *not a* is used in neutral statements of fact, while *no* is used in affirmations that are decidedly emphatic and emotively coloured. For further examples see R. W. Zandvoort, *HEG*, § 531; G. Collier/B. Shields, *Guided German-English Translation*, p. 27.

b) Alternatives

Yet intelligence	*is no safeguard against*	*folly.*
But	*affords no protection against*	*imprudence.*
		foolishness.
		silliness.
		asininity.
		stupidity.

(3) Wie auch einmal die deutschen Fluglotsen einen sogenannten Bummelstreik machten, so fingen ihre französischen Kollegen einen „Eiferstreik" an, das heißt: Um ihre Forderungen an die Fluggesellschaften und damit auch an den Staat durchzusetzen, tun sie das, was sie „Dienst nach Vorschrift" nennen und nicht einen Strich mehr.

a) Annotations

1. Wie ... so: A great deal has been written about adverb clauses of comparison, but up to now this particular type of comparative clause has received scant attention. The alternatives available in modern English are as follows:

a) *as ... so:*

As some dogs have it in the blood, or are trained, to worry certain creatures to a certain point, so – not to make the comparison disrespectfully, – Pleasant Riderhood had it in the blood, or had been

trained, to regard seamen, within certain limits, as her prey. (Charles Dickens, *Our Mutual Friend*, p. 406.)
As the criminals work out their own dooms with the *natural inevitableness* of life, so Lear and those who come within the scope of his actions must suffer to the full the consequences of his folly. (W. Shakespeare, *King Lear*, ed. A. W. Verity, p. xxiv.)
As an Englishman does not like to use more words or more syllables than are strictly necessary, so he does not like to say more than he can stand to. (O. Jespersen, *Growth and Structure of the English Language*, p. 7.)

b) *just as . . . so:*

Just as the organization will tend to pressurize him to regard himself as an 'organization man' so the union will wish him to perceive the various activities on his behalf as legitimate and to behave as a 'union man'. (David Weir (ed.), *Men and Work in Modern Britain*, p. 344.)
(. . .) just as a small rise in the output of consumer goods may result in a much larger rise in the output of capital goods, so a small fall in the output of consumer goods may result in a much larger fall in the output of capital goods. (M. Stewart, *Keynes and After*, p. 46.)
Just as the Neo-classical period earned its alternative name, the Age of Reason, so Pre-Romanticism is rightly regarded as the Age of Sensibility. (L. R. Furst, *Romanticism*, p. 27.)
Just as the machine that produces vitriol is not intrinsically better or worse than that which makes sugar, so the evil man is on the same plane as the good (. . .). (L. R. Furst/P. N. Skrine, *Naturalism*, p. 20.)
Just as France was supreme as the source of Naturalism, so within French Naturalism – and eventually far beyond – the decisive mind was that of Emile Zola (1840–1902). (*ibid.*, p. 26.)
Just as exhorting people to dig a few trenches in the London parks did not measure up to the challenge of total war then, so will the present reliance on the price mechanism to reduce petrol consumption fail to measure up to the scale of the sacrifices that the Western people are shortly going to have to face. (*The Chronicle-Herald*, 19. 7. 1979, p. 7.)

c) *just as . . . so also:*

Just as he curtails his narrative records, so also, he curtails his descriptions which are seldom as circumstantial as those of Chrestien. (M. F. Richey, *Studies of Wolfram von Eschenbach*, p. 167.)

d) *just as . . . so too:*

Just as the rights of private property and of personal freedoms are not absolute and must be reconciled when they come into conflict with the rights of others and of the public generally, so too must the rights of "free collective bargaining" be subject to limitation and coordination with social necessities. (P. A. Samuelson, *Economics*, p. 137.)

e) *just as . . . likewise:*

And just as Romantic ideas and styles existed before, and persisted after, the specifically Romantic period of the early nineteenth century, likewise Naturalism can be found well before and after the late nineteenth and early twentieth-century movement of that name. (L. R. Furst/P. N. Skrine, *Naturalism*, pp. 1–2.)

f) *just as . . . in the same manner:*

(. . .) just as an English lady will nearly always write in a manner that in any other country would only be found in a man's hand, in the same manner the language is more manly than any other language I know. (O. Jespersen, *Growth and Structure of the English Language*, p. 2.)

It will be observed that in these quotations there are only two instances of inverted word-order, namely in the sentences taken from *The Chronicle-Herald* and Samuelson's *Economics*. Here we have to do with what is known as 'balance inversion' (cf. H. W. Fowler, *A Dictionary of Modern English Usage*, s.v. inversion).
Let us look first at the example from *The Chronicle-Herald*. The writer (Miss Peregrine Worsthorne) has transferred the auxiliary verb *will* to the beginning of the clause introduced by *so*. She was evidently apprehensive lest the verb should pass virtually

unnoticed after the conspicuous eleven-word subject (*the present reliance . . . petrol consumption*). In this particular instance, however, inversion is both unnecessary and artificial. The sentence flows more easily if the verb *will* is returned to its normal place: the parallelism between the sub clause and the main clause is considerably enhanced, and the verb phrase *will fail* can hardly pass unnoticed because it is followed by the conspicuous infinitive group *to measure up to*. Journalists often display an inordinate liking for artificial inversions, and their extravagances are harmful to the prestige of the English language.

Samuelson's sentence is based on the same pattern as the example from *The Chronicle-Herald*. The auxiliary verb *must* has been separated from its infinitive (*be*) and placed before the six-word subject (*the rights . . . bargaining*). This inversion is also quite uncalled-for. A more pleasing balance can be achieved by returning the verb to its normal place.

Nonetheless, it would be wrong to assume that inverted word-order can never be countenanced in this type of clause. Cp. the following example from Fowler's *Dictionary of Modern English Usage* (s.v. inversion):

(. . .) as heels of a practical kind may be useful or indeed indispensable, so too is inversion.

This kind of balance inversion is unexceptionable. The subject (*inversion*) is three times as long as the copula (*is*), so the verb is automatically drawn to the beginning of the clause. Besides, it is perfectly natural and indeed necessary to resort to inversion in many short sentences where *so* is combined with a form of *be, have* or *do* in order to draw attention to similarities between persons or things:

I'm interested in travelling. – So am I. (A. Schmitz/E. Schmitz, *Kontakte Englisch*, p. 86.)

Note the difference between *So am I* and *So I am*. The latter is used to confirm a preceding statement:

You have called me an adventurer. So I am. (R. W. Zandvoort, *HEG*, § 429.)

In Fowler's sentence, the word *so* has been made to fulfil a double function: as a correlative it serves to underscore the complementary relationship between the parallel halves of the sentence (cf. the function of *ita* in the Latin *ut. . .ita* construction), and as a pro-form for predication (cf. R. Quirk et al., *GCE*, § 9.80) it enables the writer to telescope the two clauses through ellipsis. If we were to complete the second half of Fowler's sentence, it would read as follows: *so too inversion may be useful or indeed indispensable*. The repetition of the predicate would clearly have been intolerable, and Fowler had no choice but to resort to ellipsis.

A simpler form of ellipsis may also be possible in the first half of a comparative sentence, provided that the two clauses are closely parallel both in structure and content:

As with combinations of a negative and a positive statement into one (. . .), so with inverted and uninverted members of a sentence care is very necessary. (H. W. Fowler, *A Dictionary of Modern English Usage*, s.v. inversion.)

In this case the word-group which has been ellipted is *care is very necessary*. One wonders whether Fowler realized how interesting his own sentences were . . .

Another point worth noting is that it is possible to put the main clause before the sub clause. In this case the thought-content remains intact, but there is a shift of emphasis, the correlative conjunction (*so, likewise,* etc.) is dropped, and the rhetorical effect produced by balanced sentence-structure is lost. Cf. the following example from A. Fairlie, *Flaubert: Madame Bovary* (p. 27.):

To the end, Emma remains ironically unconscious of the devotion she has roused in him, just as she ignores the blind adoration of Charles.

However, if the comparative sub clause precedes the main clause, the insertion of a correlative such as *so* is quasi mandatory. *So* is not simply a rhetorical ornament. It is a grammatical signal. *So* indicates a comparative relationship, while the omission of *so* normally indicates a temporal relationship. Cp. the following examples:

(i) People go further and further away to reach open air and countryside which continuously recedes from them, and just as their working weeks decline and they begin to have more time for leisure, they find they cannot get to the open spaces or the recreation or the beaches which they now have the time to enjoy. (L. G. Alexander, *New Concept English*, Vol. V, p. 150.)

(ii) This is not likely, however, for, as the city grows in size, so the number of citizens is likely to grow at an ever increasing rate (. . .). (M. J. Moroney, *Facts from Figures*, p. 39.)

In sentence (i), *so* has been omitted because the relationship between the sub clause and the main clause is purely temporal. In sentence (ii), however, *so* has been inserted because the relationship between the two clauses is comparative as well as temporal. This is an interesting borderline case.

In conclusion we may consider two other special cases exemplified by the following sentences:

(i) As I said, so will I do. (P. Robertson, *Latin Prose Composition*, p. 111.)
(ii) Like as a father pitieth his children, so the Lord pitieth them that fear him. (Psalms, CIII. 13, quoted in G. O. Curme, *EG*, § 86 B.)

The inversion in sentence (i) is purely rhetorical. This usage is restricted to exalted style.

The use of *like as* in place of *as* in sentence (ii) is decidedly archaic and should not be imitated at all unless a travesty of biblical style is intended.

2. auch einmal: These two words should be treated as a single sense-unit. A rendering of the tonal particle *auch* is unnecessary since addition is implied in the second half of the sentence. The time adverbial *einmal* corresponds to *once* (in mid position). It is important to remember that *once* in mid position means 'at some indefinite time in the past', while *once* in terminal position is a frequency adjunct meaning 'on one occasion only'. For examples see Hornby, *OALDCE*, s.v. once.

3. Bummelstreik: A wide variety of alternatives is given in the German-English dictionaries, but several terms have been overlooked: *work-slowdown, job action, ca'canny, go-slow movement, work-to-rules action. Work-slowdown* is a American coinage. Here is an example from the *International Herald Tribune* of 5–6 January 1980 (p. 1):

(. . .) in 1979 there were work-slowdowns or strikes in Britain, Italy, Spain, Greece and Portugal (. . .).

For *job action* and *work-to-rules action*, cp. C. L. Barnhart/S. Steinmetz/R. K. Barnhart, *A Dictionary of New English*, s.v. job action and H. S. Sloan/A. J. Zurcher, *Dictionary of Economics*, s.v. job action; for *go-slow movement*, cp. J. Rudolph, *Langenscheidts Handbuch der englischen Wirtschaftssprache*, p. 70; and for *ca'canny*, cp. M. Marcheteau/J. Tardieu, *Business and Economics*, Vol. 2. s.v. grève.

It should, however, be noted that these terms are not always interchangeable. In this text it is necessary to distinguish a go-slow movement from a work-to-rules action (see note (3) 6 below), so it is advisable to render *Bummelstreik* by a term such as *go-slow strike* and reserve locutions such as *work-to-rules action* for *Dienst nach Vorschrift*. *Job action* should be avoided here since it is a vague catchall term that can denote all kinds of trade-union tactics ranging from the old-fashioned go-slow to the more recent and sophisticated work-to-rule.

4. machten: The expression *einen Bummelstreik machen* may be rendered by means of the verb *ca'canny* (British English), or by various verb and object phrases such as *to stage a go-slow strike, to organize a slowdown strike, to mount a work-to-rule strike, to undertake a go-slow strike, to embark on a go-slow, to begin a go-slow strike, to launch a go-slow strike* or *to engage in a work-to-rule*. Here are some examples of typical collocations:

After staging a weeklong strike, several hundred workers returned to the plant and were rehired (. . .). (*IHT,* 11. 1. 1980, p. 2.)

The groups which organized the strikes from September onwards, and the militants who toppled the Bakhtiar government in early February, will not easily accept a reimposition of capitalist control, whether represented as 'Islamic' or not. (F. Halliday, *Iran: Dictatorship and Development,* p. 321.)

South Wales miners appeared last night to be in revolt against union leaders' instructions to mount an all-out indefinite strike from Monday. (*The Times,* 22. 2. 1980, p. 1.)

a protest by workers without undertaking a general strike, such as a slow-down or work-to-rules action. (C. L. Barnhart/S. Steinmetz/R. K. Barnhart, *A Dictionary of New English,* s.v. job action.)

The men embarked on a ten-month strike (. . .). (H. Pelling, *A History of British Trade Unionism,* p. 135.)

In February the Miners Federation (. . .) began a national strike to secure a minimum wage (. . .). (*ibid.,* p. 137.)

Meanwhile the railway unions, which in April had engaged in a 'work-to-rule' to persuade the Railways Board to increase its pay offer, had suffered the impact of the Court in a different way. (*ibid.,* p. 279.)

(. . .) labour leaders (. . .) have been willing to launch economy crippling strikes rather than allow introduction of automated equipment. (M. Marcheteau/J. Tardieu, *Business and Economics,* Vol. 1, p. 63.)

Several points need to be made here:
(i) Most of the expressions listed above have a markedly ingressive character of which the German verb *machen* is in itself virtually devoid.
(ii) Journalists often use the metaphorical verbs *stage* and *mount* in order to impart a more dramatic tone to their style. The verb *stage* frequently collocates with lexical items which have unmistakably 'dramatic' associations – *demonstration* and *putsch,* for instance. Cf. the following example from John Ardagh, *The New France* (p. 610):

(. . .) the staff staged a virtual putsch (. . .).

(iii) The verb *take* does not normally collocate with *job action* or *work-to-rules action* although it *is* possible to say *take strike action*. Cf. the following example from G. M. Trevelyan, *British History in the Nineteenth Century and After: 1782–1919* (p. 420):

Under the Taff Vale judgement, Trade Unions durst not, under peril of losing all their funds in damages, take any strike action to raise wages or to prevent the lowering of wages.

Similarly, *go + on* does not normally collocate with *go-slow strike* or *slowdown strike* although the expression *go on strike* can sometimes be expanded by the insertion of an adjective such as *unofficial*. Cf. the following example from H. Pelling, *A History of British Trade Unionism* (p. 238):

The Hull dockers objected to the hand-scuttling method of unloading grain, and went on unofficial strike (. . .).

Go on strike is not an absolutely fixed expression; it is what may be termed a 'semi-idiom'.

5. fingen . . . an: This preterite requires some clarification. At first blush, *fingen . . . an* seems to refer to the remote past, but the use of the present tense (*tun*) in the last part of the sentence gives us pause.

Tun is ambiguous in aspect, just as *fingen . . . an* is ambiguous in time-reference. If the verb *tun* here refers to habitual action, then the second part of the sentence is a generalization, and the preterite *fingen . . . an* can be interpreted as referring to the remote past. If, however, the verb *tun* here refers to an action that was in progress while the text was being written, then the preterite *fingen . . . an* must refer to the recent past (i.e. recent in relation to the writer's time). A perusal of the entire text suggests that these sentences were put down on paper while the strike action was still on. Judging by the style and content, the text is an excerpt from a newspaper article, and such articles normally refer to the present or the recent past rather than the remote past. Moreover, in the second half of the sentence under discussion, there is a complete absence of frequency adjuncts such as *stets* or *immer*; and there is no connecting sentence indicating that the French air controllers got into the habit of organizing work-to-rules actions after their first attempt to imitate their German counterparts. We may therefore conclude that *fingen . . . an* refers to the recent past.

Some scholars have contended that the German preterite cannot denote an action that falls within the time-sphere of the present, but this view is clearly untenable. In German, the distinction between the perfect and the preterite has become blurred, so that the perfect is often used in reference to the remote past, while the preterite is often used in reference to the recent past. In general, the preterite is used to report facts, while the perfect is used to discuss them or to relate them in some way to the present. Hence, in German newspaper articles there is often a shift from the perfect to the preterite at the beginning of a paragraph. Here are two examples from an article published in the *Frankfurter Allgemeine Zeitung* of 4 October 1969 (reprinted in F. Kershaw/S. Russon, *German for Business Studies*, pp. 74–75):

(i) Die Einkommen aus unselbständiger Arbeit haben mit plus 11½ Prozent ebenso kräftig zugenommen wie die Einkommen aus Unternehmertätigkeit und Vermögen (plus 9½ Prozent). Das Volkseinkommen als Summe beider Einkommensquellen stieg gegenüber dem ersten Halbjahr 1968 um 10½ Prozent auf 207 Milliarden DM.

(ii) Etwa gleich stark wie das Volkseinkommen hat im ersten Halbjahr 1969 auch das verfügbare Einkommen der privaten Haushalte zugenommen (10½ Prozent Zuwachs gegenüber dem zweiten Halbjahr 1968). Die Ausgaben für den privaten Verbrauch (9½ Prozent Zuwachs) folgten relativ eng der Einkommensentwicklung.

In both quotations the preterite and perfect verb forms refer to the same time-plane, and the alternation of the two tenses merely indicates shifts in the author's viewpoint. In the case under discussion, the preterite seems to have been used for two reasons. Firstly, the facts are not commented on, but merely reported (in this sentence at least). Secondly, the use of the preterite serves to enhance the parallelism between the *wie*-clause and the *so*-clause. Having examined all the essential aspects of the verb form in question, the translator may confidently render the German preterite as a present perfect. This impairs the symmetry of the comparative sentence, but enables us to avoid an unduly abrupt transition from the past tense to the present tense.

For further information on the use of the preterite and the perfect in German, the reader is referred to the following publications: P. Grebe, *Duden Grammatik der deutschen Gegenwartssprache*, §§ 93–94; J. Erben, *Abriß der deutschen Grammatik*, pp. 54–56; M. Philipp, *Grammaire de l'allemand,* p. 118; H. Weinrich, *Tempus,* pp. 64–69; W. Rasch, ‚Zur Frage des epischen Präteritums', *Wirkendes Wort,* 3. Sonderheft (August 1961), pp. 68–81.

6. Eiferstreik: This coinage, which does not appear in any dictionary, is a calque of the French term *grève du zèle.* Such loan translations are not uncommon in the British and American press. To quote but one example, the French expression *les aiguilleurs du ciel* was rendered literally as *"the switchmen of the sky"* in the *International Herald Tribune* of 5–6 January 1980 (p. 1):

Like their counterparts elsewhere in Europe, French air traffic controllers – known as "the switchmen of the sky" – are determined to relieve the pressures of their work (. . .).

In the case under consideration, however, there is not much point in using a calque which is not in established use. The original French term sounds much more natural and elegant. After all, French words and phrases are bandied about freely in English because many Britons learn French at school and French has had a considerable prestige value in England ever since the time of William the Conqueror.

At this point it may be useful to define the term in question. In French, a distinction is sometimes made between the terms *grève du zèle* and *grève perlée. Grève perlée* is a general term for a go-slow strike, while *grève du zèle* is a more specific term denoting a particular kind of go-slow movement – the so-called work-to-rule. In other words, *grève du zèle* is a hyponym of *grève perlée.* Cf. the definitions given in M. Davau/M. Cohen/M. Lallemand, *Dictionnaire du français vivant,* s.v. grève.

In English, a similar distinction is occasionally made between *go-slow strike* (or *ca'canny*) and *work-to-rule.* Cf. the following snippet from W. Galenson (ed.), *Comparative Labour Movements,* New York, 1952, cited by G. Woodcock in *Anarchism* (p. 410):

The syndicalists have advocated as means of enforcing their demands, the sympathetic strike, the slow-down through literal observance of working rules, shoddy work, and ca'canny.

In most cases, however, the boundary between *work-to-rule* and *go-slow strike* remains hazy and imprecise.

7. das heißt: An exact reproduction of the German punctuational pattern would convey a somewhat idiosyncratic impression. On the whole, the colon is used much more sparingly in English than in German. Cf. G. Collier/B. Shields, *Guided German-English Translation,* p. 152. In normal prose, the colon is not used after expressions such as *namely* or *that is,* but it may replace these locutions. For examples see W. Friederich, *Die Interpunktion im Englischen,* p. 43. If we wish to retain the expression *that is,* we shall have to put a semicolon before it and a comma after it. Here are two typical examples of the use of the comma after *that is*:

Interspersed among the entries identifying "economic principles", schools of economic thought, and economic theories, that is, entries especially appropriate to economics as an academic discipline, there will be found not a few terms derived from the nomenclature of "practical" or "business" economics. (H. S. Sloan/A. J. Zurcher, *Dictionary of Economics,* p. vi.)

For example, under certain assumed conditions, the immediate ownership of a dwelling, when none is possessed, may, for a given individual, offer such a high marginal utility that he is willing to pay a premium for it; that is, he is willing to borrow and pay interest and thus sacrifice the marginal utility of some possession that he might otherwise acquire in the future when the loan must be repaid. (*ibid.,* p. 275.)

8. Forderungen an die Fluggesellschaften: *Claim* denotes the assertion of a right, while *demand* carries strong implications of peremptory insistence (justified or unjustified). Strictly speaking, therefore, the nouns *claim* and *demand* are not synonymous, yet *claim* is often used interchangeably with *demand* in texts about industrial relations. As for the preposition *an,* it is normally rendered as *on* or *upon,* though *against* is also possible. Cf. the following quotation from H. Pelling, *A History of British Trade Unionism* (p. 98):

Stevedores, lightermen, coal porters, and others came out in sympathy – some of them formulating their own demands upon the employers.

However, certain selectional restrictions must be taken into account. *Win* does not normally combine with *demand,* though it collocates well with *claim.* On the other hand, a verb such as *press* may co-occur with either *claim* or *demand.* Furthermore, the preposition *upon* must be replaced by *from* if the verb *win* is used. Here are some examples of typical collocations:

an intentional slowing of pace by workers in order to win their claims from their employers. (Hans G. Hoffmann, *Aufbaukurs Wirtschaft, Lehrerhandbuch,* p. 20.)

After this fiasco the union leaders were in a stronger position to press their claims, which were eventually conceded almost in full. (H. Pelling, *A History of British Trade Unionism,* p. 279.)

(. . .) the Grand National Consolidated Trades Union had not merely set out to press the demands of the workers for better conditions under capitalism (. . .). (G. Woodcock, *Anarchism,* p. 299.)

9. damit: In the German-English dictionaries this word has been rendered as *thereby, and consequently,* and *and thus.* The dictionary makers have overlooked at least three alternatives: *therefore, and hence,* and *and so.* Authors such as Rudolph Flesch object to the use of *thereby, consequently, thus* and *hence.* Translators who consider these words unduly bookish may fall back on *therefore* or *so.*

10. auch: It is a moot point whether to translate or omit this tonal particle. A case might be made out for its omission on the grounds that addition is otherwise implied in the sentence.

11. durchzusetzen: The verb *enforce* (*Der kleine Eichborn,* svv. durchsetzen, Forderung) is by far the commonest equivalent of *durchsetzen* in this sense. Here are some examples.

Labour strove to enforce its demands through strikes (. . .). (R. Sieper, *The Student's Companion to the U.S.A.,* p. 21.)

The journeymen (. . .) began to combine separately from their employers, often with the overt and presumably legal object of petitioning Parliament for the redress of their grievances, but not infrequently also with the purpose of enforcing wage demands against their employers by the direct sanction of bad work, 'go-slows', or 'turn-outs' (later known as strikes). (H. Pelling, *A History of British Trade Unionism,* pp. 18–19.)

A planned and concerted work stoppage by employees in a plant or industry, in an effort to enforce certain demands having to do with their continued employment. (H. S. Sloan/A. J. Zurcher, *Dictionary of Economics,* s.v. strike.)

For a fourth example of the collocation *enforce* + *demands,* see note (3) 6 above. Note the use of *against* after *demands* in the second quotation.

The verb *realize* (Zahn, *Euro-Wirtschaftswörterbuch,* s.v. durchsetzen) is also acceptable here. Cf. the following example from H. H. Nyszkiewicz (ed.), *Economic Texts,* p. 50:

How do power workers hope to realize their claims?

Push (*W./H.*, s.v. durchsetzen) can also be accepted as a translation equivalent of *durchsetzen*. To push claims is to persuade others to recognize them (cf. Hornby, *OALDCE*, s.v. push²). Here is a typical example from *The Economist* of 15—21 August 1981 (p. 45):

It [*sc.* Solidarity] is now likely to push its radical demand for workers' self-management.

This example, however, shows that the meaning indicated in Hornby's dictionary can shade off into other senses such as 'insist on (demands or claims)'. For this reason *push* is a less acceptable equivalent than *enforce* or *realize*. It should, of course, be borne in mind that the verb *enforce* can be ambiguous too. *Enforce* has two distinct meanings: a) 'to make effective' or 'impose'; b) 'to give force to (arguments, etc.)'. In most cases, however, the contextual meaning of *enforce* emerges quite clearly from the co-text. The verb *win*, which has been overlooked by the lexicographers, is a perfectly unambiguous equivalent of *durchsetzen*. An example has already been cited in note (3) 8.

The verb *to settle* (*Der kleine Eichborn*, s.v. Forderung) is also an acceptable equivalent of *durchsetzen*. *Settle claims* is usually followed by the preposition *against*.

The verbs *press* and *back up* often collocate with the nouns *claim* and *demand*, but they can hardly be regarded as satisfactory translation equivalents of *durchsetzen*. To press a claim is to insist that it should be accepted, and to back up a claim is to give support to it. Examples of the collocations *press* + *claim* and *press* + *demand* have already been cited in note (3) 8. An example of the collocation *back up* + *demand* may be found in C. L. Barnhart/S. Steinmetz/R. K. Barnhart, *A Dictionary of New English*, s.v. job action:

The Uniformed Fire Officers Association yesterday voted a "job action" — the refusal to perform nonfirefighting duties — to back up demands for more manpower. (*The New York Times*, 26. 7. 1968, p. 16.)

12. tun: This word, which at first blush seems to present no difficulty whatever, is a snare for the unwary translator. *Tun* must be considered in relation to the other elements in the sentence, for here we have to do with syllepsis, a rhetorical figure in which a single word is used to govern two or more words, although applying to them in different senses. Syllepsis may be distinguished from zeugma, a figure of speech in which a single word is made to refer to two or more words of a construction, although applying in sense to only one of them. The basic difference between these two forms of ellipsis is that syllepsis is grammatically correct, while zeugma, strictly speaking, entails an infraction of the rules governing normal usage. Examples:

(i) Mr. Pickwick took his hat and his leave. (Ch. Dickens, cited in *CED*, s.v. zeugma.)
(ii) Here Thou, Great Anna! whom three Realms obey,
Dost sometimes Counsel take — and sometimes Tea. (A. Pope, 'The Rape of the Lock', Canto III, vv. 7—8.)
(iii) To wage war and peace. (*RHD*, s.v. zeugma.)
(iv) See *Pan* with Flocks, with Fruits *Pomona* crown'd (A. Pope, 'Windsor-Forest', v. 37.)

Quotations (i) and (ii) are instances of syllepsis, while (iii) and (iv) are instances of zeugma.

In our German text, the yoking word *tun* governs both *Dienst* and *Strich*. *Dienst tun* and *keinen Strich tun* are standard collocations recorded in the Duden dictionaries, so that the ellipsis of the verb *tun* before the second word-group appears perfectly natural. In English, however, it is impossible to reproduce this syllepsis because *Dienst nach Vorschrift tun* and *keinen Strich tun* cannot be rendered word for word. *Dienst nach Vorschrift* is *working to rule*, and *keinen Strich tun* is *not to do a stroke of work*. The verb *do* collocates with *stroke of work*, but it does not collocate with *working to rule*, work-

to-rule, work-to-rule strike or *work-to-rules action*. Any attempt to weld such elements together would run counter to established usage: the result would be zeugma, not syllepsis, and zeugma would be quite out of place in this kind of text. In order to avoid bungling the whole sentence, we must therefore recast the sylleptic word-group, using one of the standard collocations listed in note (3) 4.

For further information on syllepsis and zeugma, the reader is referred to the following works: H. Lausberg, *Elemente der literarischen Rhetorik*, §§ 320–326; G. v. Wilpert, *Sachwörterbuch der Literatur*, svv. Syllepse, Zeugma; W. Kayser, *Das sprachliche Kunstwerk*, p. 117; P. Fontanier, *Les figures du discours*, pp. 313–315; H. W. Fowler, *A Dictionary of Modern English Usage*, svv. syllepsis and zeugma; M. H. Abrams, *A Glossary of Literary Terms*, s.v. rhetorical figures; K. Beckson/A. Ganz, *A Reader's Guide to Literary Terms*, svv. syllepsis, zeugma; A. F. Scott, *Current Literary Terms*, svv. syllepsis, zeugma; W. K. Wimsatt, *The Verbal Icon*, pp. 177–179.

The next point to consider is whether the German verb should be rendered as a simple or a progressive form. There is good reason, as we have observed (cf. note (3) 5 above), for thinking that the verb *tun* refers to an action that was in progress while the text was being written, and there are no indications that the action is considered as habitual or repetitive. The verb *tun* must therefore be rendered by a progressive form. Verbs such as *organize, mount, undertake, embark, begin* and *launch* can be used in the progressive form, but they would be inappropriate here because, owing to their markedly inchoative denotations, they would imply that the work-to-rules action had not yet really got under way when the text was written. *Engage in* or *stage* would be much more suitable in this context.

13. das, was ... nennen: In this particular instance, German and English usage coincide. 'What'-sentences, however, are often quite tricky. Cf. W. Friederich, *Technik des Übersetzens*, pp. 119–124. *Nennen* may also present difficulties in translation. Even native speakers are apt to forget that the verb *term* is used without *as*, although *describe* (in the sense of *nennen* or *bezeichnen*) combines with *as*. Cf. F.T. Wood, *Current English Usage*, s.v. term. Example:

In informal British English, the causing of damage to a factory during a labour dispute is termed rattening (*or* is described as rattening).

14. und nicht einen Strich mehr: As we have already seen (note (3) 12), it is quite impossible to ellipt the verb in this word-group. However, this is not the only difficulty presented by this syntagma. We cannot simply insert the verb *do* and translate word for word. A syntagma such as *and do not do a stroke of work more* would be conspicuously unidiomatic. The expression *not to do a stroke of work* can be used only in a limited number of patterns. We can say *I haven't done a stroke of work today* or *He never does a stroke of work*, but we cannot simply add the word *more* and leave it at that. If we write *and do not do a stroke of work more*, the English reader will naturally ask 'More than what?' So we shall have to be more explicit and write *more than is necessary* or *more than is absolutely necesssary*.

There are, of course, other ways of rendering the German idiom in question. We can substitute the noun *tap* for *stroke*, or we can use a locution such as *He didn't stir a finger, He didn't lift a finger, He didn't raise a finger*, or *He didn't lift a hand*. Yet none of these expressions will do here because a word-group introduced by *more* would sound very odd after a noun such as *finger* or *hand*.

And never do a stroke of work more than is absolutely necessary would be an acceptable rendering of the word-group under discussion, but we can make the sentence more compact by converting the finite clause into a non-finite clause. In English, a present participle is often used to explicate a preceding finite verb form. In such cases, the finite verb and the non-finite verb denote actions or processes which are co-extensive, complementary or inclusive of each other, and there is often a more or less explicit cause-and-effect relationship between the actions or processes involved. Examples:

(i) (. . .) this relative disparity between expenditures on capital, as opposed to consumer goods, continues even as production increases, the trend being aided by the effect of competition. (H. J. Sloan/A. J. Zurcher, *Dictionary of Economics,* pp. 277–278.)
(ii) From this premise it is argued that although the worker is entitled to all the value he produces, he receives only that portion necessary for his upkeep, the remainder passing to the capitalist as profit or surplus value. (*ibid.,* p. 424.)
(iii) (. . .) works like *La Chevelure* or *Le Cygne* move subtly and almost imperceptibly between outer and inner worlds, constantly enriching each by analogies with the other. (A. Fairlie, *Baudelaire: Les Fleurs du Mal,* p. 20.)
(iv) He condemned the earlier poetic technique, demanding clarity and rational form in expression (. . .). (J. W. H. Atkins, *English Literary Criticism: 17th and 18th Centuries,* p. 5.)

In examples (i) and (ii), the finite and non-finite verb forms have different subjects, while in (iii) and (iv) the subjects are identical. In both cases, however, the basic principle is the same.

The question of negation also calls for a few remarks. In this particular instance, *never* can be used in lieu of *not.* Foreign students of English are apt to overlook the fact that *never* is not only a time frequency adjunct, but also an emphatic negative. In *Usage and Abusage* (s.v. never), Eric Partridge reminds his readers that *never* as a substitute for *not* is a colloquialism which may sound incongruous in formal writing. In the case under discussion, however, the style is sufficiently informal to warrant the use of *never* as a negative minimizer, and anyhow the familiar undertones of *never* as a negative are muted owing to the absence of an adverbial which might rule out the temporal meaning of *never* through reference to a specific future time. Besides, there is at present a marked tendency towards a more relaxed tone in most types of writing, so that many words and phrases which were once confined to familiar conversation have now been admitted into good formal or semi-formal usage. For further information on the use of *never* as a means of negative intensification, the reader is referred to the following books: R. Quirk et al., *GCE,* § 8.30; R. Quirk/S. Greenbaum, *UGE,* § 8.17; J. P. Vinay/J. Darbelnet, *Stylistique comparée du français et de l'anglais,* § 59; E. Partridge, *Usage and Abusage,* s.v. never; H. W. Fowler, *A Dictionary of Modern English Usage,* s.v. never; F. T. Wood, *English Colloquial Idioms,* s.v. never.

A good alternative to the negative particle *never* is the verb *refuse,* which implies decisiveness, and even ungraciousness, thereby emphasizing the idea of obstinate and wilful rebelliousness or resistance to authority.

b) Alternatives

Just as	the German	air controllers		once	staged	a
″ ″		air traffic controllers			organized	″
″ ″		air traffic control staff			mounted	″
″ ″		controllers			undertook	″
″ ″					embarked on	″
As					launched	″
					engaged in	″

so-called	go-slow strike,		so		their French
″	go-slow,		so also		
″	slowdown strike, (U.S.)		so too		
″	slowdown, (U.S.)		likewise		
″	work-slowdown, (U.S.)		in the same manner		
″	go-slow movement,		so		
″	ca'canny				

counterparts	have begun a	*grève du zèle*; that is, in order to
colleagues		: [ ]

enforce	their	demands		on	the	airline companies	and
realize	″	claims		upon		airlines	
push	″	″	/demands	against		air transport companies	
settle	″	″		″		air-lines	
win	″	″		from		airways	
						carriers	

thus		on the	Government,	they are	engaging in	what they
thereby			State,		staging	
consequently						
therefore						
hence						
so						

term	a	work-to-rule campaign,	refusing to do	a stroke of
call		″ work-to-rules action,	never doing	
describe as	″	work-to-rule,		

work more than is	*absolutely necessary.*
	necessary.

④ Da sie eigentlich nicht streiken dürfen, ist diese Form äußerster „Pflichterfüllung" ihr Ersatz für den Streik, zu dem sie sich, wie sie immer wieder betonen, genauso berechtigt glauben, wie andere Angestellte.

a) Annotations

1. Da: The commonest translation equivalents of the causal subordinator *da* are *since, as, because* and *seeing that*. These conjunctions must be carefully distinguished from one another.

In general, the causal conjunctions *as* and *since* are used to introduce the 'logical' reason or reasons from which the statement in the main clause is deduced. *Because,* on the other hand, is normally used to introduce the 'true' reason or reasons for a statement. It follows therefore that clauses introduced by *as* or *since* have a tendency to precede the main clause, while clauses introduced by *because* have a tendency to follow the main clause. Examples:

As these elements constitute 99 per cent of all living things, including plants, they are obviously of prime importance. (G. Holister/A. Porteous, *The Environment,* p. 39.)

Since conservationists argue strongly against the throw-away philosophy, with some justification on energy consumed, a strong case can be made for bottle standardization and the enforced use of returnables so that both energy and materials are conserved. (*ibid.,* p. 41.)

Ulysses and other works by James Joyce have been excluded because the author, although fully aware of their germinal importance for modern fiction, believes that they have been more than adequately discussed and analyzed. (S. Spencer, *Space, Time and Structure in the Modern Novel,* p. xxiii.)

These examples show how the positional tendencies of various clause types reflect various types of thought progression. A writer who uses *because* invites us to accept his conclusions unquestioningly, while a writer who uses *since* or *as* invites us to follow his line of thought attentively in the hope that we shall eventually arrive at the same conclusions as he did. The use of *because* often conveys an impression of peremptoriness, while the use of *since* or *as* tends to be more persuasive.

It is also possible to make certain distinctions between *as* and *since.* R. W. Zandvoort makes an excellent point when he says that the use of *since* implies that the cause or reason is an undisputed fact (*HEG,* § 632). One might also note that *since,* unlike *as,* may easily be brought into accentual prominence. This is probably the reason why the causal conjunction *as* is not normally followed by a parenthesis. In connected speech, a parenthesis is always introduced by a distinct pause, and it is hardly possible to make a clearly audible prosodic break after an unaccented and weak word. *Since,* like *because,* is quite frequently followed by parenthetic words and phrases. Examples:

Since, on singles, the banker breaks even, his total profit on this series in which expectation is realized will be 102 units out of 1,296 units staked. (M. J. Moroney, *Facts from Figures,* p. 85.)

Historical digressions are avoided because, in the authors' view, contemporary and diachronic grammar are best treated separately. (From the blurb on the dust jacket of Zandvoort's *Handbook of English Grammar.*)

It is, of course, virtually impossible to lay down hard and fast rules for the use and discrimination of these conjunctions, especially since contemporary usage is often characterized by a certain muzziness and indecision.

Sometimes *because* is used at the opening of a sentence, though this does not necessarily mean that *because* is treated as a synonym of *as* or *since. As* and *since,* however, are often used as if they were synonymous with *because* (probably on account of their brevity), and the use of *especially as* or *especially since* after a main clause is in no way contrary to established usage. Examples:

Because he has quarrelled with the chairman he has resigned. (R. Quirk et al., *GCE,* § 9.26.)

Because the profiles are based on proportions, they both have the same area. (G. Holister/A. Porteous, *The Environment,* p.21.)

He could not work as he was ill in bed. (E. Partridge, *Usage and Abusage,* s.v. *as* for *because.*)

The ideology behind best practicable means causes much controversy as it is considered to be a loophole which may allow industry to emit noxious or injurious substances in greater amounts than would have been allowed had absolute standards been imposed. (G. Holister/A. Porteous, *The Environment,* p. 36.)

(. . .) in many cases, one has not felt it necessary to supply an English title, since most readers will know enough French to translate the names of the books in question for themselves. (S. Spencer, *Space, Time and Structure in the Modern Novel*, p. xxii.)

It is also interesting to note that clauses of reason or cause introduced by *since* are often embedded into main clauses, especially in literary English:

Her connexion with Palmer and Honor, since she did not share in the knowledge that was crucial, seemed flimsy and abstract compared with mine. (I. Murdoch, *A Severed Head*, p. 154.)

Finally, we should remember that there is a special kind of final *because*-clause which functions as a disjunct of reason:

He's drunk, because I saw him staggering. (R. Quirk et al., *GCE*, § 9.23.)
He must hate women, because he certainly treats them badly. (G. Collier/B. Shields, *Guided German-English Translation*, p. 93.)

Here the logical relationship between the main clause and the sub clause is implicit ('semantic implication'). The main clause contains an assumption, while the sub clause gives the reason for the assumption instead of the real reason for the fact assumed to be true. Comma separation is mandatory, and the substitution of *as* or *since* for *because* would be contrary to established usage.

The compound conjunction *seeing that* is rather different from *because, since* and *as. Seeing that,* which means 'considering that' or 'in the light of the fact that', introduces clauses of circumstance, that is, sub clauses which are 'semantically half-way between conditional clauses and clauses of reason' (R. Quirk et al., *GCE*, § 11.38). These clauses may precede or follow a main clause. Examples:

Seeing that the weather has improved, we shall be able to enjoy our game. (R. Quirk et al., *GCE*, § 11.38.)
Your harshness to him is strange, seeing that you have always been good friends. (G. O. Curme, *EG*, § 88 A.)

For further information on *since, as, because* and *seeing that,* the reader is referred to the following works: R. Quirk et al., *GCE*, §§ 9.23, 11,37, 11.38; R. W. Zandvoort, *HEG,* § 632; G. O. Curme, *EG,* § 88 A; H. W. Fowler, *A Dictionary of Modern English Usage,* svv. as, because; E. Partridge, *Usage and Abusage,* svv. as, because; R. Flesch, *The ABC of Style,* s.v. as.

2. eigentlich: Disjuncts such as *strictly speaking* are usually positioned at the beginning of a clause. Examples:

Strictly speaking, he should have been here by now. (G. Collier/B. Shields, *Guided German-English Translation,* p. 163.)
Strictly speaking, that's not the thing to do. (*ibid.*)

However, the locution *strictly speaking* may occupy mid-position when used as an adjunct. Example:

He is not strictly speaking a chemist. (Hornby, *OALDCE,* s.v. proper.)

3. streiken: Here it is necessary to draw a distinction between the inchoative and the durative aspects of the verb *streiken.* The inchoative aspect is rendered by expressions such as *come out on strike* (= in den Streik treten), while the durative aspect is rendered by expressions such as *to be on strike* or *to be out on strike* (= sich im Streik befinden). In the case under consideration, the aspect of the verb *streiken* is clearly inchoative, so all the durative expressions given in the dictionaries are automatically ruled out.

The next problem is to select an appropriate word or phrase capable of rendering the inchoative aspect of *streiken.*

The phrase *to strike work* (recorded in *Cassell's German and English Dictionary*, s.v. streiken) is obsolete. It was ousted by the verb *strike* in the early nineteenth century. Cf. H. Pelling, *A History of British Trade Unionism*, p. 19 (note).
Down tools would be inappropriate here because it is normally used only of workmen. The verb *strike* and practically all the other locutions listed in the dictionaries would be acceptable here. It is, however, worth noting that the verb *strike* (in the sense of *streiken*) is nowadays used almost exclusively in the infinitive. None the less, finite forms of *strike* still occasionally crop up in the works of contemporary authors whose style is otherwise very up-to-date. Examples:

They therefore struck to obtain the necessary direct recognition. (H. Pelling, *A History of British Trade Unionism*, p. 240.)

(. . .) workers have come out for better conditions – as in the Renault plant at Le Mans in 1971 – or else they have struck mainly in the declining industries in the depressed areas, where wages are below average and jobs are insecure. (J. Ardagh, *The New France*, pp. 60–61.)

4. nicht streiken dürfen: In France, strikes by controllers have been illegal since 1964.

5. diese Form äußerster „Pflichterfüllung" In this case, the translation equivalents given in the dictionaries are quite useless. Expressions such as *performance of a duty* or *fulfilment of one's duty* would sound decidedly odd in this context, and, what is more, adjectives such as *extreme, utmost* or *maximum* do not collocate well with *performance* or *fulfilment*.

However, it is possible to reproduce the pattern of the German word-group by rendering *äußerst* by an adjective such as *over-punctilious* and *Pflichterfüllung* by a phrase such as *adherence to rules and regulations*. *Observance of* could be substituted for *adherence to*, but this rendering would have an air of infelicity because it would entail the repetition of the preposition *of* (*this form* of *over-punctilious observation* of *rules and regulations*).

Pflichterfüllung can also be translated by a phrase such as *manner in which they perform their duties of employment*. Typical collocations may be found in various monolingual dictionary definitions of the verb phrase *work to rule* and the compound nouns *work-to-rule* and *job action:*

pay exaggerated attention (deliberately) to rules and regulations and so slow down out output. (Hornby, *OALDCE*, s.v. rule.)

a curtailment of output by workers by observing safety rules etc. with exaggerated care. (*PED*, s.v. work-to-rule.)

a form of industrial action in which employees adhere strictly to all the working rules laid down by their employers, with the deliberate intention of reducing the rate of working. (*CED*, s.v. work-to-rule.)

A vague term used to identify such a trade-union tactic as refusal to perform certain normal duties of employment while continuing duties essential to the public's health and security (. . .). (H.S. Sloan/A. J. Zurcher, *Dictionary of Economics*, s.v. job action.)

Expressions such as *rules and regulations* and *working rules* may, of course, be replaced by *working regulations:*

But today staff are protected by new social insurance schemes and working regulations (. . .). (J. Ardagh, *The New France*, p. 397.)

6. Ersatz: The British borrowed the noun *Ersatz* from German as early as 1875 (according to the *S.O.E.D.*), and *ersatz* (almost invariably written with a small letter) is now firmly established in the English vocabulary. It has even undergone a slight semantic shift in so far as it is used almost exclusively in a depreciatory sense, while the German word *Ersatz* is used only occasionally with pejorative connotations. In the case under consideration, the word *Ersatz* is evaluatively neutral and should therefore be rendered as *substitute*.

For further information on *ersatz* and other borrowings from German, the reader is referred to the following works: H. W. Fowler, *A Dictionary of Modern English Usage*, s.v. ersatz; J. Buchanan-Brown et al. (edd.), *Le Mot Juste*, pp. 103–114; B. Foster, *The Changing English Language*, pp. 102–112; T. Pyles, *The Origins and Development of the English Language*, pp. 332–334; C. L. Wrenn, *The English Language*, p. 68; P. Bacquet, *Le Vocabulaire anglais*, p. 112; G. J. Forgue, *Les mots américains*, pp. 54–56.

7. Wie ... betonen: The conjunction *wie* should be left untranslated here. It is necessary to draw a distinction between two different types of *wie*-clause which may be embedded inside other clauses: a) parenthetical clauses that are semantically peripheral to the superordinate clause; b) parenthetical clauses that are semantically integrated in the superordinate clause. Examples:

(i) Dabei werden, wie bei der Informationsdarstellung noch gezeigt wird, alle arithmetischen Operationen auf Additionen zurückgeführt und über diese ausgeführt. (J. Biethahn, *Einführung in die EDV für Wirtschaftswissenschaftler*, p. 42.)
(ii) Ich will lieber mit Platon irren, den du, wie ich weiß, sehr hoch schätzest. (E. Bornemann, *Lateinisches Unterrichtswerk*, p. 137.)
(iii) Der Chef, der, wie Sie sich denken können, meinem Hofrat Behrens in Äußerlichkeiten ein wenig ähnlich sah, beklopfte mich und stellte mit großer Schnelligkeit eine sogenannte Dämpfung, einen kranken Punkt an meiner Lunge fest (. . .). (T. Mann, *Der Zauberberg*, p. vii.)

In order to interpret these sentences correctly, the translator must coordinate syntactic and semantic analysis. Syntactically, all three sentences belong to the same category; yet careful analysis reveals important semantic differences. In each case, we can remove the *wie*-clause without essentially damaging the intelligibility of the statement. In sentence (ii), however, the removal of the *wie*-clause modifies the import of the statement. This is because *wie ich weiß* is semantically integrated in the structure of the relative clause *den du . . . sehr hoch schätzest*. The parenthesis *wie ich weiß* modifies the meaning of the statement by presenting the contents of the relative clause as an indisputable fact. The parenthesis in sentence (iii) seems at first sight to belong to the same class as the parenthesis is sentence (ii), especially since it is embedded within a relative clause; in fact, however, the parenthesis *wie Sie sich denken können* is semantically peripheral to the clause in which it is embedded, just like the parenthesis in sentence (i). As for the *wie*-clause in the text under discussion, it belongs to the same category as the parenthesis in sentence (ii) since it modifies the meaning of the superordinate relative clause. The parenthesis *wie sie immer wieder betonen* clearly indicates that the air controllers have given direct expression to their views about their rights, so that the author's statement about these views cannot be considered as a mere inference or conjecture.

The *wie*-clauses in sentences (i) and (iii) can be rendered more or less literally into English with the aid of the conjunction *as*, but the *wie*-clause in sentence (ii) must be rendered without *as: for whom I know you have a great regard*. Cf. the Latin equivalent: *errare malo cum Platone, quem tu quanti facias, scio*. In English, as in Latin, the relative pronoun is drawn into the sub clause embedded within the relative clause. This is the construction which German scholars describe as *relativische Verschränkung*.

The English are exceptionally fond of embedding short sub clauses within relative and other constructions, and it may be useful to attempt a classification of the resultant structures, especially since most foreign students of English find many of these structures particularly bewildering and often virtually untranslatable:

a) the simple parenthesis introduced by *as:*

Another reason why be had selected Blessed Lydwine as the subject of his first essay in hagiography was that she was a native of Holland, a country which, as has been seen, commanded his affection and hereditary loyalties. (R. Baldick, *The Life of J.-K. Huysmans,* p. 292.)

This type of parenthesis is neither semantically nor syntactically connected with the clause within which it is embedded.

b) the parenthesis without *as:*

(i) The general form of the original work has, however, been retained: a form which, I think, has justified itself with English readers who have looked to it for a survey of the literature of the German-speaking peoples. (J. G. Robertson, *A History of German Literature,* p.v.)

(ii) Another feature it has in common with its predecessor is the addition of a few carefully selected verse translations, which, it is hoped, will encourage students to attempt similar work themselves. (A. Watson Bain, *German Poetry for Students,* p.vi.)

Like the *as*-clause cited under a), this type of parenthesis is syntactically independent of the clause within which it is embedded. There is, however, a tenuous semantic link between the embedded clause and the superordinate relative clause. Such parentheses fulfil more or less the same function as the German attitudinal disjuncts *meines Erachtens* and *hoffentlich.*

c) sub clauses interlocked with relative clauses ('push-down' clauses):

(i) The *Dark Ladie* itself is a fragment of ballad which Coleridge never finished but which he tells us in *Biographia Literaria* [ii. 6] he was preparing at about the time he wrote the *Ancient Mariner.* (Wordsworth and Coleridge, *Lyrical Ballads,* edd. R. L. Brett/A. R. Jones, pp. 297–298.)

(ii) The only important parts of the text I believe I have omitted in this summary are its anti-realistic opening and concluding chapters. (R. Fowler (ed.), *Style and Structure in Literature,* p. 181.)

(iii) In Section IV I have outlined a method of free composition which I have found helps to break down the habit of translating whatever thoughts come into the pupil's mind into that sort of "German" which involves so much laborious correction for the teacher. (L. J. Russon, *Complete German Course for First Examinations,* p. vii).

(iv) What literature, then, inspired me to write those first things, which, looking back on them now, I realize were so heavily didactic? (D. Herms, *Englisch-deutsche Übersetzung,* p. 28.)

(v) It is a way of thinking (. . .) which exposes the inner dynamism that is bound to lead from capitalism to some other post-capitalist order which we have agreed to describe as a socialist one. (*ibid.,* p. 38.)

(vi) Each of the 540 engines that the British company had contracted to deliver to Lockheed at $ 840,000 would have cost more than $ 1.1 million to build. (H. G. Hoffmann, *Aufbaukurs Wirtschaft,* p. 90.)

(vii) There are some departures from the usual lay-out (. . .) which the author has found from practical experience to be useful. (C. M. Glover, *A Concise Latin Grammar,* p.v.)

(viii) This is taken so far in some cases that a whole story becomes a kind of dialogue between the narrator's view of the world and the view of the world the author assumes us to have. (R. Fowler (ed.), *Style and Structure in Literature,* p. 159.)

(ix) It must also be something that his employer wants him to communicate to himself or to others. (E. Newton, *European Painting and Sculpture,* p. 17.)

(x) Such a theory is manifestly absurd, because it leaves out of account all that we have already found to be common to all the arts. (*ibid,* p. 26.)

(xi) Based on a story from Erasmus Darwin's *Zoönomia, or the laws of Organic Life,* 2 vols., 1794–6, which Wordsworth persuaded Joseph Cottle to borrow for him in June 1797. (Wordsworth and Coleridge, *Lyrical Ballads,* edd. R. L. Brett/A. R. Jones, p. 282.)

(xii) Section I is designed to give a reasonably adequate German grammar which (. . .) will (. . .) be full enough to explain by rule and particularly by example any points of difficulty which could fairly be expected to arise at this stage of German. (L. J. Russon, *Complete German Course for First Examinations*, p.v.)
(xiii) Jonathan Culler has set out in his paper some criteria by which I would be happy for the validity of the analytical methods I have sketched out to be assessed. (R. Fowler (ed.), *Style and Structure in Literature*, p. 211.)
(xiv) I will introduce you to-morrow to the lady whose acquaintance you say you have long been anxious to make. (L. S. R. Byrne/E. L. Churchill, *A Comprehensive French Grammar*, p. 196.)
(xv) Honor was dressed in a high-necked black garment of which I could not remember afterwards whether it was a silk dress or an overall. (I. Murdoch, *A Severed Head*, p. 167.)

These examples show that dovetailing can occur in practically any kind of relative clause: contact clauses (ii and viii), and clauses introduced by *which* (i, iii, iv, etc.), *that* (vi, ix and x), *whose* (xiv), *of which* (xv) or *by which* (xiii).

The pushdown elements represent several structural types and may be embedded at various levels within the relative clause: noun clauses dependent on verbs of saying, thinking, etc. (i, ii, iii, iv and xiv), infinitives that conceal full subordinate clauses (v and vi), accusative and infinitive constructions (vii, viii, ix, x and xi), nominative and infinitive constructions (xii), non-finite verbal constructions introduced by *for* (xiii), and indirect questions introduced by *whether* (xv). Sometimes one pushdown element is embedded within another. Sentence (iv) is a relatively simple example of this embedding type, but in sentence (xiii) the process of embedding is taken to its ultimate refinement in an elaborate Chinese box arrangement of units.

In this domain of syntax it is very hard to establish satisfactory formal correspondences between German and English. It is often possible to render pushdown elements by adverbials:

I believe (ii): meines Wissens[1]
I have found (iii): nach meiner Erfahrung
we have agreed (v): einmütig
had contracted (vi): laut Vertrag, vertragsgemäß

In many cases, however, it seems advisable to recast the whole relative clause, transposing parts of speech in order to reduce the number of subordinators to a minimum. Sentence (iv) is a case in point:

Welche Art Literatur inspirierte mich denn damals zu diesen frühen Schriften, deren übertrieben lehrhaften Charakter ich erst jetzt im nachhinein erkenne?

The rendering proposed by Dieter Herms (*op. cit.*, p. 73) is somewhat more literal than mine. There are three subordinators: *die, wie* and *wenn:*

Welche Art Literatur inspirierte mich denn damals zu diesen frühen Sachen, die, wie mir klar wird, wenn ich heute auf sie zurückblicke, so stark belehrend waren?

It is a curious fact that these intricate constructions, which often daunt even the most resourceful translators, can usually be generated quite easily in monolingual coursework. The only serious problem likely to be encountered outside the circumscribed domain of translation is the choice between *who* and *whom*. This question has been a subject of much controversy between grammarians. According to G. O. Curme, H. W. Fowler, E. Gowers, E. Partridge, F. T. Wood and R. Quirk, *whom* should be used only if the relative pronoun can be proved to be the logical object of the first finite verb that follows the pushdown element. However, this nice point of grammar is seldom

---

[1] In other contexts one might also resort to solutions such as *meiner Meinung nach*.

remembered or even understood, and the rule laid down by the strict grammarians is unconcernedly infringed by the generality of native speakers, and even by contemporary writers held in high esteem. There is a widespread tendency always to use *whom* in preference to *who*, although *whom* is now on its way out in most other types of sentence (cf. W. Friederich, *Englische Morphologie*, p. 116.) In *The ABC of Style* (p. 298), Rudolph Flesch boldly maintains that 'the *whom* usage is now firmly established', and with his wonted iconoclastic fervour he has come out in favour of this usage.

It is a moot point whether one kind of usage should be considered more acceptable than another. F. T. Wood tried to justify prescriptive usage by arguing that the pushdown elements 'have the force of parentheses and could be moved to another part of the sentence' (*Current English Usage*, p. 260). However, his examples sound very strange when the pushdown elements are displaced, and Sir Ernest Gowers has shown that the parenthesis argument is fundamentally unsound (cf. H. W. Fowler, *A Dictionary of Modern English Usage*, p. 709). Yet even Gowers' arguments are assailable in so far as they are based on prescriptivist assumptions about the English nominative and accusative. It would be possible, for example, to make out a case for the use of *who* in sentences of the type *Bateman could not imagine who it was that he passed off as his nephew*. Here one might argue that *who* is the subject of *was* and not the object of *passed off*. But surely the pronoun *who* fulfils both functions? And surely the nominative and accusative forms are both justifiable? And after all, there is no reason to assume that the verb *to be* must invariably be combined with a nominative form. We say *It's me* and *That's him*, although prescriptive grammarians have obstinately maintained that the nominative forms *I* and *he* should be used here on the analogy of Latin (cf. W. Friederich, *Englische Morphologie*, p. 116; F. Palmer, *Grammar*, pp. 14–17). English is not subject to the laws of Latin grammar; and anyway, the laws of Latin grammar are every bit as arbitrary as those of any other language. In Arabic, for instance, the verb *laysa* (= not to be) requires the accusative to follow it, so that one has to translate *I'm not a student* as *lastu ṭāliban* and not **lastu ṭālibun* (cf. A. A. Ambros, *Einführung in die arabische Schriftsprache*, pp. 99–100).

Why do so many well-educated native speakers persist in violating the rules of prescriptive grammar by writing 'hypercorrect' sentences such as *The man whom we thought was guilty proved to be innocent* (F. T. Wood, *Current English Usage*, p. 259)? The main reason, I think, is the analogy between this type of construction and structures such as *The man whom we saw was guilty*. The demon of analogy is at work everywhere in language, surreptitiously sapping the defences of the prescriptivists, slowly but surely effacing obsolescent and artificial distinctions in speech sounds, syntax and vocabulary. There are remarkable parallels between English and Latin usage in this domain, but I do not believe that the present tendency to use *whom* in preference to *who* is due to Latin influence. Linguistic history sometimes repeats itself, and modern English has in some respects regenerated syntactical patterns that were common in classical Latin (cf. in particular the examples quoted in A. Linnenkugel/P. Friling, *Lateinische Grammatik*, p. 148).

In order to avoid being penalized by grimly conservative examiners, foreign students of English generally prefer to observe the rigid rules set up by prescriptivists, but these quaint academic rules, which are already widely considered as a dead letter, will probably be relegated to the dusty archives of linguistic history in the not too distant future.

For further information on *who* and *whom*, the reader is referred to the following works: F. T. Wood, *Current English Usage*, s.v. who: whom; E. Partridge, *Usage and Abusage*, s.v. *who* and *whom*; H. W. Fowler, *A Dictionary of Modern English Usage*, pp. 708–9; G. O. Curme, *EG*, § 80. E. 3; R. Flesch, *The ABC of Style*, s.v. *who* or *whom*?; R. Quirk et al., *GCE*, § 13.42.

d) Sub clauses interlocked with nominal clauses introduced by *what:*

(i) It is therefore valuable practice for you to get used to explaining what you think the passage means without referring to a set of possible answers, three of which are wrong. (W. S. Fowler, *Proficiency English*, Vol. 2, p. viii.)
(ii) Such teachers can comment upon structure and metre, but are insensitive to rhythm, read badly, and never get beyond a strictly rational account of what they think the poem is about. (M. Boulton, *The Anatomy of Poetry*, p. vii.)
(iii) 'But that is what you said all artists do', the reader may object. (E. Newton, *European Painting and Sculpture*, p. 45.)
(iv) Mr and Mrs Meier tell him what they hope they and Harvey will do then. (W. Bliemel/ A. Fitzpatrick/J. Quetz, *Englisch für Erwachsene*, Vol. 1, p. 92.)

Since *what* is here equivalent to *that which*, these nominal clauses are really relative clauses in disguise. They may be termed 'nominal relative clauses' (R. Quirk et al., *GCE*, § 11.14). In most cases, they make nasty brain-teasers for the translator. Sometimes, a *what*-clause can be rendered quite neatly by a noun phrase, but it is often necessary to resort to more complex transformations in order to produce an acceptable German translation. Sentence (iv) is a case in point:

Herr und Frau Meier sagen ihm, was sie dann zusammen mit Harvey zu unternehmen hoffen.

Here it is possible to avoid an ungainly hypotactic construction because the subjects of *hope* and *will do* are almost identical. The subject of *will do* is merely an extension of the subject of *hope:*

(i) they (= Mr Meier + Mrs Meier) hope
(ii) they and Harvey (= Mr Meier + Mrs Meier + Harvey) will do

The additional element in the second subject (*Harvey*) can be rendered as a prepositional phrase (*zusammen mit Harvey*) in order to facilitate syntactical integration.

e) sub clauses embedded within *wh*-questions:

(i) When do you think I can leave? (P. Giorgetti/J. Norman, *Italian Phrase Book*, p. 136.)
(ii) What do you think that cost? (C. P. Snow, *Last Things*, p. 203.)
(iii) What sort of shape can she think her body is? (V. Woolf, *The Voyage Out*, p. 158.)
(iv) How do you think I can do my Latin with you interrupting every few seconds? (W. Friedrich, *Technik des Übersetzens*, p. 138.)
(v) Ah, but how long do you think it'll last? (V. Woolf, *To the Lighthouse*, p. 123.)
(vi) What do you think we ought to do? (C. H. Jaffé, *Englisch für alle Fälle*, p. 77.)

In German it is sometimes possible to recast the sentence in such a way that a clumsy succession of sub clauses can be avoided. In sentence (i), for example, the 'push-down' clause *do you think* can be rendered by the particle *wohl*, and in sentence (iv) *How do you think I can* may be rendered quite simply as *Wie soll ich:*

Wann kann ich wohl abreisen?
Wie soll ich mein Latein machen, wo du mich dauernd unterbrichst? (W. Friedrich, *op. cit.*, p. 138.)

In a great many cases, however, English and German follow more or less the same pattern:

(i) Was glauben Sie, was ich Ihnen sagen kann? (D. Wellershoff, *Die Sirene*, p. 14.)
What do you think I can tell you?

(ii) Was glaubst du, wer hier war? (E. Kästner, *Drei Männer im Schnee,* p. 149.)
Who do you think was here?

Two points are worth noting here. Firstly, English uses connecters more sparingly than German: in sentence (i), *was* . . . *was* corresponds to *what,* and in sentence (ii) *was* . . . *wer* corresponds to *who.* Secondly, the anticipatory use of the interrogative pronoun *was* has no parallel whatever in English. It would be quite impossible to use the interrogative pronoun *what* to introduce a personal pronoun such as *who.*

8. immer wieder: This locution is often rendered by adverbials such as *time and again* or *time and time again.* F. T. Wood asserts that '*time and time again* is to be preferred' to *time and again* (*Current English Usage,* p. 238), but he makes no attempt to justify this somewhat arbitrary ruling.

The expression immer wieder can also be rendered quite neatly by the construction *keep (on)* + *-ing* form, which expresses continuity or frequent and persistent repetition. Adverbials such as *time and again* or *again and again* convey an impression of objectivity, while the *keep-* construction imparts a more personal tone to the style. Cf. A. Lamprecht, *GES,* § 225.

9. sich . . . berechtigt glauben: A quasi-literal reproduction of the German construction would sound somewhat stilted: *to which, they keep insisting, they believe themselves [to be] entitled just as much as other employees.* It is therefore preferable to render *berechtigt* by means of the expression *to have rights.* This conversion, of course, involves rather radical reorganization: *they believe [that] they have exactly the same rights as other employees.* The subordinating conjunction *that* is ellipted. Such ellipsis is customary at the beginning of a noun clause introduced by a 'push-down' clause within a relative clause. In this case, *they believe* is the 'push-down' clause. It is even more fully integrated in the relative clause structure than the preceding word sequence *they keep insisting,* and it is thus even more closely akin to the kind of German parenthesis dealt with in E. Bornemann's *Lateinisches Unterrichtswerk* (p. 137). Cf. the preceding note on multiple embeddings in English.

b) Alternatives

Since, strictly speaking, they are not allowed to		*strike,* *come out on strike,* *go on strike,* *go out on strike,* *walk out,* *walk off,* (U.S.) *leave work,* *stop work,*	
this form of	*over-punctilious* *over-scrupulous* *over-particular* *over-meticulous* *over-strict* *over-exact* *unduly punctilious* *exaggeratedly punctilious*	adherence to	*rules and regulations* *working rules* *working regulations*
this	*over-punctilious* *over-scrupulous* *over-particular* *over-meticulous* *over-strict* *over-exact* *unduly punctilious* *exaggeratedly punctilious* *exaggerated*	manner in which they care with which	*perform their duties of employment* *observe rules and regulations* *adhere to working rules* „ „ *working regulations*
is their substitute for the strike to which, they keep insisting, they believe			
they have	*exactly* *just*	the same rights as other	*employees.* *salaried employees.*

---

⑤ Bei solchen Unternehmungen ist der richtige Moment wichtig.

a) Annotations

1. Unternehmungen: *Action* is no doubt the most appropriate equivalent in this context. Cf. the expression *take strike action* (note (3) 4 above). The military term *operation* might also be used figuratively.

2. ist der richtige Moment wichtig: A literal translation would have an air of infelicity. *Der richtige Moment* is here equivalent to *die Wahl des richtigen Zeitpunkts*, and this expression can be rendered quite neatly by the noun *timing*. *In such actions timing is important* would be a fairly acceptable translation of the sentence under discussion, but it would be better to reformulate the statement in such a way as to bring the word *timing* into prominence. A possible solution would be to render *ist . . . wichtig* by *a great deal depends on*. This makes it possible to manoeuvre the noun *timing* into end-position.

Augmentation is also feasible, though it entails the sacrifice of the noun *timing: In such actions it is essential to choose the right moment.*

b) Alternatives

In such	*actions*	*a great deal depends on timing.*
	operations	*it is essential to choose the right moment.*
	" "	*important* " " " " " " .

⑥ Mit den Fluglotsen kommen gemeinhin weit weniger Menschen in Berührung als mit Zollbeamten.

a) Annotations

1. gemeinhin: The equivalents listed in the bilingual dictionaries are as follows: *commonly, ordinarily, usually, mostly, generally, widely, currently, vulgarly.* Unfortunately, these adverbs almost invariably occupy mid-position, so that they can hardly be made to fit into a sentence such as *Far fewer people come into contact with air controllers than with customs officers.* We can say *People usually come into contact with . . .,* but we can hardly place the adverb *usually* after a subject preceded by *few, fewer, far fewer,* etc. *Usually* does occasionally occupy front-position, but in written English it often seems rather feeble unless it is thrown into relief through retardation of the subject, as in the following sentence taken from Knud Schibsbye's *Modern English Grammar* (p. 117):

Usually, particularly in formal English, there is a mixture of these possibilities.

We have therefore virtually no alternative but to replace the dictionary equivalents of *gemeinhin* by some disjunct which can occupy front-position: *in general, generally speaking, as a rule,* or perhaps even *overall.* The adverb *overall* is still much less common than expressions such as *generally speaking,* but it has recently become a fad word and is rapidly gaining ground in the language of journalism. Cf. the following example from *Reader's Digest* (December 1979, p. 212):

Overall, verbal and spatial abilities in boys tend to be "packaged" into different hemispheres (. . .).

In *The Complete Plain Words* (pp. 152–155), Sir Ernest Gowers discusses the word *overall* in considerable detail and concludes that 'it is high time that its excursions into the fields of other words were checked'. Perhaps he is right. Time will show.

2. Mit . . . kommen . . . in Berührung: Expressions such as *get in touch with someone* would be quite inappropriate here because they imply a conscious attempt to come into contact with another person. Cf. the German expression *sich mit jemandem in Verbindung setzen.* The locution *rub shoulders with someone* would also be unsuitable here because it carries implications of close association and friendly social relations. Cf. the example sentence given in the *Random House Dictionary* (s.v. shoulder):

As a social worker in one of the worst slum areas, she rubs shoulders with the poor and the helpless.

Rub shoulders with is closely synonymous with the verb *hobnob,* but *hobnob,* unlike *rub shoulders with,* is generally followed by words or phrases denoting members of the upper class (*royalty, the rich and the famous,* etc.).

b) Alternatives

Generally speaking, far fewer people		*come into contact with air*			
In general,		"	*in*	"	" *air*
As a rule,					
Overall,					
controllers	than with	*customs officers.*			
traffic controllers		*customs officials.*			
		custom-house officers.			
		custom-house revenue officers.			
		customs guards. (U.S.)			

⑦ Wer ein Flugzeug benutzt, wird es sich leisten können, so heißt es.

a) Annotations

1. Wer: The indefinite relative pronoun *wer* should never be rendered as *who.* In the following snippet from D. Weir, *Men and Work in Modern Britain* (pp. 360–361), the word *who* is evidently a mistranslation:

Concern with the impact of bureaucratization upon the prospects for internal democracy in representative institutions, particularly trade unions, has been a prominent strain in sociological analysis since Roberto Michels' *Political Parties* first appeared in English in 1915. His aphorism 'who says organization says oligarchy' has become a sociological commonplace.

He who, he that and *whosoever* would strike the wrong note here because they are restricted to archaic and exalted style. *Any person who* would also be inappropriate because it is used mainly in officialese. In this context, the best equivalents would be *people who, anyone who, if anyone, those who* or *whoever.* Examples:

(i) People who live in glasshouses shouldn't throw stones. (Proverb.)
(ii) Anyone who wishes to become a good writer should endeavour, before he allows himself to be tempted by more showy qualities, to be direct, simple, brief, vigorous and lucid. (E. Gowers, *The Complete Plain Words,* p. 78.)
(iii) Those who jump queues may get the last swiss roll, but they will be the first to wish they hadn't. (L. Gough (ed.), *The Harrap Book of Modern Essays,* p. 23.)
(iv) (. . .) whoever (. . .) has learned his fellow-creatures outside the sheep-pens of the social dogmatists – knows that each one of them is an uncommon man and is incapable of thinking of himself or of the man next him in any other terms (*ibid.* pp. 16–17.)
(v) Whoever knows the meaning of the word 'tenderness' cannot fail to recognize that the Russian icon painter has discovered an adequate equivalent for it in paint. (E. Newton, *European Painting and Sculpture,* p. 31.)
(vi) Whoever bends his whole mind to true worthiness will be attended by good fortune and honour. (J. Wright, *A Middle High German Primer,* p. 187.)

The following points should be noted:
(i) *Anyone who* may sometimes be replaced by *anyone* + *-ing*-form. The *-ing* form is employed in reference to very specific situations, while *anyone who* is reserved for generalizations. Examples:

Anyone undertaking to revise the book will pause over the opening words of Fowler's own preface (. . .). (H. W. Fowler, *A Dictionary of Modern English Usage*, p. ix.)
Anyone not writing legal language would have avoided repeating *regulations* twice (. . .). (E. Gowers, *The Complete Plain Words*, p. 192.)

(ii) Both Sir Ernest Gowers and George O. Curme have drawn attention to the interchangeability of indefinite relative clauses and conditional clauses (Curme, *EG*, § 89. C; Gowers, *The Complete Plain Words*, p. 32), and it is interesting to note that in the glossary of Joseph Wright's *Middle High German Primer* the indefinite relative pronoun *swër* (the Middle High German equivalent of *wer*) is translated by *if anyone*. It is therefore rather surprising that contemporary lexicographers have overlooked the fact that modern German relative clauses introduced by the indefinite pronoun *wer* may be conveniently rendered as conditional clauses introduced by *if anyone*.
(iii) *Whoever* is much more formal than the other modern equivalents listed above. This should be apparent from the example sentences.

2. ein Flugzeug benutzt: This expression, which has not been recorded in the German-English dictionaries, is synonymous with *mit dem Flugzeug reisen* and may therefore be rendered as *fly, go by plane, travel by plane, go by aeroplane, travel by aeroplane, go by air, travel by air* or *take a plane*.

3. wird es sich leisten können: The periphrasis *werden* + infinitive has modal force and serves to express confident certainty or present probability, the implication being that the truth of the assumption will become apparent upon investigation.Cf. P. Grebe, *Duden Grammatik*, § 99. In English, *will* + infinitive can be used in the same way. Cf. G. O. Curme, *EG*, § 119. E. 3; A. J. Thomson/A. V. Martinet, *A Practical English Grammar*, § 228; A. Lamprecht, *GES*, § 625; R. Quirk et al., *GCE*, § 3.47; R. Quirk/ S. Greenbaum, *UGE*, § 3.51; R. W. Zandvoort, *HEG*, § 185.

4. es: The pronoun *es* points back to the word sequence *ein Flugzeug benutzt*. This kind of pro-form may often be rendered by the infinitive marker *to* or the elliptical formula *to do so*. Anaphoric *to* is particularly common in colloquial English, while *to do so* is generally restricted to more formal usage. These constructions are used after verbs of complete predication such as *want, like, hope* and *try* as well as after the auxiliaries *have, ought, need* and *be able*. Examples:

You've spoilt my letter. – Well, I didn't mean to. (A. Lamprecht, *GES*, § 703.)
He wanted to go but he wasn't able to. (A. J. Thomson/A. V. Martinet, *A Practical English Grammar*, § 228.)
Sinners should not wait for revivals. Christ nowhere tells them to do so. (K. Schibsbye, *MEG*, § 1.3.4.2.)

The use of *to* and *to do so* is generally to be recommended in cases where it is necessary to avoid the repetition of a verb or verb phrase employed in a preceding clause. However, certain selectional restrictions must be taken into account in the case under consideration. We can say *People who travel by plane can afford to do so*, but we can hardly use the formula *to do so* if *can* is replaced by *will be able to*: *will be able to afford to do so* would have an air of infelicity because of the repetition of the particle *to*. In order to avoid such an inelegancy, we must therefore render *es* as *it* or *such things*. For further information on anaphoric *to*, the reader is referred to the following works:

A. J. Thomson/A. V. Martinet, *A Practical English Grammar*, § 250; R. W. Zandvoort, *HEG*, § 61; K. Schibsbye, *MEG*, § 1.3.4.2; R. A. Close, *RGSE*, § 3.8; G. O. Curme, *EG*, § 123. F; A. Lamprecht, *GES*, § 703; K. Beilhardt/F. W. Sutton, *Learning English: Englische Schulgrammatik*, § 53; R. Quirk/S. Greenbaum, *UGE*, § 10.35; R. Quirk et al., *GCE*, § 9.81; O. Jespersen, *Growth and Structure of the English Language*, p. 197.

5. so heißt es: Source attribution at the end of sentences is an inveterate newspaper habit on both sides of the Atlantic. Cf. J. P. Vinay/J. Darbelnet, *Stylistique comparée du français et de l'anglais*, § 203. Here is a typical example from *World and Press* (2nd September issue 1981, p. 2):

Women don't live longer than men just because they have, in general, a different working life, a group of American scientists claim.

R. Flesch objects to this practice on the ground that it generally results in bathos (*The ABC of Style*, p. 259), and the evidence he has produced in support of his views can scarcely be gainsaid.

Anticlimactic effects can be avoided by putting the speech tag in the middle of the sentence. Examples:

Study of the planets, they suggest, can tell much about the origins of the solar system and galaxies, perhaps of life itself. (*World and Press*, 2nd September issue 1981, p. 1.)

That should have been lesson enough – but it wasn't – for President Herbert Hoover, who suggested in 1922, the authors say, that the U.S. Patents Office disband itself because everything had been invented. (*ibid.*, p. 5.)

Flesch objects to this device too because it breaks the rhythm of the statement that is quoted (*The ABC of Style*, p. 249). This objection, however, is not really valid. Everything depends on the way the rhythm is broken. Broadly speaking, perfect regularity of rhythm tends to be intolerably oppressive unless it is justified by special circumstances, as in a sermon, a prayer, an incantation, or a highly rhetorical political speech. Unexpected breaks in rhythm, on the other hand, are an invaluable means of relieving monotony. Such pauses can highlight key words or ideas, giving an effect of extreme flexibility and permitting subtle modulations of tone which arrest the reader's attention and enhance his appreciation of the text.

There are, of course, sentences in which it is hard to find an appropriate place for the speech tag, and in such cases it is normally advisable to indicate the source at the beginning.

Finally, it is important to remember that there are special cases in which a sudden anticlimax may be stylistically justifiable. Cf. the following example from *The Oxford-Harrap Standard German-English Dictionary* (s.v. heißen):

Er hat seinen Sohn enterbt, heißt es.
He has disinherited his son, (or) so they say.

Here the speech tag has the effect of an afterthought, and it imparts to the statement a tone of contempt, indifference or incredulity. This tone would be quite appropriate in the case under consideration since the author of the article is clearly hostile to the air controllers.

b) Alternatives

People who	travel by plane	will be able to afford	it,	or
Those who	go by plane		such things,	so
	travel by aeroplane			
	go by aeroplane			
	travel by air			
	go by air			
	take a plane			
	fly			
Anyone who travels by plane				
Whoever travels by plane				
If anyone travels by plane, he				
so they say.				
they say.				

⑧ Die armen Leute fliegen nicht.

a) Annotations

1. Die armen Leute: This expression can be rendered in two ways: *the poor* or *poor people*. The use of the definite article is normally mandatory before certain substantivized adjectives of quality which have generic reference and take plural concord, e.g. *the old, the young, the rich, the innocent, the wise*. The expression *poor people*, on the other hand, cannot take a definite determiner unless it refers to a particular group of poor people. The terse simple form *the poor* is somewhat commoner than *poor people*. For further information on adjectives as noun-phrase heads, the reader is referred to the following works: Henryk Kałuża, *The Use of Articles in Contemporary English*, pp. 43–44; R. Quirk et al., *GCE*, § 5.20.; R. Quirk/S. Greenbaum, *UGE*, § 5.6; A. J. Thomson/A. V. Martinet, *A Practical English Grammar*, § 18; R. W. Zandvoort, *HEG*, § 778; K. Schibsbye, *MEG*, §§ 2.66, 3.2.3; R. A. Close, *RGSE*, § 7.21; G. O. Curme, *EG*, § 108; A. Lamprecht, *GES*, § 187;* F. W. Sutton/K. Beilhardt, *Grundzüge der englischen Grammatik*, § 109; K. Beilhardt/F. W. Sutton, *Learning English: Englische Schulgrammatik*, § 123.

2. fliegen nicht: *Do not* or *don't?* The use of contracted verbal forms in written English has been the subject of much discussion and little agreement. In *The ABC of Style* (s.v. apostrophes), R. Flesch encourages his readers to make liberal use of colloquial contractions in order to narrow the gap between written and spoken English. However, very few authors have followed his advice, and there is still a marked bias towards the use of uncontracted forms in written prose. Here are some examples from recent academic publications:

We are told about the world before we see it. (E. Butterworth/D. Weir (edd.). *The Sociology of Modern Britain*, p. 12.)
It implies that there is freedom of choice between alternatives (. . .). (A. Seldon/F. G. Pennance, *Everyman's Dictionary of Economics*, s.v. advertising.)

I am also anxious to stress what I am *not* trying to do. (P. M. Wetherill, *The Literary Text: An Examination of Critical Methods,* p. xviii.)
It is not always possible to produce convincing evidence for the sound of a language in earlier periods. (I. A. Gordon, *The Movement of English Prose,* p. 16.)
I am greatly indebted to the Philological Society for undertaking publication (. . .). (P. M. Clifford, *Inversion of the Subject in French Narrative Prose from 1500 to the Present Day,* preface.)

In some publications, however, contracted forms alternate with uncontracted forms. Contracted forms naturally occur quite frequently in passages where the author adopts a chatty tone and addresses the reader directly. Examples:

I've arranged every page spread in the book with this thought (. . .). (P.A. Samuelson, *Economics,* p. viii.)
You will discover that harder or less important material (. . .) has been put in appendixes, or often in footnotes. (*ibid.,* p. ix.)
We have already given some answers (. . .) (*EFL bulletin,* September 1980, p. 1.)
DON'T (. . .) worry if you can't sing very well yourself. (*ibid.,* p. 2.)
Above all, don't regard a song as a 'soft option'. (*ibid.*)

Samuelson's use of the uncontracted form *you will* shows how inconsistent usage in this domain still is.

Even in press reports, contracted forms are few and far between. However, they tend to occur somewhat more frequently in the popular press than in quality newspapers. It is very hard to find examples of contracted forms in *The Times,* the *International Herald Tribune, The Economist* or *Time,* but colloquial contractions may occasionally be discovered in the *Daily Express.* Cf. the article from the *Daily Express* of 3 November 1965 reprinted in D. Crystal/D. Davy, *Investigating English Style,* p. 175.

There are even special varieties of spoken English in which the uncontracted forms tend to predominate. Some very useful material may be found in D. Crystal/D. Davy, *op. cit.,* chapter 5. Here the language of unscripted commentary is studied with reference to two texts. Text I, which is a commentary on a cricket match, is spattered with contracted forms, while text II, which is an account of a state funeral, contains no contracted forms whatever.

It is very hard to predict the future of the uncontracted forms since usage is at present in a somewhat fluid state. In *Stylistics* (p. 94), G. W. Turner takes the line that the use of uncontracted forms in writing is merely a spelling convention, and that these forms should therefore be read aloud as if they were contracted, just as the verb-ending *th* was usually read as *s* in seventeenth-century England (cf. O. Jespersen, *Growth and Structure of the English Language,* pp. 189–90). If everyone were to follow this habit, the uncontracted forms would no doubt be rapidly supplanted by the colloquial contractions. However, owing to the prevalence of spelling pronunciations in this age of mass literacy (cf. B. Foster, *The Changing English Language,* pp. 247–248), the old uncontracted forms seem unlikely to lose favour in the foreseeable future.

b) Alternatives

The poor	do not	*go by air.*
Poor people		*travel by air.*
		go by plane.
		travel by plane.
		go by aeroplane.
		travel by aeroplane.
		take a plane.
		fly.

⑨ Eine solche Maßnahme in normalen Zeiten macht also wenig Aufsehen.

a) **Annotations**

1. **Eine solche Maßnahme:** It seems advisable to explicate this word sequence in order to remind the reader of the key concept *work-to-rule*.

2. **in normalen Zeiten:** This expression, which has not been recorded in the dictionaries, may be rendered quite literally as *in normal times*. Examples:
In normal times therefore all laws must derive their validity from the constitution which is the ultimate basis of all law. (E. J. Cohn, *Manual of German Law*, Vol. I, p. 4.)
In normal times, this system of free collective bargaining is not hampered by any government interference. (D. Hamblock/D. Wessels, *Englisch in Wirtschaft und Handel*, Vol. 1, p. 42.)
The expression *at ordinary times* is also in common use. Cf. the following quotation from a text by Huxley (G. Kostuch, *Problems and Opinions*, p. 62):
That all men are equal is a proposition to which, at ordinary times, no sane human being has ever given his assent.

3. **macht ... wenig Aufsehen:** Some useful equivalents have been overlooked by the dictionary makers: *attract + notice, make + impact, have + impact, create + excitement*. Examples:
In a period which saw considerable dissension within the party on grounds of policy, the power of the union leaders to determine the issues at annual conferences by the weight of their 'block vote' attracted a good deal of notice. (H. Pelling, *A History of British Trade Unionism*, p. 245.)
In 1963 a book called *Pour une réforme de l'entreprise*, written by a distinguished civil servant, Marcel Bloch-Lainé, made a considerable impact. (J. Ardagh, *The New France*, p. 56.)
The group they founded was based in western Europe, and although it itself had no great impact, it marked the beginning of a period in which pro-Chinese policies of one sort or another were dominant within Iranian exile circles (. . .). (F. Halliday, *Iran: Dictatorship and Development*, p. 236.)
A revolutionary theory predicting that all matter will eventually disappear is creating widespread excitement among physicists. (*IHT*, 18. 12. 1979, p. 1.)
The expressions which *have* been listed in the dictionaries also call for a few remarks:
(i) The locution *to make a splash* would be inappropriate here since it is normally used with a human subject. It means 'to attract attention by making an extravagant display of wealth, wit, virtuosity, etc.' Example:
Stilpe (like Bierbaum) is a *verbummeltes Genie*, who manages to make a splash in journalism and lays about him as a Berlin critic. (J. Bithell, *Modern German Literature*, p. 61.)

(ii) The expression *to cut a dash* would also be unsuitable. *To cut a dash*, which is closely synonymous with *to make a splash*, means 'to behave or dress showily'. Unlike *splash*, *dash* is normally used of a flashy display of physical skill, and it does not normally refer to a striking or ostentatious display of wealth. A good example sentence is given in the *Random House Dictionary* (s.v. dash): *He cut a dash on the ski slopes last winter*.
(iii) The expression *to make* (or *create*) *a furore* is somewhat problematic since the noun *furore* is ambiguous. *Furore* may denote either a wild burst of enthusiasm or an outburst of public protest, indignation, controversy, or the like. It is often used of books, plays, paintings and similar objects intended for public consumption.
(iv) *Notice*, which implies a much weaker impact than *sensation*, would be quite

appropriate here since *Aufsehen* is modified by *wenig*. The expression *to create a sensation* is often used with an inanimate subject and carries implications of widespread public excitement. Cf. the following example from A. T. Q. Stewart, *The Ulster Crisis* (p. 76):

But on 9 September he was back in London, in time for the sensation created by Lord Loreburn's letter to *The Times*.

4. wenig: When used in a purely quantitative sense before a noun, *wenig* may often be rendered as *little* or *not much*. Hence we may say *I have very little time for reading* or *I have not much time for reading*. In the case under consideration, however, it is important to remember that words such as *sensation* or *furore* cannot be modified by *little* because they are are not mass nouns. Both *sensation* and *furore*, however, may be modified by the evaluative formula *not much of a*. This turn of expression is often used disparagingly before count nouns in sentences such as *He's not much of a scholar* or *It wasn't much of a dinner* (cf. Hornby, *OALDCE*, s.v. much[1]).

5. also: *Also* (used in the sense of *folglich*) may be rendered in various ways. *Thus, hence, consequently* and *accordingly* would sound rather too formal in this context. *Logically* would also appear somewhat too cumbersome. *So* and *therefore* seem much more appropriate. We could write *So in normal times . . .* or *In normal times therefore . . .* (cf. the first example sentence quoted in note (9) 2 above). *Therefore* in front-position would appear too stiff, making the sentence sound almost like a parody of a reasoned proof in a mathematics book. Possible alternatives not recorded in the dictionaries include *It follows therefore that. . .* and *From this it follows that*. Examples:

It follows therefore that (except in the rare case of artists of independent means) the artist's work of art is not merely the child of his own personal fancy (. . .). (E. Newton, *European Painting and Sculpture*, p. 17.)

From this it follows that *auswählen* is generally applicable only with such things as can be carried by hand (. . .). (R. B. Farrell, *Dictionary of German Synonyms*, p. 70.)

b) Alternatives

In normal times therefore	*an action* such as a
At ordinary times „	*a measure*
So in normal times	
It follows therefore that in normal times	
From this it follows that in normal times	

work-to-rule	does not attract much notice.
work-to-rule campaign	„ „ „ „ attention.
work-to-rule strike	„ „ make much of an impact.
	has no great impact.
	does not create much excitement.
	„ „ „ much of a sensation.
	„ „ „ „ „ *stir*.
	„ „ cause „ „ „ sensation.
	„ „ „ „ „ „ *stir*.
	„ „ make „ „ „ sensation.
	„ „ „ „ „ „ *stir*.

> ⑩ Aber zweimal im Jahr ist die Gelegenheit günstig: Anfang August, wenn die Urlauber ausfliegen, und Ende August, wenn sie heimfliegen wollen.

a) Annotations

1. Aber: In principle, there is no reason not to use *but* at the head of a sentence, although hordes of pedantic schoolmasters have vied with one another in their virulent condemnations of this practice. Three points need to be made here.
First, the use of *but* at the opening of a sentence is particularly expedient if it is necessary to forge an adversative link with more than one sentence, or to achieve the effect of a dramatic pause in speech.
Secondly, superstitious misgivings about the initial positioning of *but* should not be confused with valid objections to the illogical or superfluous use of *but* as a sentence connecter. Such confusion is evidenced by a letter published in *The Economist* of 15–21 August 1981 (p. 6).
Thirdly, it would be a gross error to assume that an initial *aber* may always be rendered by an initial *but*. It is often advisable to translate an initial *aber* by a word such as *however* in order to impart a more formal tone to the style or to express some particular nuance (careful consideration, for instance) implied in the German text.
For further information on this subject, the reader is referred to the following works: R. Quirk et al., *GCE*, §§ 10.1, 10.17, 10.32, 10.35; R. Quirk/S. Greenbaum, *UGE*, §§ 10.19, 10.22; E. Gowers, *The Complete Plain Words,* pp. 168, 170–171; H. W. Fowler, *A Dictionary of Modern English Usage,* svv. but, and; R. Flesch, *The ABC of Style,* s.v. but; E. Partridge, *Usage and Abusage,* pp. 63–64.

2. ist die Gelegenheit günstig: A literal translation of this syntactic sequence should be avoided. There are two main difficulties: (i) the use of the definite article; (ii) the use of the copula *sein.*

(i) The German article *die* is here used to generalize the noun *Gelegenheit.* The generalization, however, is restricted to a particular set of circumstances: the sentence under consideration is not a sweeping statement about a whole class of beings or concepts. This usage has no real counterpart in English. Except when it is used in a broadly generalizing sense before class names, the English article *the* transmits a sense of uniqueness in so far as it implies precise reference to something which has already been mentioned and which is presumed to be still in the mind of the reader or listener.[2] It follows therefore that if we were to use the English definite article in this context, the word *the* would be interpreted as a particularization rather than a generalization, and it would appear very unusual because the facts which are here ushered in by the article are as yet unfamiliar to the reader.

(ii) If we were to render *ist* as *is* we would imply that the opportunity in question was a palpable reality. In this case, however, the opportunity is considered as a mere potentiality. In order to express this nuance, we must use a verb that is capable of indicating the transition from potentiality to reality: *an opportunity presents itself, offers, occurs* or *arises.* These standard collocations have been recorded in various dictionaries.

---

[2] Exceptions are possible only in artistic prose or poetry, where the unexpected use of the definite article acts as a spur to the reader's imagination and results in a gradual blurring of the distinctions between fiction and reality.

3. günstig: If we render *ist* by a verb such as *offer* or *arise*, the clause must be reorganized in such a way that the predicative adjective *günstig* assumes an attributive function. In other words, *zweimal im Jahr ist die Gelegenheit günstig* becomes *zweimal im Jahr bietet sich eine günstige Gelegenheit*. The word sequence *eine günstige Gelegenheit* can be treated as a sense-unit, and the attributive adjective *günstig* can be safely left untranslated, though this is not to deny that collocations such as *a good opportunity* or *a favourable opportunity* are possible. Turns of expression such as *a propitious opportunity* or *an auspicious occasion* are also possible, but they would savour of affectation here. Johnsonese has now gone out of vogue in most varieties of journalism, although sesquipedalian words and expressions are still commonly used to achieve comic effects.

4. Anfang August, wenn: The English conjunction *when* often has the continuative function which is assumed by *wenn* in this syntactic sequence. Augmentation is therefore unnecessary. Examples:

Their first appearance can conveniently be dated in 1866, when the anthology *Le Parnasse contemporain* came out with poems by Verlaine and Mallarmé (. . .). (A. Hartley, *The Penguin Book of French Verse*, Vol. 3, p. xxxii.)
His first voyage was made in 1492, when he reached the West Indian Islands. (J. E. Mansion, *A Grammar of Present-Day French*, § 311.)

5. wollen: *Wollen* is here used in an inchoative sense. It can therefore be rendered by an expression such as *get ready to* + infinitive or *prepare to* + infinitive.

b) Alternatives

Twice a year, however,	*an opportunity* *a good opportunity* *a favourable opportunity*	*presents itself:* *offers* *occurs* *arises*	*at the* *in the* *early*
beginning of August, when *early part of August,* *in August,*	*holidaymakers* *holidayers* *tourists* *vacationists* (U.S.) *vacationers* (U.S.)	are *going away,* and *leaving,*	*at the* *towards*
end of August, *the end of August,*	when they are *getting ready* *preparing*	to *fly home.* *go home by air.*	

⑪ Dies erregt ganz besonderes Aufsehen.

a) Annotations

1. Dies: This demonstrative pronoun does not point to any particular word or word-group in the preceding sentence. It merely refers to the idea implied in the clause *Aber zweimal im Jahr ist die Gelegenheit günstig*. For reasons of clarity, we must resort to augmentation in English: *a work-to-rule at this time of (the) year*.

2. erregt ganz besonderes Aufsehen: The modifier *ganz besonderes* may be rendered fairly literally as *extraordinary* or *exceptional*. However, there are at least two other possible renderings which call for a few remarks: (i) *attracts exceptionally wide attention*; (ii) *really does cause a stir*. For the collocation *attract + wide attention*, cp. the following quotation from H. Pelling, *A History of British Trade Unionism* (p. 239):

Another strike which attracted wide attention, because of its impact on the public, was that precipitated by the maintenance men at the newspaper printing-presses.

The use of the adverb *really* in conjunction with the stressed *do*-form is a more oblique rendering which emphasizes the realization of the air controllers' intentions by pointing the contrast between a work-to-rule in August and a job action organized 'in normal times'.

b) Alternatives

```
A work-to-rule            at this time of year    really does create a stir.
  work-to-rule campaign at this time of the year     ”        ”   cause  ”  ”
  work-to-rules action                                ”        ”   make   ”  ”
                                                  makes an enormous impact.
                                                  has an extraordinary impact.
                                                  creates an extraordinary stir.
                                                  causes    ”        ”         ”
                                                  makes     ”        ”         ”
                                                  creates   ”        ”     sensation.
                                                  causes    ”        ”         ”
                                                  makes     ”        ”         ”
                                                  attracts exceptionally wide attention.
```

 Wann meldeten Zeitungen, daß Verspätungen im Flugdienst bis zu acht Stunden und darüber hinaus dauerten?

a) Annotations

1. meldeten: This German preterite implies a strong connexion with the present and should therefore be rendered as a present perfect. (Cf. the use of the present perfect in sentences of the type *Have you ever been to London?*) The adverb *ever* can be inserted here in order to emphasize the idea of doubt or incredulity that is implicit in the German original.

2. daß . . . dauerten?: Here it is advisable to recast the sentence in order to avoid a somewhat cumbrous noun clause introduced by *that*.

3. Verspätungen im Flugdienst: A literal translation would appear rather heavy. Compounds such as *air service delay* sound much more snappy. Cf. the use of the abstract compound *delivery delay* in the following quotation from C. H. Jaffé, *Englisch für alle Fälle* (p. 46):

This memo you sent me about the delivery delay on the console desks.[3]

---

[3] A console desk is a desk on which the controls of an electronic computer system are mounted.

The word sequence *the delivery delay on the console desks* could be translated into German as follows: *die Verzögerung in der Ablieferung der Steuerpulte.*

4. und darüber hinaus: Turns of expression such as *fourscore and upward* are quite common, but the word *upward* is here debarred by the proximity of *up* in the word sequence *up to eight hours*. We have therefore no choice but to use some other word such as *more* or *longer*.

b) Alternatives

When have newspapers ever	carried published reported	reports of " "	air service airline service	delays of " "
up to eight hours and	*longer?* *more?*			

 Wann sah man Szenen, in denen müde Frauen und hungrige Kinder auf nacktem Boden kauerten: das reinste Elend auf luxuriösen Flughäfen?

a) Annotations

1. sah: As in the preceding sentence, the use of the present perfect is mandatory. Cf. note (12) 1 above.

A more delicate problem is posed by word-choice. The verb *see* is debarred by the proximity of the noun *scenes*. A word sequence such as *seen scenes* would offend the ear. *See* must therefore be replaced by *witness*. In loose writing *witness* is frequently used merely as a synonym of *see* (cf. *S.O.E.D.*, s.v. witness). There are, however, some important differences between these two verbs. *See* simply means 'to perceive with the eyes', and it is often followed by nouns denoting perfectly commonplace objects – biros, ink-bottles or in-trays, for instance. *Witness,* on the other hand, can mean 'to be a witness, spectator or auditor of something of interest, importance or special concern'. Hence it is possible to say *to witness an accident* or *to witness the death of a monarch*. Another important distinction between *see* and *witness* is that *witness* belongs to a more formal register of language than *see*. Consider, for example, the quotation from Southey given in the *S.O.E.D.* (s.v. witness): *Never did I witness a more melancholy scene of devastation*. In the case under discussion, the verb *witness* is particularly appropriate since the last two sentences of our German text are markedly formal in tone. The prosaic style of the preceding sentences has given way to a decidedly oratorical manner of discourse. Witness the use of the rhetorical question and anaphora. This mode of expression must be imitated by the translator.

2. man: Generally speaking, the use of *one* and *you* is a matter of social background among native speakers. Cf. W. S. Fowler, *Proficiency English, Teacher's Book 1*, pp. 9–10. Upper-class speakers tend to prefer *one*, and countless examples of this usage may be found in the works of authors such as Virginia Woolf:

And he would go to picture galleries, they said, and he would ask one, did one like his tie? (V. Woolf, *To the Lighthouse*, p. 10.)
One must burn one's own smoke, he thought, as he took his hat. (V. Woolf, *The Years*, p. 104.)

However, since *one* is gradually becoming outmoded, and *you* often seems unconscionably informal, the pronoun *we* is now in a fair way to supplant *one* in cultivated usage, especially in writing. Examples:

In life we never know anyone but ourselves by thoroughly reliable internal signs (. . .). (W. C. Booth, *The Rhetoric of Fiction*, p. 3.)
In a formal sense, what we mean by development is first of all increase of the overall productivity of an economy to increase the surplus (. . .). (H. Bernstein (ed.), *Underdevelopment and Development*, p. 277–278.)

This usage cuts across class boundaries and is neither unduly formal nor unduly informal. The language, of course, is at present in a very fluid state, and many writers use both *one* and *we:*

(. . .) one cannot apply what one does not possess. (S. P. Corder, *Introducing Applied Linguistics*, p. 7.)
We call a particular practical activity an art when it cannot be carried out successfully by following a set of rules of thumb (. . .). (*ibid.*, p. 9.)

3. Szenen, in denen . . . kauerten: The German relative clause can be rendered quite neatly by *with* and an *-ing* form. It should, however, be noted that this kind of structural conversion is impossible if the verb in the relative clause is *sein*. For further examples, see W. Friedrich, *Technik des Übersetzens*, p. 143; R. Quirk et al., *GCE*, § 6.46.

4. müde: In this case the most appropriate equivalents are *tired, tired-out, exhausted, worn-out* and *weary*.
Fatigued is normally restricted to predicative use.
Worn-out with fatigue is debarred by the proximity of the nominal group *hungry children*, which might be misconstrued as a prepositional complement.
Spent suggests either a permanent condition resulting from senescence or prolonged illness, or a temporary condition resulting from violent physical exertion. *Spent* may thus be used attributively of worn-out old men, or of runners, swimmers or horses that have just taken part in a race.
Jaded often carries a suggestion of overindulgence and satiety. In this context it would call up a train of associations that would be at variance with the author's meaning.
Drowsy, sleepy and *sleepful* often carry implications of restfulness and would therefore be rather out of place in this context. *Sleepful* is an exceptionally rare word, even in literary English.
Tuckered out is generally restricted to informal American usage.
For further information about the English equivalents of *müde*, see *Webster's New Dictionary of Synonyms*, s.v. tire, and *The Random House Dictionary of the English Language*, s.v. tired.[1]

5. hungrige: Four equivalents have been recorded in the bilingual dictionaries: *hungry, ravenous, starving* and *famished*. A careful study of the areas of meaning covered by these adjectives shows that there is a good deal of overlapping, and the absence of clear-cut boundaries between the words often causes difficulty in translation.
Hungry is beyond a shadow of doubt the most general and ordinary word in the group. It means 'in need of food'. It normally denotes a perfectly innocuous temporary condition, but occasionally it is also used to denote a permanent pathologic condition:

It makes one hungry to see good meat (. . .). (D. H. Lawrence, *Sea and Sardinia*, p. 114.)
Sometimes, the hungry simply lose the will to live. (*Time*, 12. 11. 1979, p. 24.)

In the first example, *hungry* clearly refers to a temporary state, and there is not the slightest suggestion of chronic undernourishment. In the second example, however, the noun phrase *the hungry* refers to Cambodian refugees in the last stages of malnutrition. *Ravenous* is a more emphatic word than *hungry*. When used of humans, it means 'excessively hungry' and denotes a temporary condition. A typical example is given in the *Random House Dictionary*: *feeling ravenous after a hard day's work*.
Starving closely approaches *famished* in meaning. In informal English, both adjectives are used predicatively in the sense 'very hungry'. Examples:

What's for dinner? – I'm starving! (Hornby, *OALDCE*, s.v. starve.)
I'm famished! (*ibid.*, s.v. famish.)

Both these statements are obviously hyperbolical. In formal English, however, *starving* and *famished* can mean 'reduced to the extremities of hunger', 'dying from lack of food'. Examples:

A starving person wastes away, literally consuming himself in the process. (*Time*, 12. 11. 1979, p. 24.)
famished homeless multitudes. (*RHD*, s.v. famished.)

In the case under discussion, *hungry* is the only fully satisfactory translation equivalent.

6. auf nacktem Boden: The use of the definite article is mandatory in English.
In this kind of phrase *nackt* is normally translated as *bare* rather than *naked*. In *LEW* (s.v. nackt), however, *on the naked floor* is given as a possible rendering of *auf dem nackten Boden*.
In the case under discussion, it is rather hard to decide whether *Boden* should be rendered as *floor* or *ground*. If we write *on the bare floor*, we imply that the unfortunate air passengers were crowded together in departure lounges with inadequate seating arrangements; and if we write *on the bare ground*, we imply that the people were in the open air. Either is possible. The use of the noun *earth*, however, would hardly be acceptable in this context. *Ground* is a fairly vague word which may denote either a natural surface (mould, clay, etc.) or a man-made surface (paving stones, macadam, etc.). *Earth*, on the other hand, would here be interpreted as a synonym of *soil*, a word which denotes the natural top layer of the land surface of our planet. For further information on the English equivalents of *Boden*, the reader is referred to R. Meldau/R. B. Whitling, *Schulsynonymik der englischen Sprache*, s.v. Boden.

7. kauerten: *Cower* would be quite unacceptable here because it always implies abject fear. In certain contexts *crouch* closely approaches *cower* in meaning. *Crouch*, however, can imply aggressiveness as well as fear. For example, one can use the verb *crouch* of a beast of prey preparing to spring. The verb *squat*, on the other hand, rarely carries psychological implications. In many cases, *squat* and *crouch* are virtually interchangeable and utterly devoid of emotive colouring. Some good examples of *crouch* used as a synonym of *squat* may be found in D. H. Lawrence, *Sea and Sardinia*. In the fifth chapter of this book, the author describes men roasting meat over an open fire, and he repeatedly uses the verb *crouch* to depict the men's attitudes. One example will suffice here:

And he turned bandying words with his dark-browed mate, who was still poking the meat at the embers and crouching on the hearth. (p. 117.)

As for the verb *huddle*, it can hardly be used in this context since it means 'to crowd together, as from fear or cold'.

8. das reinste Elend: German journalists are often extremely laconic when indicating the logical connections between statements. The colon is made to perform the function of a connective word sequence. Examples:

Grundüberlegung dabei: Was nicht vorhanden ist, kann auch nicht verbraucht werden. (Heinz Gampe (*Scala*), in V. Johnson/J. A. Brooks/E. Francke, *Advanced German Comprehension*, p. 47.)

Ziel: Den Mitgliedstaaten alle erforderlichen Unterlagen zu geben, damit sie die Einhaltung gemeinsam festgelegter Vorschriften ständig überprüfen. (Hermann Bohle (*Die Zeit*), *ibid.*, p. 51.)

Gurtzwang im Auto: Unbedingt weniger Verletzte, so ... (G. Collier/B. Shields, *Guided German-English Translation*, p. 153.)

In English this particular kind of zippy telegraphic style is unusual, except in headlines. In the case under consideration, the German construction can be sacrificed without compunction. We can replace the colon by a full stop and begin a new sentence with the words *When has one ever witnessed* ... This anaphora heightens the effect of the preceding sentence and enables us to round off the passage with a rhetorical flourish.

9. reinste: The translation equivalent of this word need not be a grammatical superlative, but it must be a superlative in meaning.

10. auf luxuriösen Flughäfen: The correct preposition is *at*. Cf. the following quotation from I. Murdoch, *A Severed Head*, p. 194:

(...) I had been at London Airport all day.

The word *Flughafen* often presents difficulties in translation. The following terms should be carefully distinguished: *airport, aerodrome, air terminal, airfield, air station.*

An airport is a public landing and taking-off area for commercial use by civil aircraft, usually with surfaced runways and aircraft maintenance and passenger facilities (*Instandhaltungswerkstätten und Abfertigungsgebäude*).

Aerodrome is a somewhat dated word which gained currency in Britain about 1902 and which denotes a tract of level ground for the arrival and departure and servicing of aircraft, with hangars, workshops, etc. *Aerodrome* and *airport* were once virtually synonymous (cf. the rather old-fashioned definition of *airport* given in the Supplement to the *S.O.E.D.*). Nowadays, however, one tends to make a distinction between *aerodrome* and *airport*. When it is still used, the term *aerodrome* is generally reserved for a base which is smaller than a commercial airport and which is used mainly for private aircraft.

An air terminal is 'a building in a city from which air passengers are taken by road or rail to an airport' (*CED*). In English-German dictionaries this term is normally rendered as *Flughafenabfertigungsgebäude*. These terms, however, are not used coextensively. The German term *Flughafenabfertigungsgebäude* embraces all the passenger facilities belonging to an international airport, while the English term is normally restricted to the passenger facilities outside the airport. In order to obviate misunderstandings, it is therefore advisable to translate *air terminal* by the loan word *Air Terminal* rather than by *Flughafenabfertigungsgebäude* or *Abfertigungsgebäude*. Cf. the definition of *Flughafen* given in *Der neue Brockhaus*: Anlage zur Abwicklung des (Personen- und Güter-) Flugverkehrs, umfaßt Start- und Lande- (SL-) sowie Rollbahnen, Flugzeugabstellplätze, Abfertigungsgebäude (dazugehörig: Air Terminal, in der Stadt gelegen) und Flugsicherungsanlagen. In the same article the functions of the *Abfertigungsgebäude* are defined as follows: Das Abfertigungsgebäude erfüllt die verkehrsmäßigen und betriebl. Aufgaben eines ‚Bahnhofs'; es enthält u. U. noch Räume für Zoll- und

Paßkontrolle sowie meist für jeden einzelnen Abflug besondere Sammel- und Warteabteile. Von dort gelangen die Fluggäste zum Flugzeug (. . .). This clearly shows that *Abfertigungsgebäude* does not cover the same area of meaning as the word *air terminal*.
An airfield is a landing and taking-off area for aircraft. There are usually hard-surfaced runways and permanent buildings such as hangars, workshops and offices. Airfields are used mainly for military purposes.
An air station is an airfield usually smaller than an airport but having facilities for sheltering and servicing aircraft.
In the case under discussion, *airport* is clearly the only acceptable equivalent of *Flughafen*.

b) Alternatives

When *has one* ever witnessed scenes with	*exhausted* women and hungry
have we	*tired*
	tired-out
	worn-out
	weary
children *squatting* on the bare *floor?* When *has one* ever witnessed
crouching *ground?* *have we*
abject misery at luxurious airports?
utter misery
dire distress
dire penury

Text III*
Weiter an der kurzen Leine

Die französischen Banken werden bis Ende dieses Jahres weiterhin an der kurzen Leine gehalten. Die Leine ist jetzt sogar noch etwas verkürzt worden, denn die von den Währungsbehörden festgesetzten Koeffizienten für die Kreditvergabe im 2. Halbjahr bedeuten eine weitere Verengung des Kreditspielraums der Banken. So dürfen die Großbanken bis Ende Dezember ihr Kreditvolumen gegenüber Ende Dezember 1979 nur um 3,5% (im Vorjahr: 4%) ausweiten, die mittleren Banken immerhin um 6% (statt 7%) und die auf Verbraucherkredite und Ratenkäufe spezialisierten Institute um 7% (statt 9%). Darlehen für den Wohnungsbau, die bisher weitgehend von diesen Normen ausgenommen waren, fallen jetzt ebenfalls unter das in Bankkreisen berüchtigte "encadrement". Die bei diesen Krediten festgestellte Zuwachsrate von 27% im letzten Jahr hat der Regierung offensichtlich zu denken gegeben. Auch der unter den Banken üblich gewordene Kauf von nicht ausgenutzten Quoten eines Finanzinstituts durch ein anderes soll künftig nicht mehr toleriert werden. Dafür bleiben Kredite zur Förderung des Exportgeschäfts zur Hälfte „frei", passiver Außenhandel verpflichtet schließlich.

---

* Dolmetscher- und Übersetzerprüfung/Englisch/4. 6. 1980/Industrie- und Handelskammer zu Dortmund.

Text III
Still in leading-strings

The French banks will continue to be kept in leading-strings until the end of this year. The leading-strings have now been made even a bit shorter, for the percentages for the granting of credit in the second half of the year, percentages fixed by the monetary authorities, mean a further narrowing of the banks' lending capacity. Thus, between now and the end of December, the big banks will be allowed to expand their credit volume by only 3.5% as against the end of December 1979 (4% last year); still, the medium-sized banks will be allowed an expansion of 6% (instead of 7%), and the institutions that specialize in consumer credit and hire purchase an expansion of 7% (instead of 9%). Housing loans, which have hitherto been largely exempted from these norms, now also fall within the scope of that *encadrement* which is so notorious among bankers. The 27% rate of increase in these credits observed last year has evidently set the government thinking. Even the purchase of unused quotas of one financial institution by another, which has become a common practice in banking quarters, is no longer to be tolerated in future. On the other hand, fifty percent of export promotion credits remain 'free'; after all, a foreign trade deficit involves certain obligations.

Annotations and Alternatives

① Weiter an der kurzen Leine

a) Annotations

The German idiom *jemanden an der kurzen Leine halten* may be rendered into English in various ways: *to keep* (or *hold*) *s.o. in leading-strings, to have* (or *keep*) *s.o. in* (or *on*) *a* (or *the*) *string, to lead s.o. in a string, to hold* (or *have*) *s.o. in leash, to keep a tight leash on s.o., to hold s.o. in check* (or *restraint*), *to keep a tight hand on s.o.*
These equivalents fall into three categories: (a) locutions based on the image of the leash or string; (b) locutions based on the image of the hand; (c) locutions based on abstract concepts such as *restraint* or *check* (faded images which are unintelligible to persons who have no knowledge of French or Latin).
Before making a choice, we must consider the German text as a whole. The metaphor of the string or leash is carried on in the second sentence. The stereotyped phrase *jdn. an der kurzen Leine halten* is revitalized. The adjective *kurz* is converted into the corresponding verb *verkürzen*.
The following conclusions emerge from this observation:
(i) The clichés in group (c) must be rejected because they are too abstract.
(ii) The locutions in group (b) must also be ruled out, for our metaphors will seem incongruously mixed if we use the image of the hand in the title and then switch over to the image of the leash or string; and if we stick to the image of the hand we shall be hard put to it to revitalize the metaphor since a hand cannot be shortened in the same way as a leash.
It follows therefore that we have no alternative to using the expressions we have placed in group (a). Yet even here certain selectional restrictions must be taken into consideration. The locution *to keep s.o. on a string* often has a subjective connotation. Cf. the German equivalents given in Engeroff/Lovelace-Käufer, *An English-German Dictionary of Idioms* (s.v. string) and the definition given in *CED* (s.v. string): 'to have control or a hold over (a person), esp. emotionally.' It is therefore preferable to use an expression containing *leash* or *leading-strings*. *Leash* is a common metaphor for *control*, and the word *leading-strings* normally denotes 'a state of dependence or tutelage' (*WNCD*).
The adverb *weiter*, which expresses continuity, may be rendered as *still*.

b) Alternatives

| Still *in leading-strings* |
| *in leash* |

② Die französischen Banken werden bis Ende dieses Jahres weiterhin an der kurzen Leine gehalten.

a) Annotations

1. werden ... gehalten: Two difficulties of translation must be considered here: (a) tense; (b) selectional restrictions.

(a) In German the present tense is often used with reference to future time. This use is much less common in English. Cf. R. W. Zandvoort, *HEG*, § 129. In this particular instance, the future tense is mandatory.
(b) The expression *to have s.o. in leash* is not used in the passive, and it would be inappropriate here since it does not suggest persistence. We must use a phrase containing a verb such as *hold* or *keep: hold s.o. in leash, keep* (or *hold*) *s.o. in leading-strings.*

2. bis Ende dieses Jahres: In English the article must be inserted. Cf. *Anfang Juli* (at the beginning of July), *Ende März* (at the end of March), etc. For further examples, see H. F. Eggeling, *A Dictionary of Modern German Prose Usage*, s.v.v. article (definite), Monatsnamen.

3. weiterhin: This adverb can be safely left untranslated when it co-occurs with verbs such as *bleiben* or *stehen:*

Er wird weiterhin ungeschlagen bleiben.   He will remain undefeated. *(ibid.)*
(*LEW*, s.v. weiterhin.)
Er wird auch weiterhin an der Spitze der   He will remain (*or* stay) at the head of
Partei stehen. *(ibid.)*   the party. *(ibid.)*

In this particular instance, however, *weiterhin* must be translated since it indicates that there is to be a further tightening of credit in the immediate future. The omission of *weiterhin* could imply that there were practically no serious credit restrictions prior to the government decision under discussion.
It is sometimes possible to render *weiterhin* by an adverbial such as *in the future*. In this case, however, it is quite impossible to translate *weiterhin* in this way since the adverbial *in the future* cannot combine with a phrase such as *until the end of this year*. We have therefore no alternative to converting *weiterhin* into a verb (*continue*). Cf. A. Lamprecht, *GES*, § 225; F. W. Sutton/K. Beilhardt, *GES*, § 113.
The verb *continue* often presents difficulties in translation since it can enter into a variety of patterns. The subject may be human or inanimate, and the complement may be a substantive, an active or passive infinitive, or an -*ing* form. As Zandvoort has pointed out (*HEG*, § 68), the infinitive is employed more frequently than the -*ing* form, particularly in spoken English. However, the use of these forms is a common cause of uncertainty, even among advanced students, and some attempt must be made to define the principles that operate in this area. Consider the following examples:
(i) Despite the cease-fire, which came into force on 28th January, Vietnamese soldiers on both sides continued fighting in order to gain as much territory as possible before a final peace. (R. Sieper, *The Student's Companion to the U.S.A.*, p. 42.)
(ii) Few people like changing their habits, good or bad, and, whether it is smoking, drinking or over-eating, they continue "enjoying" them to the end, often the bitter end. (Bliemel et al., *Englisch für Erwachsene*, vol. 2, p. 107.)
(iii) She continues talking. (*ibid.*, p. 109.)
(iv) He was unable to continue making his full contribution. (*The Times*, 1955, quoted by W. Friederich, *Probleme der Semantik und Syntax des englischen Gerundiums*, p. 64.)
(v) She touched the back of Kitty's head very lightly with the brush, and stood there immobile waiting presumably, with lowered eyes, for Kitty's order to depart or to continue brushing. (I. Murdoch, *A Word Child*, p. 309.)
(vi) As the silence lengthened and as she continued to stand there some divine ferocious thrilling power out of the centre of the earth began to reach me, to rise through me. (*ibid.*, p. 312.)
(vii) If you continue to be so obstinate . . . (*ALD*, s.v. continue, quoted by W. Friederich, *Probleme der Semantik und Syntax des englischen Gerundiums*, p. 64.)

(viii) Continue to be in poor health. (W.Friederich/J. Canavan, *DEWC*, s.v. continue.)
(ix) Continue to be chairman. (*ibid.*)
(x) Prices continued to rise. (*ibid.*)
(xi) They continued to quarrel daily. (W. F. H. Whitmarsh/C. D. Jukes, *Advanced French Course*, p. 158.)
(xii) He continued to think men better than they were. (L. Gough (ed.), *The Harrap Book of Modern Essays*, p. 116.)
(xiii) Though she now chose to earn her living on the music-hall stage as a dancer and mime, she continued to write. (Raymond Mortimer, introduction to Colette, *Chéri/The Last of Chéri*, p. 7.)
(xiv) In his next two plays, he continued to portray the people and scenes of his homeland, but in a more serious vein. (H. F. Garten, introduction to C. Zuckmayer, *Der Hauptmann von Köpenick*, p. 9.)
(xv) (. . .) those of them who were discussed in the first two editions and continued to produce in exile – some of them their best work – have had this later work fully treated. (J. Bithell, *Modern German Literature*, p. xi.)
(xvi) Each type of input continues to be used for some time after it has ceased to be the most eligible (. . .). (J. Robinson, *Further Contributions to Modern Economics*, p. xii.)
(xvii) (. . .) Latin songs, often of indifferent merit, continued to be written and sung. (F. J. E. Raby, *The Oxford Book of Medieval Latin Verse*, p. xvi.)
(xviii) (. . .) Latin continued to be used as the liturgical language in all parts of Europe that paid ecclesiastical allegiance to Rome. (F. Brittain, *The Penguin Book of Latin Verse*, p. xlix.)
(xix) Latin continued to be used for degree disputations at Cambridge until about the middle of the nineteenth century. (*ibid.*, p. l.)

The following points should be noted:

(a) In examples (i), (ii), (iii) and (v), the *-ing* form clearly has descriptive force. It expresses duration, incompletion, interest in the activity as such (durative aspect).
(b) Examples (iv) and (v) are seemingly of the same ilk. In both cases there are evidently some considerations of euphony at work, for the use of the *-ing* form makes it possible for the writer to avoid the heavy repetition of *to* with the infinitive. There is, however, one important difference between (iv) and (v). The verb phrase in (iv) (*making his full contribution*) is abstract, while the verb in (v) (*brushing*) is concrete. The verb form in (v) makes a vivid impression on the reader, while the corresponding form in (iv) seems virtually devoid of descriptive or emotional force. The *-ing* form in (iv) seems to have been used merely for euphony. In a sentence such as *He continued to make his full contribution*, the infinitive construction sounds more natural than the *-ing* form.
(c) In examples (vi) – (xix) the infinitives are terminate and thus have factual force.
(d) In *Probleme der Semantik und Syntax des englischen Gerundiums* (pp. 63–64), Wolf Friederich has attempted to elucidate the problem in hand by making a distinction between the volitive and non-volitive aspects of certain verb phrases. There seems to be some truth in Friederich's hypothesis, for it is well-nigh impossible to find examples of an inanimate subject followed by the combination *continue* + *-ing* form. None the less, I am disinclined to endorse Friederich's views on the use of the *-ing* form and the infinitive in sentences with a human subject. The non-volitive aspect is readily discernible when the verb in the infinitive denotes a state, an attitude, a position or an appearance (cf. examples (vi), (vii), (viii), (ix) and (xii); but when the verb in the infinitive denotes an action, the line of demarcation between the volitive and the non-volitive aspect is vague at best (cf. examples (xi), (xiii), (xiv), (xv)). Verbs of action are generally employed in the infinitive when it seems desirable to state facts calmly and objectively, and the *-ing* form is used only when the author wishes to impart descriptive force to a statement. Two sentences quoted in Curme's *English Grammar* (pp. 261–262) illustrate this point very well:

(i) They continued fighting.
(ii) During the whole day the army continued to advance.

Sentence (i) exemplifies the durative aspect of the verb. It represents the action as going on. Sentence (ii) exemplifies the terminate aspect. It calls attention to the act as a whole.
(e) Wolf Friederich has pointed out that there are certain parallels between the aspectual systems of Russian and English (*Probleme der Semantik und Syntax des englischen Gerundiums,* p. 105). Friederich's remarks are pertinent, yet here, I think, we must speak with the greatest circumspection. It is worth recalling that the Russian imperfective forms are used to render both the progressive and the frequentative aspects of English verbs. This divergence between the two systems reveals a fundamental difference in time orientation. For a very brief but enlightening comparison of the aspectual systems of Russian and English, see Pamela Davidson/Jill Norman, *Russian Phrase Book,* p. 13. The use of the perfective and imperfective infinitives in modern Russian is explained in clear, simple terms in C.-J. Veyrenc, *Grammaire du russe,* pp. 70–71.

The whole problem thus simmers down to three basic principles which may be set forth in simplified form as follows:
(a) Inanimite subject +*continue* + infinitive
(b) Human subject + *continue* + infinitive of verb of state, attitude, etc.
(c) Human subject + *continue* + infinitive of verb of action (terminate aspect)
Human subject + *continue* + -*ing* form of verb of action (durative aspect)

b) Alternatives

| The French banks will continue *to be kept in leading-strings* |
| " " *held* " " " |
| " " *held* " *leash* |
| until the end of this year. |

③ Die Leine ist jetzt sogar noch etwas verkürzt worden, denn die von den Währungsbehörden festgesetzten Koeffizienten für die Kreditvergabe im 2. Halbjahr bedeuten eine weitere Verengung des Kreditspielraums der Banken.

a) Annotations

1. **Die Leine:** The metaphor used in the title must be continued here.

2. **jetzt:** In bilingual dictionaries such as *LEW, jetzt* is rendered as *now, at present* and *at the present time.* However, it would be a gross error to assume that these three locutions are interchangeable in a random way.
In this particular instance, the correct equivalent is *now. Now* often expresses a contrastive relation of the present to what precedes. It may occupy front-position or mid-position:

Now is the best time to visit Devon. (Hornby, *OALDCE,* s.v. now.)
Ansehen is now obsolete in this sense. (R. B. Farrell, *Dictionary of German Synonyms,* p. 27.)

At present corresponds to *zur Zeit*. *At the present time* is used in the same way as the German expression *in der heutigen Zeit*.

3. sogar noch: The additive adjunct *noch* should not be translated separately. The particles *sogar* and *noch* constitute a single thought-unit and are frequently used to intensify a comparative. The English equivalents are *even, yet* and *still*. *Even* and *yet* always precede the comparative, but *still* may be positioned before or after the comparative:

an even (*or* yet) more difficult problem. (*LEW*, s.v. sogar)
Mary is still taller. (Hornby, *OALDCE*, s.v. still)
Mary is taller still. (*ibid.*)
That would be still better. (*ibid.*)
That would be better still. (*ibid.*)

Still is often placed after a predicative adjective, but it is not normally placed after a noun. Hence we do not say **a more difficult problem still*. In *Guided German-English Translation* (p. 165), Gordon Collier and Brian Shields have dealt with the particle *noch* in considerable detail, but they seem to have overlooked this point.

4. etwas verkürzt worden: *Shorten* and *make shorter* are often freely interchangeable. In this case, however, *make shorter* is a more appropriate translation since adverbials such as *somewhat* or *a bit* combine more readily with adjectives than with verbs. The adverbial *etwas* may be rendered in various ways: *somewhat, rather, a little, a bit, (just) a little bit, slightly, a shade, a thought, a trifle*. The first four equivalents in our list have been recorded in various German-English dictionaries. The other expressions have been ignored although they are in common use.

It should be noted that the locution *a thought* does not manifest the same co-occurrence restrictions as *a bit*. *A bit* is wider in application than *a thought*. *A bit* combines freely with the positive or comparative forms of adjectives, and it can also co-occur with the adverb *too*. *A thought*, on the other hand, does not normally co-occur with the positive forms of adjectives. Hence we can say *a bit long, a bit longer* or *a bit too long*, but **a thought long* appears unacceptable because it violates selection restrictions. It should also be borne in mind that there is a stylistic difference between *a bit* and *a thought*. *A bit* has a colloquial ring, while *a thought* has a somewhat literary flavour. Here are some examples of *a thought:*

In his smart dark grey London clothes he looked elegant, taller, a thought more degenerate. (I. Murdoch, *A Severed Head*, p. 101.)
You could be a thought more enthusiastic. (*CED*, s.v. thought.)
Criticism just a thought too severe. (J. E. Mansion, *HSFED*, I, s.v. tantinet.)
(. . .) if the haire were a thought browner. (Shakespeare, quoted in the *OED*, s.v. thought.)

Nowadays the word *smidgen* is widely used in the sense of *a little bit*. It is an informal Americanism and is rapidly gaining currency in the U.K. Cp. the following example from *The Economist* (8–14 March 1980, p. 12):

Total credit demands to be financed in the United States this year are estimated at only a smidgen below the record $ 415 billion net financed in 1979.

The word *smidgen* (also spelt *smidgin*) should be used with caution. Its selectional restrictions have not yet been fully explored, and the information provided in the unilingual dictionaries is quite inadequate.

5. Koeffizienten: Readers may be somewhat puzzled by the use of the term *Koeffizient* in this context. Strictly speaking, the word *coefficient* denotes a numerical or constant factor in an algebraic term or the product of all the factors of a term excluding one or more specified variables. It should, however, be borne in mind that the text under discussion is about France and that the author in all likelihood obtained his information from French source materials, so that his choice of terms was probably determined to a considerable extent by French usage. In contemporary French, the term *coefficient* is often used very loosely in the sense of *factor* or *percentage*. Cf. *Le Petit Robert* (1978), s.v. coefficient. Robert cites the following example: *Il faut prévoir un coefficient d'erreur*. In such cases, the French *coefficient* corresponds to English words such as *percentage*. Limits are normally indicated in terms of percentages when a government introduces ceilings on bank advances or imposes a credit squeeze. Cf. the following quotation from G. Bannock/R. E. Baxter/R. Rees, *The Penguin Dictionary of Economics*, p. 96.:

In May 1968, the BANK OF ENGLAND requested banks to restrict loans to no more than 4 per cent above the level at the time of devaluation in November 1967.

As a rule, terms such as *percentage* and *rate* collocate with the verb *fix,* so the verb *festsetzen* may be rendered as *fix* in this particular instance. Cf. the following example from Michael Greener, *The Penguin Dictionary of Commerce*, s.v. minimum lending rate:

It still has a major say in fixing interest rates generally (. . .).

6. Kreditvergabe: In *O-HSG-ED*, three terms are given under the catchword *Kreditgewährung: granting, allowing, extension of credit. Granting of credit*, which is the only equivalent given in *G/C*, is by far the commonest term.Cf. the following example from M. Greener, *The Penguin Dictionary of Commerce*, s.v. tight money:

This may be the result of deliberate governmental interference, e.g. increasing the MINIMUM LENDING RATE, calling for substantial SPECIAL DEPOSITS by the banks or imposing controls on the granting of credit − particularly in the HIRE PURCHASE field.

7. im 2. Halbjahr: The term *half-year* is much less common in English than *Halbjahr* is in German. The most acceptable equivalent of the locution *im zweiten Halbjahr* is *in the second half of the year*. A typical example may be found in one of the translation exercises in R. Renner/R. Sachs, *Wirtschaftssprache*, p. 37:

The growth of production slowed down in the second half of the year.

The word-group *in the second half of the year* may also be followed by a date such as *1960*. Cf. *O-HSG-ED*, s.v. Halbjahr.

8. die von den Währungsbehörden . . . Halbjahr: In our German text, the past participle *festgesetzten* is placed immediately before the noun to which it refers (*Koeffizienten*). In English, it is impossible to imitate the German prepositive participial construction, and this gives rise to structural problems. Cp. the following more or less literal translation of the word-group in question: *the percentages for the granting of credit in the second half of the year fixed by the monetary authorities*. In this version, the past participle *fixed* has been cut off from the noun to which it refers (*percentages*). There are so many words between *percentages* and *fixed* that the relationship between the noun and the participle is no longer evident and *fixed* seems to refer to *year*. It is therefore advisable to create a more direct link between *fixed* and *percentages* by repeating the latter word, or by replacing it by a superordinate such as *rate*. Cf. the following quotation from Einar Haugen/M. Bloomfield, *Language as a Human Problem* (p. xii):

Interest in grammar arose out of the question − one which has, as we shall see, continually exercised Western man − whether languages were *natural* or *conventional,* a question connected in early Greek thought with the more general dispute over the boundaries of nature (φύσις) and of law or convention (νόμος).

In this example sentence, the author has repeated the noun *question* in order to create a direct link between this word and the past participle *connected*.

9. Kreditspielraums der Banken: *Margin available for lending* (*W/H*) does not combine with a genitive. *Margin for (further) lending* (*G/C*) may co-occur with an inflected genitive. *Lending capacity* (*G/C*) may be used with either an inflected genitive or a periphrastic genitive. In this area of difficulty, the patterns of language usage seem to be undergoing fairly rapid change. At present there is a growing tendency to use the inflected genitive with collective nouns such as those listed in R. Quirk et al., *GCE*, § 4.98 (c). Terms such as *bank* or *company* are on the borderline between animate and inanimate noun classes, and the inflected genitive, which in strictly traditional usage is used mainly with animate nouns, is now encroaching boldly upon the preserves of the periphrastic genitive, especially in journalism. In many cases, the length of the word-groups employed in the genitive is likely to play a decisive role in determining the choice made by the language-users. Cp. Françoise Dubois-Charlier, *Éléments de linguistique anglaise: la phrase complexe et les nominalisations,* pp. 127–8. In this particular instance, it may be preferable to use the inflected genitive in order to avoid the repetition of the word *of* (*a further narrowing of the lending capacity of the banks*). However, as Otto Jespersen has pointed out in *Growth and Structure of the English Language* (p. 173), the English frequently tolerate long strings of prepositions, as in *on the occasion of the coming of age of one of the youngest sons of a wealthy member of Parliament*. As G. B. Shaw once put it, 'The golden rule is that there are no golden rules.'

b) Alternatives

The *leading-strings*	*have* now been made even	*a bit*	shorter, for
” *leash*	*has*	*somewhat*	
		a shade	
		a trifle	
		a thought	
the percentages for the granting of credit in the second half of the			
year, *percentages* fixed by the	*monetary authorities,*	*mean*	
rates	*currency authorities,*	*represent*	
	financial authorities,	*constitute*	
		imply	
a further *narrowing*	of the *banks' lending capacity.*		
contraction	” *lending capacity of the banks.*		
	” *banks' margin for lending.*		
	” *banks' credit limit.*		
	” *banks' credit line.* (U.S.)		

(4) So dürfen die Großbanken bis Ende Dezember ihr Kreditvolumen gegenüber Ende Dezember 1979 nur um 3,5% (im Vorjahr: 4%) ausweiten, die mittleren Banken immerhin um 6% (statt 7%) und die auf Verbraucherkredite und Ratenkäufe spezialisierten Institute um 7% (statt 9%).

a) **Annotations**

1. **So:** The following equivalents are listed in the bilingual dictionaries: *so, thus, hence, therefore, and therefore, consequently, then, for that reason*. These logical connecters cannot be regarded as interchangeable. The following distinctions should be observed.

So has a somewhat colloquial flavour. It may be used as a result conjunct or an inferential conjunct. As a result conjunct it introduces a sentence or clause expressing the result of what precedes. As an inferential conjunct it introduces a summing-up. It always occupies head-position. Like the German conjunct *also*, *so* is rather vague, and it can be used with reference to reasons that are implied and not stated. Cf. R. B. Farrell, *Dictionary of German Synonyms*, pp. 361–2; R. Quirk et al., *GCE*, § 10.27; G. Collier/B. Shields, *Guided German-English Translation*, pp. 54, 86, 150, 171. Here are some examples:

They don't often use it over the week-end. So you can borrow it, if you want to. (R. Quirk et al., *GCE*, § 10.27.)

In consequence of the weight of the first of these two groups, interest differentials may typically be much smaller than would be the case if exchange rate expectations were fully reflected. So, as a result of interest arbitrage, the spot rate for the D-mark, in the example, will tend to jump promptly, rather than making a smooth ascent over five years at the 7 percent yearly rate. (Philip H. Trezise (ed.), *The European Monetary System: Its Promise and Prospects*, p. 95.)

So he's not coming. (R. B. Farrell, *Dictionary of German Synonyms*, p. 362.)

Sometimes the word *so* is preceded by the conjunction *and:*

And so we continue to experience the vagaries of the business cycle, sadly deriding the ingenuous optimism of an earlier decade. (Paul A. Volcker, *The Rediscovery of the Business Cycle*, p. 74.)

Thus is generally considered to be more appropriate to formal contexts. It may occupy front-position or mid-position in a main clause, and in a sub-clause it may be placed immediately after the subordinator. Its two principal meanings ('in this way' and 'so') occasionally coalesce. *Thus* is particularly emphatic when it takes initial position, and the emphatic effect produced by fronting may be heightened by comma separation. Here are some typical examples:

Thus, formerly, at the Customary Court of a manor, events relating to the copyhold lands were presented by the tenants for the information of the lord. (John Burke, *Osborn's Concise Law Dictionary*, s.v. presentment.)

Thus, to take the same example as before, the two elements in the English phrase *you do* can be inverted in interrogation: *do you*?, but no such possibility exists in Latin (. . .). (S. Ullmann, *Meaning and Style*, p. 4.)

Thus the t value measures how many classes a given class is away from the assumed mean (. . .). (M. J. Moroney, *Facts from Figures*, p. 71.)

Thus, although it was not a genuine inventory cycle, the 1973–1975 cycle was heavily dominated by inventory adjustments. (Paul A. Volcker, *The Rediscovery of the Business Cycle*, p. 85.)

Purely external history, so admirably treated in other books, is thus purposely kept to a minimum (. . .). (T. Pyles, *The Origins and Development of the English Language*, p. vi.)

It is believed that thus all pupils will be enabled to read some Latin author with understanding in the shortest possible time (. . .). (P. Robertson, *Latin Prose Composition*, p. vi.)

Hence is a shade more formal than *thus*. Unlike *thus*, it almost invariably occupies front-position. *Hence* is generally followed by a comma. It may introduce a noun phrase or a sentence:

Usually they have been simply forgotten. Hence the title of this volume. (R. De Witt Miller, *Impossible — Yet it Happened*, p. 8.)
Hence, if LINK and REFERENCE are the same at the end of the processing, no links need be written out (. . .). (P. Z. Ingerman, *A Syntax-Oriented Translator*, p. 76.)
These books are intended to facilitate rather than to forestall classroom discussion — hence, they set forth their principles briefly, without elaboration, and with modest amounts of illustration. (L. Altenbernd/L. L. Lewis, *A Handbook for the Study of Fiction*, Introduction.)

In the first example, comma separation is impossible, but in the other sentences comma separation is perfectly normal.

Therefore, which is neutral to formal, is used in much the same way as *thus*, though there are special cases where *thus* and *therefore* are not interchangeable. *Therefore* is remarkably mobile, and stylists take full advantage of its mobility in order to achieve greater elegance of expression. *Therefore* has very complicated position rules. It may appear initially, terminally or medially, and when it appears medially it may occupy several different positions: (a) after auxiliaries such as *can* or *may*; (b) between the noun subject and the verb; (c) between a subordinator and a present participle; (d) before the subordinator *that* in sentences of the pattern: anticipatory *it* + *is* + adjective + *that* + noun clause. Here are some examples:

(i) Therefore we have found it helpful to include attributive adjectives in all drills following the presentation of adjectives. (H. L. Kufner, *The Grammatical Structures of English and German*, p. 58.)
(ii) This *Smaller Dictionary*, intended for general consumption, can therefore go into any home, any school, any library. (E. Partridge, *Smaller Slang Dictionary*, p. vii.)
(iii) We may therefore assume this value, provisionally, as the mean value, and then proceed to calculate a correction to it. (M. J. Moroney, *Facts From Figures*, p. 66.)
(iv) The Administration, therefore, will have to lean heavily on its new 'jawbone' policy (. . .). (H. H. Nyszkiewicz/K. H. Rühe (edd.) *Economic Texts*, pp. 7–8.)
(v) Whilst, therefore, paying some attention to the foundations of the Bloomsbury school in the Cambridge thought of the early years of the century, I am devoting the major part of my thesis to D. H. Lawrence and Wyndham Lewis. (A. Wilson, *Anglo-Saxon Attitudes*, p. 14.)
(vi) It is false, therefore, that all our ideas come through sense. (N. Chomsky, *Aspects of the Theory of Syntax*, p. 49.)

In examples (i), (ii) and (iii), *therefore* could be replaced by *thus*. In examples (iv), (v) and (vi), it is impossible to replace *therefore* by *thus* without changing the word order (*The Administration will thus have to . . ., Thus, whilst paying . . ., It is thus false . . .*). In example (iv), we cannot substitute the pronoun *it* for the noun *Administration* without modifying the word-order (*It will therefore have to . . .*). This is because *it* is unstressed.

German students of English often confuse *therefore* and *that is why*. They almost invariably render *deshalb* and *darum* as *therefore* and tend to fight shy of the expression *that is why*. *Therefore* and *that is why* express two different aspects of the cause-and-effect relationship. Compare the following examples.

(i) Mr Smith was very untrustworthy. That's why I dismissed him.
(ii) Mr Smith was very untrustworthy and was therefore dismissed.

In both examples the first statement indicates a cause while the second statement indicates an effect or result. In the first case, however, the performer (speaker or writer) assumes that the addressee (hearer or reader) already knows about the dismissal, while in the second case the performer assumes that the addressee does not yet know about the dismissal. In the first case, the addressee's attention is focused on the cause rather than on the effect since the cause is unknown while the effect is known. In the second case, equal stress is laid on the cause and the effect since both are unknown (or assumed to be unknown) to the addressee. In the second example, *therefore* could be replaced by *and so*. A less formal version would therefore read as follows: *Mr Smith was very untrustworthy, and so he was dismissed*. In the first example, *that's why* could be rendered by *darum* or *deshalb* in initial position. In the second example, *therefore* could be rendered by *deshalb* in medial position. Cp. the example sentences in R. B. Farrell, *Dictionary of German Synonyms*, p. 361; Paul Grebe et al., *Duden Bedeutungswörterbuch*, s.vv. darum, deshalb; Günther Drosdowski, *Duden Stilwörterbuch*, s.vv. darum, deshalb.

Consequently is used in relatively formal style. *Consequently* and *as a consequence* are virtually interchangeable. They introduce an objective statement of the effect of the cause given in the preceding clause or sentence. Both locutions are normally restricted to initial position:

In German, however, such expressions are usually compounded; consequently the German language is very rich in compound nouns. (Eric V. Greenfield, *German Grammar*, p. 48.)
Consequently, Dr. Nadiri's view seems somewhat more optimistic than Mr. Volcker's (. . .). (Paul A. Volcker, *The Rediscovery of the Business Cycle*, p. 11.)
English shows no distinction between these two uses; as a consequence our students often have trouble keeping them apart. (H. L. Kufner, *The Grammatical Structures of English and German*, p. 58.)

Then is an inferential conjunct which may be classed as 'neutral to formal' and which requires comma separation to indicate that it is not a time adjunct. It is usually employed in relatively short units, and it can appear in medial or in final position. Medial positioning is generally a source of difficulty for the foreign student of English, for *then*, like *therefore*, can occur in a wide range of optional positions between the first and the last word of a clause or sentence, and experienced stylists often use the conjunct *then* very consciously with a view to achieving rhetorical effects based on intonation breaks and suspenseful retardation. It may be helpful to indicate some of the positions that can be occupied by the word *then*: (a) between a style disjunct and the subject; (b) immediately after the head noun in a periphrastic genitive construction; (c) immediately before an amplificatory pronominal tag; (d) between the subject and an auxiliary such as *must*; (e) between the subject and the copulative verb *to be*; (f) immediately before the subordinator *that*; (g) between a subordinator and the subject of a sub-clause. A few examples will suffice:

(i) Nothing to quarrel about there, then. (G. Collier/B. Shields, *Guided German-English Translation*, p. 54.)
(ii) Briefly, then, we may say that the metrical characteristics are conclusive against the date 1610 (Shakespeare, *Macbeth*, ed. A. W. Verity, p. xi.)
(iii) The story, then, of *Hamlet* was not new, nor was Shakespeare the first to dramatise it. (Shakespeare, *Hamlet*, ed. A. W.Verity, p. xv.)
(iv) Let us go then, you and I (. . .). (T. S. Eliot, 'The Love Song of J. Alfred Prufrock'.)
(v) If the poet, then, must perforce dramatize the oneness of the experience, even though paying tribute to its diversity, then his use of paradox and ambiguity is seen as necessary. (Cleanth Brooks, *The Well Wrought Urn*, p. 174.)

(vi) Wordsworth's 'Intimations' ode, then, is not only a poem, but, among other things, a parable about poetry. (*ibid.*).
(vii) Does it seem to you, then, that the Prime Minister is taking a big risk in calling for an election this year? (R. Quirk et al., *GCE,* § 10.28.)
(viii) When, then, the student tackles a passage that is to be rendered into Latin prose, he should first consider what will make a convenient period. (P. Robertson, *Latin Prose Composition,* p. 236.)

In most of these examples, *then* could be replaced by *therefore.* For instance, one might compare sentence (vi) with the following quotation from A. W. Verity's edition of Shakespeare's *Hamlet* (p. xii):

This, therefore, is a second, and a sound, argument in favour of 1602.

For that reason and *for this reason* are generally restricted to written English and almost always occupy front-position:

For that reason we hope that the occasionally lighter touch by which some of the information is conveyed may be forgiven by the perhaps unduly serious-minded student. (C. E. Eckersley/W. Kaufmann, *A Commercial Course for Foreign Students,* Vol. 1, p. iv.)
For this reason the difficult words in this work are given the pronunciations with which they are spoken by those who habitually use them (. . .). (Robert H. Hill, *Jarrolds' Dictionary of Difficult Words,* p. 6.)

2. dürfen: The use of the future tense is obligatory here. Cp. note (2) 1 (a).

3. Vorjahr: *Vorjahr* is rendered as *last year* when it refers to the twelve-month period immediately preceding the year in which the speaker or writer gives utterance to his thoughts. Expressions such as *the previous year, the preceding year* or *the year before* are used only if reference is made to a remoter period of time. Hence a person writing or speaking in 1980 will employ the locution *last year* when drawing a comparison between 1980 and 1979, but he will use *the year before* or some similar expression when comparing 1979 with 1978 or 1978 with 1977.

4. die mittleren . . . um 6%: In this particular instance the verb cannot be ellipted in English. Ellipsis of the verb is restricted to a number of special cases in modern English. Cf. R. Quirk et al., *GCE,* §§ 9.72–9.78. In order to avoid flat-footed repetition of the expression employed in the first clause, we may convert the verb *expand* into a noun (*expansion*).

5. mittleren: *Middle-sized* is much less common than *medium-sized.*

6. immerhin: *Nevertheless, in spite of that, however* and *still* are virtually interchangeable in written English. *Yet* often expresses mild surprise at the fact or facts reported. *After all* may mean 'when everything is considered' or 'in spite of expectations, efforts, etc.' (*CED*).

7. die auf Verbraucherkredite . . . um 7%: Ellipsis of the verb is possible here on account of the structural parallelism between the word-groups *die mittleren . . . (statt 7%)* and *die auf Verbraucherkredite . . . (statt 9%).*

8. Verbraucherkredite: *Verbraucherkredit* is sometimes rendered as *consumption loan* (v. Eichborn) or *consumer loan* (Zahn). The commonest term, however, is *consumer credit.* Cf. *Consumer Credit* (Crowther Report), Vol. I.

9. Ratenkäufe: Two different forms of agreement are subsumed under the term *Ratenkäufe*: (a) hire-purchase agreements (*Mietkauf*), and (b) credit sale agreements (*Kreditkauf, Abzahlungskauf, Teilzahlungskauf*). In the U.K. both kinds of agreement are covered by the Hire Purchase Act (1965).

A hire purchase agreement is an agreement to hire goods for a specified period, with an option for the hirer (known in contract law as the bailee) to purchase the goods at the end, generally for a nominal sum. As a rule, the seller retains ownership until the final instalment is paid. The U.S. equivalents of *hire purchase* are *installment buying, installment purchase, installment business, installment contract, purchase on deferred terms, purchase of goods on the deferred payment system, installment selling, installment plan.*[1] These locutions are not all interchangeable. *Installment buying, installment business,* etc., are general terms denoting the hire-purchase system of buying, while *installment contract* denotes a specific agreement concluded under the system in question. In *A Dictionary of Modern American Usage* (s.v. instal(l)ment), H. W. Horwill remarks that hire purchase business transactions are ordinarily considered in the U.S.A. from the viewpoint of the seller. This is not quite true. Horwill evidently overlooked the synonyms of *installment selling* which have been listed above. The information given in Norman Moss's *What's the Difference?* is also rather scanty. Only one American equivalent of *hire purchase* has been recorded: *installment plan.* Mr Moss spells *instalment* with one *l*, but in U.S. English it is normally spelt *installment. Installment plan* has not yet been recorded in the German-English dictionaries. Perhaps it should also be noted that the hire-purchase system of buying is denoted in informal British English as *the never-never* or *buying on the never-never* (cf. *Kaufen auf Stottern*). This is not quite the same as *buying goods on tick. Tick* is a colloquial term for *credit.*

A credit sale agreement is defined by law as 'an agreement for the sale of goods under which the purchase price is payable by five or more instalments not being a conditional sale agreement'[2]. Under a credit sale agreement the property in[3] the goods (*das Eigentum an der Ware*) passes immediately to the buyer (*geht unmittelbar auf den Käufer über*). The seller has no security since he does not reserve the property pending payment.

In the United Kingdom the institutions mainly concerned with consumer lending are the clearing banks and especially the hire purchase finance houses.[4]

For further information on hire purchase sale, credit sale agreements and the like, see J. Rudolph, *Langenscheidts Handbuch der englischen Wirtschaftssprache,* pp. 58–61; *Consumer Credit* (Crowther Report), Vol. 1; J. Burke, *Osborn's Concise Law Dictionary,* s.vv. hire-purchase agreement, credit-sale agreement; G. Bannock/R. E. Baxter/R. Rees, *The Penguin Dictionary of Economics,* s.vv. hire purchase, consumer credit, finance house, finance houses association, Crowther Committee; M. Greener, *The Penguin Dictionary of Commerce,* s.vv. hire purchase, Hire Purchase Act 1965, credit sale agreement, Consumer Credit Act 1974; A. Gilpin, *Dictionary of Economic*

---

[1] A number of international terms are listed in the third volume of the *O-HSG-ED,* s.v. Ratenkauf. See also *G/C,* s.v. Ratenkauf.

[2] Under a conditional sale agreement (*Kauf unter Eigentumsvorbehalt*) the property in the goods remains in the seller until the goods have been paid for.

[3] The preposition *of* is sometimes substituted for *in.*

[4] Jochen Rudolph has rendered this term as *Teilzahlungsbank* or *Kundenkreditbank.*

Terms, s.vv. hire purchase, credit sale, hire purchase finance houses. For information on hire purchase agreements in Germany, see E. J. Cohn, *Manual of German Law,* Vol. I, § 262. For information on the French system, see M. Marcheteau/J. Tardieu, *Business and Economics,* Vol. 1, pp. 299–300.

b) Alternatives

Thus, *between now and the end of December,* the *Hence,* *until the end of December* *Consequently,* *As a consequence,* *Between now and the end of December, therefore,* *Until the end of December, therefore,*		

big banks	will be *allowed*	to *expand* their	*credit volume*
major banking houses	*permitted*	*extend*	*volume of credit*
large		*enlarge*	*volume of credits*
			total credit outstanding
			total credits
			total loans

by *only* 3.5%	*as against*	the end of December 1979 (4% last
a mere	*as compared with*	
a meagre	*compared with*	
	in comparison with	

year); *still,*	the *medium-sized* banks will be allowed an
however,	*medium-size*
nevertheless,	
in spite of that,	

expansion of 6% (instead of 7%), and the institutions *that*	
	which

specialize in *consumer credit* and	*hire purchase*
specialise » *consumer credits*	*hire-purchase*
consumer loans	*hire purchase sale*
consumption loans	*installment buying*
consumption credit	*installment purchase*
consumption credits	*installment selling*
	installment business
	purchase on instalment terms
	purchase of goods by instalments
	purchase of goods on the instalment system
	purchase of goods on the deferred payment
	[*system*
	purchase on deferred terms
	installment contracts
	hire-purchase agreements
	credit sale agreements
	hire-purchase and credit sale agreements

an expansion of 7% (instead of 9%).

(5) Darlehen für den Wohnungsbau, die bisher weitgehend von diesen Normen ausgenommen waren, fallen jetzt ebenfalls unter das in Bankkreisen berüchtigte „encadrement".

a) Annotations

1. Darlehen ... Wohnungsbau: This word-group must be translated as a lexical unit. Cf. the compound *Wohnungsbaudarlehen*.

2. ausgenommen waren: Time adverbials such as *so far, up to now,* and *till now* normally occur with the present perfect – the so-called perfect of experience (cf. R. W. Zandvoort, *A Handbook of English Grammar*, § 141) – because they indicate a past with current relevance:

All the policemen I've met so far were unfriendly and didn't even try to help me. (W. Bliemel/A. Fitzpatrick/J. Quetz, *Englisch für Erwachsene*, Vol. 2, p. 63.)

When this type of statement is set back into the past, the present perfect is replaced by the past perfect:

(. . .) up to now he had never had an accident. (M. Bianchi/W. Bliemel/A. Fitzpatrick/J. Quetz, *Englisch für Erwachsene*, Vol. 3, p. 91.)

3. das ... „encadrement": The French term ought to be retained in an English translation. English-speaking authors often interlard their writings with French words and phrases, for the British revere French culture as the Romans revered Greek culture:

But the greatest influence of all, at least in my view, is what used to be called the *trahison des clercs,* the moral betrayal by those who ought to be upholders of the traditional virtues, qualities, and institutions, and of the truths and values which it was their duty to maintain. (Lord Hailsham in: P. Hutber (ed.), *What's Wrong With Britain?* p. 42.)
The methodology of this approach is to examine whether the demand-pull prediction stands up to empirical scrutiny and, should it fail to do so, to deduce, *faute de mieux,* that cost-push factors were responsible for inflation. (J. A. Trevithick/C. Mulvey, *The Economics of Inflation,* p. 38.)
Though at first under no more respectable leadership than that of Wilkes, it proved a formidable opponent both to Crown and aristocracy, because it found a *point d'appui* in London. (G. M. Trevelyan, *British History in the Nineteenth Century and After:* 1782–1919, p. 32.)
A *fou rire* had got hold of her. (I. Murdoch, *The Bell,* p. 253.)
Annette's education, which was less important, and in the course of which she had learnt four languages and little else, had been picked up *un peu partout* (. . .). (I. Murdoch, *The Flight from the Enchanter,* p. 8.)
The list of examples could be lengthened.
In the case under discussion, *encadrement* is short for *encadrement du crédit* (= credit squeeze, tightening of credit).
The translation of the definite article *das* poses a rather intricate problem since the attributive phrase *in Bankkreisen berüchtigte* is restrictive inasmuch as it introduces a closer specification of the credit squeeze described in the opening sentences. If we render the German definite article by the English definite article, the word *the* will be interpreted as a defining element suggesting the possible existence of another, different, *encadrement*. Thus, in order to avoid conveying a false impression, we have no choice but to use the demonstrative determiner *that*. It should be borne in mind that

words such as *this* and *that* frequently carry pejorative implications. On the affective use of the demonstrative determiners in English see J. P. Vinay/J. Darbelnet, *Stylistique comparée du français et de l'anglais*, § 239.

In *Guided German-English Translation* (p. 24), Gordon Collier and Brian Shields point out that demonstrative determiners do not normally co-occur with restrictive postmodification, but they concede that exceptions are possible. Useful examples are given on p. 59 (5.3.5b). Despite the comparative infrequency of this construction type, the co-occurrence of demonstrative determiners with restrictive postmodification seems to be an intrinsic element of traditional English usage. Cf. the following example from John Milton's famous sonnet on his blindness (xix):

And that one talent which is death to hide
Lodged with me useless (. . .).

The translation of the adjective *berüchtigt* also calls for a few remarks. German premodification must be replaced by English postmodification, so we cannot employ adjectives that are normally used attributively (*ill-famed, ill-reputed*). Locutions which are used only as postqualifiers must also be ruled out (*of bad repute, of evil repute, of ill repute*). *Disreputable, infamous* and *flagitious* are contextually impermissible. *Disreputable* generally collocates with nouns such as *bar, club, fellow, house* or *locality*, while *infamous* and *flagitious* both imply atrocious wickedness. *Flagitious* is 'somewhat less rhetorical and more closely descriptive' than *infamous* (*WNDS*, s.v. vicious). It would, however, be possible to employ *in bad repute* since this expression is used predicatively. In this case, of course, augmentation by *such* would be needed. *Notorious* (= unfavourably known) would also be acceptable here. Augmentation by *so* would be required. For examples see R. Meldau/R. B. Whitling, *Schulsynonymik der englischen Sprache*, s.v. berühmt; H. W. Klein/W. Friederich, *Englische Synonymik* s.v. bekannt.

b) Alternatives

Housing loans, *House-building loans,* *Loans for house-building,*	which	*have hitherto* *have so far* *up to now have* *up to the present have* *till now have* *thus far have* *up to this time have* *until now have*	*been largely*

exempted from these	*norms,*
	standards,
	laws,
	principles,
	rules,
		now also *fall within the scope of*
		    likewise come ″ ″ ″ ″
		                come under
		                fall under
		                fall within the ambit of
		                come within the range of
		are now also *covered by*
		  ″ ″ *likewise* ″ ″	

that *encadrement* which is	*so notorious*
	in such bad repute
		among bankers.
		  ″ *bank experts.*
		in banking quarters.
		  ″ ″ *circles.*	

> ⑥ Die bei diesen Krediten festgestellte Zuwachsrate von 27% im letzten Jahr hat der Regierung offensichtlich zu denken gegeben.

a) Annotations

1. bei diesen Krediten: In this type of pattern *bei* is normally rendered as *in*. Cf. the following sentence from D. Hamblock/D. Wessels, *Englisch in Wirtschaft und Handel: Übersetzungstexte* (p. 29):
Das ergibt eine Zuwachsrate von 19,2 Prozent bei den Stückzahlen und 25,5 Prozent dem Werte nach.
This represents a rate of increase of 19.2 per cent in volume and 25.5 per cent in value. (D. Hamblock/D. Wessels, *Englisch in Wirtschaft und Handel: Übersetzungstexte – Lösungen*, p. 29.)

b) Alternatives

The 27% rate of increase in these credits observed last year
has *evidently*   set   the government thinking.
obviously   given „   „   food for thought.
clearly   given pause to the government.
manifestly given the government pause.
apparently

> ⑦ Auch der unter den Banken üblich gewordene Kauf von nicht ausgenutzten Quoten eines Finanzinstituts durch ein anderes soll künftig nicht mehr toleriert werden.

a) Annotations

1. unter den Banken: In this particular instance, *unter den Banken* is virtually synonymous with *in Bankkreisen*. Cf. sentence (5) above.

2. der ... üblich gewordene Kauf: German premodification must be replaced by English postmodification.

3. nicht ausgenutzten: These two words must be rendered as a single lexical unit. Cf. *unausgenutzt*.

4. Quoten: The quotas referred to here are credit quotas.

5. Finanzinstituts: The term *finance house* is contextually impermissible since it is a hyponym and not a synonym of *financial institution*. Cf. J. Rudolph, *Langenscheidts Handbuch der englischen Wirtschaftssprache*, p. 248; G. Bannock/R. E. Baxter/R. Rees, *The Penguin Dictionary of Economics*, s.v. finance house; M. Greener, *The Penguin Dictionary of Commerce*, s.v. finance house.

6. ein anderes: The use of the pro-form *one* is optional here. Cf. Hornby, *OALDCE*, s.v. another.

7. künftig: *In future* is synonymous with *from now on*. *In the future* means 'in the time yet to come':

Try to live a better life in future. (Hornby, *OALDCE*, s.v. future.)

Although industry has so far not committed itself to using jojoba oil in the future, the signs are that once it is available in commercial quantities, its use will soon become widespread. (W. S. Fowler, *Proficiency English*, Vol. 1, p. 61.)

Henceforth, henceforward and *hereafter* would sound unduly formal in this context. *From this time forward,* which has not been recorded under the catchword *künftig* in the bilingual dictionaries, would sound rather too solemn and literary. The same goes for the expression *from this time on.*

b) Alternatives

Even the	*purchase*	of	*unused*	quotas of one	*financial institution*
	purchasing		*unfilled*		*finance institution*
	buying				*financial enterprise*
	acquisition				
by	*another,*	which has become a common practice in			*banking quarters,*
	another one,				*banking circles,*
is no longer to be tolerated	*in future.*				
	from now on.				

⑧ Dafür bleiben Kredite zur Förderung des Exportgeschäfts zur Hälfte „frei", passiver Außenhandel verpflichtet schließlich.

a) Annotations

1. Dafür: *On the contrary* is not synonymous with *on the other hand*. *On the contrary* is an expression used to render a denial or contradiction more emphatic. *On the other hand* is a phrase used to indicate contrasted points of view, facts, arguments, etc.

2. bleiben: *Remain* should be used in preference to *stay*. *Stay* is employed in a strictly local sense, while *remain* (often followed by an adjective, a present participle or a noun) can mean 'to continue unchanged'. Cf. H. W. Klein/W. Friedrich, *Englische Synonymik*, s.v. bleiben; S. I. Hayakawa, *Cassell's Modern Guide to Synonyms & Related Words*, s.v. remain.

3. Kredite ... Exportgeschäfts: This word-group should be rendered as a single lexical unit. Cf. *Exportförderungskredit.*

4. passiver Außenhandel: This expression, which has not been recorded in the dictionaries, is synonymous with *Außenhandelsdefizit.*

5. verpflichtet: Verbs such as *oblige* cannot be used without a direct object in English. The proverb *Adel verpflichtet* is undoubtedly the commonest example of *verpflichten* used absolutely, but the lexicographers have overlooked the fact that *verpflichten* may also be used absolutely with noun subjects such as *der Name* or *passiver Außenhandel*. In such cases, it is possible to convert the verb into a noun (*Verpflichtung:* obligation). A verb such as *involve* or *entail* can then be used to establish a link with the sentence subject.

6. schließlich: *Schließlich* is rendered as *finally* when it draws attention to the various stages of what precedes. In this case, however, it implies an inference drawn from a number of facts or arguments considered as a whole. It must therefore be translated by some phrase such as *after all* or *all things considered* (= wenn man es recht bedenkt). Cf. *LEW,* s.v. schließlich; R. B. Farrell, *Dictionary of German Synonyms,* s.v. last, The expression *all things considered* may be expanded: *when everything is considered* (*CED,* s.v. after).

b) Alternatives

On the other hand, fifty *percent* of export promotion credits *per cent*	
remain 'free'; *after all,* *all things considered,* *when everything is considered,*	*a foreign trade deficit* *an export deficit*
involves certain *obligations.* *entails* ” *responsibilities.*	

Text IV*

Konjunkturprognosen

Kein Zyklus gleicht dem anderen. Dafür sind die materiellen und psychologischen Ursachen der Schwingungen jeweils zu verschieden; insbesondere sind die einen Aufschwung bestimmenden Faktoren jedesmal andere, was für seine Länge und Stärke entscheidend, für seine gewünschte Vorausberechnung aber das größte Hindernis ist. Trotzdem mühen sich die Konjunkturforschungsinstitute um die Aufgabe, den Konjunkturverlauf in seinen Veränderungsraten und den Zeitpunkt des Wechsels von einer zur anderen Lage vorauszusagen. Hierbei kann aus geschichtlicher Erfahrung über das Gewisse der Wechsellagen hinaus nicht allzuviel mit Sicherheit geschlossen werden. An wissenschaftlichen Anstrengungen, die Konjunkturerfahrungen für Konjunkturprognose und Konjunkturpolitik nutzbar zu machen, fehlt es nicht. So vermutete z. B. der russische Nationalökonom Nicolai Kondratjew, die damals rund zehn-, heute rund fünfjährigen Zyklen (immer von einer Wiederbelebung bis zur nächsten gerechnet) würden durch lange Wellen überlagert; diese würden alle fünfzig Jahre einen Wechsel im Überwiegen von Aufschwungs- und Stockungsjahren bringen. Als Ursache hierfür erkannte Professor Kondratjew den nur alle fünfzig Jahre auftretenden Belebungseffekt durch grundlegende Erfindungen im Maschinen- und Energiebereich, die nachhaltige Kostensenkung versprechen und dadurch nachhaltige Neuinvestitionen auslösen.

---

* Dolmetscher- und Übersetzerprüfung/Englisch/7. 10. 1980/Industrie- und Handelskammer zu Dortmund.

Text IV
Economic Forecasting

No two cycles are alike. This is because there are appreciable differences between the material and psychological causes of the various oscillations; above all, the determinants of an upswing are always different, a fact which is decisive for the length and intensity of the upturn, though it is the greatest obstacle to making the requisite forecasts about it. Nonetheless, the economic research institutes endeavour to predict rates of change in the cyclical trend and to identify turning points in advance. In this field of research, few definite inferences can be drawn in the light of historical experience, except that some kind of economic fluctuation is bound to occur.

There is no lack of scientific attempts to utilize accumulated knowledge of trade cycles for economic forecasting and cyclical policies. Thus, for example, the Russian economist Nikolai Kondratieff conjectured that cycles, which in those days had a duration of about ten years, and which nowadays are about five years in length (always calculated from one trade revival to the next) were overlaid with long waves; every fifty years, he surmised, these long waves caused periods with a preponderance of high years to alternate with periods in which recession years predominated. Professor Kondratieff believed this was due to an effect that could be observed only once every fifty years, the reinvigorating effect of fundamental discoveries in technology and energy which held out hopes of effective cost reduction, thereby inducing effective new investment.

Annotations and Alternatives

① Konjunkturprognosen

a) Annotations

Expressions such as *business outlook* and *outlook for the economy* are unacceptable unless *Konjunkturprognose* is used loosely in the sense of *Konjunkturaussichten*. In the U.K., the word *forecast,* in the economic sense, is still in current use, but in the U.S.A. it has recently been ousted by *scenario.* Cf. the following quotation from *World and Press* (1st March issue 1981, p. 2):

The gem (. . .) is that in the Reagan Administration the word "forecast", in the economic sense, is out; it's regarded as too Keynesian. The new "in" word? "Scenario".

b) Alternatives

> *Economic Forecasting*
> *Business Forecasting* (U.S.)
> *Economic Forecasts*
> *Business Forecasts* (U.S.)
> *Business Predictions*
> *Business Scenarios* (U.S.)

② Kein Zyklus gleicht dem anderen.

a) Annotations

The dictionary equivalents given under the catchword *gleichen* are unacceptable in this particular instance. In some dictionaries, however, workable equivalents may be found under the catchword *gleich*:

(i) No two have been alike. (*W/H.*)
(ii) No fingerprint is exactly like another. (*O-HSG-ED.*)
(iii) No two fingerprints are exactly alike. (*ibid.*)

In sentence (iii), *exactly alike* could be replaced by *quite the same.* Cp. the following quotation from Paul A. Samuelson, *Economics,* p. 237:

No two business cycles are quite the same.

b) Alternatives

> *No two cycles are alike.*
>   „ „ „ „ *quite the same.*
> *No cycle is exactly like another.*

③ Dafür sind die materiellen und psychologischen Ursachen der Schwingungen jeweils zu verschieden;

a) Annotations

1. Dafür: The translations offered by the bilingual dictionaries would not make much sense if used in this context. The most satisfactory solutions are *The reason for this is that* and *This is because*. Examples:

The reason for this is that we believe Chomsky's main contribution has been as a system-builder (...). (N. Smith/D. Wilson, *Modern Linguistics*, p. 10.)
(...) this was largely because Chomsky was proposing to draw conclusions from the nature of language to the nature of the human language-user (...). (*ibid.*, p. 9.)

In the first example sentence the word-group *for this* can be deleted without affecting sense or acceptability.
In informal style, *for this* is often replaced by *why*. In *The Elements of Style* (pp. 23–24), W. Strunk and E. B. White admit that the expression *the reason why is that* is in common use, but they suggest that it ought to be replaced by *because*. Owing to their preoccupation with the ideal of concision, they have evidently failed to notice that *because* and *the reason why is that* are not really interchangeable.
As a rule, one uses *because* if the focus of information is the fact stated or the idea expressed in the main clause. The sub clause is normally quite short:

Leave me because you want someone else. (I. Murdoch, *A Severed Head*, p. 26.)
Their style is not the less vicious because we find it curious. (J. Middleton Murry, *The Problem of Style*, p. 11.)

However, the subordinating conjunction *because* proves totally inadequate whenever one wishes to give thematic and focal prominence to the reasons that are to be furnished or the arguments that are to be advanced in support of the fact stated in the main clause. In such cases, one must resort to an expression such as *the reason for this is that*. If the explanation is particularly lengthy, and hypotaxis inevitable, one may have to construct several sentences introduced by a phrase such as *for this reason:*

We may say that the critic should make clear by his context the sense in which he is using the word; the fact remains that he seldom does – for this reason. The critic, unless he is that very rare and valuable thing, a technical critic, must be to some extent a creative artist in his criticism. The first part of his work is to convey the effect (...). (J. Middleton Murry, *op. cit.*, p. 7.)

2. Schwingungen: The most appropriate term is *oscillation*. Cp. the following quotation from the *PDE* (s.v. trade cycle):

Trade cycle. Regular oscillations in the level of business activity over a period of years.

3. jeweils: The 'literal' translation *in each case* (*LGS*) is only marginally possible since it is an obstacle to smooth reading. The most acceptable solution is a class-shift: the adverb *jeweils* may be converted into the adjective *various* (= jeweilig). Cf. *O-HSG-ED*, s.v. jeweilig.

4. zu verschieden: *Too* + *different* is a low-probability collocation, so the translator has to resort to a clause-structure shift entailing a class-shift:

the (...) causes (...) are *too different*

there are *appreciable differences* between the (...) causes (...)

Note that 'existential sentences', i.e. sentences introduced by *there is* or *there are*, are much more common in English than in German. Cp. the examples quoted in W. S. Fowler's *Proficiency English* (*Teacher's Book 1*, p. 6).

b) Alternatives

| *This is because*   there are *appreciable*   differences between |
| *The reason is that*   *considerable* |
| the material and psychological causes of the various oscillations; |

④ insbesondere sind die einen Aufschwung bestimmenden Faktoren jedesmal andere, was für seine Länge und Stärke entscheidend, für seine gewünschte Vorausberechnung aber das größte Hindernis ist.

a) Annotations

1. insbesondere: This adverb offers a variety of possibilities in English translation: *in particular, above all, particularly, (e)specially, in especial* and *principally*. However, it is well to remember that these locutions are not always freely interchangeable.
The particularizers *in particular* and *above all* can fulfil two types of syntactic function:

a) They function as adjuncts when they are integrated within the structure of the clause, i.e. when they serve to focus attention on specific clausal constituents rather than on the clause as a whole. Examples:

We have lots of brown and black and yellow Britons who were born and educated here, in particular the present younger generation (. . .). (*World and Press,* 1st February issue 1981, p. 2.)
In the U.S.A. in particular, the problem is causing great concern. (R. Arvill, *Man and Environment,* p. 22.)
(. . .) there is (. . .) vast scope for improvement in the structure and content of central and local government; in the size of areas, membership of governing bodies and the quality of staff; in delegation at all levels; in the arrangements for cooperation between public and private enterprise; and, perhaps above all, in the ways of getting citizens to participate in decision-making. (*ibid.,* p. 25.)
For it is her unfavourable background and the harsh, uncomprehending treatment she receives which encourage the more dangerous aspects of her character − her tendency towards outbursts of violent anger and vengefulness in the face of injustice, her romantic yearning for perfection and an escape from the realities of life, and above all her intense secret pride. (T. Fontane, *Grete Minde,* ed. A. R. Robinson, pp. xxix−xxx.)
He wanted above all to go to sleep (. . .). (A. Sillitoe, *Saturday Night and Sunday Morning,* p. 77.)

b) They function as disjuncts when they are not integrated within the clause, i.e. when they serve to focus attention on the clause as a whole rather than on its constituents. Examples:

Surplus stocks of food in the major exporting countries, which have 'cushioned' the world against adversity, had nearly gone; in particular, cereal stocks were the lowest for 20 years. (R. Arvill, *Man and Environment,* p. 17.)

In particular, we should like to express our gratitude to Broder Carstensen (. . .). (R. Quirk/S. Greenbaum, *UGE*, p. vi.)
In particular, I have to acknowledge my indebtedness to the following: (. . .). (M. J. Moroney, *Facts from Figures*, p. vi.)
Above all there are neologisms which are springing up in large numbers, owing to the present rapid pace of progress, and for which there is in most cases no equivalent, (*G/C*, p. xi.)
Above all, we have to thank Miss G. Prowe for her meticulous arrangement and editing of the draft material (. . .). (*O-HSG-ED*, Vol. II, p. v.)
Until recently it was Government policy to favour take-overs on the grounds that the bigger a company was, the stronger and more competitive it would be abroad, an analysis that may sometimes be justified but often overlooks disadvantages, above all because no one has worked out systematically why the majority of mergers take place. (W. S. Fowler, *Proficiency English*, Vol. 1, p. 43.)

In the case under discussion, *insbesondere* modifies the clause *sind . . . andere*, so the adverb phrases *in particular* and *above all* can be accepted as suitable translation equivalents.

The other English equivalents of *insbesondere* would be inappropriate here since they are normally used only as focusing adjuncts that serve to restrict words and phrases rather than entire clauses. Examples:

particularly:

(. . .) the greatly increased study (particularly in Europe) of the impact of English on other languages has meant a considerable extension of Chapter 2 (. . .). (R. Quirk, *The Use of English*, p. v.)
And quite often, even if we don't habitually speak with our original local dialect, we may feel the need to retreat into it on occasion – as into our own home, when we want to be particularly private and personal, or when we want to declare our basic loyalties. (*ibid.*, p. 90.)

especially:

As an amateur in linguistics, I am especially indebted to those who have readily responded to my appeals for expert guidance (. . .). (H. W. Fowler, *A Dictionary of Modern English Usage*, p. xi.)
Especially marked in the last decades of the century was the rapprochement between aristocrats and Jews (. . .). (T. Fontane, *Die Poggenpuhls*, ed. D. Barlow, p. xii.)
The trouble with most laws, of course, and especially those concerning nationality, is that there are always borderline cases who may suffer considerable hardship. (*World and Press*, 1st February issue 1981, p. 2.)

For detailed information about the words *especially* and *specially*, see H. W. Fowler, *A Dictionary of Modern English Usage*, s.v. especial(ly); R. Flesch, *The ABC of Style*, s.v. especially. Fowler has pilloried the tautological phrase *more especially*, but this locution is so firmly rooted in modern usage that it may prove ineradicable. The same holds true for the expression *more particularly*. Cp. the following example from Derrick Barlow's edition of Theodor Fontane's *Die Poggenpuhls* (p. x):

Owing to an unusual combination of circumstances, too complex to be analysed here, the German nobility, and more particularly the Prussian, succeeded in retaining a number of social prerogatives which its French and English counterpart had long relinquished.

in especial:

There are three problems, in especial, that confront the compiler of such a dictionary as this. (H. W. Horwill, *A Dictionary of Modern American Usage*, p. viii.)

This expression has not been listed as an equivalent of *insbesondere* in the bilingual dictionaries, although it is a close synonym of *in particular*.

principally:

His treatment of psychological and social problems was frank and fearless, and at the same time he presented for us a whole world in miniature, principally the world of his own day and his own familiar milieu. (T. Fontane, *Grete Minde,* ed. A. R. Robinson, p. xxiv.)

2. die einen Aufschwung bestimmenden Faktoren: Syntactically, this word-group may be rendered in two ways: a) *the factors which determine an upswing*; b) *the determinants of an upswing*. As far as style is concerned, the second solution is preferable since it makes for greater concision. The word *determinant* is particularly common in economic parlance. Cp. the following example from the *PDE* (s.v. Stabilization policy):

The determinants of the timing and amplitude of these fluctuations are analysed in that part of economics known as the theory of the trade cycle.

3. Aufschwung: The lexicographers have overlooked two translation equivalents of this term: *turn-up* and *burst of expansion.* Cp. the following examples from M. Stewart, *Keynes and After:*

Other economists, again, took a more positive view about the reasons for the turn-up, arguing that new investment was stimulated not only by the lower costs of doing it, but also by the greater profitability of doing it. (p. 43.)
Then it [*sc.* the down-swing] would level off, and the stage would be set for another burst of expansion. (p. 40.)

Upturn and *upswing,* which may also be used to translate *Aufschwung,* are usually unhyphenated, but the hyphenated forms are quite acceptable, too. Cp. the following examples from M. Stewart, *Keynes and After:*

There was, however, a compensation for the inevitability of the down-turn: the up-turn was inevitable too. (p. 48.)
On the up-swing everything would expand (. . .). (p. 40.)

4. was: Here we have to do with a typically German sentential relative clause. As a rule, short, straightforward sentential relative clauses can be rendered literally into English, but clauses as long as this one are apt to present difficulties in translation. In contemporary English, sentential relative clauses tend to be relatively short. Cp. the following example from R. M. Davis, *The Novel: Modern Essays in Criticism* (p. 27):

It has been, historically, the most various and changeable of literary disciplines, which means that it has been the most alive.

For further examples, see R. Quirk/S. Greenbaum, *UGE,* § 13.12; R. Quirk et al., *GCE,* § 11,52.
Lengthy and complex sentential relative clauses seem contrary to accepted modern usage since they tend to be ungainly and ineffectual. The pronoun *which* by itself is insufficient to give the remainder of the sentence the fresh push-off that the introduction of a comparatively complex idea requires. In order to arrest attention and prevent the sentence from tailing off into hazy insignificance, it is customary to resort to various rhetorical stratagems:

a) the use of the demonstrative pronoun *this* as an anaphoric signal:

The pay of government workers, teachers, employees in regulated industries, and others lags behind the rise in prices, and this makes it difficult to recruit and hold good workers. (C. A. Dauten/L. M. Valentine, *Business Cycles and Forecasting,* p. 5.)

b) the reduction of the sentential relative clause to a nominal group thrown into relief by comma separation or dashes:

Until the mid seventeenth century compositors generally sat to their work, but from then on it became more usual to compose standing up, an easier position for fast work. (P. Gaskell, *A New Introduction to Bibliography*, p. 43.)

Sheets of copy were put up on the case, either folded into a special clip called a 'visorium' – the normal continental method up to the nineteenth century – or held against the right-hand side of the upper case by an arrangement of weights and string, as was usual in England in the later handpress period and probably before. (*ibid.*)

c) the insertion of a factive abstract noun before the relative pronoun *which*:

Mountains and forests made Ulster inaccessible from the central plain, a factor which remained important until the seventeenth century. (A. T. Q. Stewart, *The Ulster Crisis*, p. 26.)

The divergencies between German and English usage in this problem area may be accounted for in two ways:

a) German syntax is closely modelled on Latin syntax, so that on the whole German is not quite so disjointed from sentence to sentence as is English. Most British and American writers use connecters so sparingly that their prose often conveys an impression of desultoriness. (Cp. George Saintsbury's remarks on English prose style in *A Short History of French Literature* (p. 614) and Jacques Duron's comments on Saintsbury's own prose style in *Langue française langue humaine*, p. 175 (note 27).) Indeed, the authors of some English style manuals go the length of advocating an airy disregard for the correct use of the connecting words and phrases that link sentences and paragraphs together. Rudolph Flesch's remarks on 'transitions' are an extreme instance of this tendency:

Don't fret over how to make a transition from one topic or one paragraph to the next. Just start the next thought naturally and the transition will take care of itself. (R. Flesch, *The ABC of Style*, p. 282.)

Flesch's strictures, it is true, are directed mainly against the overuse of the more ponderous connecters that abound in formal style, particularly in legal parlance, but it seems to me that his treatment of connecters in general is unduly off-hand. More serious authors, especially those who have specialized in the teaching of English as a foreign language, readily admit the importance of connecters in continuous English prose, and W. S. Fowler has given great prominence to this problem area in *Proficiency English*.

The principal points to note in this connection are as follows:

(i) German, owing to its Latin heritage, relies more heavily on logical connecters than does English.

(ii) In addition, German makes liberal use of a complex system of tonal particles which have no exact counterparts in English, and which function not only as connecters, but also as indicators of the subjective attitudes and evaluations of the language-user.

(iii) German prose usage, however, is not so close to classical Latin usage that characteristically Latin linking devices such as the relative connection (*der relativische Anschluß*) can invariably be rendered literally into German. The relative connection is normally translated by a demonstrative (*dieser*, for instance) and a particle such as *und, aber, nun, daher, also* or *denn*. Cp. E. Bornemann, *Lateinisches Unterrichtswerk*, p. 125; A. Linnenkugel/P. Friling, *Lateinische Grammatik*, § 102.

b) The second explanation for the divergencies between German and English usage is as follows. In English, the relative pronoun *which* can introduce either a sentential relative clause or a non-sentential relative clause. Hence ambiguity may arise if the last word in the head clause is a noun, and the almost complete absence of verb endings characteristic of person and number may also be a fruitful source of confusion.

In German, however, this kind of ambiguity is virtually impossible since the word *was* is not normally used as a substitute for the relative pronouns *der* and *welcher*. Some exceptions are cited in H. F. Eggeling, *A Dictionary of Modern German Prose Usage* (s.v. *was* (relative)), but the usage in question is so rare and so unorthodox, to say the least, that such border-line cases can safely be disregarded in a study devoted to the translation-problems that arise in connection with contemporary German texts on politics and economics. Besides, German verbs, unlike their English counterparts, frequently change their form according to their grammatical function in a sentence.

There are several constraints upon the use of the linking devices enumerated above. The following points are worth noting:

a) In cases where no ambiguity can arise, the writer can choose between a sentential relative clause and a main clause introduced by a demonstrative pronoun. In our example sentence from R. M. Davis, *The Novel: Modern Essays in Criticism* (p. 27), no ambiguity can arise because the noun *disciplines* is plural and the verb *means* is clearly recognizable as a singular form. The relative pronoun *which* has been employed in order to establish a closer link with what has preceded. The use of subordination involves a greater and more explicit degree of control, while coordination allows more structural flexibility, a looser and more spontaneous form of thought progression. In the following examples, the demonstrative *this* has been used in order to preclude misunderstanding:

The imitative, rationalistic view of art offered no real scope for the individual imagination: this was the cardinal source of its inadequacy and the eventual cause of its decline in the eighteenth century. (L. R. Furst, *Romanticism*, p. 19.)

With the abandonment of the old system, its sense of security was lost in life as in art. This is a break of such far-reaching consequences that its effects, even today, can hardly be overestimated. (*ibid.*)

b) The reduction of the sentential relative clause to a nominal group is possible only when the sentential relative clause consists of the copula *to be* followed by a predicate. The sense remains intact after deletion of the relative pronoun and the link verb.

c) The insertion of a factive abstract noun before the relative pronoun *which* is a very useful means of enhancing the coherence of a statement. However, there are sharp constraints upon this form of sentence-linkage:
(i) It is normally restricted to formal usage.
(ii) It can be used only when the head clause is so constituted that its content may be summed up in a general factive noun such as *fact, factor, point, view* or *complaint*.
(iii) In certain cases, the sentential relative clause has to be recast before a factive abstract noun can be inserted. Consider the following example:

Or an author may hope to move us by a series of crudely sensational or sentimental appeals, which is what F. R. Leavis objects to in *Le Père Goriot*.

If we wish to insert the factive noun *complaint*, we have to re-word this sentence as follows:

Or an author may hope to move us by a series of crudely sensational or sentimental appeals – a complaint which F. R. Leavis levels at *Le Père Goriot*. (P. Dixon, *Rhetoric*, p. 5.)

(iv) The device in question ought to be avoided if the sentential antecedent is disproportionately long in relation to the relative clause. In such cases it is advisable to start a new sentence with a demonstrative pronoun. Cp. the following example from M. Stewart, *Keynes and After* (p. 46):

For after a while it goes into reverse; just as a small rise in the output of consumer goods may result in a much larger rise in the output of capital goods, so a small fall in the output of consumer goods may result in a much larger fall in the output of capital goods. This can be seen if we go back to our example.

The statement beginning with the words *This can be seen* could be converted into a sentential relative clause introduced by *a fact that*, but the resultant sentence would appear absurdly ill-balanced.

5. für... entscheidend: Two constructions can be used here: *decisive for* + noun, and *decisive in* + *-ing* form + noun. The dictionary makers have overlooked the second possibility. Here is an example:

This tardiness was due to two factors, which, together, were decisive in shaping French Romanticism (...). (L. R. Furst, *Romanticism*, p. 49.)

It is interesting to note that the adjective *important* can be used in exactly the same way:

The pursuit of the natural was also important in shaping the Romantic lyric (...). (R. L. Furst, *op. cit.*, p. 56.)

6. seine Länge: For the sake of clarity, we can use an *of*-genitive instead of a possessive adjective.

7. für seine ... aber: Medial *aber* is rarely translated by *but*, the commonest equivalents being the conjunct *however* (with bracketing commas) and the subordinating conjunction *though*. In this particular instance, *aber* is a concessive conjunction and introduces a nuance of careful consideration. *But* would be too weak and unspecific in this context[1], and *however* must also be ruled out since it cannot be made to fit into the sentence, so we have no choice but to use a concessive clause introduced by *though*.

8. für seine gewünschte Vorausberechnung ... das größte Hindernis: Several points need to be made here:

a) In this word-group we have a typical instance of what Charles Bally described as *la séquence anticipatrice* ('the anticipatory sequence')[2]: the least important words come first, while the most important words come last. In this case, phrase inversion is mandatory: the English equivalent of *Hindernis* must be placed before its complement.

b) The preposition *für* is yet another potential source of difficulty. *Obstacle, impediment* and *bar* are all followed by *to*:

the elimination of all obstacles to the free movement of goods, services, capital and labour. (*PDE*, p. 146.)
Constant inflation through wage arbitration has been a main impediment to British economic advance. (R. Renner/R. Sachs, *Wirtschaftssprache*, p. 54.)
Poor health may be a bar to success in life. (Hornby, *OALDCE*, s.v. bar.)

c) *Obstacle, impediment* and *bar* are appropriate in this context since they are frequently used in a figurative sense and followed by abstract nouns. *Stumbling-block* and *hindrance* are almost always used figuratively, but they are not normally followed by prepositional phrases. *Barrier* is used in phrases such as *barriers to educational progress* (Hornby), but it is more restricted in application than *obstacle, impediment* and *bar*. *Difficulty* would be too vague and too weak in the case under discussion.

---

[1] *But* is sometimes used to join two relative clauses, but the repetition of the relative pronoun is apt to sound unduly stiff and formal.
[2] Cf. Charles Bally, *Linguistique générale et linguistique française*, pp. 193–281.

Obstruction would be inappropriate because it is normally used in a literal sense[3], and *snag* would also be inappropriate since it implies the intervention or discovery of something unexpected. For example sentences see H. W. Klein/W. Friederich, *Englische Synonymik*, s.v. Hindernis.

d) The word-group *seine gewünschte Vorausberechnung* cannot be translated literally. Before attempting a translation, it is necessary to ascertain the exact nature of the relationship expressed by the possessive adjective *seine*. The upswing is the object, not the subject of the activity denoted by the noun *Vorausberechnung*, so *seine* must be rendered by a prepositional phrase such as *about it*.

The use of the preposition *about* also calls for a few remarks. The prepositions *of* and *about* can be used interchangeably to establish a link between *forecast* and another noun, but only *about* can be used to create a link between *forecast* and the pronoun *it*. For an example of the use of the preposition *of*, cp. C. A. Dauten/L. M. Valentine, *Business Cycles and Forecasting*, p. 345:

In making forecasts of gross national product, it is necessary to keep in mind the major factors that cause shifts in economic activity.

It is interesting to note that in certain contexts there are similar constraints upon the use of the prepositions *at* and *with*. Hence we say *deposits at the central bank*, but *deposits with it*.

Some writers replace *about* by *as to*, and in recent years this practice has spread apace in many forms of utility writing. Scholarly works on politics, economics, the social sciences and literature are no exceptions:

Hence two additional conditions have commonly been made a part of perfect competition: resources are mobile among uses; and their owners are informed as to yields in these various uses. (H. Townsend (ed.), *Price Theory*, p. 314.)

An action for injury could also be brought against a retailer who, for example, might sell goods in a dangerous condition or without the necessary warnings and guidance as to the dangers in use. (D. Swann, *Competition and Consumer Protection*, p. 298.)

These two Achilles come and go in the *Iliad*, but the fact that they are combined into a figure of absorbing interest does not deceive us as to their origins. (A. T. Hatto, *The Niebelungenlied*, pp. 307–308.)

Language experts have animadverted at length upon this form of expression, and they have produced a fair amount of evidence in support of the view that the misuse of the compound preposition *as to* begets verbosity and makes for flabby writing.

There are, however, certain uses of *as to* that are recognized as legitimate: (i) *as to* followed by an infinitive construction denoting result or purpose; (ii) *as to* placed at the head of the sentence in order to bring into prominence a word-group that otherwise would have to stand later. For further information, see H. W. Fowler, *A Dictionary of Modern English Usage*, s.v. as; Sir Ernest Gowers, *The Complete Plain Words*, pp. 87–89; F. T. Wood, *Current English Usage*, s.v. as to; R. Flesch, *The ABC of Style*, s.v. as to; W. Strunk/E. B. White, *The Elements of Style*, p. 41; A. S.Hornby, *OALDCE*, s.v. as[2].

In the word-group under discussion, the abstract noun *Vorausberechnung* denotes an action rather than the result of an action, so the most appropriate rendering is a gerund

---

[3] I mean *obstruction* as a synonym of *obstacle*, not *obstruction* as a synonym of *stonewalling*.

followed by a noun such as *forecast, prediction* or *precalculation*. These nouns all collocate with the verb *make*. Examples:

Since forecasting is still much more of an art than a science, it is to be expected that economists will use varying approaches in making forecasts. (C. A. Dauten/L. M. Valentine, *Business Cycles and Forecasting*, p. 324.)
However, it is extremely hazardous to make predictions as to the date of such a monetary union. (H. G. Grubel, *The International Monetary System*, p. 154.)

The noun *forecast* also collocates with the verbs *develop* and *obtain*. Examples:

Their reactions to the situation in their fields are, however, valuable background in developing a forecast by any method or combination of methods. (C. A. Dauten/L. M. Valentine, *Business Cycles and Forecasting*, p. 326.)
They are, however, valuable to the forecaster because they provide a check on forecasts obtained by other methods. (*ibid.*, p. 336.)

e) The adjective *größte* can be rendered as *greatest, biggest* or *most important*. For the collocation *most important impediment,* cp. the following example sentence from H. W. Klein/W. Friederich, *Englische Synonymik*, s.v. Hindernis:

The most important impediment to reform, perhaps, is the number and diversity of the plans which have been submitted as possible cures (R. Dawson).

It is well to remember that the adjectives *great* and *big* are often synonymous with *important*. *Great* can be used with *obstacle, impediment* or *bar*. *Big* can combine with *obstacle,* but does not collocate well with *impediment* or *bar*. For further information on *great, big* and other adjectives of size, see H. W. Klein/W. Friederich, *Englische Synonymik*, s.v. groß; R. Meldau/R. B. Whitling, *Schulsynonymik der englischen Sprache*, s.v. groß; E. Leisi, *Der Wortinhalt*, pp. 44, 102−105.

b) Alternatives

above all, in particular,	the determinants of an	*upswing* up-swing upturn up-turn turn-up boom burst of expansion uptrend	are always
different, *a fact which* and this	is decisive for the length and intensity of		
the upturn, though it is the	greatest *obstacle* " impediment " bar most important obstacle " " impediment " " bar biggest obstacle		to *making* developing obtaining
the requisite *forecasts* predictions precalculations	about it.		

⑤ Trotzdem mühen sich die Konjunkturforschungsinstitute um die Aufgabe, den Konjunkturverlauf in seinen Veränderungsraten und den Zeitpunkt des Wechsels von einer zur anderen Lage vorauszusagen.

a) Annotations

1. Trotzdem: Here the translator has a considerable choice of expressions, but he must not take it for granted that the dictionary equivalents for *trotzdem* are interchangeable. The words and phrases normally used to translate *trotzdem* vary in the degree of their formality, and in some cases there are sharp constraints upon word-order.
The adverb *notwithstanding* is a ponderous and rather musty word that is much used in legal parlance, but it is apt to sound stilted in ordinary prose. The example cited in *The Random House Dictionary* (s.v. notwithstanding) sounds rather unnatural:
We were invited notwithstanding.

Nonetheless and *nevertheless* are neither unduly formal nor unduly informal. Both words are usually in initial position, though they can also occupy mid-position or end-position. Examples:
Nonetheless, people insist that they do their best. (P. A. Samuelson, *Economics,* p. 249.)
Nevertheless, the inescapable fact is that, in a world recession and amid restrictive economic policies in many countries, after Ottowa the deflationary pressures are likely to increase. (*World and Press,* 2nd August issue 1981, p. 1.)
Nevertheless, despite a long-term favourable outlook, the oil industry in the present day has to deal with some complex problems. (M. Marcheteau/J. Tardieu, *Business and Economics,* Vol. 1, p. 23.)
(. . .) any Frenchman will understand us when we make this slip, but he may shudder nevertheless because we are failing to conform with conventions by which he sets great store. (R. Quirk, *The Use of English,* p. 110.)
Alternatively, it may be (and still frequently is) argued that, although we have no '*dog-em*' and '*dog-i*' correspondence with the Latin accusative and dative, we nevertheless express the same distinctions in English as are expressed in Latin by means of cases (. . .) (*ibid.,* p. 116.)
The purpose of this second American revolution, dimly realised, spasmodically formulated, too slowly and reluctantly pursued, but pursued nevertheless, is the same as that of the first: to create what could be the working model of a world society. (H. J. Lechler/F. Ungerer (edd.), *Modern Life,* p. 147.)

Still is a shade less formal than *nonetheless* and *nevertheless,* and it generally establishes a close link with what precedes:
It was futile, still they fought. (*RHD,* s.v. still[1].)
Even if I concede that our statistics did not embrace a sufficient number of extracts to give fully reliable results, still it is indisputable that English shows more regularity and less caprice in this respect than most or probably all cognate languages (. . .). (O. Jespersen, *Growth and Structure of the English Language,* p. 11.)

Yet has been a subject of much controversy between language experts. Students of English are often exhorted to forswear the use of this word at the beginning of a sentence. Cp. P. Bacquet/D. Keen, *Initiation au thème anglais,* pp. 79, 101; R. Flesch, *The ABC of Style,* s.v. yet. According to Flesch, *yet* at the opening of a sentence is 'used

(. . .) only in pompous rhetorical prose'. He uses the adjective *rhetorical* as a term of abuse for a style of tinsel ornament and forgets that good prose can be rhetorical without lapsing into pomposity. H. W. Fowler's remarks on the use of the word *yet* are more objective and reasonable. Fowler concedes that the adversative adverb *yet* can be used legitimately in initial position in order to point a contrast, but he insists that 'the opposition between the fact it introduces and that which has gone before should be direct and clear' (H. W. Fowler, *A Dictionary of Modern English Usage*, s.v. yet). Here are some specimens of *yet* sentences from the works of accomplished stylists:

It means poverty and obscurity and a constant struggle to make ends meet as a working artist without other source of income. Yet there is an immense relief of the spirit, a sense of homecoming. (Eoghan Ó Tuairisc, quoted in Terence Conway (ed.), *Ireland and its Problems*, p. 25.)
With the moral issues involved in human action he is no more concerned than the naturalist who observes a battle between two tribes of ants, and for the susceptibilities of Mrs Grundy he has as little regard as the other members of the group of 'realists' to which he belongs. Yet among his tales there are some forty or fifty to which not even Mrs Grundy – were that lady known in France – could possibly object (. . .). (J. E. Mansion (ed.), *Contes choisis de Guy de Maupassant*, p. 9.)
The historical records of English do not go so far back as this, for the oldest written texts in the English language (in 'Anglo-Saxon') date from about 700 and are thus removed by about three centuries from the beginnings of the language. And yet comparative philology is able to tell us something about the manner in which the ancestors of these settlers spoke centuries before that period (. . .). (O. Jespersen, *Growth and Structure of the English Language*, p. 17.)

For all that occurs both in written and in spoken English and may be placed at the opening or at the end of a sentence. A specimen of informal American usage is given in *The Random House Dictionary* (s.v. for):

He's a decent guy for all that.

In spite of it can also be used as a translation equivalent for *trotzdem*, but the pronoun *it* often has to be replaced by a demonstrative in order to establish a closer link with what precedes. *In spite of* is a shade less formal than *despite*.

The adversative phrase *at the same time* occurs both in written and in spoken English. It is used to introduce an idea which has hitherto been left out of consideration. Examples:

At the same time you must not forget that (. . .). (Hornby, *OALDCE*, s.v. same.)
The new hazards are neither local nor brief. (. . .) At the same time the permissible margin for error has become very much reduced. (H. J. Lechler/F. Ungerer (edd.), *Modern Life*, p. 262.)

Still and all is restricted to American and Irish English. A typical example is cited in *The Random House Dictionary* (s.v. still[1]):

Even though you dislike us, still and all you should be polite.

The phrase *even so* is used both in spoken and in written English. As a rule, it is positioned initially:

It has many omissions; even so, it is quite a useful reference book. (Hornby, *OALDCE*, s.v. even[2].)

After all occupies end-position when it means 'in spite of circumstances, expectations, efforts, etc. It is as common in spoken English as in written English. Examples:

Was it reality, after all? (Jack London, *Love of Life*, p. 56.)
He won the race after all! (*CED*, s.v. after.)
He failed after all. (Hornby, *OALDCE*, s.v. after[4].)
He came in time after all. (*RHD*, s.v. all.)

However, if *after all* means 'when everything is considered' (*schließlich*), it may occupy front-position or mid-position:

After all, why worry about it? (*CED*, s.v. after.)
They are, after all, still here. (*World and Press*, 2nd August issue 1981, p. 1.)

The phrases *all the same* and *just the same* are interchangeable. They are frequently used in spoken English and normally introduce or conclude a fairly short sentence. Examples:

He's not very reliable, but I like him all the same. (Hornby, *OALDCE*, s.v. same.)
You don't have to go but we wish you would, all the same. (*RHD*, s.v. same.)
It was a success, but it could easily have failed, just the same. (*ibid.*)

Though, which invariably occupies end-position when used in the sense of *trotzdem*, is generally restricted to informal usage:

His food is rather a problem. He looks fit, though. (R. Quirk et al., *GCE*, § 8.90.)
It's very lovely, though, with the sun shining through the trees. (W. Friedrich, *Technik des Übersetzens*, p. 138.)

2. mühen sich: A wide variety of equivalents is given in the bilingual dictionaries, and the translator may have difficulty in selecting the right words or expressions.
In some works of reference (such as Kißling's *Lexikon der englischen Unterrichtssprache*), *sich mühen* is rendered as *to trouble oneself*. In this context, however, *to trouble oneself* would be quite inappropriate. *To trouble oneself* is normally used only in sentences which are explicitly or implicitly negative, e.g.

He had never troubled himself ... to understand the question. (*SOED*, s.v. trouble.)

To put onself out suggests inconvenience rather than prolonged and arduous physical or intellectual exertion. Examples:

She has certainly put herself out to see that everyone is comfortable. (*RHD*, s.v. put.)
Uncle George put himself out to give us a good time while we were staying with him. (F. T. Wood, *English Verbal Idioms*, s.v. put out.)

To exert oneself does not normally imply sustained or exceptional efforts or burdensome duties:

To exert oneself to arrive early. (Hornby, *OALDCE*, s.v. exert.)

The locution *try and try* would be unsuitable here since it is too subjective and since it does not normally introduce an infinitive construction. (*Try*, of course, is generally followed by an infinitive.) In modern English, identical verb forms are often coordinated to express wearisome repetition, sustained but fruitless efforts. Cp. 'They knocked and knocked' (R. Quirk et al., *GCE*, § 9.128). *Try and try* and *knock and knock* have strong emotional connotations. They are good examples of what Vinay and Darbelnet describe as the 'successive aspect' (*l'aspect successif*). Cp. J. P. Vinay/J. Darbelnet, *Stylistique comparée du français et de l'anglais*, § 139.
The verb *struggle* implies vigorous and strongly motivated attempts to overcome physical, mental or moral difficulties – exhaustion, opposition, temptations, etc.

The thief struggled to get free. (Hornby, *OALDCE*, s.v. struggle.)
Simon held onto the edge of the pool and struggled to pull himself up. He felt limp with exhaustion and sick from swallowing water. (I. Murdoch, *A Fairly Honourable Defeat*, p. 373.)
One thinks of Dylan Thomas, struggling
    to twist the shapes of thoughts
        Into the stony idiom of the brain (...) (R. Quirk, *The Use of English*, p. 262.)

The verb *to strive*, like *sich mühen*, is frequently used in formal contexts. It means 'to make a great and tenacious effort'. Like *struggle*, it carries heightened implications of difficulty, but unlike *struggle*, it is rarely used of attempts to surmount physical obstacles. Examples:

She strove to keep her self-control. (*SOED*, s.v. strive.)
The mere fact that Faust "strives" to participate in the "Werden" of the universe does not make him either a scholar or a philosopher. (J. W. Goethe, *Faust I*, edd. R.-M. S. Heffner et al., p. 72.)

To labour means 'to exert one's powers of body or mind, especially with painful or strenuous effort' (*WNCD*). An example of *labour* followed by an infinitive construction is given in Hornby's *OALDCE* (s.v. labour): 'labour to complete a task'. This construction is restricted to formal usage.

To toil is closely synonymous with *to labour*. Elderly dialect speakers in Northern Ireland sometimes use *toil* as a colloquial synonym for *work*. In standard English, however, *toil* is restricted to formal usage. *To toil* means 'to engage in hard and continuous mental or physical work' or 'to struggle mentally' (*SOED*). It is a very strong word, and it often occurs in combinations such as *toil to death*, e.g. '. . .toiling to death in forests, mines and quarries, many for no more than indulging in freedom of thought' (K. Schibsbye, *MEG*, § 11.1.1.). In the case under discussion, it would sound overemphatic as well as over-literary. These comments may be extended to the phrase *toil and moil*, which is the verbal counterpart of reduplicated nouns such as *hurlyburly* and *huggermugger*.

To endeavour is at present used in two distinct senses: a) to try; b) to strive, to attempt strenuously. *Endeavour* is apt to sound stuffy, pompous, or even ludicrous when it is used merely as a formal synonym for *try*, especially if the efforts referred to are very undignified. The comic effect is probably intentional in the following sentence from Iris Murdoch's novel *A Severed Head* (p. 111):

On her back now, she came against me with both hands pushing and clawing, and endeavoured to drive her knee into my stomach.

This is from a description of a rather unseemly tussle between an upper-class English gentleman and a distinguished Cambridge don. The effect produced by the use of the verb *endeavour* is quite different in a staid Victorian novel such as Anthony Trollope's *The Warden* (p. 178):

The warden endeavoured to appear unconcerned as he said, "Oh, indeed! I'll go upstairs at once (. . .)".

Here the word *endeavour* is in perfect harmony with the character of the churchwarden and his highly conventional surroundings.

It may be possible to make out a case for rejecting the word *endeavour* in non-ironic informal contexts (cf. R. Flesch, *The ABC of Style*, s.v. endeavor), but there is absolutely no reason to castigate the use of *endeavour* in highly formal contexts such as the following:

Instead then of endeavouring by uniform and fixed systems of education, to keep mankind always the same, let us give free scope to everything which may bid fair for introducing more variety among us. (Joseph Priestly, quoted in: R. Ridout, *English Today*, Vol. 5, p. 15.)

For further information see *Webster's New Dictionary of Synonyms*, s.v. attempt; H. W. Klein/W. Friederich, *Englische Synonymik*, s.v. sich bemühen.

To try one's level best is a relatively informal expression meaning 'to try very hard' or 'to do everything possible'.

We tried our level best to drive there in three hours, but there was an unexpected detour. (*RHD*, s.v. level.)

To take much trouble means 'to make a considerable effort'. This expression is used both in spoken and in written English.

To take pains to (+ infinitive) and *to be at pains to* (+ infinitive) mean 'to make a great effort'. *To take pains* is normally used to represent the act as a whole (terminate aspect), while *to be at pains* normally represents the act as going on (progressive aspect). Examples:

Great pains have been taken to finish the project. (*RHD*, s.v. pain.)
He was at pains to assure me that the eye operation had been completed. (C. P. Snow, *Last Things*, p. 152.)
No, the measure of the generative poetics hypothesis, as both Zholkovsky and Scheglov are normally at pains to make clear, is in its explanatory adequacy and descriptive power. (R. Fowler (ed.), *Style and Structure in Literature*, p. 171.)

In the third example, the progressive force of the expression *to be at pains* is weakened by the frequentative adverb *normally*. It should also be noted that the noun *pains* may be replaced by the singular form of the noun *trouble* in the expression *to take pains*. However, this kind of substitution is not possible in the expression *to be at pains*. These locutions are used both in spoken and in written English.

The expressions *to try hard* and *to work hard* are self-explanatory.

The locutions *to make an effort* and *to make some effort* generally imply that relatively little energy is expended. Cf. the following example from David Weir (ed.), *Men and Work in Modern Britain* (p. 355):

Fitfully and haltingly most of the major unions have responded to changing conditions by recognizing shop stewards and making some effort to equip them.

3. die Konjunkturforschungsinstitute: The term *Conjuncture Institute* has been overlooked by the lexicographers. Here is an example from C. A. Dauten/L. M. Valentine, *Business Cycles and Forecasting*, p. 285:

A theory of long waves in economic activity was developed by N. D. Kondratieff while he was director of the Conjuncture Institute of Moscow.

4. um die Aufgabe: This word sequence can be safely left untranslated since it merely serves to herald the non-finite object clause *den Konjunkturverlauf. . . vorauszusagen*. Cf. the use of *darauf, darin, davon,* etc. before a clause which is a prepositional object of a verb. Examples:

Er freut sich darauf, daß du ihn besuchst: He is looking forward to your visiting him. (L. J. Russon, *Complete German Course for First Examinations*, p. 124.)
Die Aufgabe des Statistikers besteht darin, (+ infinitive): The statistician's job is to . . . (M. J. Moroney, *Facts from Figures*, p. 120.)

5. den Konjunkturverlauf in seinen Veränderungsraten: In English, as in German, the preposition *in* is sometimes used as a substitute for *of*. Examples:

(i) Similar analyses of the activities of unions in their more official aspect and of the attitudes of participants on both management and workers' sides appear to indicate that the role of the shop steward is well regarded and is of positive benefit to the system of industrial relations as a whole. (David Weir (ed.), *Men and Work in Modern Britain*, p. 346.)
(ii) The British trade-union movement, both in its history and in its present-day characteristics, reflects many of the special features of society and politics in this country. (H. Pelling, *A History of British Trade Unionism*, p. 290.)

In the foregoing sentences, replacement of *in* by *of* would entail rather radical reorganization of the initial catenations:

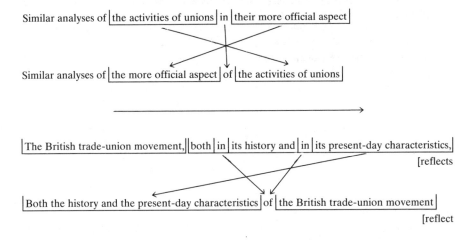

In the first example the use of *in* has evidently been motivated by a desire to avoid excessive formal repetitiveness (the threefold repetition of the preposition *of*). In the second example, however, the motivation is less obvious. The author presumably wanted to bring into prominence the nominal group *the British trade-union movement*, In our German text the use of the preposition *in* seems rather arbitrary, for the sentence still reads quite smoothly if the *in*-construction is replaced by a genitive: *die Veränderungsraten des Konjunkturverlaufs*.
Let us now consider the various avenues open to the translator. A literal translation such as *the cyclical trend in its rates of change* is grammatically possible, but it sounds a trifle unusual. *Rates of change of the cyclical trend* seems more in keeping with the spirit of English, but fastidious language-users will doubtless object to the repetition of the preposition *of*. It is therefore advisable to replace the second *of* by *in*, thus establishing a closer link between the two nominal groups. No one is likely to take exception to a word sequence such as *rates of change in the cyclical trend*.
The term *Veränderungsrate,* which has not been recorded in the dictionaries, is normally rendered as *rate of change*. *Rate of change* is connected to its noun complement by means of the preposition *in*. The repetition of the word *of* would jar on the ear. Cf. the following example from A. Seldon/F. G. Pennance, *Everyman's Dictionary of Economics,* s.v. Phillips, Alban William H.:

For many years thereafter it was widely held that the lower the amount of unemployment, the larger the rate of change in wages.

This substitution of *in* for *of* involves no change in word-order. It should be carefully distinguished from the kind of substitution illustrated by the quotations from Weir and Pelling given at the beginning of this section.

6. den Zeitpunkt ... vorauszusagen: A literal translation would have an air of infelicity. The idea expressed in this word sequence may be rendered freely in various ways: *to identify turning points in advance, to forecast the turns of business activity,* or *to predict the date when business will turn generally*. Cf. the following quotations from P.

A. Samuelson, *Economics:*

Warren Persons, Geoffrey Moore, Arthur F. Burns, and Julius Shiskin found that certain series (. . .) can give some help in identifying turning points in advance (. . .). (p. 249.)
And there is no magical method of forecasting the turns of business activity. (p. 252.)
Researchers long looked for a statistical series (or group of series) that would manifest a turn a *fixed* number of months *before* business turned generally. (p. 249.)

The expression *to identify in advance* is synonymous with *to predict*. It would therefore be grammatically possible to merge the word sequences *to predict rates of change in the cyclical trend* and *to identify turning points in advance* to produce a complex such as: *to predict rates of change in the cyclical trend and turning points*. However, this kind of sequence is stylistically unsatisfactory because it is front-heavy. In order to redress the balance we must either reverse the objects of the verb *predict* or render *voraussagen* first by *predict*, then by *identify in advance*. The second solution is preferable since it enables us to reproduce the emphasis and movement of the thought progression in the original text.

b) Alternatives

Nonetheless,	the	economic research institutes	endeavour
Nevertheless,		Economic Research Institutes	take much trouble
Still		institutes for economic research	take pains
Yet		business research institutes	try hard
For all that,		Conjuncture Institutes	work hard
In spite of that,			
to predict	rates of change in the	cyclical trend	and to
forecast		cyclical course	and
prognosticate		economic trend	
		economic course	
		trend of economic activity	
		course of economic activity	
		trend of business activity	
		course of the business cycle	
		course of the trade cycle	
		business cycle	
		economic cycle	
		run of business	
		development of business	
		economic development[4]	
		path of the economy	
identify turning points in advance.			
the date when business will turn generally.			

---

[4] Note the omission of the article.

> **⑥** Hierbei kann aus geschichtlicher Erfahrung über das Gewisse der Wechsellagen hinaus nicht allzuviel mit Sicherheit geschlossen werden.

a) Annotations

1. Hierbei: There is no standard translation equivalent for this word. Each case has to be treated on its merits. Some useful phrases have been given in the bilingual dictionaries (*in this connection, in doing so,* etc.), but none of these solutions would be really satisfactory in the present context.

2. kann . . . nicht allzuviel mit Sicherheit geschlossen werden: A literal rendering of this word sequence could hardly be accepted without demur. Translation into English entails a radical reorganization of the word-material: a clause-structure shift, complex class-shifts, and a shift in viewpoint resulting in the suppression of meiosis. The subject is brought forward to the beginning of the clause, the verb *schließen* is converted into a verb-noun phrase (*draw inferences*), the adverbial *mit Sicherheit* is converted into an attributive adjective (*definite*), and the conventionalized meiotic formula *nicht allzuviel* is converted into the stylistically neutral determiner *few*.

3. aus geschichtlicher Erfahrung: In this case a word for word translation would be possible, but a freer rendering is preferable for stylistic reasons. The phrase *in the light of* is a faded image meaning 'taking into account' or 'with the help gained from'.

4. über das Gewisse der Wechsellagen hinaus: A word for word translation of this word sequence would sound very peculiar in English. The most natural solution is to render the entire prepositional phrase as a sub clause introduced by *except that*. The substantivized adjective *das Gewisse* can be converted into a verb phrase (*to be bound to occur*), while the plural noun *Wechsellagen* (not recorded in any dictionary) can be translated by a less abstract noun phrase such as *some kind of economic fluctuation*.

b) Alternatives

In this field of research, few definite	*inferences* *conclusions*	can be drawn in the	
light of historical experience,	*except that* *beyond the fact that*	some	*kind* *sort* of economic
fluctuation is bound to *change*		*occur.* *take place.*	

> **⑦** An wissenschaftlichen Anstrengungen, die Konjunkturerfahrungen für Konjunkturprognose und Konjunkturpolitik nutzbar zu machen, fehlt es nicht.

a) Annotations

1. Konjunkturerfahrungen: There is no standard translation equivalent of this term, and this is probably one of the reasons why it has not been recorded in the dictionaries.

Possible renderings include *accumulated knowledge of trade cycles* and *past experience of trade cycles*. For the collocations *accumulated knowledge* and *past experience*, see *CED*, svv. experience, heuristic.

b) Alternatives

There is no lack of scientific attempts to	*utilize accumulated*		
	employ past experience of		
knowledge of trade cycles	for	*economic forecasting*	and
	business cycles	*business forecasting* (U.S.)	
		economic forecasts	
		business forecasts (U.S.)	
		business predictions	
		business scenarios (U.S.)	
cyclical policies.			
cyclical policy.			
trade cycle policy.			
stabilization policy.			
economic policy.			
policies for controlling the	*level of economic activity.*		
„ „ „	„ *trade cycle.*		

⑧ So vermutete z. B. der russische Nationalökonom Nicolai Kondratjew, die damals rund zehn-, heute rund fünfjährigen Zyklen (immer von einer Wiederbelebung bis zur nächsten gerechnet) würden durch lange Wellen überlagert; diese würden alle fünfzig Jahre einen Wechsel im Überwiegen von Aufschwungs- und Stockungsjahren bringen.

a) Annotations

1. So: *So* is often used as a result conjunct. In this case, however, it merely serves to introduce an example. *So* and *z. B.* constitute a sense-unit. The most appropriate English equivalent is therefore the adverb *thus*, which can mean 'as an example' or 'for instance' (cf. *RHD*, s.v. thus). When used in this sense, *thus* always occupies front-position.

2. z. B.: In declarative sentences the locutions *for example* and *for instance* often stand in the second place. Examples:

In his Berber section, for example, Mr. Mitchell points out that any consonant may be syllabic in Berber. (J. R. Firth in: *Studies in Linguistic Analysis*, p. vii.)

The Wadi al Ain, for instance, was marked as flowing into the sea near Abu Dhabi. (W. Thesiger, *Arabian Sands*, p. 176.)

A useful stylistic variant is *by way of example* (cf. Hornby, *OALDCE*, s.v. instance).

3. der russische Nationalökonom Nicolai Kondratjew: Several points need to be made here. To begin with, appositives denoting a person's profession are often placed after

the proper noun in English. In this case, however, there is no need to re-position the appositives since the information unit *der russische Nationalökonom* seems contextually more important than *Nicolai Kondratjew*.
Secondly, lexicographers often render the term *Nationalökonom* as *political economist* (*LGS*) or *public economist* (v. Eichborn). In point of fact, however, these terms are comparatively rare. Just as *political economy* has been supplanted in most cases by *economics*, so *political economist* has been supplanted in most cases by *economist*. For information on the term *political economy*, see E. Partridge, *Usage and Abusage*, s.v. Political Economy, and David W. Pearce (ed.), *The Dictionary of Modern Economics*, s.v. Political Economy. Here are some examples of the use of the term *economist* in the sense of *Nationalökonom:*

Named after the Russian economist N. D. Kondratieff, who made important contributions in the 1920s to the study of long-term fluctuations. (G. Bannock/R. E. Baxter/R. Rees, *The Penguin Dictionary of Economics*, s.v. Kondratieff cycle.)

Russian economist who discovered long-term (50–60-year) fluctuations or waves in economic activity, prices and exchange: hence Kondratieff Cycle. (A. Seldon/F. G. Pennance, *Everyman's Dictionary of Economics*, s.v. Kondratieff, N. D.)

Thirdly, the name of the Russian economist must be anglicized. For examples see the sentences quoted above. See also P. A. Samuelson, *Economics*, p. 241; C. A. Dauten/ L. M. Valentine, *Business Cycles and Forecasting*, pp. 285–6; D. W. Pearce, *The Dictionary of Modern Economics*, s.v. Kondratieff, Nikolai D. (1892–).

4. die: The subordinating conjunction *that* cannot be ellipted here because the dependent declarative clause is long and complicated. For further information on the omissibility of *that* in nominal clauses, see R. Quirk et al., *GCE*, § 11.17.

5. die damals ... Zyklen: Expressions such as *zehnjährige Zyklen* can be translated literally: *ten-year cycles, five-year cycles*, etc. Cp. the word-group *(50–60-year) fluctuations* in the quotation from *Everyman's Dictionary of Economics* in note (8) 2, above. In this particular instance, however, one-to-one lexical matching is out of the question because the compound adjectives *zehnjährig* and *fünfjährig* are modified by the time adverbs *damals* and *heute* and this type of bracketing is not customary in English. The elliptical word sequence *die damals ... Zyklen* is equivalent to two conjoined relative clauses dependent on the antecedent *die Zyklen: die Zyklen, die damals rund zehn Jahre dauerten, und die heute rund fünf Jahre dauern.* It is necessary to realign the original sentence segment in this way in order to produce an adequate English translation.
The author of the source text has resorted to ellipsis in order to avoid flatfooted repetition of the combining form *-jährig*. In the target text ellipsis is not feasible, but repetition can be avoided by the use of two different phrases expressing the idea of duration, e.g. *whose length* + [form of *to be*] + numerical indication, and *which had a duration of* + numerical indication. Cp. the following quotations from P. A. Samuelson, *Economics*:

Kuznets cycles should not be confused with alleged *very long waves* – the so-called Kondratieff cycles – whose complete cycle length is about half a century. (p. 241.)
The American experience indicates that the major business cycle has had an average duration of a little over eight years. (p. 239.)
Most observers had no trouble in agreeing on the major cycles, which were about 8 to 10 years in length. (*ibid.*)

Some final words should be said about clause linkage. In the suggested version the two relative clauses are connected by *and which*. The use of this linking device is sometimes considered a stylistic lapse. In *The ABC of Style,* for instance, R. Flesch affirms that '*and which* is always awkward and usually wrong', and he goes on to suggest that either *and* or *which* should be deleted. In principle, however, there is no aprioristic reason why precisians should blench at *and which* or *and who,* provided that these coordinators are used to introduce a second relative clause with the same antecedent as one that has just preceded it.

Let us consider some examples:

(i) Our island produced the best wool in Europe, and had for centuries supplied the Flemish and Italian looms with material with which they could not dispense for luxury production, and which they could get nowhere else. (G. M. Trevelyan, *English Social History*, p. 21.)

(ii) It is only the exceptional reader, certainly, who in the course of time comes to classify and compare his experiences, to see one in the light of others; and who, as his poetic experiences multiply, will be able to understand each more accurately. (T. S. Eliot, *The Use of Poetry and the Use of Criticism,* pp. 18–19.)

In example (i) the deletion of *and* or *which* would throw the grammar out of gear. In example (ii), on the other hand, it would be possible to omit the relative pronoun *who* without overriding grammar, but such deletion could hardly be vindicated on stylistic grounds. Deletion is inhibited by the presence of an adverbial clause of time (*as . . . multiply*) between the subject (*who*) and its predicate (*will be . . . accurately*).

However, it is quite normal to ellipt the relative pronoun when the second relative clause is brief and uncomplicated:

(. . .) the reader, bewildered, gropes about for what is absent, and puzzles his head for a kind of 'meaning' which is not there, and is not meant to be there. (T. S. Eliot, *The Use of Poetry and the Use of Criticism,* p. 151.)

Another point worth noting is that the conjunction *and* is usually deleted before *which* when a full relative clause is coordinated with a reduced relative clause. Examples:

These facts will emerge in a Government-sponsored report to be published in two volumes early next year which will provide statistical evidence that women are second-class citizens, underprivileged and underpaid. (M. Marcheteau/J. Tardieu, *Business and Economics,* Vol. 1, p. 87.)
Things essential to our recovery which we ourselves could not produce. (E. Gowers, *The Complete Plain Words,* p. 169.)

It would, of course, be a gross error to assume that the deletion of *and* is mandatory in such sentences. Each case has to be decided on its own merits.

Sir Ernest Gowers, who has descanted upon clausal and phrasal coordination in *The Complete Plain Words* (pp. 168–9), conjectures that the old grammatical rules 'may be destroyed eventually by usage', but with his customary shrewdness he advises his readers to defer to tradition for the time being.

A relative clause is occasionally found coordinated with a noun, as in the sentence from Nelson's correspondence quoted by Sir Ernest Gowers (*op. cit.,* p. 168). The generality of educated Englishmen, however, would balk at resorting to such forms of coordination.

Finally, it is important to stress that this domain of usage is rife with confusion, contradictions and irrational inhibitions. Many language-users simply put their faith in rules of thumb and hope for the best; and even seasoned stylists are often beset by doubts and fight shy of coordination with *and which* except in cases where this form of clause linkage is absolutely necessary to ensure comprehensibility and give a fresh push-off to the final segment of an intricate sentence.

For further information on *and which* and similar 'kittle cattle', the reader is referred to the following works: H. W. Fowler, *A Dictionary of Modern English Usage*, s.v. which with and or but; E. Gowers, *The Complete Plain Words*, pp. 168–9; R. Flesch, *The ABC of Style*, s.v. and which; F. T. Wood, *Current English Usage*, s.v. and.; E. Partridge, *Usage and Abusage*, s.v. and which.

6. würden ... überlagert: This is an instance of indirect style, so *würden ... überlagert* must be rendered as a preterite.
The verb *überlagern* sometimes presents difficulties in translation. The dictionary equivalents (*overlap, super(im)pose* and *overlay*) are not interchangeable.
Overlap must be ruled out here because it is not used in the passive voice.
The verb *superimpose* can be used in the passive, but it is not normally followed by a *by*- or *with*-phrase functioning as a means or instrument adjunct. *Superimpose* combines with the prepositions *on* and *upon*. Cp. the following example from M. Stewart, *Keynes and After* (p. 40):

The cycle was superimposed, however, on a rising trend (...).

If we wished to use the verb *superimpose* in our translation, we should have to turn the sentence round and write: *long waves are superimposed upon cycles, which in those days* ... This solution would be quite acceptable if the German sentence ended with the word *überlagert*. Unfortunately, however, the sentence goes on after the semi-colon, and the demonstrative pronoun *diese* refers back to the noun phrase *lange Wellen*. Thus, if we realign the sentence in the manner that has just been indicated, we shall subsequently be confronted with difficulties of the jigsaw type, and we shall be hard put to it to create a satisfactory link between the English equivalents of *diese* and *lange Wellen*.
The verb *superpose* must also be rejected. For the difference between *superpose* and *superimpose*, see *Webster's New Dictionary of Synonyms*, s.v. overlay.
We have therefore no choice but to employ the verb *overlay*. This word is often used figuratively and is usually followed by *with*. Cf. the following example from L. R. Furst/P. N. Skrine, *Naturalism* (p. 3):

So even though the earliest equation of Naturalism with materialism has in the last hundred years or so been overlaid with various elaborations, this first sense of the term has by no means died out (...).

7. diese: This demonstrative pronoun might be rendered as *the latter*. The *former-latter* device, however, is somewhat stilted and has incurred the censure of Rudolf Flesch and Sir Ernest Gowers. Cp. R. Flesch, *The ABC of Style*, svv. former ... latter, latter; E. Gowers, *The Complete Plain Words*, p. 194. In the case under discussion, the sentence flows more easily if the nominal group *long waves* is repeated. For further information on *the latter*, see H. W. Fowler, *A Dictionary of Modern English Usage*, s.v. latter.

8. würden ... bringen: One can insert a parenthesis (*he surmised*) in order to indicate that this statement is in indirect style.
It is hard to establish position rules for short parenthetical expressions used in reporting words or thoughts. However, the positioning of such parentheses seems to be subject to certain unwritten laws, and it may be useful to specify some of the positions in which parentheses most commonly occur:

a) between a noun subject and a verb:

The Arabs, he added, would give us milk so that we need not touch our food and water. (W. Thesiger, *Arabian Sands*, p. 134.)

'A discussion of the word Style', it has been suggested, 'if it were pursued with only a fraction of the rigour of a scientific investigation, would inevitably cover the whole of literary aesthetics and the theory of criticism (. . .).' (R. Quirk/A. H. Smith (edd.), *The Teaching of English*, p. 36.)

The foreign student, they say, should as far as possible adopt the same method. (*EFL bulletin*, March 1981, p. 2.)

b) between a demonstrative pronoun and a verb:

That, I suppose, is the result of treating form and content as though they were separate entities (. . .). (R. Quirk/A. H. Smith (edd.), *The Teaching of English*, p. 36.)

c) between an adverbial and a sentence subject:

'Once upon a time', wrote Cecil Day Lewis, 'poetry and science were one, and its name was Magic.' (R. Quirk/A. H. Smith (edd.), *The Teaching of English*, p. 110.)

'In one of the poems', the reviewer points out, 'the name of a village called *Snettisham* (. . .) is introduced'. (*ibid.*, p. 40.)

d) between a verb and its complement:

'We hope', he says, '*never to hear* this unpleasing sound again in verse'. (R. Quirk/A. H. Smith (edd.), *The Teaching of English*, p. 40.)

(. . .) it could, I take it, be used effectively in verse (. . .). (*Ibid.*)

This word order is particularly common when the subject of the sentence is an unstressed pronoun such as *I, he, she, it, we* or *they*. The insertion of a parenthesis between an unstressed pronoun and its verb would run counter to normal usage. If the verb is negated, the parenthesis is inserted after the particle *not*:

It is not, say its critics, 'good, plain English', it is not, they say, the kind of English which Civil Servants, ought to use. (R. Quirk/A. H. Smith (edd.), *The Teaching of English*, p. 44.)

If a verb consists of two closely linked elements (e. g. *do better*) and is followed by a dependent infinitive construction, then the parenthesis is inserted between the second element of the verb and the dependent infinitive. It would be quite wrong to place the parenthesis between *do* and *better* in a sentence such as the following:

We would do better, I think, to take the model of the learner referred to above (the linguistically gifted idiot), and turn it upside down. (*EFL bulletin*, March 1981, p. 6.)

e) between a conjunction and a sentence subject:

'Yet', he goes on to say, 'second language teaching as an art or science is in its main principles universal (. . .). (R. Quirk/A. H. Smith (edd.), *The Teaching of English*, p. 138.)

9. würden . . . einen Wechsel . . . bringen: In German an excessive reliance on the abstract noun at the expense of the verb (e.g. *Wechsel* for *wechseln*) often befogs the author's meaning. A literal translation of the word sequence *würden . . . einen Wechsel . . . bringen* would sound unduly ponderous and abstract. It is therefore advisable to realign the clause in a manner which is likely to be more congenial to English readers. The noun *Wechsel* (= alternation) may be transposed to a verb (*alternate*). This class-shift entails a clause-structure shift, for the preposition *in* must be eliminated and its complement (*Überwiegen . . . Stockungsjahren*) must be split up into two parts linked by the preposition *with*. This grammatical adjustment involves the explication and reduplication of certain elements which have been ellipted in the source text: the word *years* must be repeated, and so must the notion expressed by *Überwiegen*. Fastidious readers might take exception to the repetition of the word sequence *with a preponder-*

ance of (. . .), so it may be expedient to introduce a variant at the end of the statement, e.g. *in which there was a preponderance of (. . .)*. This relative clause adds weight to the final segment of the sentence and helps to round it off quite neatly.

b) Alternatives

Thus, *for example,*
    for instance,
    by way of example,
	the Russian economist Nikolai Kondratieff				

conjectured that cycles,	*which in those days had a duration of about*				
surmised	„ *at that time* „ „ „ „ „				
speculated	„ „ „ „ *were about ten years in*				
presumed	*whose length in those days was about ten*				
assumed	„ „ *at that time* „ „ „				
supposed	*which in those days lasted about ten years*				
had an idea	„ *at that time* „ „ „ „				
ten years, and	*which nowadays are about five years in length*			(always	
length,	„ „ *have a duration of about five years*				
years,	*whose length nowadays is about five years*				
	which nowadays last about five years				
calculated from one trade revival to the next) were overlaid with long					
reckoned					
waves; every fifty years, he surmised, these long waves caused					
periods with a *preponderance* of *high*			*years* to alternate with		
preponderancy		*booming*	„		
predominance					
predominancy					
periods in which *recession years predominated.*					
there was a predominance of recession years.					
„ „ „ *predominancy* „ „ „					
„ „ „ *preponderance* „ „ „					
„ „ „ *preponderancy* „ „ „					

⑨ Als Ursache hierfür erkannte Professor Kondratjew den nur alle fünfzig Jahre auftretenden Belebungseffekt durch grundlegende Erfindungen im Maschinen- und Energiebereich, die nachhaltige Kostensenkung versprechen und dadurch nachhaltige Neuinvestitionen auslösen.

a) Annotations

1. Als Ursache . . . Belebungseffekt: The author of the source text has spotlighted the notion of causality by the initial placement of the word-group *als Ursache hierfür,* and his sentence moves in the impressionistic order that is characteristic of modern

German. English, in contradistinction to German, tends to adopt a more analytical order of exposition, placing the subject before the verb and the verb before its complement. The translator is therefore obliged to remake the discourse pattern in a way that English readers will find more congenial. However, it is not sufficient to shift the subject to the beginning of the sentence and then attempt one-to-one lexical matching. The result of such a procedure would be a very awkward-sounding and disjointed word sequence: *Professor Kondratieff saw as the origin of this the reinvigorating effect (. . .).* The words are English, but the syntax is unmistakably German, for in English one does not normally separate the verb *see* from its complement. In order to correct this woefully misbegotten sentence, one must realign the entire sequence and attempt to achieve an approximation to the original *démarche* by means of controlled transposition (class-shift plus clause-structure shift). The noun *Ursache* may be transposed to an adjective (*due*), and the original word sequence may be split up into two main parts: a brief reporting clause containing a verb of belief or assumption (*Professor Kondratieff believed*) and a zero *that*-clause indicating the result of Kondratieff's cogitations (*this was due to* + [complement]). The omission of *that* is feasible because the nominal clause is relatively uncomplicated.

2. den nur . . . Energiebereich: Here we are confronted with an array of intricate problems which must be resolved by a series of complicated lexical and grammatical manipulations. The attributive participial phrase (*nur. . . auftretenden*) must be converted into a relative clause and tacked on to the English equivalent of *Belebungseffekt*. This change in word-order now brings further difficulties in its train. The translation equivalent of *Belebungseffekt* must not be separated from its complement (*durch . . . Energiebereich*). We have therefore no alternative but to resort to repetition. This translation operation must be effected in three stages. First, the notion expressed by *Belebungseffekt* is introduced by means of the noun *effect* preceded by the indefinite article. Secondly, the relative clause corresponding to the German participial construction is attached to its antecedent (*effect*). Thirdly, the idea rendered by *Belebungseffekt* is taken up again and expanded. The definite article is here substituted for the indefinite article because the reader has now been familiarized with the concept in question. This resumptive device is somewhat more common in English than in German. This is because English favours right-branching structures, while in German there is a marked tendency to use anticipatory medial branching ('nesting'). On the use of 'right-tending' structures in English, see R. Quirk et al., *GCE*, § 11.81.

3. auftretenden: The dictionary equivalents of this verb include *to be found* and *to be encountered*. In this context, however, *to be observed* seems more appropriate. The verbs *find* and *encounter* do not normally collocate with the noun *effect*.

4. Belebungseffekt: This compound, which has not been recorded in the dictionaries, must be decomposed into its lexical elements and rendered by a present participle plus a noun: *reinvigorating effect*. German compounds consisting of two nouns are often translated by combinations of the type present participle + noun or adjective + noun. Cp. *Saisonschwankungen* (seasonal variations).

5. im Maschinen- und Energiebereich: This word sequence is a typical instance of that proliferative spatial imagery which is used for the rendition of intellectual conceptions in almost every variety of present-day language. This type of imagery can be traced back to the later part of the eighteenth century, but it did not really gain momentum until the beginning of the twentieth century. Its spread has undoubtedly been fostered by the headlong progress of inventions and the consequent geometrizing of our environment. Contemporary thinking is dominated by spatial concepts. Even time is now considered by physicists and mathematicians as an aspect of space. Broadly speaking, all the countries in Western Europe have evolved along much the same lines during the past few decades. It is therefore quite natural that spatial metaphors should nowadays be equally common in German and English. Cp. the figurative use of words such as *sector, area, zone, sphere, radius, circumference, pole, axis, Bereich, Bezirk, Sektor, Zone, Sphäre, Umkreis, Pol* or *Achse*. There are, however, certain divergencies of which the translator ought to be aware. Two examples will suffice here:

(i) Sonst würde sie [sc. die Labour-Regierung] alle Stabilisierungserfolge zunichte machen, die sie im letzten halben Jahr erreicht und die eine aktive Zahlungsbilanz in den Bereich des Möglichen gebracht hat [sic!]. (K. C. Horton, *German Economic Extracts*, p. 46.)

(ii) Mit der Roßkur einer Reduzierung der Belegschaft um 25 000 Mitarbeiter bis 1981 will Sir Michael Edwardes, Chairman der British Leyland Ltd., den seit Jahren dahinsiechenden staatseigenen britischen Autokonzern wieder in die Gewinnzone bringen. (IHK Dortmund, Dolmetscher- und Übersetzerprüfung, 18. 10. 1979.)

The spatial metaphor in sentence (i) has no figurative counterpart in English. The normal English equivalent of the expression *etwas in den Bereich des Möglichen bringen* is *to make something possible*.

The spatial metaphor in sentence (ii) (*den . . . Autokonzern wieder in die Gewinnzone bringen*) poses more intricate problems. Literal translation is out of the question. In order to render the German expression adequately, we must resort to an extreme form of modulation which consists in substituting one image for another. R. v. Eichborn has translated this locution as *to bring back into the black* (*Der kleine Eichborn*, s.v. Gewinnverband). This is a very deft modulation. *In the black* means 'operating at a profit or being out of debt' (as opposed to 'being in the red'). The only thing one might object to here is the use of the verb *bring*. English *bring* always implies motion toward the speaker, while German *bringen* does not carry this implication. Hence a sentence such as *Er brachte mich nach Hause* (meaning 'to my home') must be rendered as *He took me home*, and not **He brought me home*. Cf. H. L. Kufner, *The Grammatical Structures of English and German*, p. 91. In the case under discussion, the verb *put* would be more appropriate than *bring*. Cf. the following example sentence from the *Random House Dictionary* (s.v. black):

New production methods put the company in the black.

Another possible rendering of *wieder in die Gewinnzone bringen* is the nautical image *to put back on an even keel*. Cf. the following quotation from *Reader's Digest* (March 1980, p. 133):

Mexican president José López Portillo, a 59-year-old former law professor with 20 years' experience in public administration, has put the Mexican economy back on an even keel after six free-spending years under his predecessor, Luis Echeverría Alvarez.

The expression *to put back on an even keel* is elegant and picturesque, but if it is used to translate *wieder in die Gewinnzone bringen* the focus is somewhat skewed. *On an even keel* means 'in a state of balance'. It expresses a concept which is wider than that represented by *wieder in die Gewinnzone bringen,* and it might be taken to mean 'showing neither profit nor loss' rather than 'showing an excess of returns over the outlay of capital'.

The words *Maschinenbereich* and *Energiebereich* are borderline cases. Expressions such as *the energy sector* are in common use, but there is at present a tendency in some quarters to react against the overuse of *sector* and its near-synonyms. Cf. R. Flesch, *The ABC of Style*, svv. area, field. Thus metaphorical German compounds such as *Energiebereich* may often be rendered by non-metaphorical simplex words like *energy*. Cf. the use of the noun *energy* in the following snippet from P. A. Samuelson, *Economics* (p. 748):

The crisis in energy is perhaps an omen of a bigger crisis yet to come, some will argue.

It is also interesting to note that *Energiebereich* has been glossed as *electricity and fuels* in C. A. Gunston/C. M. Corner, *Deutsch-Englisches Glossarium finanzieller und wirtschaftlicher Fachausdrücke*.

The term *Maschinenbereich* may be treated in a similar manner. Only the non-metaphorical element in this compound need be reproduced in an English translation, and this element (*Maschinen-*) may be modulated to the noun *technology* or the adjective *technological* when *Maschinenbereich* occurs in a syntagma such as *Erfindungen im Maschinenbereich: discoveries in technology* or *technological discoveries*. Cf. the use of the words *technology* and *technological* in the following quotations:

Recent advances in science and technology are making it increasingly possible for man to influence his environment. (H. J. Lechler/F. Ungerer (edd.), *Modern Life*, p. 248.)
Another prefers to attribute the cycle to fluctuations in the rate of technological inventions and innovations (. . .). (P. A. Samuelson, *Economics*, p. 243.)
As could be expected from the deepening of capital and from technological advance, Q/L has risen steadily. (*ibid.*, p. 689.)

In the present instance, however, the translator has no choice but to render the word *Maschinenbereich* as a noun because it is coordinated with *Energiebereich* and *Energiebereich* cannot be translated with the aid of the adjective *energetic*. *Technological* means 'pertaining to technology', but *energetic* does not mean 'pertaining to energy'. If we were to use different parts of speech to translate *Maschinenbereich* and *Energiebereich*, the resultant word sequence would be unpleasantly asymmetrical.

For further information on spatial imagery, the reader is referred to Georges Matoré, *L'espace humain,* a brilliant and profound study which can be warmly recommended to anyone interested in sociolinguistics.

6. versprechen: Two points need to be made here. First, the present tense should be rendered as a preterite since the introductory verb in the head clause (*erkannte*) is in a past tense. Traditional tense sequences are frequently disregarded by journalists. Cf. the example sentence quoted by André Tellier in *Grammaire de l'anglais* (p. 7). In this particular instance, however, it is advisable to observe the rules about sequence of tenses.

Secondly, the verb *versprechen* need not be rendered as *promise*. Expressions such as *hold out hopes of* (+ noun) or *bid fair to* (+ infinitive) seem more appropriate in this context. The use of the locution *bid fair to* entails a double transposition: the nominal element *-senkung* must be converted to a verb (*reduce*), and the adjective *nachhaltig* must be converted to an adverb (*effectively*).

7. und dadurch . . . auslösen: A literal translation would sound rather flat. The most elegant solution is a non-finite clause introduced by *thereby*. For the collocation *induce + investment,* cp. the following snippet from P. A. Samuelson, *Economics* (p. 225):

Induced investment means that anything increasing national income is likely to be good for the capital-goods industries.

b) Alternatives

Professor Kondratieff believed	*this*		was due to an effect	*that*
		that this		*which*
could be observed only once every fifty years, the reinvigorating				
effect of	*fundamental*	*discoveries*	in technology and energy which	
	basic	inventions		
held out hopes of	*effective*	*cost reduction,*	*thereby*	inducing effective
		" cutting,	thus	
bade fair	to reduce costs effectively,			
seemed likely "	"	"	"	

new investment.
" capital expenditure.
"   "   projects.
reinvestment.
dishoarding.

Text V*

Das auf der Weltwährungskonferenz von Bretton Woods (USA) im Jahre 1944 beschlossene Währungssystem sah für die beteiligten Länder feste Wechselkurse gegenüber dem als Leitwährung dienenden Dollar vor, für den selbst wiederum ein festes Austauschverhältnis zum Gold festgesetzt war (Gold-Devisen-Standard).
Außerdem wurde die freie Austauschbarkeit (Konvertibilität) der Währungen vereinbart, die in verschiedenen westlichen Industrieländern einschließlich der Bundesrepublik Deutschland zunächst für den Waren- und Dienstleistungsverkehr eingeführt und 1958 auch auf den Kapitalverkehr ausgedehnt wurde.
Ungleichgewichte auf dem Devisenmarkt (Angebots- oder Nachfrageüberschüsse bei festgesetztem Kurs) lösten bei Überschreiten einer vereinbarten Bandbreite (1% über oder unter dem Festkurs) Interventionen der betroffenen Zentralbank aus.
Die Interventionspflicht erforderte es, daß die Zentralbanken Angebotsüberschüsse aus dem Markt zu nehmen oder Angebotslücken durch Auflösung von Devisenreserven zu schließen hatten. Um dieser Interventionspflicht auch dann genügen zu können, wenn die eigenen Devisenreserven nicht ausreichen, gewährte der Internationale Währungsfonds (IWF) Kredite (Ziehungsrechte der Mitgliedsländer).

---

* Rainer Ertel, *Volkswirtschaftslehre: Einführung am Beispiel der Bundesrepublik Deutschland* (R. Oldenbourg)

Text V

A new monetary system was adopted at the international monetary conference held at Bretton Woods (U.S.A.) in 1944. Under this system, the countries concerned were required to observe exchange rates fixed in relation to the dollar, which was to serve as a key currency, and which in turn was linked to gold by a fixed exchange value relationship (the gold exchange standard).

In addition, it was agreed that currencies would be freely exchangeable (convertible). To begin with, this convertibility was established for goods and service transactions in various western industrial countries including West Germany, and in 1958 it was extended to capital transactions.

Disequilibria in the foreign exchange market (excess supply or demand under a system of fixed exchange rates) triggered interventions by the central bank directly affected whenever a stipulated fluctuation limit ($\pm$ 1 per cent around the fixed rate) was exceeded.

The obligation to intervene meant that central banks had to take surplus offers off the market or fill gaps in supplies by liquidating foreign currency reserves. In order to enable member countries to fulfil this obligation to intervene even when their own foreign exchange reserves were insufficient, the International Monetary Fund (IMF) granted credits (member states' drawing rights).

Annotations and Alternatives

① Das auf der Weltwährungskonferenz von Bretton Woods (USA) im Jahre 1944 beschlossene Währungssystem sah für die beteiligten Länder feste Wechselkurse gegenüber dem als Leitwährung dienenden Dollar vor, für den selbst wiederum ein festes Austauschverhältnis zum Gold festgesetzt war (Gold-Devisen-Standard).

a) Annotations

1. Das ... Währungssystem: A literal rendering of the attributive participle would result in a most unwieldly construction involving the insertion of a long string of words between the sentence subject *monetary system* and one of the English equivalents of the verb *vorsehen*. The German sentence needs to be broken apart and replaced by two or more shorter grammatical units.

2. auf der Weltwährungskonferenz: In this kind of phrase *auf* must be rendered as *at*. Cf. *at the conference* (auf der Tagung) (E. Weis/E. Haberfellner, *Business Vocabulary for All*, s.v. conference).

3. von Bretton Woods: In this type of phrase the preposition *von* may be rendered in various ways. Cf. the following examples:
(i) The U. K. Treasury submitted proposals for the establishment of an International Clearing Union for discussion at the Bretton Woods Conference in 1944. (G. Bannock/R. E. Baxter/R. Rees, *The Penguin Dictionary of Economics*, s.v. Keynes Plan.)
(ii) The Conference of Bretton Woods, 1944, established the dollar as the world currency together with gold (. . .). (R. Sieper, *The Student's Companion to the U.S.A.*, p. 95.)
(iii) an international monetary conference held in 1944 at Bretton Woods in New Hampshire (. . .). (*CED*, s.v. Bretton Woods Conference.)

The use of *in* and *at* before place-names often causes difficulty. In the case under discussion, *at* should be used in preference to *in*. Cf. the following examples:
(i) (. . .) the establishment at Bretton Woods of the World Bank and the International Monetary Fund (. . .). (M. Stewart, *Keynes and After*, p. 23.)
(ii) Like so many human institutions, the International Monetary Fund (I.M.F.), set up at Bretton Woods just before the end of the Second World War, was essentially designed to deal with the problems of the past. (H. G. Grubel, *The International Monetary System*, p. 134.)
(iii) The International Monetary Fund was created by international agreement at Bretton Woods, New Hampshire, in July 1944 (. . .). (*ibid.*, p. 158.)

It is virtually impossible to lay down any hard-and-fast rule for the use of *in* and *at*. For an interesting discussion of present-day usage, see F. T. Wood, *English Prepositional Idioms*, s.v. at.

4. im Jahre 1944: Adverbials of place usually precede adverbials of definite time if both types of adjunct cluster within the same clause. See R. Quirk et al., *GCE*, § 8.77; R. A. Close, *RGSE*, § 15.17; A. Lamprecht, *GES*, § 246; R. W. Zandvoort, *HEG*, § 718. This principle is exemplified in H. G. Grubel, *The International Monetary System*, p. 158 (quoted in the preceding note). However, the expected word-order is sometimes reversed for the sake of balance, emphasis or information focus:

a) *Balance:*
Long place adjuncts tend to follow short time adjuncts. Cf. the example from *CED* cited in the preceding note.

b) *Emphasis:*
She went with him the next day to the hotel. (W. Somerset Maugham, quoted in A. Lamprecht, *GES,* § 246.)

c) *Information focus:*
People stayed for months in the same house without stirring from it even for a night. (Viscount Grey, quoted in R. W. Zandvoort, *HEG,* § 718.)

In this example the author has moved the place adjunct *in the same house* to the end of the main clause in order to establish a closer relationship with the place reference *from it* in the non-finite clause introduced by *without.* There may also be some considerations of balance at work here since the time adjunct *for months* is much shorter than the place adjunct *in the same house.*

5. sah ... vor: In German one often encounters transitive verbs with inanimate objects. This type of animism is possible in English, too, yet it is much less common than in German[1] or French. Here are a few examples of animism in modern English:

(i) Section A of this chapter shows how our mixed economy tackles the three problems of economic organization that must be met by any society. (Paul A. Samuelson, *Economics,* p. 37.)
(ii) The late twelfth century saw the composition of *Artes poeticae* which greatly influenced vernacular writers. (F. J. E. Raby, *The Oxford Book of Medieval Latin Verse,* p. xviii.)
(iii) The early seventeenth-century shift from tight Senecan structures to the opener movement of the 'loose and free' sees once again the written prose of educated Englishmen reverting to the movement of speech. (Ian A. Gordon, *The Movement of English Prose,* p. 116.)
(iv) It [*sc.* cooperation] requires that Other countries agree, through political bargaining, on which should do the adjusting by how much and how frequently. (H. G. Grubel, *The International Monetary System,* pp. 142–3.)
(v) The Rome Treaty also provides that during the transition period restrictions which limit the ability of nationals of one member-state to set up in business in another member-state shall be removed. (D. Swann, *The Economics of the Common Market,* p. 79.)
(vi) The Bill provides for the eventual self-government of the territory. (A. P. Cowie/R. Mackin, *Oxford Dictionary of Current Idiomatic English,* Vol. 1, s.v. provide for[3].)
(vii) A clause in the agreement provides for the arbitration of all disputes by an independent body. (*ibid.*)

In the case under discussion, it is advisable to avoid the constructions employed in example sentences (iv), (v), (vi) and (vii). If we use the constructions exemplified in sentences (iv) and (v), the result will sound rather odd because *The system provides that* ... and *The system requires that*... are collocationally somewhat abnormal. And if we use the constructions exemplified in sentences (vi) and (vii), we shall land ourselves in an even more awkward situation. We shall be confronted once more with the problem of collocational abnormality, and on top of that we shall run the risk of becoming hopelessly mired in the second part of the sentence. If it comes to the pinch, we can say: *The system provided for exchange rates fixed in relation to the dollar,* but the insertion of a word-group corresponding to *für die beteiligten Länder* is bound to prove grammatically and stylistically disruptive, to say the least of it.
We have therefore no choice but to recast the sentence, using a prepositional phrase such as *under this system.* Cf. the following examples:

---
[1] Cf. W. Friederich, *Technik des Übersetzens,* pp. 65–72.

Under the present system, the U.S. holds about 23 per cent of the voting strength (. . .). (G. Bannock/R. E. Baxter/R. Rees, *The Penguin Dictionary of Economics*, s.v. International Monetary Fund.)
In this system the central bank will not exchange its currency for gold on demand (. . .). (*ibid.*, s.v. gold exchange standard.)
Under such a system she [*sc.* the U.K.] would remain autonomous in respect of tariffs on goods emanating from outside the free trade area. (D. Swann, *The Economics of the Common Market*, p. 26.)

6. beteiligten: The adjective *concerned* is postposed when it means 'interested', 'guilty' or 'involved'. It is preposed when it means 'worried', 'troubled', 'anxious' or 'solicitous':

(i) I shall find the boy concerned and punish him. (*CED*, s.v. concerned.)
(ii) with a concerned look. (Hornby, *OALDCE*, s.v. concern^2.)

The postpositive adjective in sentence (i) can be regarded as a reduced relative clause. It should be noted that in American English attributive and postposed *concerned* and *involved* are interchangeable if the head of the noun phrase is *party* or *parties* (legal usage). Cf. R. Quirk et al., *GCE*, § 5.18. However, American and British usage are identical with regard to the adjectives *absent* and *present*, which belong to the same group as *concerned* and *involved*.
Another point worth noting in this connection is that certain highly charged adjectives which can occur attributively or predicatively are occasionally postposed in exalted style:

The same fundamentals of British character and temperament that we observed in the quiet old eighteenth century – British common sense and good nature, British idiosyncrasy and prejudice – when brought face to face with this prolonged and terrible crisis in human affairs, have produced, after labours, errors, and victories innumerable, the strange world in which we live today. (G. M. Trevelyan, *British History in the Nineteenth Century and After: 1782–1919*, p. 18.)

This type of postposition is generally restricted to poetry.

7. Wechselkurse: The English equivalent of this noun collocates with verbs such as *observe* and *maintain*. Examples:

Under the I.M.F.'s articles of agreement, member countries are required to observe an exchange rate, fluctuations in which should be confined to ± 1 per cent around its par value. (G. Bannock/R. E. Baxter/R. Rees, *The Penguin Dictionary of Economics*, s.v. International Monetary Fund.)
These rates were declared and registered legally with the I.M.F. and every country committed itself to maintain them within a margin of maximum plus or minus one per cent unless 'fundamental' payments disequilibrium required a change of the parity rate. (H. G. Grubel, *The International Monetary System*, p. 159.)
(. . .) it ought to be possible for them simultaneously to run huge balance-of-payments surpluses by maintaining advantageous exchange rates (. . .). (*The Economist*, 8–14. 3. 1980, p. 22.)

8. gegenüber: *Gegenüber*, which is synonymous with *im Verhältnis zu*, may be rendered in various ways:

a) *in relation to:*

Under the rules of the International Monetary Fund, established at the Bretton Woods Conference towards the end of the Second World War, exchange rates have been fixed at a par value in relation to the dollar (. . .). (G. Bannock/R. E. Baxter/R. Rees, *The Penguin Dictionary of Economics*, s.v. Exchange rate.)
Bis 1973 war das Kursrisiko nicht unbegrenzt, sondern durch die Interventionspunkte (*intervention points*) begrenzt (*limited*), die im Verhältnis zum Dollar als Leitwährung festgelegt waren

(*established in relation to the dollar as the key currency*). (J. Rudolph, *Langenscheidts Handbuch der englischen Wirtschaftssprache*, p. 280.)
During the depression of the thirties, competitive devaluations of national currencies in relation to gold had the effect of endowing gold with capital value gains and a resultant positive rate of return, which tended to exceed that available in foreign currencies. (H. G. Grubel, *The International Monetary System*, pp. 132–134.)

b) *in terms of:*

This par value is quoted in terms of the U.S. dollar, which is in turn linked to gold. (G. Bannock/R. E. Baxter/R. Rees, *The Penguin Dictionary of Economics*, s.v. International Monetary Fund.)
Die Amerikaner erklärten sich bereit, den Dollar gegenüber dem Gold um rund acht Prozent abzuwerten (*devalue the dollar in terms of gold by eight per cent*) und die Einfuhrzusatzabgabe abzuschaffen (*remove the import surcharge*). (J. Rudolph, *Langenscheidts Handbuch der englischen Wirtschaftssprache*, p. 54.)
(. . .) Banker's exchange rates in terms of gold must never be changed. (H. G. Grubel, *The International Monetary System*, p. 134.)
In December 1971 the Smithsonian Agreement was reached among the ten largest industrial nations of the Western world (. . .) to devalue the dollar in terms of gold to $ 38 from $ 35 per ounce and to increase the value of most currencies in terms of dollars. (*ibid.*, p. 150.)
If quotations were not in dollars, Canadian, German, French or United States importers who wanted to compare the current and expected future prices of coffee from the various sources would have to gather and evaluate information about the current and expected future exchange rates of each of these currencies in terms of their own. (*ibid.*, p. 152.)

c) *against:*

In analogy with the Despres-Kindleberger-Salant argument, any country which wished to reduce or slow down the growth in its dollar holdings should be expected to appreciate its exchange rate against the dollar. (H. G. Grubel, *The International Monetary System*, p. 150.)
Now assume that the franc depreciated to a maximum of 2.25 per cent against the dollar (. . .). (*ibid.*, p. 204.)
The Swiss franc tendency to appreciate against all other currencies seems to be due to the low inflation rate (. . .). (I. de Renty, *Lexique quadrilingue des affaires*, p. 262.)
The dollar was devalued against other currencies by increasing the official price of gold from $ 35 to $ 38 an ounce. (R. Sieper, *The Student's Companion to the U.S.A.*, p. 96.)
cross rate. (e.g., in BRD, for $ against £) (*G/C*, s.v. Usancekurs.)

d) *relative to:*

All they would have had to do in the presence of large U.S. deficits was to revalue upwards their currencies relative to the dollar. (H. G. Grubel, *The International Monetary System*, p. 140.)

e) *vis-à-vis:*

The dollar and the pound sterling have continued in their historic roles as leading reserve currencies, although in recent years their positions have been undermined because of persistent balance of payments deficits in both the U.S. and the U.K., which gave cause for speculation as to their long-term exchange value *vis-à-vis* gold. (G. Bannock/R. E. Baxter/R. Rees, *The Penguin Dictionary of Economics*, s.v. reserve currency.)

The French phrase *vis-à-vis* was appropriated by the English language as early as the eighteenth century and is quite common in formal usage. However, it has not yet been wholly absorbed and is not always used correctly by native speakers. Foreign terms and phrases are becoming increasingly popular in present-day English, and a useful collection of such borrowings has been published under the title *Le Mot Juste* (edd. John Buchanan-Brown et al.). The languages which have been taken into consideration in this new lexicon include French, German, Italian, Spanish, Latin, Greek, Russian, Arabic, Chinese, Hebrew, Persian, Turkish and Sanskrit.

9. Leitwährung: This compound is normally rendered as *key currency* or *reserve currency*. These terms are closely allied in meaning, yet they are not always interchangeable. *Reserve currency* (= *Reservewährung*) is wider in application than *key currency*. Strictly speaking, a key currency is a key reserve currency, a leading reserve currency. For precise definitions of the term *reserve currency,* see G. Bannock/R. E. Baxter/R. Rees, *The Penguin Dictionary of Economics* and A. Gilpin, *Dictionary of Economic Terms.*

10. dienenden: The attributive phrase *dem als Leitwährung dienenden* is non-restrictive, so it must be rendered by a non-restrictive relative clause. Restrictive relative clauses are often replaced by present participle clauses, but this type of substitution is not possible with non-restrictive relative clauses. In the case under discussion, the translator must use the verb *to be* (= *sollen*) in order to eke out the sense of the participle *dienenden.* Finite verb forms are by necessity more precise than non-finite verb forms.

11. für den ... festgesetzt war: In contemporary English there is a marked tendency to avoid relative clauses initiated by prepositions (*for which, about which,* etc.). This type of relative clause construction is felt to be stiffly formal and is often replaced by an infinitive clause. Cp. R. Quirk et al., *GCE,* § 14.29. If it is impossible to use an infinitive, it may be possible to recast the relative clause in such a way that the introductory preposition can be dispensed with. The relative clause *für den ... festgesetzt war* is a case in point. Cf. the following quotation from G. Bannock/R. E. Baxter/R. Rees, *The Penguin Dictionary of Economics* (p. 226):

This par value is quoted in terms of the U.S. dollar, which is in turn linked to gold.

12. selbst: This word can be safely left untranslated. Cp. the example sentence quoted in the preceding note.

13. Austauschverhältnis: *Terms of trade* (Eichborn) would be quite unacceptable in this context. The expression *terms of trade* denotes the ratio of export prices to import prices.

14. festgesetzt: The verb *festsetzen* must be considered in conjunction with the wordgroup *ein festes Austauschverhältnis zum Gold.* The basic idea conveyed by these words may be expressed quite simply by means of the verb *peg,* which means 'to stabilize by legislation', and which is commonly used with reference to the prices of commodities, exchange rates, etc. Cp. the following example from H. G. Grubel, *The International Monetary System* (p. 147):

These bonds (. . .) provided the equivalent of a gold guarantee to countries which chose not to devalue their currencies in case the United States did so, but provided only a guarantee of fixed value in national currency for those which kept their exchange rates pegged to the dollar.

15. Gold-Devisen-Standard: The commonest English equivalent of this compound is *gold exchange standard.* Cp. J. Rudolph, *Langenscheidts Handbuch der englischen Wirtschaftssprache,* pp. 51,53; G. Bannock/R. E. Baxter/R. Rees, *The Penguin Dictionary of Economics,* s.v. Gold exchange standard; A. Gilpin, *Dictionary of Economic Terms,* s.v. Gold Standard. However, the term *dollar-gold exchange standard* occasionally crops up in economic textbooks. Cp. the following example from H. G. Grubel, *The International Monetary System* (p. 127):

This meant a dismantling of the dollar-gold exchange standard and the removal of the U.S. dollar from its central position in this post-war international monetary system.

b) Alternatives

A new monetary system was adopted at the international monetary
conference held *at Bretton Woods (U.S.A.) in 1944.* *Under* this system, *in 1944 at Bretton Woods (U.S.A.).* In
the countries concerned were required to *observe* exchange rates *maintain*
fixed *in relation to* the dollar, which was to serve as a *key* *in terms of* *reserve* *against* *relative to* *vis-à-vis*
currency, and which in turn was *linked to gold by a fixed exchange* currency *pegged to gold*
value relationship *(the gold exchange standard.)* *(the dollar gold exchange standard.)*

② Außerdem wurde die freie Austauschbarkeit (Konvertibilität) der Währungen vereinbart, die in verschiedenen westlichen Industrieländern einschließlich der Bundesrepublik Deutschland zunächst für den Waren- und Dienstleistungsverkehr eingeführt und 1958 auch auf den Kapitalverkehr ausgedehnt wurde.

a) Annotations

1. Außerdem: It is necessary to insist on a number of distinctions between the phrases *into the bargain* and *in addition,* especially since the information given in the unilingual dictionaries is inadequate and misleading.
Into the bargain is an additive-intensifying phrase meaning 'over and above what is agreed, stipulated, considered, expected or generally regarded as reasonable'. Cf. the German expressions *obendrein* and *dazu noch,* or the French locution *par-dessus le marché. Into the bargain* is much used in conversation, and often has an emotional connotation. Examples:

If you have anything to do with such a scheme you'll endanger your good name, and probably lose your money into the bargain. (F. T. Wood, *English Colloquial Idioms,* s.v. bargain.)
He's stupid and lazy into the bargain. (Cf. G. Collier/B. Shields, *Guided German-English Translation,* p. 165.)

In addition is decidedly more formal and has no subjective colouring whatever. Cp. the following example from G. Bannock/R. E. Baxter/R. Rees, *The Penguin Dictionary of Economics* (pp. 146–147):

Under the treaty, the European Investment Bank was formed, with powers to lend money for the development of backward regions of the community, including associate members. In addition, a European Social Fund was set up to assist the redeployment of workers thrown out of work (. . .).

2. wurde . . . vereinbart: A literal translation would sound unduly stiff. It is preferable to convert the abstract nouns into adjectives and introduce the main statement by means of anticipatory *it.* Cf. the following quotation from G. Bannock/R. E. Baxter/R. Rees, *The Penguin Dictionary of Economics* (p. 226):

(. . .) it was agreed that discussions would be held to review the whole problem of international liquidity.

3. der Währungen: Zero article is mandatory since in this particular instance *Währungen* is a noun with generic reference, i.e. a noun denoting a class as a whole. Cp. the following examples:

As Chapter 36 will show, the Bretton Woods Conference of 1944 (. . .) defined in its Charter the parities of currencies not simply in terms of gold, but also in terms of dollars (. . .). (Paul A. Samuelson, *Economics,* p. 613.)
In December 1971, the 'Group of Ten' (. . .) agreed on new 'central values' of currencies in order to achieve a dollar devaluation of 10 per cent with a permissible margin of ± 2.25 per cent. (G. Bannock/R. E. Baxter/R. Rees, *The Penguin Dictionary of Economics,* p. 226.)

4. die . . . ausgedehnt wurde: The antecedents of the relative pronoun *die* (*Austauschbarkeit* and *Konvertibilität*) have been converted into adjectives, so we have no choice but to split the German sentence into two independent statements.

5. Bundesrepublik Deutschland: The commonest English equivalent is *West Germany.* Cp. the following example from D. Swann, *The Economics of the Common Market* (p. 87):

The common grain price issue was also important because it brought France and West Germany directly into conflict.

The variant spelling *W. Germany* is also quite common. Cp. G. Dalton, *Economic Systems and Society,* p. 179. English-speaking authors occasionally write *Germany* when they mean *West Germany.* Cp. the following example from H. G. Grubel, *The International Monetary System* (p. 150):

In December 1971 the Smithsonian Agreement was reached among the ten largest industrial nations of the Western world, the Group of Ten consisting of Belgium, Canada, France, Germany, Italy, Japan, the Netherlands, Sweden, the United Kingdom and the United States, to devalue the dollar in terms of gold to $ 38 from $ 35 per ounce and to increase the value of most currencies in terms of dollars.

This usage is misleading and ought not to be imitated. The expression *the German Federal Republic* is sometimes used in highly formal writing. Cp. the following example from a letter by Professor T. W. Hutchison (Birmingham):

More recently, after World War II, the economy of the German Federal Republic, the outstanding western economic success of recent decades, started with the advantage of sensible, and quite restrictive, trade union legislation. (*The Times,* 18. 1. 1980, p. 15.)

The expression *Federal Republic of Germany* (*LGS, LEW, S/W, W/H*) is comparatively rare. *Federal Republic (W/H)* is somewhat more common, yet it can be used only when the context makes it quite clear that the state referred to is West Germany.

6. Waren- und Dienstleistungsverkehr: This word-group should be rendered as a lexical unit. A wide variety of alternatives is given in the bilingual dictionaries, but the phrase *movement of goods and services* has been overlooked, although the expression *free movement of goods* has been recorded in R. Renner/R. Sachs, *Wirtschaftssprache.* The phrase *movement of goods and services* is usually preceded by the adjective *free* and is generally employed with reference to the European Common Market. It is interesting to note that in this kind of word-group the English adjective *free* corresponds to a German noun (*Freiheit* or *Freizügigkeit*). Examples:

the free movement of goods, services, capital and labour between the member countries. (G. Bannock/R. E. Baxter/R. Rees, *The Penguin Dictionary of Economics*, s.v. European Economic Community.)
Freiheit des Personen-, Dienstleistungs- und Kapitalverkehrs. (F. Bülow/H. Langen, *Wörterbuch der Wirtschaft*, s.v. Europäische Wirtschaftsgemeinschaft.)
die Freizügigkeit des Güterverkehrs. (W. Henrichsmeyer/O. Gans/I. Evers, *Einführung in die Volkswirtschaftslehre*, p. 221.)

7. eingeführt: *Establish* and *establishment* collocate well with word-groups such as *movement of goods*. Cp. the following quotation from D. Swann, *The Economics of the Common Market* (p. 69):
The Community approached the establishment of free movement of labour in stages.

8. auch: This additive tonal particle can be safely left untranslated since the information provided in the sentence makes further emphasis or coloration redundant.

b) Alternatives

In addition, it was agreed that currencies would be freely exchangeable (convertible). To begin with, this convertibility was established for	*goods and service transactions* *the movement of goods and services* *the exchange of goods and services* *the circulation of goods and services* *commerce in goods and services* *trade and services*	in various western	
industrial countries *industrial states* *industrial nations* *industrialized countries*	including	West Germany, W. Germany, the German Federal Republic, the Federal Republic of Germany,	and
in 1958 it was extended to	*capital transactions.* *movements of capital.* *capital movements.*		

③ Ungleichgewichte auf dem Devisenmarkt (Angebots- oder Nachfrageüberschüsse bei festgesetztem Kurs) lösten bei Überschreiten einer vereinbarten Bandbreite (1% über oder unter dem Festkurs) Interventionen der betroffenen Zentralbank aus.

a) Annotations

1. Ungleichgewichte: The noun *imbalance* is not normally used with reference to the foreign exchange market. The commonest term is *disequilibrium*. Examples:
How to cure the disequilibrium? (Paul A. Samuelson, *Economics*, p. 611.)

The system envisaged a change in exchange rates only when a fundamental disequilibrium had become apparent after the use of stop-gap measures. (A. Gilpin, *Dictionary of Economic Terms*, s.v. Bretton Woods Agreement.)

2. auf: A distinction may be made between *on the market* and *in the market*. *On the market* means 'available for purchase' (*CED*, s.v. market). *To be in the market for something* means 'to wish to buy or acquire something'. Cf. the following example from Hans G. Hoffmann, *Aufbaukurs Wirtschaft* (p. 84):

(. . .) you are in the market for 30 electronic desktop calculators.

In a market means 'in an area of economic activity in which buyers and sellers come together'. In the case under consideration, *in* is clearly the correct preposition. Cp. the following examples:

The actual rate at any one time is determined by supply and demand conditions for the relevant currencies in the market. (G. Bannock/R. E. Baxter/R. Rees, *The Penguin Dictionary of Economics*, s.v. Exchange rate.)
(. . .) America was beginning to face up realistically to the need to curtail its appetite for imported oil by allowing the price mechanism to begin to work again in the American market (. . .). (*The Economist*, 8.–14. 3. 1980. p. 20.)

3. Devisenmarkt: In the bilingual dictionaries, this term has been translated as *foreign exchange market* and *currency market*. The term *exchange market* has been overlooked. Cp. the following example from G. Bannock/R. E. Baxter/R. Rees, *The Penguin Dictionary of Economics* (s.v. Exchange rate):

If there were no government control over the exchange market (such as the U.K. exercises through the exchange equalization account), there would be a *free* or *floating exchange rate* in operation.

4. Angebots (. . .) überschüsse: A wide variety of possible renderings is given in the bilingual dictionaries, but one translation equivalent has been overlooked: *excess of supply*. Cp. the following example from Paul A. Samuelson, *Economics* (p. 610):

Such an excess of supply would bid the rate back down to E, where the market of foreign currency for dollars is just cleared.

5. bei festgesetztem Kurs: Here, as in most cases, the translation of the preposition *bei* causes difficulty despite thorough treatment in various bilingual dictionaries. The following example sentences illustrate a number of possibilities which the dictionary makers have not yet taken into account:

(i) Keynes was not alone in inquiring into the repercussions of an exogenous increase in aggregate expenditure at full employment. (J. A. Trevithick/C. Mulvey, *The Economics of Inflation*, p. 20.)
(ii) Under floating exchange rates, in the longest run it is the *monetary policies* of the different countries that ultimately determine their price levels and thereby strongly influence the trends of their exchange rates. (Paul A. Samuelson, *Economics*, p. 610.)
(iii) (. . .) it explains why, despite ripples of relatively minor magnitude, inflation is, under a system of fixed exchange rates, essentially a worldwide phenomenon. (J. A. Trevithick/C. Mulvey, *The Economics of Inflation*, p. 6.)

In the case under consideration, the preposition *at* would sound odd, but *under* or *under a system* would be quite acceptable. Generic reference must be indicated by pluralization.

6. lösten . . . aus: In this particular instance, the most appropriate equivalent is the verb *trigger*. Cp. the following quotation from H. G. Grubel, *The International Monetary System* (p. 191):

These indices are to be used to trigger automatic changes in the official exchange rate of a country and force its government to maintain this rate within specified margins through appropriate intervention in the foreign market.

The verb *trigger*, generally followed by *off*, collocates with nouns such as *disagreement, argument, discussion*, etc. For further details, see A. P. Cowie/R. Mackin, *Oxford Dictionary of Current Idiomatic English*, Vol. 1, s.v. trigger off.

7. bei Überschreiten: The word-group introduced by the preposition *bei* can be rendered as a time clause. The temporal conjunction *whenever* may be used to express the frequentative aspect.
Überschreiten can be translated by the metaphorical verb *overshoot*. Cp. the following quotation from *The Economist* of 8–14 March 1980 (p. 57):
But the EMS should continue to minimise short-term fluctuations and the "overshooting" from which non-EMS currencies such as the yen and sterling have suffered.

Exceed collocates well with *limit* (cf. the phrase *exceed the speed limit*), and *go beyond* collocates quite well with nouns such as *band* or *margin*. *Go beyond*, however, is not normally used in the passive.

8. Bandbreite: A wide variety of alternatives in given in the bilingual dictionaries: *band, (fluctuation) margin, margin of fluctuation (for a currency), range of variation* and *spread*. This list, however, is far from complete. The dictionary makers have overlooked the following translation equivalents: *range of fluctuations, range of permitted fluctuations, margin of permitted fluctuations, margin of exchange rate fluctuation, permitted fluctuation limit,* and *intervention margin*. Examples:

(i) Within the total permitted range of fluctuations against the dollar of 4½ per cent ('the tunnel'), the rates for the participating currencies at any one time were restricted to a band of 2¼ per cent ('the snake'). (A. Gilpin, *Dictionary of Economic Terms,* s.v. Smithsonian Agreement.)
(ii) (. . .) the Bank of England (q.v.) progressively narrowed the range of permitted fluctuations until 1939 when the rate was effectively fixed at $ 4.03. (*ibid.,* s.v. Floating Exchange Rate.)
(iii) In addition, it was agreed that, as a temporary measure, the margin of permitted fluctuations should be ± 25 per cent. (G. Bannock/ R. E. Baxter/R. Rees, *The Penguin Dictionary of Economics,* s.v. Exchange rate.)
(iv) Agreement reached by the Group of Ten (q.v.) countries in Washington in December, 1971, to re-establish a system of fixed rates of exchange embodying a major re-alignment of parities and a widening of the margins of exchange rate fluctuation. (A. Gilpin, *Dictionary of Economic Terms,* s.v. Smithsonian Agreement.)
(v) Both [*sc.* the Danish krone and the Belgian franc] have, at different times, rung the alarm bells of the "divergence indicator"[2] (set at 75% of the permitted fluctuation limit of each currency against the ecu). (*The Economist,* 8–14. 3. 1980, p. 54.)
(vi) Under this scheme, a country experiencing a persistent balance-of-payments deficit can let its exchange rate drift lower within the margin and as it does so the pegged rate, together with its intervention margin, also drifts lower through time. (H. G. Grubel, *The International Monetary System,* p. 192.)

---

[2] The divergence indicator, one of the new elements of the European Monetary System created in March 1979, is a kind of early warning device designed to detect community currencies that deviate from the Community average represented by the ECU. Cf. P. H. Trezise (ed.), *The European Monetary System: Its Promise and Prospects,* pp. 14–15, 52–53.

9. (1% über oder unter dem Festkurs): The word-group *über oder unter* may be rendered by means of the sign ± and the preposition *around*. Cp. the following example from G. Bannock/R. E. Baxter/R. Rees, *The Penguin Dictionary of Economics* (s.v. International Monetary Fund):

Under the I.M.F.'s articles of agreement, member countries are required to observe an exchange rate, fluctuations in which should be confined to ± 1 per cent around its par value.

10. Interventionen der betroffenen Zentralbank: The German genitive (*der*) must be rendered by means of a preposition. Cp. the following example from P. H. Trezise, *The European Monetary System: Its Promise and Prospects* (p. 18):

It holds that every nation should pursue appropriate domestic macroeconomic policies and then permit currency values to be determined in the foreign exchange market without intervention by central banks or governments.

The phrase *on the part of* is less suitable than *by*. *By* is used to introduce instrumental and agentive phrases in passive clauses, while *on the part of* is normally used to establish a link between a concrete agentive noun and an abstract non-agentive noun. Examples:

(. . .) a much shorter, and completely original Covenant was drafted by Thomas Sinclair. (A.T.Q. Stewart, *The Ulster Crisis*, p. 61.)
In Abraham Fraunce's *Arcadian Rhetorike* each of the figures is illustrated by a quotation from Sidney's poetry or prose. (P. Dixon, *Rhetoric*, p. 60.)
(. . .) 'a short phase of excessive and at times naïve enthusiasm for science on the part of men of letters'. (L. R. Furst/P. N. Skrine, *Naturalism*, p. 22.)
There was no objection on the part of the owner of the land. (Hornby, *OALDCE*, s.v. part.)

On the distinction between *by* and *with*, see R. Quirk et al., *GCE*, § 6.41.

11. betroffenen: Word-order and word-choice call for a few remarks. Postmodification is mandatory here. *Affected* is more appropriate than *concerned*. *Affected* differs from *concerned* in suggesting a higher degree of concern and often a need for action. For information on the German equivalents of the verb *affect*, see R. B. Farrell, *Dictionary of German Synonyms*, pp. 11−15. In the case under consideration, we may add the adverb *directly* in order to reinforce the sense of the past participle.

12. Zentralbank: In *Langenscheidts Handbuch der englischen Wirtschaftssprache* (p. 280), Jochen Rudolph has pointed out that in English-speaking countries central banks are often referred to vaguely as *the authorities*. In the case in question, however, it is preferable to use the term *central bank* in order to avoid ambiguity.

b) Alternatives

Disequilibria in the	*foreign exchange market*	*(excess supply*	or
	currency market	*(excessive supply*	”
	exchange market	*(an excess of supply*	”

demand	*under a system of* fixed exchange rates)	*triggered*
”	*under*	*triggered off*
”		

| interventions by the central bank directly affected whenever a |

stipulated	*fluctuation limit*	(± 1 per cent around
	fluctuation margin	
	margin of fluctuation	
	margin of permitted fluctuations	
	margin of exchange rate fluctuation	
	margin	
	intervention margin	
	range of variation	
	range of fluctuations	
	range of permitted fluctuations	
	band	
	spread (U.S.)	

| the fixed rate) was | *exceeded.* |
| | *overshot.* |

(4) Die Interventionspflicht erforderte es, daß die Zentralbanken Angebotsüberschüsse aus dem Markt zu nehmen oder Angebotslücken durch Auflösung von Devisenreserven zu schließen hatten.

a) Annotations

1. erforderte es: As already pointed out (cp. note (1) 5 above), the English are often loath to resort to animistic constructions in non-literary contexts. In this case, it is advisable to replace the verb *require* by *mean* in order to avoid a sequence which might be considered incompatible with the spirit of contemporary English.

2. durch Auflösung von Devisenreserven: In order to make the sentence run more easily, we may render the abstract noun *Auflösung* as a gerund. The verb *liquidate* has a wide range of meanings, including 'convert assets into cash'.

b) Alternatives

The obligation to intervene meant that central banks had to take		
surplus offers off the market or *fill* gaps in supplies by *surpluses of offers* *close* *bridge* *stop*		
liquidating *foreign currency reserves.* *foreign exchange reserves.* *currency reserves.*		

⑤ Um dieser Interventionspflicht auch dann genügen zu können, wenn die eigenen Devisenreserven nicht ausreichten, gewährte der Internationale Währungsfonds (IWF) Kredite (Ziehungsrechte der Mitgliedsländer).

a) Annotations

1. Um . . .Kredite: The grammatical relationship between the infinitive clause and the main clause calls for a few remarks. In general, a purpose clause introduced by *damit* is replaced by an infinitive clause when the main clause and the dependent clause have the same subject. Cf. P. Grebe (ed.), *Duden Grammatik der deutschen Gegenwartssprache,* § 1041,6. In modern German, however, this distinction is not absolute, but rather in the nature of a cline, with well marked poles, but a good deal of overlap in between. Hence, a finite clause is often tolerated even when the subjects are identical, and a finite clause is mandatory when the subject is brought into prominence:

(i) Er eilt, damit er den Anschlußzug noch erreicht. (J. Erben, *Abriß der deutschen Grammatik,* p. 187.)

(ii) Jeden wichtigen Angeklagten verhört er allein . . ., damit er, nur er und nicht einmal seine Unterbeamten, die entscheidenden Einzelheiten erfahre. (St. Zweig, quoted in J. Erben, *op. cit.,* p. 73.)

None the less, according to the Duden grammar (§ 1041,6), loosely attached infinitive clauses should be tolerated only when the subject of the infinitive is immediately apparent from the context; and in the case under discussion it is a moot point whether the subject of the infinitive group *genügen zu können* can be said to emerge at once from the co-text. The subject of *genügen zu können* is *die Zentralbanken der Mitgliedsländer,* while the subject of *gewährte* is *der Internationale Währungsfonds.* It would no doubt have been preferable to use a finite clause introduced by *damit* in order to obviate misunderstandings. At any rate the sentence must be recast in English since the kind of syntactic looseness so frequently tolerated in contemporary German would run counter to established English usage. Cf. the use of *afin de* and *afin que* in French, or *per* and *perché* in Italian. The translator may choose between a non-finite clause introduced by *in order to* and a finite clause introduced by *in order that.* However, since sub-clauses introduced by *in order that* are apt to be somewhat unwieldly, it seems preferable to use an infinitive clause. We shall therefore have to reword the sentence in such a way that the subjects of both clauses will be identical.

2. nicht ausreichten: These two words must be treated as a single thought-unit. In the suggested version, the negative prefix *in-*corresponds to the negative adverb *nicht,* the element *-sufficient* corresponds to *ausreich-,* and the copula *were* corresponds to the tense ending *-ten.*

b) Alternatives

| In order to enable *member countries* to *fulfil* this obligation to |
| *member states* *meet* |
| intervene even when their own *foreign exchange reserves* were |
| *foreign currency reserves* |
| *insufficient,* the International Monetary Fund (IMF) granted credits |
| *inadequate* |
| (*member states'* drawing rights). |
| *member countries'* |

Text VI*
Antizyklische Haushaltspolitik

Die Variation von Staatsausgaben und -einnahmen zur Inflationsbekämpfung geht von dem Nachfragesoginflationsmodell aus. Die Inflation entsteht demnach primär aus einem Nachfrageüberhang. Die dadurch ausgelösten Preissteigerungen lassen sich nur verhindern, wenn entweder eine freiwillige oder eine erzwungene Zurücknahme von Nachfrageplänen die Lücke zwischen Produktionsmöglichkeiten und gesamtwirtschaftlicher Nachfrage schließt. In einer solchen Situation kann der Staat, der ja selbst mit seiner Nachfrage nach Investitionsgütern (Schulgebäude, Straßenbauten) oder nach öffentlichem Konsum (Käufe für die Verwaltung, Bildungseinrichtungen, Bundeswehr) eine wichtige Größe in der gesamtwirtschaftlichen Nachfrage darstellt, durch Kürzung seiner Ausgabenpläne den Preisauftrieb verhindern oder verlangsamen.

Darüber hinaus kann er versuchen, die Nachfragepläne der privaten Wirtschaftssubjekte dadurch zu beeinflussen, daß er ihnen eine höhere Steuerbelastung auferlegt und damit das verfügbare Einkommen bzw. die Nettogewinne verringert. Dies kann er durch höhere Steuersätze, so z. B. im Fall der Lohn- und Einkommensteuer oder durch Änderung der Bemessungsgrundlagen, so z. B. im Fall der Veränderung des Abschreibungsmodus für Investitionen, erreichen. Legt er die so erhaltenen Steuereinnahmen bei der Bundesbank still, dämpft er nicht nur die Nachfrage, sondern er entzieht dem Wirtschaftskreislauf auch Liquidität, d. h. er verkleinert die Geldmenge.

---

* Wolfgang Ströbele, *Inflation: Einführung in Theorie und Politik* (R. Oldenbourg)

Text VI
Cyclical Budgeting

The idea that inflation can be combated through variations in government expenditure and government receipts is based on the demand-pull model of inflation. According to this model, inflation is mainly due to an excess of demand over supply. The only way to prevent the resultant price increases is to bridge the gap between potential production and overall economic demand by means of a voluntary or compulsory cancellation of demand projects. In a situation of this kind, the Government can prevent or slow down the upsurge in prices by putting a lid on spending. After all, owing to its demand for capital goods (schools and roads) or public consumption (sales contracts for public administration, educational establishments or the Federal German Armed Forces), the Government itself plays an important rôle in determining overall economic demand.

In addition to retrenching expenses, the Government may attempt to influence the demand projects of private economic subjects through higher taxation, thereby paring down their disposable income or net profits as the case may be. The State can attain this object by putting up tax rates, as in the case of income tax, for instance, or by modifying the bases of assessment, as in the case of alterations in the system of granting investment allowances, for example. If the Government immobilizes the tax receipts obtained in this way by placing them on special deposit at the Bundesbank, it not only curbs demand, but also withdraws liquid resources from the economy, i. e. it tightens up the money supply.

———————→

Annotations and Alternatives

① **Antizyklische Haushaltspolitik.**

a) Annotations

1. Antizyklische: Headlines should be as succinct as possible. *Tending to counteract the effect of the business cycle* (*G/C*) would be much too long for a headline.

2. Haushaltspolitik: The plural (*budgetary policies* (*LEW*)) is preferable to the singular since the headline refers to budgetary policies in general.

b) Alternatives

Cyclical	*Budgeting*	
Anticyclical	*Budgetary*	*Policies*
Anti-cyclical	*Budget*	"
Countercyclical	*Budgetary*	*Practices*
Contracyclical	"	"

② **Die Variation von Staatsausgaben und -einnahmen zur Inflationsbekämpfung geht von dem Nachfragesoginflationsmodell aus.**

a) Annotations

1. Die Variation ... Inflationsbekämpfung: A literal translation would sound unduly abstract and obscure. Augmentation is needed since *variation* alone cannot support two successive noun-centred prepositional phrases followed by a verb and yet another prepositional phrase. Besides, *variation* as a *nomen actionis* does not collocate well with *to be based on* (= ausgehen von). Collocational abnormality can be avoided by making the factive noun *idea* the subject of the sentence. This results in a clause-structure shift that entails a number of class-shifts. Several distinct formal operations have to be performed sequentially in order to generate the terminal string in the target language. First, the nominal groups *Die Variation von Staatsausgaben und -einnahmen* and *zur Inflationsbekämpfung* are reduced to their respective deep structures:

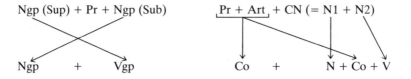

Ngp = nominal group; Sup = superordinate; Sub = subordinate; Pr = preposition; Vgp = verbal group; Art = article; CN = compound noun; N = noun; Co = conjunction; V = verb.

These abstract constructs may be translated into German as follows:

Die Variation von Staatsausgaben und -einnahmen

Staatsausgaben und -einnahmen werden variiert.

zur Inflationsbekämpfung

um Inflation zu bekämpfen

Second, formal correspondences are established between the source language and the target language by means of quasi-literal rank-bound translation:
Public spending and public revenue are varied
in order to combat inflation

Third, an embedding transformation is applied to the intermediate string *public spending and public revenue are varied in order to combat inflation*. In other words, the intermediate string is converted into an appositive clause whose head is the factive abstract noun *idea*. *Idea* is now the grammatical subject of the matrix sentence; and the link between the embedded sentence and the matrix sentence in provided by the subordinating conjunction *that*:

The idea that public spending and public revenue are
varied in order to combat inflation

Fourth, we must make a number of permutations in order to explicate certain ideas which are implicit in the German sentence. The 'variations' referred to in the German original are potential rather than actual, i. e. the author is merely referring to the *possibility* of varying public spending and public revenue. In order to take account of this nuance, we must therefore insert some form of the modal auxiliary *can* or use some equivalent phrase such as *it is possible to*.

The insertion of such lexical elements entails yet another alteration. Strictly speaking, two possibilities are referred to: the possibility of varying public spending and public revenue, and the possibility of combating inflation by such measures. The fight against inflation is the end, and the varying of public spending and public revenue is the means by which this end is to be achieved. The context requires that thematic and focal prominence be given to the end rather than the means, so it is advisable to mention the end before the means. For easy reference, we may use the symbol E for the syntagma denoting the end, and the symbol M for the syntagma denoting the means. M is subordinated to E by means of the preposition *through*[1], and the potential aspect of the

---

[1] Cf. the following quotation from J. A. Trevithick, *Inflation*, p. 77: '(...) aggregate demand can most effectively be regulated through variations in the size or rate of change of the money stock.'

resultant complex is expressed by the use of *can* or *it is possible to* (denoted by the symbol P (= potentiality)). The structure of the terminal string in the target language may therefore be represented diagrammatically as follows:

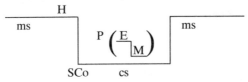

ms = matrix sentence; cs = constituent sentence (= embedded sentence); H = head of appositive clause; SCo = subordinating conjunction; P = word or phrase expressing potentiality; E = syntagma denoting the end; M = syntagma denoting the means
N. B. Syntactical subordination is indicated by vertical straights.

2. Staatsausgaben: A wide variety of alternatives is given in the bilingual dictionaries. Usage differs considerably, yet at present *public spending* and *government expenditure* seem to be gaining popularity at the expense of the other expressions recorded in the dictionaries:

U.S. politics is now coming into a profoundly interesting time as the traditional ideas about public spending are suddenly ordered to stand up and account for themselves. (*World and Press,* 1st March issue 1981, p. 1.)

In September de Gaulle's young finance minister, Valéry Giscard d'Estaing, launched an austerity plan that involved a credit squeeze, a wage and price freeze and severe curbs on public spending. (J. Ardagh, *The New France,* p. 34.)

One running cause of union discontent over the years has been the Government's choice of priorities for public spending (. . .). (*ibid.,* p. 76.)

In his classic pamphlet *How to Pay for the War* (1940), Keynes addressed himself to one central problem: how to finance the government expenditure and private investment necessary for the successful completion of the war effort while at the same time avoiding the evils of inflation. (J. A. Trevithick/C. Mulvey, *The Economics of Inflation,* p. 17.)

However, the evidence presented here is, by necessity, inconclusive.

3. und -einnahmen: In the bilingual dictionaries, *Staatseinnahmen* has been rendered as *public* (or *national*) *revenue, state revenue, revenue,* etc. The term *government receipts* has been overlooked:

Fiscal policy is the deliberate manipulation of the relation between government expenditure and government receipts with a view to manoeuvring the level of aggregate demand in the desired direction. (J. A. Trevithick, *Inflation,* p. 78.)

Note that Trevithick has repeated the modifier *government* in order to avoid ambiguity.

4. Inflationsbekämpfung: This compound noun may often be rendered nominally as *fight against inflation*. In this case, however, it is preferable to use a verb phrase such as *battle inflation, combat inflation* or *fight inflation*. Examples:

(. . .) we believe that such policies can play an important role in combating inflation provided that they are part of a larger package. (J. A. Trevithick/C. Mulvey, *The Economics of Inflation,* p. 170.)

(. . .) "you can mark that on your calendar as a black day for fighting inflation." (*Time,* 12. 11. 1979, p. 63.)

The phrase *fight inflation* has not yet found its way into the dictionaries.

5. geht von . . . aus: The equivalents offered in the bilingual dictionaries are only marginally possible in this particular instance.

6. Nachfragesoginflationsmodell: This compound, which does not appear in the dictionaries, may be rendered as *demand-pull model of inflation* or *demand-inflation model*. The expression *model of inflation* is much more common than *inflation model*, except in compounds such as *demand-inflation model*, whose constituent parts fit together like a set of cylinders that slide into one another:

demand-inflation + inflation model > demand- inflation model

Here are some examples of the expression *model of inflation:*
Lastly, the remarkably complete dynamic model of inflation of Hansen, which has been much neglected, is outlined. (J. A. Trevithick/C. Mulvey, *The Economics of Inflation*, p. 7.)
(. . .) the expectations hypothesis is introduced to complete the excess demand/expectations model of inflation. (*ibid.*, p. 41.)
The latter model therefore is quite consistent with the two-gap macroeconomic model of inflation. (*ibid.*, p. 83.)
For the locution *demand-inflation model*, cp. A. J. Hagger, *Inflation: Theory and Policy* (p. 44):
Demand-inflation models are models whose data consist exclusively of 'demand' variables (. . .).
The use of italics in Hagger's text shows that the link between the elements *inflation* and *demand* is felt to be stronger than the link between *inflation* and *model*.
The locution *demand-pull model* (Hagger, *op. cit., ibid.*) would be somewhat inappropriate in our text since it is not sufficiently explicit.
Note that the terms *demand inflation* and *demand-pull inflation* are interchangeable.
(. . .) demand inflation is due to the *pull* on prices as output is insufficient to meet the total claims which are being made on it (. . .). (P. Donaldson, *Guide to the British Economy*, p. 203.)
(. . .) it is not 'demand' or 'demand-pull' inflation that has been the real trouble, but 'cost' or 'cost-push' inflation. (M. Stewart, *Keynes and After*, p. 215.)

b) Alternatives

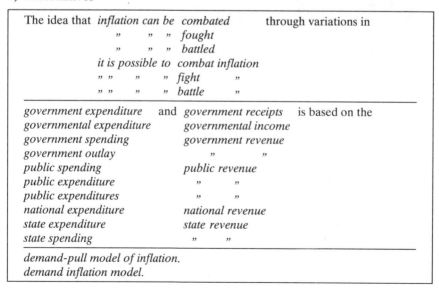

> **③** Die Inflation entsteht demnach primär aus einem Nachfrageüberhang.

a) Annotations

1. demnach: In bilingual dictionaries this adverb is sometimes rendered as *according to this* or *according to that*. In this case, however, it is advisable to replace the deictics *this* or *that* by a more specific phrase such as *this model* in order to eke out the sense of *demnach*.

2. Nachfrageüberhang: *Buyers over* would be inappropriate here since it is a Stock Exchange term for a situation where there are more buyers than sellers. Cf. M. Greener, *The Penguin Dictionary of Commerce*, s.v. buyers over.

b) Alternatives

According to this model, inflation is	*mainly* *chiefly* *primarily* *principally*	*due to* *caused by*	*an* *"* *a*	*excess* *excess* *surplus*
of demand over supply. *of demand.* *demand.*				

> **④** Die dadurch ausgelösten Preissteigerungen lassen sich nur verhindern, wenn entweder eine freiwillige oder eine erzwungene Zurücknahme von Nachfrageplänen die Lücke zwischen Produktionsmöglichkeiten und gesamtwirtschaftlicher Nachfrage schließt.

a) Annotations

1. dadurch ausgelösten: These two words may be rendered by a single lexical unit in English: *resultant*.

2. lassen sich nur verhindern, wenn . . .: A clause-structure shift is the best course here. A quasi-literal translation would be grammatical, but lifeless.

3. entweder . . . oder: Correlative conjunctions are used more often in German than in English. As has already been pointed out in the introductory chapter, German academic prose tends to be overtly rhetorical and heavily Latinate, while English prose is generally more direct, relaxed and spontaneous. It follows therefore that sophisticated linking devices such as correlative conjunctions must often be rendered by simple coordinating conjunctions in English.

4. erzwungene: The adjective *compulsory* sounds much more natural than a past participle such as *compelled*. It should be noted that the past participle of the verb *compel* is hardly ever used adjectivally. The past participle of *coerce*, however, may be used adjectivally with a noun such as *confession*. Cp. *WNCD*, s.v. throw out.

5. Produktionsmöglichkeiten: The term *production facilities* is contextually impermissible since *Produktionsmöglichkeiten* is here used in an abstract sense. The collective plural noun *facilities* generally denotes concrete objects. There is no precise translation equivalent in German. Examples:

Transport facilities: Transportwesen. (W. Friedrich, *Technik des Übersetzens*, p. 44.)
Language Laboratory facilities (title of a book by H. S. Hayes.)
Liverpool already has extensive roll-on/roll-off facilities[2] (for loaded vehicles) and packaged timber berths. (from a publication of the Central Office of Information, London 1968, quoted by Wolf Friedrich in *Lebende Sprachen*, No. 3/May–June 1969, p. 66.)
A few days later an official letter was handed to me and the morning after I introduced myself to many turbulent fellows whose aspects and manners soon convinced me that I would not be able to endure the life of the Beaux Arts, and that the facilities[3] the schools afforded were not those I sought for. (George Moore, *Confessions of a Young Man*, p. 11.)
Working in Istanbul with limited library facilities, he [*sc.* Auerbach] was increasingly forced back to concentrate on the texts themselves (. . .). (Graham Hough, *Style and Stylistics*, p. 69.)

It is interesting to compare Hough's formulation with Auerbach's own words:

Dazu kommt noch, daß die Untersuchung während des Krieges in Istanbul geschrieben wurde. Hier gibt es keine für europäische Studien gut ausgestattete Bibliothek; die internationalen Verbindungen stockten, so daß ich auf fast alle Zeitschriften, auf die meisten neueren Untersuchungen, ja zuweilen selbst auf eine zuverlässige kritische Ausgabe meiner Texte verzichten mußte. (Erich Auerbach, *Mimesis*, p. 518.)

The sentence *Hier gibt es (. . .) Bibliothek* could be rendered into English with the aid of the word *facilities:* 'Here there are no proper library facilities for European studies'.

6. gesamtwirtschaftlicher: English lacks a term of such wide application as the adjective *gesamtwirtschaftlich*, so that while *gesamtwirtschaftliche Nachfrage* may be translated as *overall economic demand (E)*, the expression *der gesamtwirtschaftliche Ablauf* must be rendered as *the general functioning of the economy (D/R*, p. 52). For further examples see *G/C*, s.v. gesamtwirtschaftlich.

b) Alternatives

The only way to *prevent* *forestall*	the resultant	*price increases* *rise in prices* *advance in prices* *enhancement in prices* *appreciation in prices* *price advances* *increase in prices* *price rises*	is to	*bridge* *close* *fill*
the gap between *potential production* *production possibilities*		and overall economic demand		
by means of a voluntary or compulsory cancellation of demand projects.				

---

[2] (Anlagen für) kranlose Verladung bzw. Direktverladung.
[3] Studienmöglichkeiten.

> (5) In einer solchen Situation kann der Staat, der ja selbst mit seiner Nachfrage nach Investitionsgütern (Schulgebäude, Straßenbauten) oder nach öffentlichem Konsum (Käufe für die Verwaltung, Bildungseinrichtungen, Bundeswehr) eine wichtige Größe in der gesamtwirtschaftlichen Nachfrage darstellt, durch Kürzung seiner Ausgabenpläne den Preisauftrieb verhindern oder verlangsamen.

a) **Annotations**

1. In einer ... verlangsamen: This is a fairly typical example of Latin-based German academic prose. A lengthy and cumbersome relative clause (*der ja ... darstellt*) is embedded inside a comparatively short main clause. This type of sentence-structure detracts from the readability of the passage, for we are in danger of losing the train of thought begun in the superordinate clause. As we have already seen, the English generally prefer shorter-winded loosely jointed speech-based sentence-structures; so we shall do well to split the German sentence into two independent statements before attempting a translation into English. Our first English sentence will be based on the main clause, and our second sentence will be based on the dependent clause.

2. mit: *Owing to* is more precise than *with*. Yet this is not the only reason why *owing to* is preferable to *with* in this particular case. *Owing to* (a synonym of *because of*) usually occupies front-position, and it may therefore be followed by two or three nominal groups. The preposition *with,* on the other hand, indicates a relationship which is both causal and instrumental. It expresses a shade of meaning which cannot be fully conveyed by locutions such as *owing to, because of* or *by means of.* When *with* is used in this particular sense, it is normally placed after the sentence subject, and can only be followed by a relatively short nominal group since the English are chary of inserting long strings of words between the subject and its verb. Cp. the following example from an article by A. Knight in the *Saturday Review* (issue dated 4 October 1969, p. 34):

(...) the film with its broader canvas, vividly contrasts the aseptic, impersonal manipulations of Britain's blundering High Command with the miseries and horrors of trench warfare in World War I.

It should however be noted that *with* (used to indicate cause) often occupies initial position when it is followed by a participial phrase or a verbless word-group corresponding to a causal clause containing the copula *to be.* Cf. the examples given in W. Friederich, *Technik des Übersetzens,* pp. 138–139.

The use of the locutions *owing to* and *due to* also calls for a few remarks. Despite objections raised by orthodox grammarians, *due to* is now commonly employed as a synonym of *owing to* on both sides of the Atlantic. Some liberal-minded linguists have recently taken up the cudgels on behalf of the offending usage, yet dyed-in-the-wool purists stoutly affirm that it is quite wrong to use the adjectival phrase *due to* as a compound preposition introducing an adverb phrase of reason. Traditional usage is rapidly losing ground, but there is still plenty of room for debate on this point. An orthodox viewpoint has been adopted by F. T. Wood, W. Strunk and E. B. White. Cp. F. T. Wood, *English Prepositional Idioms* (s.v. due); F. T. Wood, *Current English Usage* (s.v. due to); W. Strunk/E. B. White, *The Elements of Style* (p. 45). A moderately liberal stance has been adopted by Sir Ernest Gowers in *The Complete Plain Words* (pp. 187–189) and *Fowler's Modern English Usage* (s.v. due to). Professor Frank Palmer has ducked the issue (*Grammar,* p. 14), but it is quite clear that he inclines to permissiveness in matters of usage. Brian Foster and Rudolph Flesch have come out quite openly in favour of the prepositional use of *due to* (Cp. B. Foster, *The Changing English Language* (p. 226); R. Flesch, *The ABC of Style*, s.v. *due to* and *owing to*). Professor Foster, who is a first-rate stylist, has even gone the length of conforming to the offending usage:

Probably due to the inventiveness of some unknown journalist, the English abbreviation rapidly established itself in our vocabulary (. . .). (B. Foster, *The Changing English Language*, p. 110.)

Personally, I am still a trifle reluctant to give *de facto* recognition to the prepositional use of *due to*, especially since the traditional distinction between *owing to* and *due to* is still observed by many careful exponents of the language. It is therefore a moot point whether foreign students of English should be advised to follow the new trend.

3. (Schulgebäude, Straßenbauten): In this case the word *Schulgebäude* should not be rendered as *school-houses* or *school buildings* since the author is here referring to government spending projects in general rather than to specific buildings considered as physical objects. In this kind of context, the more abstract word *schools* is clearly the best translation. *Straßenbauten* might be rendered as *road building projects (LGS)*, but *roads* is a better translation because the use of the phrase *road building projects* in conjunction with the noun *schools* would produce a somewhat lopsided word-group. The syntagma *schools and roads* is much more pleasing to the ear because both the nouns are monosyllables, so that the balance of ideas is reinforced by a balance in sound. For the use of the words *schools* and *roads* in an economic context, cp. the following quotation from a book by John Ardagh (*The New France*, p. 76):

It [sc. the *force de frappe*] is eating up funds that could better be spent on schools, houses, roads, hospitals.

In this sentence, Ardagh's use of asyndeton has a rhetorical effect rather like that produced by aposiopesis. The author breaks off suddenly in the middle of a list as if to suggest that there is no need for him to multiply his examples any further. However, it is worth while noting that asyndetic coordination is much less common in English than in German. It is advisable to insert the conjunction *and* between the nouns *schools* and *roads*. For further discussion of asyndetic coordination, the reader is referred to G. Collier/B. Shields, *Guided German-English Translation*, pp. 151–2.

4. (. . .Bildungseinrichtungen, Bundeswehr): The last two elements in the list should be joined by the conjunction *or*. Cf. the preceding note on asyndetic constructions.

5. eine wichtige Größe . . . darstellt: The metaphoring conventions of the SL and the TL are out of phase. In English, the figurative use of the mathematical term *quantity* is generally restricted to the expression *an unknown quantity*. In this particular instance, the mathematical metaphor may be replaced by a theatrical metaphor (*play a rôle/part*).

6. in der gesamtwirtschaftlichen Nachfrage: English tends to strain prepositions in much the same way as German. In this case, however, English prefers greater explicitness of expression. A word for word translation would be unduly obscure. The simplest solution is to insert an *ing*-form (*determining*) between the preposition *in* and the nominal group *overall demand*.

7. durch Kürzung seiner Ausgabenpläne: This word-group may be rendered in various ways.

It may be translated quite freely by the idiomatic expression *put a lid on spending* (cf. Ivan de Renty, *Lexique quadrilingue des affaires*, p. 548). In present-day English, *lid* is often used figuratively to express the idea of restraint. Cf. the following example from *World and Press* (December 1979, p. 1):

President Carter deserves both praise and support for keeping the lid on an excruciatingly difficult situation.

Other possible free variants are *by means of a retrenchment policy* (cf. Ivan de Renty, *op. cit., ibid.*) and *by retrenching expenses* (cf. H. W. Klein/W. Friederich, *Englische Synonymik*, s.v. abkürzen).

A more literal translation would also be acceptable: *through cuts in its expenditure plans*. *Cut* in the sense of *reduction* is now fully acclimatized in Britain although it was originally a neologism imported from the United States during the financial and economic crisis of 1931 (cf. H. W. Horwill, *A Dictionary of Modern American Usage*, p. viii).

Finally, in order to make the sentence run more easily, we may also use a gerundial construction (*by making cuts . . .*). For the collocation *make + cut,* cf. Friederich/Canavan, *DEWC*, s.v. cut.

The term *Ausgabenpläne*, which has been overlooked by most lexicographers, may be rendered as *spending plans, spending projects* or *expenditure plans:*

The European Commission is to discuss today proposals to create a special fund within the EEC budget to pay for spending projects in Britain. (*FT,* 30. 1. 1980. p. 1.)

This hypothesis introduces an asymmetry into the expenditure plans of different groups. (J. A. Trevithick/C. Mulvey, *The Economics of Inflation,* p. 21.)

b) Alternatives

In a situation	*of this kind,* *like this,*	the	*Government* *State*	can prevent or
slow down *retard* *delay*	the	*upsurge in prices* *price upsurge* *uptrend in prices* *price uptrend* *price upcreep* *upward price trend*	*by putting a lid on spending.* *by means of a retrenchment policy.* *by retrenching expenses.* *through cuts in its spending plans.* „ „ „ „ *spending projects.* „ „ „ „ *expenditure plans.* *by making cuts in its spending plans.* „ „ „ „ *spending projects.* „ „ „ „ *expenditure plans.*		
After all, owing to its demand for			*capital goods* (schools and roads) *investment goods* *producers' goods* *fixed-capital goods*	
or public consumption (sales contracts for public administration,				
educational „ „	*establishments* *institutions* *services*	or the Federal German Armed Forces),		
the Government itself plays an	*important* *essential* *vital* *considerable*	*rôle in determining overall*		
economic demand.				

> ⑥ Darüber hinaus kann er versuchen, die Nachfragepläne der privaten Wirtschaftssubjekte dadurch zu beeinflussen, daß er ihnen eine höhere Steuerbelastung auferlegt und damit das verfügbare Einkommen bzw. die Nettogewinne verringert.

a) Annotations

1. **Darüber hinaus:** Owing to the divergencies between the German and English sequencing patterns in sentence (5), it is necessary to resort to augmentation here in order to establish a closer link with the idea expressed in the sequence *the Government can prevent . . . lid on spending.*

2. **er:** It is advisable to use a noun in order to achieve greater clarity.

3. **kann:** *May* should be used instead of *can* since *kann* here expresses possibility rather than ability. Cf. R. B. Farrell, *Dictionary of German Synonyms*, pp. 217–218; A. Lamprecht, *Grammatik der englischen Sprache*, § 453.

4. **eine höhere Steuerbelastung:** If *Steuerbelastung* is rendered as *taxation*, *höhere* should be rendered as *increased*. If *Steuerbelastung* is rendered as *tax burden* or *tax load*, *höhere* should be rendered as *heavier* in order to avoid a mixed metaphor. *Increased taxation* is more idiomatic than *heavier tax burden*.

5. **daß er ihnen . . . auferlegt:** The sentence structure may be simplified by the use of a prepositional phrase: *through increased taxation.*

6. **und damit . . . verringert:** Participle clauses are often used to indicate logical or causal sequence when two verbs stand in similar relation to a common sentence subject. In such cases the connectives *thereby, thus* and *so* are used without the conjunction *and:*

He can live a life of ease and splendor as a friend of the local establishment, or he can write the story as he sees it, thereby inviting exclusion from all fashionable dinner parties, continual nasty harassment and possible exile. (R. Flesch, *The ABC of Style,* s.v. thereby.)
The choir division normally speaks from the chancel area, and the echo division from the rear of the nave, thus providing an antiphonal effect. (*ibid.,* s.v. thus.)
American scholarship has seen to the publication of her letters and of her biography, so increasing sympathy with her personality and enhancing respect for the range of her mental capacity. (Ifor Evans, *A Short History of English Literature,* p. 246.)

In these example sentences, finite verb forms are used to express causes, while present participles are used to express effects. Sometimes, however, the connectives (*thereby, thus* and *so*) are dispensed with, and the cause-and-effect relationship remains implicit, as in the following example from Leon T. Dickinson, *A Guide to Literary Study* (p. 29.):

(. . .) more commonly it [*sc.* theme] is only implied, requiring the reader to infer it.

In *The ABC of Style* (pp. 276, 278–280), R. Flesch suggests that the connectives *thereby* and *thus* should be banished altogether from contemporary English because they seem 'stiff' and 'bookish'. Here, as in many other cases, Flesch's views are unduly extreme and dogmatic. When no participles are used, it may even be advisable to insert a connective such as *hence* in order to draw attention to a cause-and-effect relationship:

The justification for studying literature in a college class is that such study can help us to read more perceptively, and hence increase our understanding and enjoyment of what we read. (Leon T. Dickinson, *A Guide to Literary Study,* p. 6.)

Such details will not individualize a character, but they put him in a group, and hence set him off from many other people. (*ibid.*, p. 15.)

Hence, of course, is another of those 'bookish' words which Mr Flesch has pilloried in *The ABC of Style.*

It should be noted that participle clauses are normally avoided when verbs do not stand in the same relation to a common sentence subject. Cf. the following example from A. W. Verity's edition of Shakespeare's *King Lear* (p. xxii):

Edmund indeed passes from the one sphere of crime to the other and thus forms the main connection between the two plots.

In this example sentence, the verb *passes* denotes an action performed by Edmund, while the verb *forms* merely serves to express Verity's opinion about the function which Edmund fulfils in the play. It would therefore be inadvisable to substitute *thus forming* for *and thus forms.*

7. verringert: In contemporary English there is a marked tendency to replace abstract verbs such as *reduce* or *diminish* by concrete verbs such as *pare down* or *whittle down:*

The committee have pared his travelling allowance down to the bare minimum. (A. P. Cowie/R. Mackin, *Oxford Dictionary of Current Idiomatic English,* Vol. 1, s.v. pare down.)
The Community content was therefore whittled down. (D. Swann, *The Economics of the Common Market,* p. 108.)

b) Alternatives

In addition to retrenching expenses, the	*Government* *State*	may	*attempt* *try* *endeavour* *make an attempt* *„ „ effort.*
to *influence* *bring its influence to bear on*	the demand projects of private economic subjects		
through higher taxation,	*thereby* *thus* *so*	*paring down* *whittling down* *cutting down* *reducing* *diminishing*	their *disposable* *personal* *discretionary*
income or net *profits* *„ gains* *„ earnings*	as the case may be.		

⑦ Dies kann er durch höhere Steuersätze, so z. B. im Fall der Lohn- und Einkommensteuer oder durch Änderung der Bemessungsgrundlagen, so z. B. im Fall der Veränderung des Abschreibungsmodus für Investitionen, erreichen.

a) Annotations

1. Dies kann er . . . erreichen: Unlike German, English has already shed most of its inflexional endings, so that the principles of English word-order are comparatively rigid. As everyone knows, the normal order in a declarative sentence is: subject, verb and object. However, in choice language, the object occasionally heads the sentence:
(i) This I know. (G. O. Curme, *English Grammar*, p. 104.)
(ii) Much of what you say I agree with, but I cannot go all the way with you. (F. T. Wood, *English Verbal Idioms*, s.v. go all the way.)
(iii) The last two items on the agenda we will hold over until the next meeting. (*ibid.*, s.v. hold over.)
(iv) A chronicle of literary events, which seeks to show not only what happened but why it happened, we call a literary history. (Leon T. Dickinson, *A Guide to Literary Study*, p. 3.)
(v) Stories that render faithfully these outward circumstances of life we call *realistic* because they are true to reality (. . .). (*ibid.*, p. 12.)
(vi) (. . .) certain selected recesses of experience he explores very well (. . .). (E. M. Forster, *Aspects of the Novel*, p. 148.)
In all these sentences, the object has been put in initial position for reasons of emphasis. Sentence (ii) provides a good example of the artifice known as chiasmus. No ambiguity can arise since in each sentence the subject is a personal pronoun whose nominative and accusative forms are easily distinguishable (*I/me, we/us, he/him*). Besides, the subject invariably precedes the verb. Noun objects rarely occupy front-position except in highly formal usage. Cf. the following example from G. M. Trevelyan, *English Social History* (p. 57):
One branch of their duties, the proper control of the Spiritual Courts, the bishops neglected with unfortunate results.

In the case under consideration, however, the subject should be placed at the beginning of the sentence in order to avoid incongruity of style.

2. Dies: It is advisable to resort to augmentation here in order to make the sense quite clear.

3. kann: In this particular instance, *kann* should be rendered as *can* since it expresses ability rather than possibility. Cp. note (6) 3 above.

4. er: We may use a noun for added clarity.

5. höhere: In order to enhance the symmetry of the sentence, we may render both the adjective *höhere* and the noun *Änderung* as *-ing* forms. It is, of course, possible to render *höhere Steuersätze* by *higher taxation*.

6. Lohn- und Einkommensteuer: *Lohnsteuer* is levied on wages and salaries, *Einkommensteuer* on all other income. However, the two terms overlap to a certain extent. *Einkommensteuer* is often employed as a superordinate of *Lohnsteuer*.
Lexicographers have suggested a wide range of translation equivalents for *Lohnsteuer*: *wages tax, wage tax, tax on wages, tax on salary, tax on wages or salary*, etc. *Lohnsteuer* does not exist in Great Britain or the United States, so that English lacks a standard lexical item with a correspondingly restricted range of contextual meaning. Here we have to do with the problem of oligosemy.
Einkommensteuer, on the other hand, is wider in application than the English term *income tax*. *Einkommensteuern* are sometimes deemed to include *Kirchensteuer* and

the like. Cf. the notes on *Einkommensteuer* in C. A. Gunston/C. M. Corner, *Deutsch-Englisches Glossarium finanzieller und wirtschaftlicher Fachausdrücke* and R. Renner/ R. Sachs, *Wirtschaftssprache. Deutsch/Englisch. Englisch/Deutsch*. Here we have to do with the problem of polysemy.

For a discussion of the translation problems posed by polysemy and oligosemy see J. C. Catford, *A Linguistic Theory of Translation*, pp. 94—98; F. R. Palmer, *Semantics*, pp. 76—78; S. Pit Corder, *Introducing Applied Linguistics*, pp. 72—74. For a very brief simplified account of the German system of taxation see K. C. Horton, *German Economic Extracts*, p. 62. For information on the British system of taxation prior to 1975 see J. Rudolph, *Langenscheidts Handbuch der englischen Wirtschaftssprache*, pp. 90—94. For information on recent changes in the British system see *La nouvelle économie anglaise*, pp. 201—202; Wilfried Kratz, 'Die eiserne Lady setzt Rost an', *Die Zeit*, 29. 2. 1980, p. 17.[4]

In the case under consideration, the English term *income tax* can be used to render *Lohn- und Einkommensteuer*.

7. Bemessungsgrundlage: Several equivalents have been suggested: *basis of taxation, basis of assessment, basis of valuation, tax base, assessment base, basis of computation, basis for determination (of amount payable), determination basis, assessment basis*. The commonest term in British English is doubtless *basis of assessment*. Cf. the following quotations from the *Daily Mail Income Tax Guide 1968—1969*:

For each of the two previous tax years the normal basis of assessment is the profits of the preceding year. (p. 40.)

In the early years of ownership of every new source of income and in the closing years special bases of assessment apply. (p. 68.)

8. im Fall der Veränderung: In this particular instance it is impossible to render *Veränderung* as an *-ing* form. *In the case of* is invariably followed by a noun. Cf. the following example from the *Daily Mail Income Tax Guide 1968—1969* (p. 45):

The investment allowance ceased to be available for expenditure incurred on and after January 17th, 1966, except in the case of certain contracts entered into before this date.

Veränderung should be rendered by a plural since it refers to alterations in general rather than to one particular alteration.

9. Abschreibungsmodus für Investitionen: This expression, which has not yet been recorded in the dictionaries, may be rendered as *the system of granting investment allowances*. Cf. the following quotation from the *Daily Mail Income Tax Guide 1968—1969* (p. 48):

The system of granting investment allowances was discontinued for expenditure incurred on and after January 17th, 1966, and replaced, in part, by the provision of investment grants.

Only the expression *Abschreibung für Investitionen* (investment allowance) has been recorded in *Der kleine Eichborn*.

---

[4] The relevant passage has been reprinted in J. D. Gallagher, *Cours de Traduction allemand-français*, p. 134.

b) Alternatives

The State can	attain	this	object	by	putting up	tax rates,
	achieve	"	"		raising	rates of taxation,
	achieve	"	goal			rates of tax,
	attain	"	"			
	"	"	aim			
	"	"	purpose			
	"	"	end			
	achieve	"	"			

as in the case of income tax, *for instance,* or by *modifying* the bases of
for example, *changing*
assessment, as in the case of alterations in the system of granting
investment allowances, *for example.*
for instance.

⑧ Legt er die so erhaltenen Steuereinnahmen bei der Bundesbank still, dämpft er nicht nur die Nachfrage, sondern er entzieht dem Wirtschaftskreislauf auch Liquidität, d. h. er verkleinert die Geldmenge.

a) Annotations

1. er: It is advisable to use a noun for added clarity. Cf. note (7) 4.

2. so: The phrase *in this way* must be placed after the past participle. *So* and *thus,* on the other hand, normally precede the past participle:

(. . .) all vowels not so marked are short (. . .). (L. Forster (ed.), *The Penguin Book of German Verse,* p. xli.)
Besides being thus diversified horizontally into regional dialects, the language is also diversified vertically, into class dialects. (K. E. Schuhmacher (ed.), *English-A World Language,* p. 30.)
(. . .) the disturbing resonance thus set up is expressive of his deepest sense of what life is like. (A. E. Dyson (ed.), *Dickens: Bleak House,* p. 234.)

3. erhaltenen: *Receive* and *obtain* are not interchangeable. *Receive* implies no effort on the part of the recipient. It simply means 'to take something offered into one's possession'. *Obtain,* on the other hand, means 'to gain possession of something by a conscious effort'. For example sentences, see H. W. Klein/W. Friederich, *Englische Synonymik,* s.v. bekommen.

4. bei der Bundesbank: In this case the preposition *bei* should be rendered as *at.* Cf. the following quotation from G. Bannock/R. E. Baxter/R. Rees, *The Penguin Dictionary of Economics* (p. 35):
Deposits at the central bank are regarded by the commercial banks as cash (. . .).
However, *at* is normally replaced by *with* when a noun such as *central bank* is replaced by the pronoun *it*:
By buying and selling securities in the open market (open-market operations), the central bank can directly affect the level of the commercial banks' deposits with it (. . .). (*ibid.*)

The term *Bundesbank* may conveniently be left untranslated. Cf. the following snippet from the *International Herald Tribune* of 3 October 1979 (p. 9):

The recent tensions in the European monetary system and in dollar-DM trading caused reserves to rise 9.5 billion DM from Bundesbank interventions in September compared to a 2.5-billion-DM drop in August, the Bundesbank said.

Federal Reserve Bank should be used only with reference to the U.S. banking system. The Federal Reserve Banks are twelve regional banks under the control of the Federal Reserve Board in Washington. Cf. J. Rudolph, *Langenscheidts Handbuch der englischen Wirtschaftssprache*, pp. 251–253; Robert C. Bingham, *Economic Concepts*, p. 195.

5. Legt ... still: *Geld stillegen* is normally translated as *immobilize, sterilize* or *neutralize money*. However, literal translation is hardly possible in the case of a wordgroup such as *Steuereinnahmen bei der Bundesbank stillegen*. Augmentation is needed. Cf. the translation of the phrase *Stillegung von Steuereinnahmen* in *G/C:* 'immobilisation of tax receipts (by placing them on special deposit at the Bundesbank).'

6. Liquidität: In this case a term such as *liquid resources* should be used in preference to *liquidity* since *Liquidität* is here used in a fairly concrete sense.

7. verkleinert: In this type of context the abstract verb *reduce* is often replaced by the metaphorical verb *tighten up*. Cf. the following quotation from *World and Press* (1st August issue 1981, p. 1):

On monetary policy she [*sc.* Mrs Thatcher] has striven to tighten up the money supply.

b) Alternatives

If the Government	*immobilizes* *sterilizes* *neutralizes*	the	*tax receipts* *tax returns* *tax revenue* *tax revenues* *revenue from taxation* *tax yield* *yield of taxes* *inland revenue* *internal revenue* (U.S.)			
obtained in this way *thus obtained* *so obtained*	by placing	*them* *it*	on special deposit at the			
Bundesbank, *Federal Bank,*	it not only curbs demand, but also withdraws liquid					
resources *assets* *funds* *means*	from	*the economy,* *economic circulation,*	i.e. it	*tightens up* *reduces*	the	*money* *money* *volume of*
supply. *stock.* *money in circulation.*						

Text VII*
Beschäftigung

Den ausgeprägten Schwankungen des Sozialproduktwachstums entsprechen gegenläufige Entwicklungen im Beschäftigungsgrad, d. h. im Auslastungsgrad der volkswirtschaftlichen Produktionskapazität. Als einen Teilindikator des Beschäftigungsgrades hatten wir die Arbeitslosenquote genannt. Ihren höchsten Stand erreicht die Arbeitslosenquote mit 30,5% (1932) in der Weltwirtschaftskrise. Ein Vergleich der jährlichen Wachstumsraten des realen BSP mit den jeweiligen Arbeitslosenquoten für die BRD zeigt, daß rückläufiges oder stagnierendes Wachstum mit relativ hohen Arbeitslosenquoten einhergeht (z. B. in der Weltwirtschaftskrise und den Rezessionen 1967 und 1974/75). In den 50er Jahren wird die konjunkturbedingte Beziehung zwischen Wachstumsgeschwindigkeit und Arbeitslosigkeit überlagert durch ein beträchtliches Maß von „struktureller" Arbeitslosigkeit, das im wesentlichen aus den Kriegsnachwirkungen resultiert. Insgesamt zeigt sich, daß mit der zunehmenden „Verstetigung" des wirtschaftlichen Wachstums in der Nachkriegszeit auch das Ausmaß der konjunkturell bedingten Arbeitslosigkeit zurückgeht. Zwischen 1960 und 1973 lag die Arbeitslosenquote bei durchschnittlich nur 1,0%. In der Rezession des Jahres 1974 stieg die Arbeitslosenquote allerdings auf 2,6%, im Jahre 1975 sogar auf 4,7% an.

In vielen Ländern sind aus verschiedenen Gründen höhere Arbeitslosenquoten zu beobachten (im wesentlichen strukturbedingt); z. B. lag die Arbeitslosenquote der USA in den letzten Jahren bei 5% bis 6%, im Jahre 1975 sogar bei 8,5%, wobei jedoch Unterschiede der statistischen Erfassung zu berücksichtigen sind.

---

* Wilhelm Henrichsmeyer, Oskar Gans, Ingo Evers, *Einführung in die Volkswirtschaftslehre* (Eugen Ulmer)

Text VII
Employment

The strongly marked fluctuations in the growth of the national product are correlated to contrary developments in the level of employment, i. e. in the extent to which the productive capacity of the economy is utilized. We have referred to the unemployment rate as a partial indicator of the level of employment. The unemployment rate reached an all-time peak of 30.5% (1932) during the Great Depression. A comparison of the annual growth rates of real GNP and the unemployment figures for West Germany during a given period shows that a decline or standstill in growth is the concomitant of relatively high unemployment rates (as in the Depression years and during the recessions of 1967 and 1974/75). In the fifties the cyclical relation between the rate of economic growth and unemployment was fogged over by a substantial measure of structural unemployment basically due to the aftermath of the War. On the whole there is evidence that the increasing stability of economic growth during the post-war period is coupled to a drop in cyclical unemployment. Between 1960 and 1973 the unemployment rate averaged a mere 1.0%. During the recession of 1974, however, the unemployment rate rose to 2.6%, shooting up to as much as 4.7% in 1975.

For various reasons, higher rates of unemployment may be observed in many countries (In most cases the unemployment is structural.); in recent years, for instance, the unemployment rate in the U.S.A. has ranged between 5% and 6%, rising to no less than 8.5% in 1975, though allowance must be made for differences in the ways statistical surveys have been made.

Annotations and Alternatives

Annotations

In this particular case, *Beschäftigung* must be rendered by *employment* since it means 'the state of being employed'. The use of the word *occupation* in this context would be an elementary blunder since *occupation* denotes the activity in which the person engages – *eine Beschäftigung* as opposed to *Beschäftigung* as an abstract economic term.

② Den ausgeprägten Schwankungen des Sozialproduktwachstums entsprechen gegenläufige Entwicklungen im Beschäftigungsgrad, d. h. im Auslastungsgrad der volkswirtschaftlichen Produktionskapazität.

a) Annotations

1. Den ... Sozialproduktwachstums: This syntagma refers back to the preceding section of the book from which this passage has been taken. The definite article (*Den*) should therefore be retained.

2. ausgeprägten: A wide variety of equivalents is given in the two-language dictionaries. In the present instance the most appropriate solutions are *marked, strongly marked* or *pronounced*. *Marked* and *pronounced* mean 'obvious', 'evident' or 'noticeable' (*markant, auffallend, deutlich hervortretend*). *Distinctive* would be unsuitable here since it means 'peculiar', 'individual', 'characteristic':

A language (...) may have lost most of its distinctive word-endings like modern English. (C. L. Wrenn, *The English Language*, p. 13.)

The adjective *distinct*, on the other hand, might be used in the present context, for *distinct* may signify 'recognizable' or 'definite' as in the phrase *a distinct improvement* (*CED*, s.v. distinct) or *two distinct collocational ranges* (J. C. Catford, *A Linguistic Theory of Translation*, p. 11). *Defined* in the sense of *deutlich hervortretend* is normally applied to concrete objects:

The hills were sharply defined against the sky. (*DEWC*, s.v. define.)

Decided is applied to phenomena whose reality is indisputable: *a decided victory or superiority* (*FMEU*) or *a decided drop in attendance* (*CED*). *Prominent* in the sense of *ausgeprägt* generally collocates with nouns denoting parts of the face (*cheekbones, chin*, etc.).

3. Schwankungen des Sozialproduktwachstums: In this instance, the German genitive must be rendered by the preposition *in*. Examples:

cyclical fluctuations in employment. (H. G. Grubel, *The International Monetary System*, p. 22.)
variations among occupational groups in political attitudes, life expectancy, interests, intelli-

gence, insanity, reading tastes, family size and standards of conduct. (D. Weir (ed.), *Men and Work in Modern Britain*, p. 19.)
variations in spelling forms. (*CED*, p. xix.)
variations in pronunciation. (*ibid.*, p. xxiii.)

Fluctuation and *variation* can enter into similar patterns, and they are equally acceptable in this context.

4. Sozialproduktwachstums: This kind of polysyllabic nonce word is typical of German academic prose, for scientific style tends to single-word classifications in its expositions and descriptions. Such coinages are by no means rare or impossible in English, and in recent years there has been a steady increase in the number of nonce words formed by the juxtaposition of existing terms. For example:

Who, for instance, has heard of a pro-co-generation lobby or an anti-conversion-loss lobby? (*RD*, July 1980, p. 81.)

Yet, on the whole, English does not manifest quite the same genius for compound associations as German, so the translator often has to interpret the German compounds and construct explanatory word sequences. Cf. the following quotation from *Reader's Digest* (August 1979, p. 98):

Their amendment (. . .) would limit federal spending increases to the growth in the Gross National Product.

In point of style *growth of* and *growth in* are equally acceptable. In our case, however, the preposition *in* is debarred by the proximity of *in* the preceding word-group (*fluctuations in*).

5. entsprechen: The bilingual dictionaries give a wide range of equivalents. The most appropriate solution in this particular case is *to be correlated to,* for the verb *correlate* implies a causal relationship between parallel developments. Cp. the use of the word *correlation* in the following quotation from a recent book edited by P. Hutber (*What's Wrong With Britain?*, p. 36):

(. . .) nor at the national level is there any correlation between expenditure on research and economic growth.

Note the differences between the grammatical patterns of the source language and the target language:

Den (. . .) Schwankungen (. . .) entsprechen (. . .) Entwicklungen (. . .)
[complement]   +   [verb]   +   [subject]
The fluctuations (. . .) are correlated to (. . .) developments (. . .)
[subject]   +   [verb phrase]   +   [complement]

The complement of the German sentence has become the subject of the English sentence, and vice versa, but the word-order and the basic meaning are the same in both cases.

6. Beschäftigungsgrad: *Rate of employment* is less common than *level of employment.* Examples:

The volume of physical goods and services available to a community, the level of employment, and the goods and services earned in exchange for work (the *real* wage) are all determined by the community's natural resources, physical capital and labour supply (. . .). (A. D. Bain, *The Control of the Money Supply*, p. 14.)

Prior to the Second World War, it was observed that capitalist economies were subject to regular patterns of expansion and contraction in the scale of output and hence in the level of employment. (J. A. Trevithick, *Inflation*, p. 10.)

7. d. h.: It is sometimes possible to replace *i.e.* by *meaning*. Cp. the following example from J. K. Galbraith, *The Affluent Society*, p. 122:

The immediate though not the ultimate cause of depression is a fall in the aggregate demand – meaning in the purchasing power available and being used – for buoying the output of the economy.

8. Auslastungsgrad: *Utilization* is clearly the best word for *Auslastung* in this particular case. Cp. K. Hawkins, *Unemployment*, p. 116:

By enabling firms to maintain a relatively high level of capacity-utilization, employment subsidies can contribute to lower unit costs and thus help firms to survive a recession.

We may repeat the word *level* (or *rate*) in order to underline the parallel between the concepts *Beschäftigungsgrad* and *Auslastungsgrad*.

9. der volkswirtschaftlichen Produktionskapazität: The adjective *volkswirtschaftlich* can be converted into a noun. Cp. the following quotation from J. A. Trevithick, *Inflation*, p. 10:

Provided the economy was not subjected to any further external shock such as war or famine, and provided that the government acted in a responsible manner by refraining from putting undue strain on the productive capacity of the economy, the price level would remain more or less stable.

The expression *productive capacity* has been overlooked by the dictionary makers, though it has been recorded in J. Rudolph, *Langenscheidts Handbuch der englischen Wirtschaftssprache* (p. 3). *Produktionskapazität* is sometimes rendered as *manufacturing capacity*, but this term would not do here because it is restricted to the mass production of finished or half-finished goods by machinery. *Production capacity* and *output capacity*, on the other hand, would be quite suitable in this context since they are terms of wide comprehension which may be used in reference to raw materials as well as processed goods.

b) Alternatives

The *strongly marked fluctuations* in the growth of the national
    marked   variations
    pronounced
    distinct

product are correlated to contrary developments in the *level of*
                                                                                     rate   "

employment, i. e.	in the	*extent to which*		the	*productive capacity of*	
"	– *meaning*	*level of utilization*	of	the	*productive capacity of*	
		rate of utilization	"	"	*production capacity*	"
		extent of utilization	"	"	*output capacity*	"
		degree of utilization	"	"	"	"	"

the economy is utilized.
the economy.

③ Als einen Teilindikator des Beschäftigungsgrades hatten wir die Arbeitslosenquote genannt.

a) Annotations

1. Teilindikator: The first element of this compound may be rendered by means of the adjective *partial*. The second element (*-indikator*) should be translated as *indicator* or *index*. Examples:

T. R. Saving: Monetary-Policy Targets and Indicators, in: *The Journal of Political Economy*, 75 (1967), pp. 446–65.
M. J. Hamburger: Indicators of Monetary Policy: The Arguments and the Evidence, in: *Monetary Aggregates and Monetary Policy,* Paper of the Federal Reserve Bank of New York, New York 1974, pp. 20–27.
Leading indicators call the turns of the business cycle – usually! (P. A. Samuelson, *Economics*, p. 250.)
The fertility of the land is an index of the country's wealth. (*WNCD*, s.v. index.)

In *Inflation: Theory and Policy*, A. J. Hagger discusses six *indexes* which may be used to measure inflation: the implicit deflator of G.N.P., the implicit deflator of non-farm G.N.P. at factor cost, etc. (pp. 5–11). He occasionally encloses the word *index* in quotation marks (p. 10) to remind the reader that the indexes referred to are neither alphabetical lists nor mathematical exponents.

2. hatten wir ... genannt: German authors frequently use the pluperfect when harking back to statements made in previous sections of a treatise. In such cases, English-speaking authors generally prefer the simple past tense or the present perfect. Examples:

We mentioned in 1.0 that our approach to the *levels* of language and linguistic analysis was somewhat different from that of Halliday (. . .). (J. C. Catford, *A Linguistic Theory of Translation*, p. 11.)
In the previous chapter we examined in general terms the factors which bear upon the determination of the money supply in a country (. . .). (A. D. Bain, *The Control of the Money Supply*, p. 51.)
We have already discussed the notion of a transactions demand for cash, and it can be extended to a wider group of financial assets. (*ibid.*, p. 154.)

The simple past tense is normally used with time indicators such as *in the previous chapter,* while the present perfect is normally used with adverbials such as *already.*
German writers have no qualms about leaping from the present to the pluperfect, while British and American authors are generally averse to such abrupt changes of tense. When they wish to direct their readers' thoughts backwards in time, they proceed step by step, from the present to the present perfect, from the present perfect to the past tense, and from the past tense to the past perfect. Thus, as a rule, the English past perfect is used only of an action or state anterior to the period in the past which is engaging our attention. Here are some typical examples from *Translation,* a recent novel by Stephen Marlowe:

He was at the top of his profession, and he hadn't got over the shock of Catherine's death. (p. 41.)
He'd had no qualms about sending her to France for the summer, and she returned, if anything, more radiant. (*ibid.*)
The sky had cleared, and a steady cold wind blew across the big Commons. (p. 43.)
She had almost decided to rejoin them when Craig let loose another whoop. (p. 51.)
Whatever it was had fallen into a patch of wild rose bushes. (p. 52.)

3. Arbeitslosenquote: In *Guided German-English Translation* (p. 39), G. Collier and B. Shields maintain that the only 'idiomatic' English equivalent of *Arbeitslosenquote* is *unemployment figure*. I should like to take Collier and Shields up on this point. It is beyond doubt that *unemployment figure* is perfectly acceptable English, yet it is obviously wrong to assert that all other variants must be rejected as 'unidiomatic'. Terms such as *unemployment ratio* and *jobless rate* are admittedly somewhat rare, yet *unemployment rate, level of unemployment* and *unemployment* (in the sense of *unemployment rate*) are all in common use. Examples:

In 1962, for example, an annual rise in output of 1.1 per cent was achieved with an official unemployment rate of 1·8 per cent. (K. Hawkins, *Unemployment*, p. 17.)
First, recession and inflation combined to push the unemployment rate to a 35-year high. (*RD*, November 1979, p. 161.)
Between 1921 and 1939 the average level of unemployment in Britain was 14% (. . .). (P. Donaldson, *Guide to the British Economy*, p. 153.)
Unemployment is over 20 percent. (*RD*, August 1979, p. 132.)
Unemployment was high (. . .). (*RD*, December 1979, p. 225.)

b) Alternatives

We have referred to	the	*unemployment rate*	as a	*partial*	*indicator*
	"	*rate of unemployment*		"	*index*
	"	*unemployment figure*			
	"	*level of unemployment*			
		unemployment			
	the	*unemployment ratio*			
	"	*jobless rate*			
of the	*level*	*of*	*employment.*		
	rate	"	"		

④ Ihren höchsten Stand erreicht die Arbeitslosenquote mit 30,5% (1932) in der Weltwirtschaftskrise.

a) Annotations

1. Ihren höchsten Stand: For idiomatic equivalents of this expression, see note (4) 3 below.

2. erreicht: In this particular case, the German present tense should be rendered by the English past tense. The historic present is less common in English than in German.

3. mit: In this type of phrase, the preposition *mit* cannot be rendered by *with*. Cp. the following example sentences:

Between 1967 and 1974 registered unemployment never fell below half a million and during the severe recession of 1975−8 it rose to a peak of 1·37 million (. . .). (K. Hawkins, *Unemployment*, p. 16.)
In the future, it [sc. the Third World labour force] will speed up to 2·1 per cent a year between 1980 and 1985, reaching an all-time peak of 2.23 per cent ten years later. (P. Harrison, *Inside the Third World*, p. 178.)

Note that the expression *highest level* (= *höchster Stand*) can hardly be substituted for *peak* in this kind of phrase. *Highest level* is normally followed by the preposition *in* with a non-numerical adjunct. For example:

(. . .) taxes have surged to the highest peacetime level in America's history. (*RD*, August 1980, p. 72.)

It should also be noted that the locution *hit a peak* is less formal than *reach* (or *rise to*) *a peak*. Cp. the following example from S. Marlowe, *Translation* (p. 64):

That was when the religious persecution hit its peak.

4. in: In this type of syntagma, *during* is preferable to *in*. Cp. K. Hawkins, *Unemployment* (p. 16): *during the severe recession of 1975—8.*

5. Weltwirtschaftskrise: Equivalents such as *world-wide economic crisis* or *world economic crisis* may be accepted at a pinch, but the crisis referred to here is generally known in English as *the Great Depression*. The phrase *the Depression years* is also in common use. *The Great Contraction* (J. Rudolph, *Langenscheidts Handbuch der englischen Wirtschaftssprache*, p. 39) is a very rare expression. Examples:

Once the new plant was built, the company had agreed to change the six-hour shift – adopted during the Depression years – to a standard eight-hour shift. (*RD*, March 1980, p. 146.)

They are intent upon sweeping away delusions – from the impression that the Great Depression was a failure of capitalism (. . .) to the idea that advertising misleads the public (. .). (*RD*, February 1980, p. 166.)

b) Alternatives

The	*unemployment rate*	*reached*	*an all-time peak*	of 30.5% (1932) during
”	*rate of unemployment*	*rose to*	*a peak*	*per cent*
”	*unemployment figure*			*percent*
”	*level of unemployment*			
	Unemployment			
The	*unemployment ratio*			
”	*jobless rate*			
the	*Great Depression.*			
”	*Depression years.*			
”	*Depression.*			
”	*world-wide economic crisis.*			
”	*” ” depression.*			
”	*world depression.*			
”	*international economic crisis.*			
”	*world economic crisis.*			
”	*trade depression.*			
”	*world slump.*			
”	*Great Contraction.*			

⑤ Ein Vergleich der jährlichen Wachstumsraten des realen BSP mit den jeweiligen Arbeitslosenquoten für die BRD zeigt, daß rückläufiges oder stagnierendes Wachstum mit relativ hohen Arbeitslosenquoten einhergeht (z. B. in der Weltwirtschaftskrise und den Rezessionen 1967 und 1974/75).

a) Annotations

1. Ein Vergleich der ... Wachstumsraten ... mit: We say *to draw a comparison between two things*. In this case, however, the preposition *between* would be somewhat inappropriate. The schema of the syntagma in our German text is as follows: *Ein Vergleich* + [noun X (genitive case)]*mit* [noun Y (dative case)]. This type of schema corresponds to two distinct patterns in English:

(i) a comparison of [noun X] and [noun Y]
(ii) a comparison of [noun X] with [noun Y]

For examples based on these patterns, cp. *OALDCE, DEWC* and *WNDS*.

2. Wachstumsraten: In this particular instance, *growth rate* is preferable to *rate of growth* since the repetition of the preposition *of* would jar on the ear.

3. des realen BSP: *BSP* stands for *Bruttosozialprodukt* and must be rendered as *GNP*. The definite article should be omitted. Cp. the following example randomly culled from an article in *Reader's Digest* (March 1980, p. 87):

Instead, the Soviets have continued to pour an estimated 11 to 13 percent of GNP into defense.

The adjective *real* may be rendered as *real, in real terms* or *in terms of real value:*

It [*sc.* Confidence] will be won (. . .) by keeping money growth in true proportion to the real growth of the nation's output (. . .). (*RD*, December 1979, p. 149.)
(. . .) "we are spending less on defense in real terms today than we did at the time of the '62 Cuban missile crisis." (*RD*, March 1980, p. 87.)

For the expression *in terms of real value,* cp. C. A. Gunston/C. M. Corner, *Deutsch-Englisches Glossarium finanzieller und wirtschaftlicher Fachausdrücke,* s.v. real. Note that the phrase *real economic growth* means 'apparent growth less the current inflationary increment' (*WNCD,* s.v. real).

4. jeweiligen: The equivalents given in the dictionaries are somewhat unsatisfactory. In this case, the adjective *jeweilig* may be rendered by an adverbial group such as *during a given period.*

5. BRD: This abbreviation is not used in English. One normally writes *West Germany*. The abbreviation *FRG* is comparatively rare.

6. rückläufiges ... Wachstum: A literal translation would be somewhat unidiomatic. It is advisable to make the adjectives into nouns.

7. einhergeht: The equivalents given in the bilingual dictionaries would be unacceptable in this context. There are at least three possible solutions: *to accompany, to go along with* and *to be the concomitant(s) of:*

(. . . .) the outbreaks of that permissiveness and violence which always seems to accompany national decay (. . . .). (P. Hutber, *What's Wrong With Britain?*, p. 43.)
Along with this suspicion goes a colossal ignorance of the facts. (*RD*, December 1979, p. 108.)
Unemployment is the concomitant of a financial panic. (*WNCD,* s.v. accompaniment.)

8. den Rezessionen 1967 und 1974/75: G. W. Turner claims that *recession* is merely a euphemism for *depression* (*Stylistics*, p. 116). Strictly speaking, however, the words *recession* and *depression* are not freely interchangeable. A recession is 'a temporary depression in economic activity or prosperity' (*CED*). *Rezession* is sometimes trans-

lated as *business decline*. In the present instance, however, this locution is debarred by the proximity of the word *decline* in the syntagma *a decline or standstill in growth*. In English, a time-indicator such as *1967* cannot be placed after the noun *recession*, but it is possible to put the time-indicator before the noun. Cp. *the 1973 Arab oil embargo* (*RD*, February 1980, p. 87). The preposition *of* may also be used in such cases. Cp. *the natural-gas shortage of 1977* (*RD*, February 1980, p. 91).
In this particular instance one might also use an expression of time such as *back in*. Cp. the following examples from *Reader's Digest:*

Back in 1921, there were some 178 U.S. tire companies (. . .). (*RD*, March 1980, p. 146.)
Back in 1972 the Mc Govern people threw Dick Daley's white ethnic Chicago delegates out of the Democratic convention. (*RD*, July 1980, p. 97.)

Way back in is also in regular literary and colloquial use, especially in American English:

The highest annual rate was 7·1 percent, way back in 1950. (*RD*, December 1979, p. 108.)

In *LGS*, the word sequence *back in 1900* has been rendered as *schon im Jahre 1900*. It should, however, be noted that in many cases *back in* merely suggests remoteness in time. Phrases such as *schon im Jahre* may be rendered unambiguously by *as long ago as, as far back as, as early as,* or *already in*. For *as long ago as*, cp. P. Hutber (ed.), *What's Wrong With Britain?*, p. 31:

As long ago as the 1870 s and 1880 s, when Britain still comfortably led the world in sheer volume and value of exports, we had already contracted 'the English disease'.

For *as far back as*, cp. W. Strunk/E. B. White, *The Elements of Style*, p. xv:

Clearly, Will Strunk had foreseen, as far back as 1918, the dangerous tonsillectomy of a prince, in which the surgeon removes the tonsils and the *Times* copy desk removes the final *s*.

For *as early as* and *already in*, cp. B. Foster, *The Changing English Language*, p. 80.

b) Alternatives

A comparison of the annual growth rates of	*real GNP*					
	GNP in real terms					
	GNP in terms of real value					
and the *unemployment figures* for	*West Germany*					
with " *rates*	*W. Germany*					
" *ratios*	the *German Federal Republic*					
	the *Federal Republic of Germany*					
during a given period shows that a decline or standstill in growth						
is the concomitant of relatively high *unemployment rates*	(as *in*		the			
goes along with " *figures*	" *during*	"				
accompanies " *ratios*						
Depression years and during the *recessions*	of *1967 and 1974/75*).					
Great Depression	*downturns* " " " " "					
	1967 and 1974/75 recessions.)					
	recessions back in 1967 and 1974/75).					

⑥ In den 50er Jahren wird die konjunkturbedingte Beziehung zwischen Wachstumsgeschwindigkeit und Arbeitslosigkeit überlagert durch ein beträchtliches Maß von „struktureller" Arbeitslosigkeit, das im wesentlichen aus den Kriegsnachwirkungen resultiert.

a) Annotations

1. wird: It is advisable to substitute the past tense for the historic present. Cf. note (4) 2 above.

2. konjunkturbedingte: In this context *cyclical* sounds more natural than *cycle-induced*, *cyclically induced* or *cyclically conditioned*. Highly specific German double compounds often correspond to imprecise non-compound words in English. Thus the compound adjective *praxisbezogen* may be rendered by the simple adjective *practical* in a phrase such as *praxisbezogene Ergebnisse der arbeitspsychologischen Forschung* (D. Hamblock/D. Wessels, *Englisch in Wirtschaft und Handel: Übersetzungstexte*, p. 30).
The adjective *economic* would be too vague in this context, and expressions such as *due to cyclical fluctuations*, *for cyclical reasons* or *due to the economic situation* (or *trend*) would make no sense.

3. überlagert: *Conceal* (*LEW*) is an acceptable translation, but *fog over* is more vivid. Cp. the following quotation from *Reader's Digest* (November 1979, p. 163):
This would fog over the link between the payroll tax and Social Security benefits (...).

4. „struktureller" Arbeitslosigkeit: *Structural unemployment* is 'unemployment created by some basic long-term change in the demand or technological conditions in an economy, e.g. unemployment of coal miners as a result of the decline in demand for coal' (*PDE*, s.v. structural unemployment). The term *technological unemployment* is also in current use. For further information on this question, see P. A. Samuelson, *Economics*, p. 319, and A. Seldon/F. G. Pennance, *Everyman's Dictionary of Economics*, s.v. unemployment.

5. das ... resultiert: We may resort to structural conversion in order to avoid a somewhat unwieldly relative clause.

6. Kriegsnachwirkungen: It is impossible to render this term by means of a compound.

b) Alternatives

In the fifties the cyclical relation between the	*rate of economic growth* *growth rate* *growth velocity*		
and unemployment was *fogged over* by a *concealed*	*substantial* *considerable*	measure of	
structural *technological*	unemployment *basically* " *essentially* *chiefly* *fundamentally* *due in the main to* *due for the most part to*	*due to* " " " " " "	the aftermath of the War.

⑦ Insgesamt zeigt sich, daß mit der zunehmenden „Verstetigung" des wirtschaftlichen Wachstums in der Nachkriegszeit auch das Ausmaß der konjunkturell bedingten Arbeitslosigkeit zurückgeht.

a) Annotations

1. zeigt sich: Two acceptable renderings are supplied in the bilingual dictionaries: *it appears (that)* (*LGS* and *W/H*) and *we see (that)* (*W/H*). However, there are some other possible variants which the dictionary makers have overlooked: *There are signs (that)* and *There is evidence (that)*. Examples:

(. . .) there are signs that *do not* will eventually be written only when a pronunciation with two separate words is to be suggested. (G. W. Turner, *Stylistics*, p. 94.)
But in recent years there have been increasing signs that the system may be breaking down. (*RD*, March 1980, p. 133.)
But there is evidence that the people of Britain are beginning to tumble to the fact that if they want to enjoy the fruits of life then rights must be balanced by duties and individual effort must be made. (P. Hutber, *What's Wrong With Britain?*, p. 9.)

It is also possible to recast the whole sentence, making the verb *zurückgeht* into a noun (*decrease*): *(. . .) there appears to be a relationship between the increasing stability (. . .) and the decrease in cyclical unemployment.* For the construction *There appears to be* + indefinite article + noun, cp. G. W. Turner, *Stylistics*, p. 111:

There appears to be an increase in the use of *-ness* among the young as familiarity with Latin becomes less common.

2. mit . . . zurückgeht: Here we must resort to a clause-structure shift:

daß mit der zunehmenden [noun X (dative)] (. . .) auch das Ausmaß der [noun Y (genitive)] zurückgeht
that the increasing [noun X] is coupled to a drop in [noun Y]

The verb phrase *is coupled to* corresponds to the preposition *mit*, while the noun *drop* corresponds to the verb *zurückgeht*.
Coupled to and *linked with* are more or less interchangeable in this context. Cp. the following example sentences:

(. . .) economists believed that the size of the nation's energy input was directly coupled to the size of its output of goods and services (. . .). (*RD*, July 1980, p. 78.)
Productivity growth is intimately linked with investment. (*RD*, December 1979, p. 110.)

3. „Verstetigung": This kind of parasynthetic coinage is typical of contemporary German. One is constantly reminded of the words of Ludwig Reiners, the well-known German stylistician: *Deutsch kann man nur gestaltend, nur individuell schreiben* (*Stilkunst*, p. 21). *Verstetigung* has not been recorded in any dictionary, though the verb *verstetigen* (= to make permanent) may be found in C. A. Gunston/C. M. Corner, *Deutsch-Englisches Glossarium finanzieller und wirtschaftlicher Fachausdrücke*. *Verstetigung* consists of the prefix *ver-*, the adjective *stetig* and the suffix *-ung*. The basic idea expressed by *Verstetigung* is thus *Stetigkeit* (= constancy, steadiness, continuity). The prefix *ver-* expresses the inchoative aspect (cp. P. Grebe, *Duden Grammatik der deutschen Gegenwartssprache*, § 778), and the suffix *-ung* expresses action (cp. P. Grebe, *op. cit.*, § 695). In English it is virtually impossible to coin a corresponding term, so we have to make do with a conventional noun such as *stability* or *steadiness*. The inchoative aspect may be expressed by the present participle *increasing*.

4. Nachkriegszeit: The equivalents given in the bilingual dictionaries are perfectly acceptable, but two possible variants have been overlooked: *the post-war years* and *the post Second World War period.* Examples:

This vast improvement has only been partly due to the more buoyant economic conditions of the post-war years (...). (P. Donaldson, *Guide to the British Economy,* p. 153.)
Throughout the post Second World War period politicians have searched for some mechanism (...) that would accelerate the rate of growth. (P. Hutber, *What's Wrong With Britain?,* p. 37.)

5. konjunkturell bedingten Arbeitslosigkeit: Cyclical unemployment is unemployment which results from the trade cycle. For further information, see A. Seldon/F. G. Pennance, *Everyman's Dictionary of Economics,* s.v. unemployment; G. Bannock/R. E. Baxter/R. Rees, *The Penguin Dictionary of Economics,* s.v. cyclical unemployment.

b) Alternatives

On the whole	*there is evidence that*	the	increasing	stability		of economic			
	there are signs that	"	"	steadiness	"	"			
	we see that	"	"	"	"	"			
	it appears that	"	"	"	"	"			
	there appears to be a relationship between the increasing								
growth	*during*	*the*	*post-war period*			*is*	*coupled to*	*a drop*	*in*
"	"	"	*postwar period*				*linked with*	*decrease*	
"	"	"	*post-bellum era*						
"	"	"	*post-war years*						
"	"	"	*post Second World War period*						
"	"	"	*afterwar period*						
	after the war								
stability of economic growth in the post-war period and a drop in cyclical									
cyclical unemployment.									
unemployment.									

⑧ Zwischen 1960 und 1973 lag die Arbeitslosenquote bei durchschnittlich nur 1,0%.

a) Annotations

1. lag ... bei durchschnittlich: These three words constitute a lexical unit and may be rendered by the verb *average.* However, a class-shift is also possible: in other words, we may convert the adverb *durchschnittlich* into the adjective *average.* In this case, the concrete linking verb *lag* must be replaced by the abstract copula *was: the average employment rate was ...*

2. nur: a class-shift is stylistically more satisfactory than a literal translation. The adverb *nur* may be rendered as an adjective (*mere*). Cp. the following quotation from *Reader's Digest* (December 1979, p. 108):

(. . .) according to the Federal Trade Commission, manufacturing corporations' after-tax profits averaged a mere 5.4 percent of sales (. . .).

A literal translation, however, is by no means impossible. Cp. the following quotation from F. Halliday, *Iran,* p. 143:

(. . .) the former raised the price of oil by 10 per cent and the latter by only 5 per cent.

b) Alternatives

> Between 1960 and 1973 the *unemployment rate*   *averaged a mere 1.0%.*
>   "   *figure*
>   *average unemployment rate was a mere 1.0%.*

(9) In der Rezession des Jahres 1974 stieg die Arbeitslosenquote allerdings auf 2,6%, im Jahre 1975 sogar auf 4,7% an.

a) Annotations

1. In . . . 1974: See note (5) 8 above.

2. stieg: The verb *steigen* may be rendered as *rise,* but British and American authors often employ more graphic terms suggesting the nature of the upward motion involved – rapidity, gradualness, etc. Verbs such as *shoot up* or *jump* express rapid movement, while *edge up* expresses gradual movement. Here are some examples:

(. . .) taxes have surged to the highest peacetime level in America's history. (*RD,* August 1980, p. 72.)
Gasoline prices jumped by five to eight percent. (*RD,* February 1980, p. 87.)
(. . .) within two years Atlantic's annual electricity bill shot from $ 250,000 to $ 1 million. (*RD,* July 1980, p. 79.)
From December to March, those sales had shot up from 19 million barrels a day to a record 21 million. (*RD,* February 1980, p. 87.)
(. . .) Soviet defense spending has soared to at least 15 percent of its GNP. (*RD,* December 1979, p. 87.)
Inflation edged up over 200 percent annually (. . .). (*RD,* February 1980, p. 112.)

3. im Jahre: In order to create smoother sentence-flow, we may supply the 'understood' verb in the form of a present participle: *shooting up to as much as 4.7% in 1975.* The present participle group is equivalent to a co-ordinate clause. In this type of syntactic configuration, the participle commonly expresses an action posterior to that denoted by the preceding finite verb. Examples:

India's 2.6 million registered unemployed in 1966 climbed steadily every year, reaching 9.6 millions in 1976. (P. Harrison, *Inside the Third World,* p. 177.)
In 1939 he took up a visiting professorship at Princeton University, retiring to California in 1941 and becoming a U.S. citizen in 1944. (A. Thorlby (ed.), *The Penguin Companion to Literature,* Vol. 2. p. 505.)

4. sogar: Before numerals the word *even* is often replaced by *as much as, as many as* or *as high as.* Examples:

(...) waste and fraud could amount to as much as ten percent of federal assistance programs. (*RD,* May 1980, p. 84.)
The gross national income went up by as much as 8 per cent in 1962. (R. Renner/R. Sachs, *Wirtschaftssprache,* p. 37.)
Sometimes unpaid bills run to as much as £ 300. (H. G. Hoffmann, *Lebendiges Englisch,* I, p. 42.)
By 1976 the Iranian army had ordered or acquired nearly 3,000 modern tanks, and by the early 1980s may have as many as 6,000. (F. Halliday, *Iran,* p. 95.)
(...) in poorer countries the income elasticity of demand for food may be as high as 0.6 to 0.8 (....). (*ibid.,* p. 126.)

b) Alternatives

During the *recession of 1974,* *1974 recession,* *recession back in 1974,*		however, the *unemployment rate* *unemployment figure*	
rose	to 2.6 %,	*shooting up* to as much as 4.7 %	in 1975.
soared	per cent,	*rising*	per cent
jumped	percent,	*soaring*	percent
shot		*jumping*	
shot up		*shooting*	
surged		*surging*	

⑩ In vielen Ländern sind aus verschiedenen Gründen höhere Arbeitslosenquoten zu beobachten (im wesentlichen strukturbedingt); z. B. lag die Arbeitslosenquote der USA in den letzten Jahren bei 5% bis 6%, im Jahre 1975 sogar bei 8,5%, wobei jedoch Unterschiede der statistischen Erfassung zu berücksichtigen sind.

a) Annotations

1. sind ... zu beobachten: This periphrasis is a substitute for a passive infinitive introduced by a modal auxiliary. Cp. M. Philippe, *Grammaire de l'allemand,* p. 101; P. Grebe, *Duden Grammatik der deutschen Gegenwartssprache,* § 111. In English the passive is generally used in such cases. Cp. F. W. Sutton/K. Beilhardt, *Grundzüge der englischen Grammatik,* § 47; A. Lamprecht, *GES,* § 685. For exceptions see A. Lamprecht, *op. cit.,* §§ 686, 688. The only way to avoid the passive construction here would be to employ the verb *to be* with an adjective ending in *-able (observable).* The suffix *-able* always expresses the passive voice. Cp. the French suffixes *-able* and *-ible,* the Latin suffix *-bilis* and the German suffixes *-bar* and *-lich.* On the German suffixes *-bar* and *-lich,* see M. Philippe, *op. cit.,* p. 102.

2. (im wesentlichen strukturbedingt): Brevity does not always make for clarity, and in this particular instance it merely obfuscates the authors' meaning. There is no point in attempting to reproduce the clipped style of the German original in an English translation, for in good English scientific prose ease of comprehension is at a premium. The compound adjective *strukturbedingt* refers back to the syntagma *höhere Arbeitslosenquoten* and may be rendered quite aptly by the simple adjective *structural.* Cp. our translation of the compound adjective *konjunkturbedingt* (note (6) 2 above). In order to make the meaning perfectly clear, we can expand the elliptical German parenthesis into a complete English clause.

3. lag: In English, as in German, verbs denoting abstract relationships often tend towards a picture, reflecting a physical type of vision. Thus, in German, the verb *liegen* is commonly used of mathematical figures. In English, however, it is not possible to employ the verb *lie* in this way. If *liegen* is used in a purely static sense, it can be rendered as *stand,* while the verbs *run* and *range* can be used to express the idea of constant fluctuation or development:

After the strikes it [*sc.* the official minimum legal wage] was dramatically raised by 35 per cent, and after further increases it now stands at over four francs. (J. Ardagh, *The New France,* p. 377.)
At the time of writing, the unemployment rate in Britain stands at its highest level for thirty years and shows every sign of increasing still further. (J. A. Trevithick, *Inflation,* p. 117.)
But by early 1980 it [*sc.* inflation] was running at an annual rate of 18 percent. (*RD,* August 1980, p. 74.)
Food imports were running at $ 2·6 billions in 1977 (. . .). (F. Halliday, *Iran,* p. 128.)
(. . .) the halcyon years of 1964 to 1969, when the rate of profit ranged between 6·9 percent and 9 percent. (*RD,* December 1979, p. 110.)

N.B. The verb *range* is not normally used in the progressive form when it means 'to fluctuate within specific limits'.

The tense of the verb also calls for a few remarks. In British English, time-indicators such as *in recent years* are normally associated with the present perfect. American usage, however, is quite different from British usage in this respect. The American variety of English has been Germanized to such an extent that the simple past is commonly substituted for the present perfect. According to Quirk and Greenbaum (*UGE,* § 3.30 Note), this type of substitution is generally restricted to informal usage, yet there are increasing signs that the tendency to replace the present perfect by the simple past has already begun to invade the written language as well, at least in journalism. For example:

Over the past nine years, the dollar lost about half its value in comparison with the West German mark (. . .). (*RD,* December 1979, p. 146.)

And here are some examples of informal American usage:

(i) We already put an ad in the paper (. . .). (*RD,* January 1980, p. 100.)
(ii) We just buried Charlie. (*ibid.,* p. 102.)
(iii) I said I already took out the garbage (. . .). (*RD,* February 1980, p. 84.)

All these sentences are examples of direct speech. The first two examples are from dialogue passages; the third example is from a joke told by a music-hall comedian. In example (ii) the reference is to an action which the speaker has just accomplished with the aid of a friend. Example (iii) is particularly interesting since it violates the principle of the sequence of tenses and at the same time illustrates the use of the simple past with the time relationship adjunct *already.*

The increased incidence of this type of construction in written American English doubtless stems from the relatively informal character of most present-day writing, profoundly influenced by colloquial style. The British, however, seem loath to follow the American habit of bringing the simple past tense into play when a very recent action is referred to. Cp. B. Foster, *The Changing English Language,* p. 219. Here are some examples of British usage:

(. . .) in recent years, the priority given to full employment as a policy objective has come under attack from a number of economists (. . .). (P. Donaldson, *Guide to the British Economy,* p. 153.)

Mr Wedgwood Benn appears to have altered his views considerably in the past few years. (P. Hutber, *What's Wrong With Britain?*, pp. 36–37.)

It is also interesting to note that some older American authors such as Professor John Kenneth Galbraith (born in Canada in 1908) still adhere to British usage:

In recent years, this has come extensively into discussion under various proposals for guaranteed income or a negative income tax. (J. K. Galbraith, *The Affluent Society*, p. 243.)

It should, of course, be borne in mind that in many respects Canadian English follows British rather than United States practice.

For further information on the use of the present perfect and the simple past, see G. Collier/B. Shields, *Guided German-English Translation*, p. 184, and the article by G. Vanneck in *Word* (Journal of the Linguistic Circle of New York), Vol. 14, No. 2–3, 1958, pp. 237–242.

4. im Jahre 1975 sogar bei 8,5%: See notes (9) 3 and (9) 4 above. In this case, the present participle (*rising*) may be used to express an action that falls within the timesphere denoted by the finite verb. Cp. the following example taken from P. Harrison's book, *Inside the Third World* (p. 182):

Third-World industry continued its beanstalk-like growth in the seventies, averaging 7 per cent a year between 1971 and 1975 (. . .).

In sentence (9) we rendered *sogar* by *as much as*. In this case, we may employ *no less than* as a stylistic variant. Cp. the following example sentence from G. Barraclough's *Introduction to Contemporary History* (p. 88):

No less than twenty-six (. . .) were in Asia (. . .).

5. wobei: This relative adverb poses many problems for the translator, and the bilingual dictionaries offer very few really workable equivalents. In *Technik des Übersetzens* (pp. 133–135), Wolf Friederich points out that *wobei* may often be rendered by *with* + participle. This is perfectly correct, and the examples instanced by Friederich are extremely useful. In this particular case, however, it is not possible to employ the type of construction recommended by Friederich.

Let us compare one of Friederich's examples with the German sentence which is engaging our attention:

Deweys Kabinettssitzungen sind lange Runden von Schlagwechseln, *wobei* Dewey eine ganze Menge Schläge einstecken muß.

Dewey's cabinet sessions are a prolonged round of give and take *with* Dewey *subjected* to lots of taking.

For convenience, we shall refer to Friederich's German sentence as [F] and to Henrichsmeyer's sentence as [H].

In both [H] and [F], an obligation or necessity is indicated in the sub clause introduced by *wobei*. In [F], this notion is expressed by the modal auxiliary *müssen* + active infinitive; in [H], a similar idea is expressed by the periphrasis *sein* + *zu* + active infinitive[1]. In English this kind of idea is normally rendered by *must* or *have to*, and this type of verbal expression might be used to translate the sub clause in [F]: (. . .) *with Dewey having to* + [active infinitive]. In sentence [H], however, we cannot proceed in the same manner since *zu berücksichtigen sind* is a periphrasis for a passive construction: *Unterschiede sind zu berücksichtigen* is equivalent to *Unterschiede müssen*

---

[1] At the beginning of sentence (10) the same type of periphrasis is used in a different sense (*können* + passive infinitive).

berücksichtigt werden. If we attempt to render this construction with the aid of the device recommended by Friederich, the grammar of the sentence is thrown out of gear and we find ourselves in a quandary. A word sequence such as *with differences (. . .) having to be allowed for* would be abnormal or deviant. And if we try to obviate the difficulty by using an active construction, we land ourselves in an even more awkward predicament since the active subject of the verb *berücksichtigen* is not specified in the source text.

It is often advisable to avoid the '*with* + participle' construction in cases in which the use of such a device entails the introduction of the passive present participle of the defective auxiliary *must*.

The sub clause in [H] is practically equivalent to a concessive clause, the concessive nuance being expressed by the adverb *jedoch*. The simplest solution is therefore to use a finite clause introduced by the subordinating conjunction *though*.

6. Unterschiede der statistischen Erfassung: In this case the German genitive must be rendered by the preposition *in*. Cp. the following examples:

In the various forms that Standard English now takes there are, in fact, only very slight differences in grammar (. . .). (*CED,* p. xxiii.)

National differences in word choice. (T. Pyles, *The Origins and Development of the English Language,* p. 247.)

It is, however, worth bearing in mind that *difference of* features in a number of partially lexicalized syntagmata:

Elements of regional differences of pronunciation are evident today (. . .). (*CED,* p. xix.)
It will be clear from what has been said that there remains a great diversity in the pronunciation of English in Britain, reflecting differences of region, social class, and generation. (*ibid.,* p. xx.)
But these differences of phonetic quality, of which the speaker is usually unaware, do not distinguish meaning. (*ibid.*)

In may be substituted for *of* before abstract singular nouns such as *pronunciation* or *quality*. *Of* is normally used before concrete terms such as *region* or semi-abstract terms such as *social class* or *generation*. The use of *in* is mandatory if the second noun in the syntagma is preceded by the definite article:

The differences that are nowadays observable between the northern and southern dialects arise for the most part from differences in the substratum of Gaelic speech. (*CED,* p. xxv.)

7. statistischen Erfassung: There is a close syntagmatic relationship between the word-group *statistischen Erfassung* and the preceding head word *Unterschiede,* so it is advisable to translate *Unterschiede der statistischen Erfassung* as a contextual unit. *Unterschiede* means *unterschiedliche Methoden* or *unterschiedliche Verfahrensweisen* and may thus be rendered in English as *differences in the ways . . .* The term *statistische Erfassung* has no exact counterpart in English. In order to render the semantic features realized in this lexical item, one must therefore resort to periphrasis. Periphrasis involves grammatical relations, so the basic problem posed by the expression *statistische Erfassung* is what is known as 'level shift' − a shift from lexis to grammar or vice versa. The best way to translate *statistische Erfassung* in this kind of context is to employ a phrase such as *make a statistical survey (of* + noun) or *include* [noun] *in a statistical survey*. Cp. the examples cited by Trevor Jones (*HSG-ED*). In the present case, the phrase *make a statistical survey* can be conveniently linked to the preceding word sequence by means of a relative clause. *The ways in which* may be shortened to *the ways*. Cp. the following example from S. Pit Corder, *Introducing Applied Linguistics,* p. 72:

Languages evidently do differ in the way they symbolically reflect the world (. . .).

b) **Alternatives**

For various reasons, higher	*rates of unemployment*	*may be observed*
	unemployment rates	*are observable*
	unemployment figures	

| in *many countries* | (In most cases the unemployment is |
| *a large number of countries* | |

| structrual.); *in recent years,* | *for instance,* | the *unemployment* |
| *in the past few years,* | *for example,* | *rate of unem-* |

rate	in the U.S.A. *has ranged between* 5% *and* 6%,
ployment	" " *from* " " *to* " "
	" *been running at between* 5% *and* 6%,

| *rising* | to *no less than* 8.5% in 1975, though allowance must be |
| *shooting up* | *as much as* |

| made for differences in the ways | statistical surveys have been |
| | *in which* |

| made. |

Text VIII*

Europa-Parlament lehnt EG-Haushalt ab

Zum ersten Mal in der Geschichte der Europäischen Gemeinschaft hat das Europäische Parlament einen EG-Haushalt global abgelehnt. Die am Donnerstag in Straßburg mit großer Mehrheit getroffene Entscheidung, den Budget-Entwurf für 1980 zurückzuweisen, wird weithin als der Versuch einer Kraftprobe der Versammlung mit dem Brüsseler Ministerrat angesehen, die zu einer institutionellen Krise in der Gemeinschaft führen könne. Das neue Rechnungsjahr der Europäischen Gemeinschaft beginnt am 1. Januar nunmehr ohne eine Finanzregelung. Die Institutionen der EG dürfen bis zur Vorlage und Verabschiedung eines neuen Haushaltsentwurfs, wie er von dem Straßburger Parlament gefordert worden ist, monatlich nur über ein Zwölftel der Ausgaben des abgelaufenen Rechnungsjahres verfügen.

Bei der Bekanntgabe des Abstimmungsergebnisses von 288 gegen 64 Stimmen bei einer Enthaltung für die vom Haushaltsausschuß des Parlaments empfohlene Ablehnung durch die Präsidentin des Hauses, Simone Veil, hatte es lang anhaltenden Beifall gegeben. Zugunsten des Ratsentwurfs hatten ungeachtet parteipolitischer Zugehörigkeiten im wesentlichen französische Abgeordnete, Gaullisten und Kommunisten, votiert. Der Abstimmung waren am Dienstag eine sechsstündige Debatte des Parlaments sowie in der Nacht zum Donnerstag ein fünfzehn Stunden währender Einigungsversuch zwischen einer Parlamentarier-Delegation und dem Rat der Finanzminister vorausgegangen. Die vom Rat unterbreiteten Vorschläge im Rahmen dieses sogenannten Konzertierungsverfahrens zur Überwindung der Meinungsverschiedenheiten waren am Donnerstagvormittag von den meisten Rednern der Fraktionen als unzureichend bezeichnet worden.

Vor der Entscheidung in Straßburg hatte der designierte irische Außenminister Lenihan als amtierender Präsident des Ministerrats das Parlament eindringlich davor gewarnt, den Haushalt abzulehnen. Dies wäre eine „ernste Angelegenheit", durch die „ein tiefgreifender Konflikt in der Gemeinschaft" offenbar würde. Lenihan kündigte die Möglichkeit eines juristischen Konflikts vor dem Europäischen Gerichtshof im Zusammenhang mit den Auslegungen der Haushaltsbefugnisse des Parlaments an. In seiner Auseinandersetzung mit dem EG-Rat war von den Straßburger Abgeordneten immer wieder darauf hingewiesen worden, daß dem Europa-Parlament mit der Direktwahl eine neue Souveränität zugewachsen sei. Wer, wie der Europäische Rat, Vorschläge des Parlaments einfach „abschmettere" oder allenfalls zu zaghaften Zugeständnissen bereit sei, mißachte den Willen von Millionen europäischer Wähler.

Der Brüsseler Rat hatte in dem von der Versammlung im letzten November aufgestockten Vierzig-Milliarden-Etat für das kommende Jahr die Mittel für die Sozial-, die Regional- und die Energiepolitik erheblich gekürzt und die geforderten „ersten Schritte zur Eindämmung der Agrarausgaben" abgelehnt.

---

* F.A.Z., 14. 12. 1979

Text VIII
European Parliament rejects EEC budget

For the first time in the history of the European Community the European Parliament has thrown out an EEC budget as a whole. The decision to reject the draft budget for 1980 was taken by a big majority in Strasbourg on Thursday and is widely viewed as a trial of strength between the Assembly and the Council of Ministers in Brussels, a showdown that may lead to an institutional crisis within the Community. The European Community's new financial year will now begin on 1st January without a financial settlement. Pending the submission and adoption of a newly-drafted budget to the liking of the Parliament in Strasbourg, the EEC's institutions will each month be allowed only one twelfth of the amount spent in the current financial year.
There had been long and vociferous applause when Mrs Simone Veil, the President of the House, announced the voting result − 288 votes to 64, with one abstention, in favour of the rejection recommended by the Parliament's budget committee. Those who had voted for the Council's draft were mostly French MPs − Gaullists and Communists, who had acted without regard to differences in party political allegiance. Before the vote there had been a six-hour Parliamentary debate on Tuesday as well as a fifteen-hour attempt at conciliation between a Parliamentary delegation and the Council of the Finance Ministers on the night of Wednesday to Thursday. On Thursday morning most of the speakers of the political groups had described as insufficient the proposals submitted by the Council in the course of this so-called group discussion procedure designed to overcome the dissensions.
Before the decision in Strasbourg, Mr Lenihan, the Irish Foreign Minister designate, in his capacity as acting chairman of the Council of Ministers, had urged the Parliament not to reject the budget. This would be a "serious matter" which would reveal "a deep-rooted conflict within the Community". Mr Lenihan intimated the possibility of a legal conflict before the European Court in connection with the interpretations of the Parliament's budgetary powers. In the dispute between the Parliament and the EEC Council it had been pointed out time and time again by the MPs in Strasbourg that with direct election a new sovereignty had accrued to the European Assembly. People who acted like the European Council, simply massacring the Parliament's proposals or at best consenting to cautious concessions, showed no regard for the wishes and aspirations of millions of European electors. Last November the Assembly had raised the budget for the coming year to forty milliards, but the Council in Brussels had slashed the funds set aside for the social, regional and energy policies, as well as rejecting demands for the initial steps towards putting a budgetary limit on agricultural spending.

Annotations and Alternatives

① Europa-Parlament lehnt EG-Haushalt ab

a) **Annotations**

1. **Europa-Parlament:** This term may be rendered as *European Parliament* or *European Assembly*. *European Parliamentary Assembly* (*R/S*) is now obsolete.

2. **lehnt . . . ab:** In this context, *ablehnen* may be rendered into English by *reject* or *throw out*. *Reject* is somewhat more formal than *throw out*. For illustrative contextual examples of *reject* and some related words, cp. H. W. Klein/W. Friederich, *Englische Synonymik*, s.v. ablehnen. The expression *to throw out a budget* has not yet been recorded in the dictionaries. The locution *to throw out a Bill* (einen Gesetzentwurf/eine Gesetzesvorlage ablehnen) figures in several bilingual dictionaries (*LEW, O-HSG-ED, E, W/H, LGS*), yet the other collocates of *throw out* (= reject) have been overlooked. A useful list of possible collocates in given in A. P. Cowie/R. Mackin, *Oxford Dictionary of Current Idiomatic English* (Vol. 1), s.v. throw out[2]: *Bill, amendment, proposal, suggestion, idea. Throw out* may also collocate with a noun such as *confession* (cp. *WNCD*, s.v. throw out).
It should be noted that the use of the phrasal verb *throw out* may occasionally result in ambiguity, especially if *throw out* is followed by a noun such as *proposal*. *To throw out a proposal* may mean 'to reject a proposal' or 'to put forward a proposal'. Cp. the example sentence given in *CED,* s.v. throw out: 'The chairman threw out a new proposal'. For the various shades of meaning expressed by *throw out*, cp. F. T. Wood, *English Verbal Idioms*, s.v. throw out; J. Seidl/W. Mc Mordie, *English Idioms*, p. 164. *Throw out* is by no means the only phrasal verb that may give rise to ambiguity. Cp. the expression *Boarders Taken In* (F. T. Wood, *English Verbal Idioms*, s.v. take in).
For an example of the collocation *throw out + budget,* cp. the following headline from *The Times* of 14 December 1979 (p. 1):

Europe MPs throw out budget by big majority

The more formal verb *reject* was used in the *International Herald Tribune* (14 December 1979, p. 1):

EEC Parliament Overwhelmingly Rejects Budget

Note that the European Parliament is here referred to as the *EEC Parliament*. The new abbreviation (*EC*), has not yet established itself in the Anglo-American vocabulary although German journalists now almost invariably use the abbreviation *EG* instead of *EWG*. In a recent issue of *The Economist* (4–10 April 1981) there is a section entitled *European Community* (p. 66), yet the abbreviation *EEC* is used throughout the articles in this section.

3. **EG-Haushalt:** This compound may be translated by *the EEC budget* or *the EEC's budget. The budget of the European Economic Community* is also possible, but is too long for use in headlines. Here are some examples:

As a result, subsidies to agriculture have grown each year and now take 73 percent of the EEC budget. (*International Herald Tribune,* 14. 12. 1979, p. 1.)

These rises will cost the EEC budget about 650 ecus (£ 346 m) in 1981 (. . .). (*The Economist*, 4–10. 4. 1981, p. 66.)
Cheering, clapping, and waving their order papers in the air, European MP's rose to their feet in jubilation here today after voting by an overwhelming majority to throw out the EEC's draft budget for next year. (*The Times*, 14. 12. 1979, p. 1.)
The European Parliament voted overwhelmingly today to reject the $ 23.5-billion budget of the European Economic Community for next year in a protest against increasing subsidies given to farmers. (*International Herald Tribune*, 14. 12. 1979, p. 1.)

b) Alternatives

European Parliament	rejects	EEC	budget
European Assembly	throws out	”	”
EEC Parliament	”		Budget

② Zum ersten Mal in der Geschichte der Europäischen Gemeinschaft hat das Europäische Parlament einen EG-Haushalt global abgelehnt.

a) Annotations

1. Europäischen Gemeinschaft: British and American journalists use *European Community* and *European Economic Community* as stylistic variants:

The European Community passed into the age of democracy. (*International Herald Tribune*, 15–16. 12. 1979, p. 6.)
In a dramatic antitrust crackdown of unprecedented severity, the European Economic Community today took a confidential decision to fine a major Japanese-controlled, hi-fi multinational and its distributors in leading Common Market countries a total of $ 9.55 million. (*ibid.*, p. 1.)

2. das europäische Parlament: The use of the definite article is mandatory if the nouns *Parliament* and *Assembly* are preceded by the adjective *European*. Headlines, of course, are excepted from this rule:

European Assembly Condemns France (*International Herald Tribune*, 15–16. 12. 1979, p. 2.)

When the adjective *European* is dropped, *Parliament* and *the Parliament* are used in free variation. Cp. the following sentences from a newspaper article about the EEC Parliament (*International Herald Tribune*, 15–16. 12. 1979, p. 6):

The members of the Parliament were annoyed.
First, Parliament insisted that less money should go to creating, storing, dumping and destroying food surpluses.
Indeed, the Council's massacre of Parliament's amendments has been rather greater this year than in recent years before the Parliament was directly elected.

In the first example sentence the article has been inserted; in the second sentence it has been dropped; and in the third sentence both phrase types can be observed. It may not be amiss to add that we have no reason to doubt the authenticity of this uneven usage. The author of the article from which our examples have been taken is Lord Kennet (alias Wayland Young), who was a member of the European Parliament until 1979. Perhaps Lord Kennet has been influenced by American usage, for in American English the noun *Congress* (as a proper name) may be used with or without the article. Cf. A. Lamprecht, *GES*, § 126; G. O. Curme, *EG*, § 106.

The European Parliament appears to be a very special case as far as syntax is concerned. As a rule, the noun *Parliament* takes no definite article when used as a proper name without an attributive adjective. Cp. the following example sentence in which the noun *Parliament* denotes the highest legislative authority in Britain:

At that time (. . .) yet another Bill had just been introduced into Parliament to put new controls on the influx of immigrants. (*World and Press,* 1st February issue 1981, p. 2.)

The definite article is not inserted unless the noun *Parliament* is preceded by an adjective, as in the example quoted in A. Lamprecht's *Grammatik der englischen Sprache,* § 126: 'the opposition in the British Parliament.'

3. einen EG-Haushalt: The only possible translation is *an EEC budget. The budget of the European Economic Community* cannot be transformed into **a budget of the European Economic Community's* because the postmodifier in a double genitive construction must be personal. Cp. *a friend of his father's* (Quirk et al., *GCE,* § 4.105). *The EEC's budget* cannot be transformed into **an EEC's budget* because *the EEC's budget* is a possessive genitive, not a descriptive or classifying genitive. The word group *EEC's budget* cannot be considered as a fixed expression of the type *a women's college, a summer's day* or *a doctor's degree.* For a list of the various types of genitive used in contemporary English, the reader is referred to Quirk et al., *GCE,* § 4.94. For an interesting discussion of the transformational restrictions of certain kinds of genitive, cf. A. Tellier, *Grammaire de l'anglais,* pp. 25–27. Tellier's taxonomy is similar to Quirk's, yet his terminology is rather different and may give rise to some confusion. Tellier's *génitif déterminatif* corresponds to Quirk's *possessive genitive* (*his father's car*), and the *génitif générique* corresponds to Quirk's *descriptive genitive* (*his doctor's degree*).

b) Alternatives

For the first time in the history of the	*European Community*	
	European Economic Community	
the *European Parliament* has *thrown out* an EEC budget	*as a whole.*	
„ *European Assembly* „ *rejected*	lock, stock [*and barrel.*	

③ Die am Donnerstag in Straßburg mit großer Mehrheit getroffene Entscheidung, den Budget-Entwurf für 1980 zurückzuweisen, wird weithin als den Versuch einer Kraftprobe der Versammlung mit dem Brüsseler Ministerrat angesehen, die zu einer institutionellen Krise in der Gemeinschaft führen könne.

a) Annotations

1. Die am Donnerstag . . . angesehen: Owing to certain divergencies between the sequencing conventions of German and English, it is quite impossible to copy the elaborate architectonic construction of the original sentence. The major obstacle to smooth translation is the prepositive participial phrase *am Donnerstag . . . getroffene.* This type of syntactic constituent may often be converted into a relative clause, but in this particular instance we cannot resort to such an expedient because of the infinitive clause which has been tacked on to the sentence subject *Entscheidung*. The meaning is quite clear if we write: 'The decision, which was taken by a vast majority in Strasbourg on Thursday, is widely viewed (. . .).' In this case, there can be no doubt that the relative pronoun *which* refers to the noun *decision*. The meaning, however, is obscured as soon as the infinitive clause is inserted between the relative pronoun *which* and its antecedent *decision*: 'The decision to reject the draft budget for 1980, which was taken by a vast majority in Strasbourg on Thursday, is widely viewed (. . .).' In this case the relative pronoun seems to refer to the nominal group *the draft budget for 1980* although the verb *take* does not normally collocate with a noun like *budget*. The best way to resolve this knotty problem is to simplify the general syntactic design of the sentence by constructing two main clauses hitched together with the aid of the connective *and*.

2. mit großer Mehrheit: In this case, *groß* may be rendered as *large* (= angemessen groß und darum tauglich), *big* (= auffallend groß) or *vast* (= riesengroß). These three words are scalar[1] adjectives and should not be confused with the vectorial[1] adjective *tall*. For further details concerning the English equivalents of *groß*, the reader is referred to E. Leisi, *Der Wortinhalt*, pp. 86, 104, 105; H. W. Klein/W. Friederich, *Englische Synonymik*, s.v. groß.

3. Budget-Entwurf: *Budgetary draft* (*LEW*) is a comparatively rare term. *Budget estimates* (*G/C*) is in current use, especially in the U.K., where it denotes the figures supplied each year by the Chancellor of the Exchequer showing the possible national expenditure, etc. (var.: *the Estimates*). In this particular instance, however, the most acceptable translation equivalents are *draft budget* and *budget draft*. *Draft budget* has been recorded in Zahn's *Euro-Wirtschaftswörterbuch* as well as in his *Wörterbuch zur Politik und Wirtschaftspolitik*, but *budget draft* has not yet been listed under the headword *Budget-Entwurf*. Here are some illustrative examples:

These three demands had been repeatedly incorporated in amendments to the draft budget over recent months (. . .). (*IHT*, 15–16. 12. 1979, p. 6.)

One of the most striking statements came from Herr Martin Bangemann, German leader of the Liberal group, who accused the Council of treating the Parliament as an inferior body that could be fobbed off with a few legalistic amendments to the budget draft. (*The Times*, 14. 12. 1979, p. 1.)

4. zurückzuweisen: Vide supra (1) 2.

5. den Versuch . . . Ministerrat: German genitive constructions of the type *Versuch einer Kraftprobe* are normally rendered with the aid of the preposition *at*. Cf. the following quotation from *The Times* of 14 December 1979 (p. 1):

A tired and bitter Mr Lenihan, who had spent all night with the Parliament's budget committee in a hopeless attempt at appeasement (. . .) told a radio interviewer (. . .) that the Parliament was rapidly becoming "a rabble without responsibility".

In this case, however, the word *Versuch* may be left untranslated since the phrase *Versuch einer Kraftprobe* is tautological. A 'trial of strength' *is* an 'attempt'.

The second genitive (*der Versammlung*) should be translated with the aid of the preposition *between*.

---

[1] Scalar adjectives express magnitude, but not direction. Vectorial adjectives express both magnitude and direction.

6. Brüsseler Ministerrat: There is no hard and fast rule for the translation of the adjective *Brüsseler*. *Organisation des Brüsseler Vertrages* is rendered as *Brussels Treaty Organization,* and *Brüsseler Kommission* is rendered as *Brussels Commission,* but *Brüsseler Ministerrat* is normally translated as *the Council of Ministers[2] in Brussels.* A calque of the German phrase would be front-heavy. The use of capitals is virtually obligatory. Cf. the following quotation from *The Times* of 1 April 1981 (p. 1):

Thousands of angry farmers, mainly from France and Italy, who were besieging the headquarters of the EEC's Council of Ministers in Brussels in support of their demands for higher Community farm prices were dispersed by riot police using tear gas.

7. die: The relative pronoun *die* has been separated from its antecedent *Kraftprobe.* This type of construction should not be imitated in English since it is neither elegant nor clear. In order to give the remainder of our sentence a fresh push-off, we may repeat the antecedent or use another, closely allied word. Here are some examples of this device:

(i) Early Christian Latin poetry is for the most part the work of writers who were trained in the schools of grammar and rhetoric, schools whose tradition was continued with changes and modifications throughout the Middle Ages. (F. J. E. Raby, *The Oxford Book of Medieval Latin Verse,* p. x.)
(ii) He had the genius to see in the simple iambic dimeter the measure for his purpose, a measure which was soon to be adapted for rhythmical and rhymed compositions – the so-called Ambrosian hymns. (*ibid.,* p. xi.)
(iii) Both models, however, were based upon the laws of classical physics, laws which were assumed to be applicable to micro- as well as macroscopic bodies. (J. H. Bryant, *The Open Decision,* p. 13.)
(iv) Penda's allies against Northumbria were the Christian Welsh under their King Cadwallon, savage mountaineers who revenged the wrongs of their race on the Northumbrian Christians with a cruelty far exceeding that of the heathens of Mercia against their brother Saxons. (G. M. Trevelyan, *A Shortened History of England,* p. 62.)

In all these example sentences, lucidity has been achieved through duplication of the antecedent. In examples (i), (ii) and (iii), the nucleus of the antecedent has simply been repeated literatim: (i) *schools,* (ii) *measure,* (iii) *laws.* In example (iv), however, the antecedent has been replaced by an amplificatory noun phrase: the head-word *Welsh* has been replaced by the appositive group *savage mountaineers.* The result is excellent. Nevertheless, it would be wrong to assume that in English it is never possible to separate the relative pronoun from its antecedent. Consider the following example sentences:

(. . .) poetical texts were included which became available for the student of literature as well as for the historian. (F. J. E. Raby, *The Oxford Book of Medieval Latin Verse,* p. ix.)
It was soon realized that this vast body of Latin verse, secular as well as religious, which was the product of a thousand years of assiduous composition, was important (. . .). (*ibid.,* p. x.)

In these sentences there can be no ambiguity since there are no nouns between the relative pronouns and their antecedents. In the first example, the relative pronoun is separated from its antecedent by a short verb phrase (*were included*), and in the second example the relative pronoun is separated from its antecedent by a short postpositive adjective phrase (*secular as well as religious*). Both sentences are grammatically and stylistically acceptable.

In our German sentence, however, there is a very long string of formatives between the relative pronoun and its antecedent, and the intercalated string of formatives includes two nouns. It is thus clear that the sentence must be restructured in English. The most

---

[2] The expression *executive council* (v. Eichborn) is comparatively rare.

elegant solution is to repeat the antecedent by synonymic substitution. *Trial of strength* may be replaced by *showdown,* a terse, breezy Americanism which is now quite firmly established in British English. This informal word may be frowned upon by some adamant purists, but it should be borne in mind that the British press, including the august London *Times,* now extends a wide hospitality to such terms, even in articles on serious subjects[3].

There are, of course, two other forms of anaphoric signal which may be employed if one is unwilling to repeat the antecedent literatim or by synonymic substitution. Consider the following sentences:

(i) A momentous question is now beginning to surface in Washington, one that could profoundly alter America's future. (*RD,* July 1980, p. 73.)

(ii) He will make it clear to Moscow that any Soviet intervention in Poland would immediately scuttle any further prospect of agreement on limiting nuclear weapons in Europe, something the Russians now consider an urgent priority. (*The Times,* 1. 4. 1981, p. 6.)

In the first example, the pro-form *one* refers back to the noun *question,* and in the second example the pro-form *something* refers back to the idea expressed in the word-group *would immediately . . . Europe.*

b) Alternatives

The decision to	*reject* *throw out*	the	*draft budget* *budget draft*	for 1980 was taken by a		
big large vast	majority in Strasbourg on Thursday and is widely				*viewed regarded considered*	as
a	*trial of strength* *test of strength* *trial of endurance* *test of endurance* *endurance test*	between the Assembly and the Council of				
Ministers in Brussels,	*a showdown* *something* *one*	that may	*lead to* *result in* *eventuate in*			an
institutional crisis within the Community.						

 Das neue Rechnungsjahr der Europäischen Gemeinschaft beginnt am 1. Januar nunmehr ohne eine Finanzregelung.

a) Annotations

1. beginnt: In English, as in German, the present tense is often used to indicate future events:

What time is the train? (I. Murdoch, *A Severed Head,* p. 52.)

---

[3] It is, of course, advisable to keep within the appropriate bounds. On the limits of breeziness, see W. Strunk/E. B. White, *The Elements of Style,* pp. 73–74.

However, this use is limited to cases in which a future action is regarded as part of a fixed programme or a predictable pattern of natural events. Cp. R. W. Zandvoort, *HEG*, § 129; K. Schibsbye, *MEG*, § 1.7.1.2; R. A. Close, *RGSE*, § 13.26.

2. nunmehr: The time adverb *now* often occupies front-position, as in the following example given in the *O-HSG-ED,* s.v. nunmehr:

My report is finished − now the practical work can begin.

In our case, however, the word *now*, placed at the beginning of the sentence, would sound unduly emphatic and convey an inapposite impression of immediacy. Remember that our *F.A.Z.* article was published on 14th December, 17 days before 'the new financial year' began.

Now may also occupy end-position, but as a rule this is possible only in relatively short sentences such as 'Where are you living now?' (Hornby, *OALDCE,* s.v. now).

It follows therefore that *now* will have to occupy mid-position. It should be positioned between the auxiliary verb *will* and the lexical verb *begin.* Cf. the rules for indefinite time adjuncts given in F. W. Sutton/K. Beilhardt, *GEG*, § 192.

3. Finanzregelung: This term, which has not yet been recorded in the dictionaries, may be rendered as *financial arrangement* or *financial settlement.* The first element of such German compounds is normally translated by an adjective. Cf. *Finanzlage* (= financial position), *Finanzmisere* (= financial difficulties) or *Finanzplanung* (= financial planning).

b) Alternatives

The European Community's new	*financial year*	will now begin on
	fiscal year	
	account year	
	accounting year	
1st January without a	*financial settlement.*	
	financial arrangement.	

⑤ Die Institutionen der EG dürfen bis zur Vorlage und Verabschiedung eines neuen Haushaltsentwurfs, wie er von dem Straßburger Parlament gefordert worden ist, monatlich nur über ein Zwölftel der Ausgaben des abgelaufenen Rechnungsjahres verfügen.

a) Annotations

1. Die Institutionen . . . verfügen: It would be futile to try to reproduce the periodic structure of the German sentence in an English translation. The sentence must be recast in such a way as to bring the principal elements of the main clause closer together. A long string of formatives (*bis . . . worden ist*) has been inserted between the auxiliary verb *dürfen* and its complement. The segment *bis . . . worden ist* should be placed at the head of the sentence before any attempt is made to render the entire sequence into English prose.

2. Die Institutionen der EG: We may use either an -*s* genitive or an *of*-genitive. The word-groups *European Community* and *European Economic Community* admit both genitive constructions, but the *of*-genitive is often preferred for reasons of euphony. On the other hand, the acronym *EEC* is almost invariably constructed with the -*s* genitive since writers who are fond of acronyms generally favour a snappy style:

the $ 23.5-billion budget of the European Economic Community. (*IHT*, 14. 12. 1979, p. 1.)
the people of the Community. (*The Times*, 14. 12. 1979, p. 1.)
the EEC's budget commissioner. (*The Economist*, 4–10. 4. 1981, p. 66.)
the EEC's founding fathers. (*The Guardian*, 11. 12. 1979, p. 10.)

The second example ('the people of the Community') is particularly interesting, for in this case the inflected genitive cannot be used interchangeably with the periphrastic genitive. We say 'the people of the Community', but we do not say *'the Community's people'. By the same token, we say 'the people of the United States', but we do not say *'the United States' people', although we do say 'the United States' attitude' (Quirk et al., *GCE*, § 4.98). These examples show that the rules governing the use of the inflected genitive and the periphrastic genitive are much more complex than students of English generally assume. Anglicists normally proceed on the blithe and uncritical assumption that the genitive construction is determined almost exclusively by the nature of the modifier[4] (personal or non-personal, for instance).[5] However, it is often equally important to consider the relationship between the modifier and the head.[6] Compare the following constructions:

Genitives	Analogues
(a) the United States' attitude	The United States adopted an attitude[7]
(b) the people of the United States	People live in the United States.

A very little consideration shows that the deep structures of (a) and (b) are basically different: (a) is a subjective genitive, while (b) is what might be described as a 'locative genitive' since the modifier (*of the United States*) indicates the location of the head (*the people*). It should be noted that the 'locative genitive' can be used only in a strictly limited number of cases. For example, we cannot say *'the books of the bookshelf'. We must say 'the books on the bookshelf.'[8] Professor Quirk and his colleagues have pointed out that it is impossible to say *'the bookshelf's books' but they do not seem to have realized the true reason why the genitive must be ruled out in this case. The whole point is that the 'locative genitive', which is used mainly with the names of towns and countries, can have only one form, namely: head noun phrase + *of* + modifying noun phrase.

---

[4] Terms such as *head* and *modifier* are explained in the glossary at the end of the book.
[5] Professor Quirk and his colleagues have studied modifiers in considerable detail and proposed a very useful classification of modifying noun phrases. Cp. R. Quirk et al., *GCE*, pp. 198–201. This is clearly the best study of the subject to date.
[6] Professor Quirk and his colleagues have already shown to what extent commutative restrictions may be determined by the nature of the relationship between the head and the modifier (*GCE*, § 4.98 Note; §§ 13.27–13.29). Nevertheless, a good deal of work still remains to be done in this field of research.
[7] There are, of course, several other possibilities: 'The United States *have adopted* an attitude', 'The United States *had adopted* an attitude', etc.
[8] German students of English often use the wrong preposition here. They say *in* instead of *on*. Cf. the German construction 'im Regal'. In this case there is a curious divergence between spatial concepts in English and German.

3. dürfen: The future tense should be used in English since *dürfen* is here used with reference to future time.

4. bis zur Vorlage: In this particular instance, the most elegant translation equivalent of *bis* is *pending* (= until), a preposition which is often used with reference to the law and legal forms:

pending his decision. (Hornby, *OALDCE*, s.v. pending).
pending final settlement: bis zur endgültigen Entscheidung. (*LEW*, s.v. bis.)
pending the final decision: vorbehaltlich der endgültigen Entscheidung. (Gilbertson, *HG*, s.v. vorbehaltlich.)

5. Vorlage: *Budget draft* collocates well with the verb *submit* and the nouns *submission* and *submittal*. Cf. the following quotation from *The Times* of 14 December 1979 (p. 1):

Undeterred, the Parliament proceeded to vote by 288 votes to 64, with one abstention, in favour of rejecting the budget and asking for a new draft to be submitted.

6. Verabschiedung: *Budget draft* also collocates frequently with such lexical items as *adopt* and *adoption*. Cp. the following quotations:

The immediate effect is that the EEC will in principle be prohibited under emergency rules from spending any more money next year than it has done this year – at any rate, until a newly-drafted budget can be adopted. (*The Times*, 14. 12. 1979, p. 1.)
The committee said last week it could not recommend adoption of the 1980 budget (. . .). (*IHT*, 6. 12. 1979, p. 2.)

7. neuen Haushaltsentwurfs: In the bilingual dictionaries *Haushaltsentwurf* is translated as *proposed budget* and *draft budget*. *Draft budget* collocates well with the adjective *new*, but *proposed budget* does not normally combine with attributive adjectives:

The Parliament has asked that a new draft budget to its liking should be submitted as soon as possible. (*The Times*, 14. 12. 1979, p. 1.)
Strong sections of the parliament have spoken out against the proposed budget. (*IHT*, 13. 12. 1979, p. 4.)

However, *a new draft budget* is not the only possible translation equivalent of *ein neuer Haushaltsentwurf*. The word-group *ein neuer Haushaltsentwurf* may be treated as a single thought-unit and rendered as *a newly-drafted budget*. Cf. the example sentence from *The Times* quoted in the preceding section ((5) 6).

8. wie er . . . gefordert worden ist: A literal translation would be clumsy and unidiomatic. The neatest solution is to use the phrase *to the liking of* + noun. Cf. the example sentence from *The Times* quoted in the preceding section ((5) 7).

9. monatlich . . . verfügen: A literal translation would run as follows: 'to dispose each month *of* only a twelfth *of* the expenditure *of* the financial year (. . .)'. This rendering is clearly unsatisfactory since there is a pile-up of prepositional phrases introduced by *of*. We may circumvent this difficulty by re-wording the entire sequence as follows: '(. . . the EEC's institutions will each month be allowed only one twelfth of the amount spent in the financial year (. . .).' The verb *dispose of* may be omitted since *to allow someone to dispose of a sum of money* means practically the same thing as *to allow someone a sum of money;* and the syntagma *the expenditure of* may be replaced by *the amount spent in.* Cp. the following quotation from *The Times* of 6 December 1979 (p. 8):

In the meantime, the Commission would have to use an emergency procedure whereby it is empowered to dole out on a month-by-month basis the same amount of money as was spent in the previous year.

The positioning of the time frequency adjunct *each month* offers a tricky problem to the translator. This type of time adverbial is normally placed at the beginning or at the end of the sentence. In this particular instance, however, the sentence structure is so complex that the time adverbial can occupy neither front-position nor end-position. If we place *each month* before *only*, there will be a pile-up of adverbials in the middle of the sentence, so we have no alternative to placing *each month* between the auxiliary verb *will* and the infinitive *be allowed*. It is noteworthy that English adverbials which are usually in initial position often have to be shifted to mid-position when the clause is hedged about with prepositional phrases and elaborate dependent constructions. A good example is provided by the following excerpt from an official document quoted in Henry Pelling's *History of British Trade Unionism* (p. 30):

That the laws have not only not been efficient to prevent Combinations, either of masters or workmen; but, on the contrary, have in the opinion of many of both parties, had a tendency to produce mutual irritation and distrust, and to give a violent character to the Combinations, and to render them highly dangerous to the peace of the community.

In this passage, the viewpoint adjunct *in the opinion of many of both parties* has been inserted between the verbs *have* and *had* because it is virtually impossible to place it anywhere else in the sentence without committing a stylistic error. In a short simple statement, of course, a viewpoint adjunct would normally appear initially.

Similar constructions may often be found in legal instruments. Cp. the following example from an endowment assurance[9] policy reproduced by David Crystal and Derek Davy in *Investigating English Style* (pp. 195–196):

(. . .) this policy (. . .) witnesseth that (. . .) the funds of the Society shall on the expiration of the term of years specified in the Schedule hereto or on the previous death of the Life Insured become and be liable to pay (. . .) the sum due (. . .).

In this case, two complex time adverbials linked by *or* have been intercalated between the auxiliary *shall* and the infinitives *become* and *be*. In legal documents, sentences tend to assume gargantuan proportions, and the authors of these highly intricate structures take full advantage of adverbial mobility in order to clarify meaning. Finespun elegance of expression is of secondary importance.

10. des abgelaufenen Rechnungsjahres: The translator must exercise great care in order to avoid misunderstandings. The financial year in question (1979) had not yet reached its close when the German text was written. The past participle *abgelaufen* must therefore be rendered as *current* (= *laufend*).

At first sight, the German sentence looks like a general statement, especially since the verb *dürfen* is in the present tense. However, the subsidiary clause *wie er von dem Straßburger Parlament gefordert worden ist* shows that the author is referring specifically to the problems that arose in connection with the draft budget for 1980. It follows therefore that the verb *dürfen* cannot be in the neutral present: like the verb *beginnt* in the preceding sentence, it is used with reference to future time.

The solutions we have rejected call for a few remarks:

---

[9] Lebensversicherung auf den Erlebensfall.

(a) If our German sentence were a general statement, it would be possible to render the past participle *abgelaufen* as *previous*. Cp. the example sentence from *The Times* cited in the preceding subsection ((5) 9).
(b) If the German text were dated 'January 1980', we should have to render the word *abgelaufen* by means of a participial construction: *the financial year ended 31st December 1979*. Cp. the following quotation from Hans G. Hoffmann, *Aufbaukurs Wirtschaft* (p. 56):

The following are some of the points mentioned in the Chairman's Address to the Stockholders in respect of the year ended 31st December, 1970.

b) Alternatives

Pending the *submission* *submittal*	and adoption of a	*newly-drafted budget* *new draft budget*
to the liking of the Parliament in Strasbourg, the		*EEC's insti-* *EEC insti-* *institutions of*
tutions *tutions* *the EEC*	will each month be allowed only	*one* *a* twelfth of the
amount *amount of money*	spent in the current	*financial year.* *fiscal year.* *account year.* *accounting year.*

(6) Bei der Bekanntgabe des Abstimmungsergebnisses von 288 gegen 64 Stimmen bei einer Enthaltung für die vom Haushaltsausschuß des Parlaments empfohlene Ablehnung durch die Präsidentin des Hauses, Simone Veil, hatte es lang anhaltenden Beifall gegeben.

a) Annotations

1. Bei . . . gegeben: The reader may have some difficulty in picking his way through the labyrinthine grammar of this sentence. A careful syntactic analysis is therefore an essential preliminary to translation. Two major sources of difficulty may be distinguished:
(i) The first main section of the sentence (*Bei . . . Hauses*) seems disproportionately long in relation to the second section, which consists of only six words.
(ii) Genuine confusion may result from the 'Chinese box' arrangement of the constituents in the first part of the sentence. The framework of this section is like a maze through which the thread of the author's discourse winds and loops like Ariadne's clew. The following breakdown into component elements may provide a convenient guide to the syntactic structure:

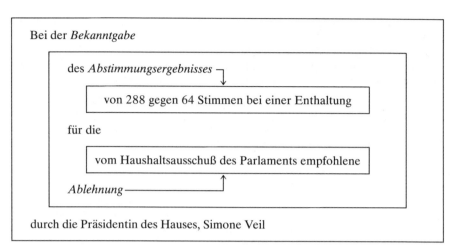

Note: The three principal concepts have been italicized.
The outer framework comprises the word-group *Bei der Bekanntgabe durch die Präsidentin des Hauses Simone Veil*; the inner frame comprises the group *des Abstimmungsergebnisses für die Ablehnung*; and the two main concepts in this group (*Abstimmungsergebnis* and *Ablehnung*) are modified by subsidiary units which have been enclosed in smaller frames (*von 288 . . . Enthaltung* and *vom Haushaltsausschuß . . . empfohlene*).
This inordinately intricate structure makes no concessions whatever to the convenience of the reader, who may be initially somewhat bemused by the juxtaposition of the words *Ablehnung* and *durch*. *Durch* is linked to *Bekanntgabe*, not to *Ablehnung*, but there are so many words between *Bekanntgabe* and *durch* that this link can hardly be discerned unless the sentence is construed like a Ciceronian period.
The translator would be ill-advised to imitate this buckram style, for contemporary English does not favour a periodic structure to the same extent as literary German or classical Latin. Except in legal documents and the like, the English are disinclined to conflate, by means of elaborate linking devices, grammatical units which in normal discourse would be more likely to appear as a series of loosely connected sentences. As a rule, the English do not try to say everything at once.
It is fairly obvious from all this that we shall have to recast the whole sentence before attempting a translation. Two major alterations may be recommended:
(i) The shorter section, which constitutes the gist of the sentence, should be placed before the longer section in order to achieve a more natural balance.
(ii) The tangled skein of the first section must be sedulously unravelled in order that the strings of formatives may be rearranged in serial order.

2. Bei der Bekanntgabe . . . durch die Präsidentin des Hauses, Simone Veil: As we have noted, the German sentence appears unduly obscure and disequilibrated because the constituents of this word-group have been wrenched asunder. Clarity and balance may be enhanced by putting the component elements together again and by replacing the abstract German nominal construction by a concrete English verbal construction. If the nominalized verb *Bekanntgabe* is converted back into its original form (*bekanntgeben: announce*), the other elements may be rearranged to form a time clause.

3. die Präsidentin des Hauses, Simone Veil: Three points require special attention: (a) the capitalization of the English equivalent of *Haus*; (b) the position of the proper noun in apposition; (c) the use of certain titles in English.

(a) *House* is normally capitalized when it denotes a parliamentary assembly. Cp. the following quotations from an article about the privileges of British MPs:

(. . .) I wager that the Committee, drunken members as well as sober ones, would almost certainly make the same ruling, and perhaps even invite the offender to come to the Bar of the House (not the one where they get drunk) and apologize (. . .). (*The Times*, 9. 4. 1981, p. 14.) I fear that the House might well have made a collective fool of itself. (*ibid.*)

(b) In *Deutsch-englische Übersetzungsübungen* (Vol. 2, p. 120), Philippine Schick asserts that in English, appositives denoting a person's rank, role, profession, etc., are generally placed after the proper noun, e.g. *Rembrandt, the painter*. There can be little doubt that this principle is observed in a great many cases, yet it would be a mistake to assume that contemporary usage with regard to the position of appositives is fixed. Word order is often determined to a large extent by considerations of euphony or emphasis. In the following example sentences the appositives have been italicized:

(i) It [*sc.* Sidney's *Arcadia*] remained popular until the eighteenth century, and when *Richardson, the bourgeois printer*, named his serving-maid heroine, he called her 'Pamela', in memory of a character in Sidney's story. (I. Evans, *A Short History of English Literature*, p. 208.)
(ii) C. M. Doughty (1843–1926), *the explorer*, whose prose records of travel, *Arabia Deserta* (1888), influenced T. E. Lawrence, published in 1906 the beginning of his long poem, *The Dawn in Britain*, (*ibid.*, 108.)
(iii) It [*sc. The Quarterly Review*] was followed by *Blackwood's Edinburgh Magazine*, in which *J. G. Lockhart, Scott's son-in-law and biographer*, was a leading spirit and one of the most virulent of contributors. (*ibid.*, 328.)
(iv) *Carl Akeley, the American naturalist*, led two expeditions in the nineteen-twenties (. . .). (L. G. Alexander, *New Concept English*, Vol. V, p. 17.)
(v) *Q. D. Leavis, the magazine's specialist in fiction*, in her *Fiction and the Reading Public*, has written an invaluable socio-literary study of the decline of popular taste in England since 1600 (. . .). (S. E. Hyman, *The Armed Vision*, p. 273.)
(vi) The last speaker before the historic vote was *Brian Lenihan, the new Irish Foreign Minister*, whose role it was to speak for the Council of Ministers. (*IHT*, 15/16. 12. 1979, p. 6.)
(vii) *John Hinckley, the accused would-be assassin*, was having psychiatric tests to determine his fitness to stand trial. (*Financial Times*, 2. 4. 1981, p. 1.)
(viii) The Irish Republic's ruling Fianna Fail party will tomorrow elect a successor to *Mr Jack Lynch, the Prime Minister*, who yesterday announced his resignation after 13 years as party leader. (*The Times*, 6. 12. 1979, p. 1.)
(ix) Other likely contenders for the post include *Mr Michael O'Kennedy, Minister for Foreign Affairs, a possible compromise candidate, Mr Neil Blaney, an Independent Fianna Fail member with strong republican views, Mr Brian Lenihan, Minister for Fisheries, Mr Desmond O'Malley, Minister for Industry and a respected senior member of the party*. (*ibid.*)
(x) Extreme instances are the characters who people the meaningless world of Samuel Beckett's dramas – *the tramps. Vladimir and Estragon*, in *Waiting for Godot*, or *the blind and paralyzed old man, Hamm*, who is the protagonist in *Endgame*. (M. H. Abrams, *A Glossary of Literary Terms*, p. 176.)
(xi) The minor characters, such as *the deaf veteran Ruysum, the contemptible demagogue Vansen*, and *the timid tailor Jetter*, are not mere wooden figures, but show individuality, just as many unimportant actors in Shakespeare's plays are coloured by creative power and breathe the breath of life. (Goethe, *Egmont*, ed. J. T. Hatfield, pp. xvi–xvii.)
(xii) *Iris Murdoch's first hero Jake Donaghue* (*Under the Net*) does retain his integrity (. . .). (J. S. Rippier, *Some Postwar English Novelists*, p. 9.)

(xiii) In an early chapter of John Le Carré's *The Spy who came in from the Cold* the hero, Leamas, returns home after spending the evening with his girl. (J. Raban, *The Technique of Modern Fiction*, p. 67.)

(xiv) With this, the reader new to a unique author can better appreciate the group of novels, which includes *Headlong Hall* (1816), *Nightmare Abbey* (1818), *Crotchet Castle* (1831), and *Gryll Grange* (1861), whose concentrated flavour became an ingredient in so much work that was to follow; notably in the early books of *Peacock's son-in-law George Meredith*, as well as in those of Disraeli and Bulwer Lytton. (Richard Church, *The Growth of the English Novel*, p. 114.)

In sentences (i)–(ix), the proper name is placed before the appositive denoting rank, profession, etc., but this order is reversed in sentences (x)–(xiv). Nevertheless, all the appositional groups in these sentences have certain elements in common: in each case, the appositives have different information value, and in each case the superordinate information unit is placed first. There is a marked tendency to place the proper noun first if there is reason to assume that the reader is familiar with the name of the person under discussion; and in certain contexts there may be some considerations of inter-sentence linkage at work. No. (xiv) is a case in point. The sentence we have quoted is the final section of a paragraph devoted entirely to a discussion of the life and works of Thomas Love Peacock. It is therefore appropriate that George Meredith should be referred to as 'Peacock's son-in-law'; it is clear that the word-group *Peacock's son-in-law* is contextually more relevant than the unit *George Meredith*; and it is natural that the appositive constituted by the proper name should be placed last.

(c) Present-day usage with regard to certain titles is somewhat inconsistent. None the less, there can be little doubt that titles such as *Mr, Mrs* and *Miss* are employed much more extensively in the British and American press than in the German press. In English, as in French, the use of such titles conveys an impression of gracious urbanity; in German, however, the effect tends to be ironic. Cf. H. Mundschau, *Übersetzungskurs Französisch-Deutsch*, p. 44 (Note 5). Here are some typical examples:

The generally conciliatory tones of Mr Brezhnev's speech may have been inspired by the desire to repair the damage done to East-West detente by the Soviet invasion of Afghanistan without withdrawing his troops from that country. (*The Observer*, reproduced in *World and Press*, 2nd March issue 1981, p. 1.)

Is Mrs Thatcher secretly afraid that President Reagan is already going soft on Communism (. . .)? (*ibid.*)

In the past, it often seemed that Mr Carter was attempting to slap together a policy by combining the mutually exclusive ideas of Mr Vance and Mr Brzezinski (. . .). (*IHT*, reproduced in *World and Press*, 2nd May issue 1980, p. 1.)

Mrs Thatcher warns Russia of disaster if Poland is invaded. (headline in *The Times*, 9. 4. 1981, p. 1.)

Mrs Margaret Thatcher warned the Soviet Union in a major speech yesterday that intervention in Poland would be a disaster for Russia as well as the Polish people (. . .). (*ibid.*)

However, usage sometimes varies, even within a single paragraph, and there is a marked tendency to omit titles in headlines:

Vance resigns (headline, *IHT*, reproduced in *World and Press*, 2nd May issue 1980, p. 1.)
Reagan may be at work next week (headline, *Financial Times*, 2. 4. 1981, p. 1.)
Furthermore, his outlook varied greatly from that of Zbigniew Brzezinski, the president's national security advisor (. . .). (*IHT*, reproduced in *World and Press*, 2nd May issue 1980, p. 1.)
Perhaps Reagan's economics and belt-tightening really will bring my weight down to where I've wanted it for several years. (*World and Press*, 2nd March issue 1981, p. 2.)

Titles such as *Mr, Mrs, Miss, Sheikh, Lady, Dr*, etc. frequently occur in sequences based on the pattern: *Mr* (etc.) + proper name + comma + appositive word-group denoting rank or office. In this kind of sequence the proper name is the head-word. The

structure of the first appositive is comparatively rigid, and the use of the definite article in this type of word-group is extremely rare, except in court circulars and the like.[10] The second appositive, however, may assume a wide range of forms, and it is therefore quite difficult to set up reliable rules for the use of the article in such word-groups.
The principles most commonly observed are as follows:

(i) The article is inserted when the word-group denoting the person's rank is preceded by a nationality adjective. In such cases, the nationality adjective serves as a restrictive modifier indicating uniqueness and answering the question 'which one?' Cf. Henryk Kałuża's remarks on partly explicit contexts in *The Use of Articles in Contemporary English* (p. 29). Here are two examples:

Sheikh Ali Khalifa, the Kuwaiti Oil Minister (*Financial Times*, 30. 1. 1980, p. 1.)
Mr Masayoshi Ohira, the Japanese Prime Minister (*The Times*, 6. 12. 1979, p. 1.)

(ii) The article must be omitted when the word-group denoting rank or office is preceded by the name of a country or state in the genitive:

Mr Abol Hassan Bani-Sadr, Iran's President-elect (*Financial Times*, 30. 1. 1980, p. 1.)

(iii) The article is frequently dispensed with when the office or position in question is usually held at one time by one person only. Cf. R. W. Zandvoort, *HEG*, § 349; H. Kałuża, *The Use of Articles in Contemporary English*, p. 58. Here are a few examples:

Mr Bill Sirs, general secretary of the ISTC (*Financial Times*, 30. 1. 1980, p. 1.)
Dr Mundawarara, deputy Prime Minister in Bishop Muzorewa's Government (*The Times*, 6. 12. 1979, p. 1.)
Mr Mark Carlisle, Secretary of State for Education and Science (*ibid.*)
Lady Jeger, chairman of the Parliamentary Labour Party (*ibid.*)
Sir Geoffrey Howe, Chancellor of the Exchequer (*ibid.*)
Mr David Steel, leader of the Liberals (*ibid.*, p. 2.)
Mr Arthur Scargill, left-wing leader of the Workshire miners (*ibid.*)

(iv) The article may be used with an affective or emphatic value. In this type of appositional group, the article shows that the apposition is not intended to convey information, but to remind us of a fact assumed as known. The word or word-group denoting rank or office becomes a 'non-title' (cf. H. Kałuża, *op. cit.*, p. 58):

Mr Ali Reza Nowbari, the Governor of Bank Markazi, the Iranian central bank (*Financial Times*, 30. 1. 1980, p. 1.)
Mr George Colley, the Finance Minister (*The Times*, 6. 12. 1979, p. 1.)
Mr Len Murray, the Trades Union Congress general secretary (*Financial Times*, 30. 1. 1980, p. 1.)

At present there is a growing tendency to preface a person's rank to his name. In this type of construction, the article is invariably omitted:

U.S. President Ronald Reagan may return to the White House as early as next week. (*Financial Times*, 2. 4. 1981, p. 1.)
British Trade Secretary John Nott warned businessmen in Hong Kong that the UK Government would probably have to resort to "temporary protectionism" against textile imports from Hong Kong and elsewhere because of growing unemployment in the home industry. (*Financial Times*, 30. 1. 1980, p. 1.)

---

[10] Cf. the following examples from *The Times* of 9 April 1981 (p. 16): 'the Lady Mary Fitzalan-Howard', 'the Princess Margaret, Countess of Snowdon'. Titles such as *Czar*, *Emperor*, *Archduke* and *Pharaoh* are discussed in H. Kałuża, *The Use of Articles in Contemporary English*, p. 56.

Rhodesian Nationalist leader Robert Mugabe came under attack from dissident members of his party (. . .). (*ibid.*)

(. . .) there is an intriguing contrast between her public advice and the warmer interest initially shown by the President and Secretary of State Haig in Mr Brezhnev's important policy speech to the Soviet Communist Party Congress. (*The Observer*, reproduced in *World and Press*, 2nd March issue 1981, p. 1.)

With the Conservative Party led by Prime Minister Margaret Thatcher and the Labor Party headed by Michael Foot, the center of British politics was up for grabs. (*IHT*, reproduced in *World and Press*, 2nd March issue 1981, p. 1.)

West German Chancellor Helmut Schmidt went to Moscow with three main themes on his mind (. . .). (*IHT*, reproduced in *World and Press*, 2nd July issue 1980, p. 1.)

This usage was originally restricted to titles held by politicians, but it has now been extended to cover almost any conceivable occupation:

"Their potential is enormous", says chemist Morris Wayman (. . .). (*Newsweek*, reproduced in *World and Press*, 2nd March issue 1981, p. 6.)

The appositives are never separated by commas, and the first main information unit is normally quite short. The construction becomes unconsciously ponderous when the first unit comprises more than three words. Cp. the following example cited by R. Quirk et al. in *GCE*, § 9.153 (Note):

25-year-old television singer Mary Cordwell is being invited to the reception.

Some writers overdo this structure, cramming modifiers into the sentence until it is chock-full. A particularly ludicrous example is quoted by David Crystal and Derek Davy in *Investigating English Style* (p. 186):

said tall, grey-haired, blue-eyed, 32-year-old ship's carpenter Andrew Jones.

Front-heavy restrictive appositives have been lambasted on both sides of the Atlantic, but the worst offenders have remained undaunted.

Some authors are content to use only one modifier before a noun denoting rank or profession, but in most cases the adjective is superfluous and the effect infelicitous. Cp. the use of the compound adjective *white-thatched* (= *white-haired*) in the following sentence quoted by Rudolph Flesch in *The ABC of Style* (p. 13):

The world's biggest baker of cookies, as well as a pantryful of other goods from arrowroot biscuits to zwieback, Nabisco has increased its sales 27% in the past five years, to $ 526 million in 1962, and *white-thatched* president Lee Smith Bickmore, 55, has reported that sales for 1963's first three quarters are a cracking good 7% ahead of last year's.

This appositional type is generally restricted to journalism. It is considered highly fashionable in popular newspapers and magazines, and it is now making inroads upon the preserves of what Brian Foster describes as 'the more thoughtful press' (*The Changing English Language*, p. 107). Cf. the examples from the *Financial Times* and *The Observer* quoted above.

The construction seems to have made its way into British English by way of such American magazines as *Time*. However, it is a moot point whether the prototype was German or American. In *The Changing English Language* (p. 107), Brian Foster takes the line that the journalistic habit in question is of German provenience, while Broder Carstensen expresses exactly the opposite opinion in *Spiegel-Wörter, Spiegel-Worte* (p. 116). In view of the infinite complexity of latter-day American-German cultural interchange, it is virtually impossible to settle this question in a fully satisfactory manner. At all events, the consensus seems to be that the principal culprits are the newsmagazines *Time* and *Der Spiegel*.

4. Abstimmungsergebnisses: A wide variety of equivalents is given in the bilingual dictionaries: *result of the voting, result of the vote, voting result, ballot result, result of the* (or *a*) *poll, referendum vote.*

Result of the poll would be inappropriate in the present context since *poll* and its derivatives are normally used with reference to elections or public opinion surveys:

Mr Abol Hassan Bani-Sadr, Iran's President-elect, said immediately after his victory at the polls, that he would work towards closer economic ties with Europe. (*Financial Times*, 30. 1. 1980, p. 1.)

A poll has found that more than half the Britons surveyed believe the European Economic Community is an unnecessary and expensive bureaucracy. (*World and Press*, 2nd March issue 1981, p. 5.)

Ballot result would not fill the bill either, for *ballot* and its derivatives have ethical undertones which are absent from the German text. Moreover, the word *ballot* implies secrecy, and the vote in question was not secret. Cf. the note on *ballot* in *Webster's New Dictionary of Synonyms*, s.v. suffrage. An abridged version of this note may be found in H. W. Klein/W. Friederich, *Englische Synonymik*, s.v. Wahlrecht.

Referendum vote would be quite unacceptable here since a referendum is a plebiscite (*Volksabstimmung, Volksentscheid*).

Result of the voting, result of the vote and *voting result* are acceptable since in the text under consideration the emphasis is clearly on the power of the European MPs to express their opinions in the approved way. Cf. the notes on the term *vote* in *Webster's New Dictionary of Synonyms*, s.v. suffrage, and H. W. Klein/W. Friederich, *Englische Synonymik*, s.v. Wahlrecht. For examples of the terms *vote* and *voting*, cf. the following quotation from *The Times* of 14 December 1979 (p. 1):

Explaining their positions before the vote, which was carried out amid some confusion with the aid of a new electronic voting apparatus, leaders of the main political groups rose one after another to assert the Parliament's democratic right to control the budget.

5. von: The preposition *von* fulfils more or less the same function as the link verb *sein*, for the word-group *des Abstimmungsergebnisses von 288 gegen 64 Stimmen* is a nominalized transform of a *be*-sentence: *Das Abstimmungsergebnis war 288 gegen 64 Stimmen.*

This type of correspondence is quite common in English, too. However, it is generally restricted to three classes of nouns:

(a) ameliorative or pejorative terms such as *angel, fool, idiot, rogue, scoundrel, rascal, devil* or *prude*:

The angel of a girl (Quirk et al., *GCE*, § 13.27.)
The fool of a policeman (*ibid.*)
That idiot of a postman (*LEW*, s.v. von.)
A regular rascal of a boy (L.S.R. Byrne/E. L. Churchill, *A Comprehensive French Grammar*, § 408.)
A poor devil of a beggar (*ibid.*)
A fool of a custom-house official (*ibid.*)
A little prude of a girl (*ibid.*)

(b) terms denoting various kinds of verbal information: *news, rumour,* etc.:

The news of the team's victory (Quirk et al., *GCE*, § 13.27.)
Vague rumours of defeat (Mansion/Ledésert, *HNSFED*, vol. 2, s.v. rumeur.)

(c) terms denoting specific numerical information: *average, figure, score, record,* etc.:

In order to get the mean difference, we calculate the several differences of the items from their average value of 8 and sum them, thus (. . .). (M. J. Moroney, *Facts from Figures*, p. 60.)

The figure of 2·2 children per adult female was felt to be in some respects absurd (. . .). (*ibid.*, p. 34.)
The forty boys make an average score of 76%. (*ibid.*, p. 55.)
(. . .) the previous record of $ 37.044 billion (. . .) (*IHT,* 3. 10. 1979, p. 9.)
The union is demanding a weekly minimum of $ 175 (. . .). (*ibid.*).
(. . .) a surplus of 2·6 billion DM (*ibid.*).

The nouns in class (a) are normally preceded by the definite or indefinite article or by a demonstrative pronoun.

The nouns in class (b) are used with the zero or definite article. The word or word-group introduced by the preposition *of* corresponds to a noun clause (*that the team had won, that the enemy had been defeated,* etc.).

The nouns in class (c) are used with the definite article, the indefinite article, or determiners such as *his, her, their,* etc. Certain peculiarities should be noted:

(i) *Average of. . .* is not always used to express an equivalence relationship. Compare *the average of 8* and *the average of the numbers 1 to 3* (Moroney, *op. cit.*, p. 54). In the first case the average is equal to *8*, while in the second case the average (calculated as an arithmetic mean) is *2*. The deep structures of the two word-groups are quite different in spite of the similarity of the surface structures.

(ii) The use of the preposition *of* is mandatory when a noun such as *average* or *figure* is preceded by a determiner such as *his*.

(iii) The use of the preposition *of* is optional when a noun such as *average* or *figure* is preceded by the definite article. There is, however, a tendency to dispense with the word *of* unless the figure in question has been previously specified in the text or in some other document of which the reader is reminded or with which he is presumed to be familiar. Compare the following examples:

We may say that the census count in a certain country taken on a certain day comes to 43, 574, 205, but it would be nothing short of silly to keep quoting the last little figure 5 for the next ten years (. . .). (Moroney, *op. cit.*, p. 46.)
As previously shown, the average of the items is

$$\bar{x} = \frac{\Sigma x}{n} = \frac{11 + 8 + 6 + 7 + 8}{5} = \frac{40}{5} = 8$$

In order to get the mean difference, we calculate the several differences of the items from their average value of 8 and sum them, thus (. . .). (*ibid.*, p. 60.)

In our first example, the figure 5 is considered in isolation for the first time. In our second example, the figure 8 occurs twice – first as the result of a computation represented with the aid of mathematical notation, then as part of a complete sentence. Let us now return to the problem in hand. Expressions such as *voting result* clearly belong to class (c), and the set of figures introduced by the preposition *von* has not been previously specified in the text. It is therefore advisable to avoid the *of*-construction by substituting a dash for the preposition *von*.

6. 288 gegen 64 Stimmen: This use of the preposition *gegen* has not yet been recorded in the bilingual dictionaries. The correct English equivalent is *to*. Cf. the quotation from *The Times* of 14 December 1979 given above in subsection (5) 5.

7. bei einer Enthaltung: The lexicographers have overlooked this use of the preposition *bei*. The correct English equivalent is *with*. Cf. the quotation from *The Times* of 14 December 1979 given above in subsection (5) 5.

8. Haushaltsausschuß: A wide variety of equivalents may be found in the bilingual dictionaries: *budget committee* (also capitalized), *budgetary committee, Budget Commission, Appropriations Committee, Senate* (or *House*) *Appropriations Committee, Select Committee on Estimates, Estimates Committee, committee of ways and means* (also capitalized), *ways and means committee, Committee of Supply*, etc. In this particular instance, the most apposite term is *budget committee*. Cf. the following quotations from the press reports on the rejection of the EEC draft budget for 1980:

(. . .) Mr Lenihan, who had spent all night with the Parliament's budget committee in a hopeless attempt at appeasement (. . .). (*The Times*, 14. 12. 1979, p. 1.)

(. . .) the budget committee of the assembly today reaffirmed its recommendation that the 1980 budget as it stands should be thrown out (. . .). (*The Times*, 6. 12. 1979, p. 8.)

(. . .) the 14-hour overnight session with the parliamentary budget committee (. . .). (*The Times*, 14. 12. 1979, p. 7.)

Then at dawn, the Parliamentary delegation reported to the Parliament's Budget Committee. (*IHT*, 15–16. 12. 1979, p. 6.)

The European Parliament is almost certain to force a confrontation with Common Market governments next week by rejecting the 1980 community budget, members of its Budget Committee said today. (*IHT*, 6. 12. 1979, p. 2.)

As can be seen from these examples, usage with regard to capitalization is not fixed.

9. des Parlaments: This unit may be rendered by an inflected genitive, a periphrastic genitive or an adjective (*Parliamentary*). Cf. the examples quoted in the preceding subsection ((6) 8).

10. lang anhaltenden Beifall: This fixed phrase has no exact equivalent in English and must be translated according to whether it approximates closer to *cheering* or *clapping*. *Beifall* is wider in application than *applause*. *Beifall* may denote clapping, cheering or stamping. There is no emphasis on clapping. *Applause*, however, is generally used in reference to appreciation or praise shown by clapping the hands. Cf. the use of the Latin verb *plaudere* in phrases such as *manus in plaudendo consumere*. Reference to other manifestations of approval is comparatively rare. Cf. the quotation from Shakespeare's *Hamlet* given in the *O.E.D.* (s.v. applaud).

When Mrs Veil announced the rejection of the EEC draft budget, there was cheering as well as clapping. Cf. the following quotations from *The Times* of 14 December 1979 (p. 1):

The EEC draft budget for 1980 was thrown out by the European Parliament yesterday amid cheers and applause.

Cheering, clapping, and waving their order papers in the air, European MPs rose to their feet in jubilation (. . .).

In the absence of a satisfactory global term corresponding to *Beifall*, we must attempt to render *lang anhaltenden Beifall* indirectly by means of some expression such as *long and vociferous applause* (Williams, quoted in H. W. Klein/W. Friederich, *Englische Synonymik*, s.v. Beifall). *Long* corresponds to the premodifier *lang anhaltend*, and *vociferous applause* renders the two notions expressed by the head word *Beifall*: *applause* conveys the idea of clapping, while *vociferous*, which comes from the Latin deponent *vociferari* (= to cry aloud, bawl, shout), conveys the idea of cheering.

Other possible renderings are *prolonged* (or *sustained*) *cheering and clapping, prolonged* (or *sustained*) *cheering and applause* and *prolonged* (or *sustained*) *cheers and applause*. *Cheering* is preferable to *cheers* since the gerundial form underscores the continuous aspect of the action. The noun *cheers*, of course, has both terminate and progressive force, yet the terminate aspect tends to preponderate over the progressive aspect, especially in locutions such as *Bronx cheer* (an Americanism denoting a vulgar sound or expression of disapproval or rejection). Cf. the following quotation from *World and Press*, 1st February issue 1981, p. 5:

Their most likely reaction is three Bronx cheers.

Prolonged cheers (*W/H*) and *rounds and rounds of cheers* (*LGS*) would be acceptable in other contexts, but they must be rejected here because they exclude the idea of clapping. *Prolonged applause* (*LEW*) and *sustained applause* (*O-HSG-ED*) are less acceptable than equivalents such as *prolonged cheering and clapping,* but one might justify them by citing an authoritative work such as *Webster's New Dictionary of Synonyms*. The authors of this dictionary point out that applause 'often carries its literal implication of clapping hands', yet they concede that 'it may be used to designate any other noisy or emphatic expression of approval (as stamping of feet, cheering, or waving of flags).' They quote an example sentence from a work by the English historian James Anthony Froude (1818–1894). Still, it is very hard to find examples of this usage in present-day English. It might be argued that the expression *cheers and applause* (used in the above-mentioned article in *The Times* of 14 December 1979) is an instance of hendiadys, a rhetorical device which is exceptionally common in contemporary English (cf. W. Friederich, *Technik des Übersetzens,* pp. 46–50). However, the balance of probability is against such an assumption. In my opinion, the odds are that the author of the article in *The Times* added the noun *cheers* because he felt that the idea conveyed by *cheers* was not adequately expressed by *applause*. An expression such as *round after round of applause* (*WNDS*, s.v. applause) would be an excellent rendering of *lang anhaltender Beifall* if Froude's usage could be accepted as authoritative and genuinely modern, but since Froude was a nineteenth-century author we must consider his usage with the utmost circumspection.

A comment is required upon the word *plaudits* (usually plural), which is a close synonym of *applause.* In the text under discussion, the noun *plaudits* would be inappropriate since it has a decidedly literary and old-fashioned flavour. Moreover, in contemporary English, *plaudits* is generally used figuratively in reference to praise bestowed by critics in book reviews and the like. Cf. the example cited in *WNCD*, s.v. plaudit. In nineteenth-century English, however, the word *plaudits* was commonly applied to cheering, clapping, and other signs of approval. The editors of *Webster's New Dictionary of Synonyms* (s.v. applause) point out that *plaudits* 'may suggest polite or gracious rather than demonstrative, expressions of approval', and they quote a sentence from Thackeray in support of their assertion. None the less, it should be noted that the noun *plaudits* was also used of more obstreperous demonstrations of approval. Cf. the quotation given in the *Shorter Oxford English Dictionary: the noisy plaudits of the pit and gallery* (1883). Hornby, Garmonsway, Simpson, H. W. Klein, W. Friederich and most other lexicographers have overlooked the fact that *plaudits* is obsolescent. Rudolph Flesch is an exception. In *The ABC of Style* (s.v. plaudits), he suggests that *plaudits* should invariably be replaced by *applause*. Personally, I feel that Flesch's views on archaic and obsolescent words are unduly extreme. The word *plaudits* is still serviceable, but its use should be left to accomplished writers.

b) Alternatives

There had been	*long and vociferous applause*	when Mrs Simone Veil,
	prolonged cheering and clapping	
	sustained " " "	
	prolonged cheering and applause	
	sustained " " "	
	prolonged cheers and applause	
	sustained " " "	
	prolonged applause	
	sustained "	
the President of the House, announced	*the voting result –*	288
	" result of the voting –	
	" result of the vote –	
votes to 64, with one abstention, in favour of the rejection recommend-		
ed by	*the Parliament's budget committee.*	
	" " Budget Committee.	
	" parliamentary budget committee.	
	" budget committee of the assembly.	

⑦ Zugunsten des Ratsentwurfs hatten ungeachtet parteipolitischer Zugehörigkeiten im wesentlichen französische Abgeordnete, Gaullisten und Kommunisten, votiert.

a) Annotations

1. Zugunsten . . . votiert: For reasons of emphasis, the subject with its modifier (*im wesentlichen . . . Kommunisten*) has been manoeuvered into the penultimate position in the sentence. In English, however, the subject must be brought into prominence by means of some other device because English structure demands that the subject precede the finite verb form in this type of declaratory statement. The emphasis and movement of the German thought pattern can be reproduced, after a fashion, by sentence-splitting and duplication of the subject nucleus. In our model version, the word-group which constitutes the grammatical subject of the German sentence has been split up into two distinct elements: the demonstrative pronoun *those* and the syntagma *mostly French MPs – Gaullists and Communists*. These two elements have been linked by means of the copulative verb form *were*, and the remaining components of the sentence have been accommodated in two symmetrical relative clauses: *Zugunsten des Ratsentwurfs hatten . . . votiert* has been rendered by a restrictive relative clause tacked on to the subject nucleus *those*, while *ungeachtet parteipolitischer Zugehörigkeiten* has been rendered by a non-restrictive relative clause tacked on to the predicate nucleus. By using a copula type of sentence, we have succeeded in preserving the basic circuitry of the German original. The link verb occupies the central position, thus ensuring both lucidity and the grammatical balance of the construction. The dissipative effect of sentence-splitting has been further counteracted by the symmetrical arrangement of the two attributive clauses; and the equivalent of the German subject nucleus has been thrown into relief by a demonstrative pronoun in front-position as well as a nominal group in end-position.

2. zugunsten: *For* and *in favour of* are equally acceptable in this context. In the bilingual dictionaries, however, *for* has not yet been listed among the translation equivalents of *zugunsten*. For the use of this preposition, cf. the following quotation from the *International Herald Tribune* (15–16 December 1979, p. 6):

Most of the French members of the Socialist group voted with their colleagues for rejection.

3. Ratsentwurfs: This new compound, which has not been recorded in the dictionaries, may be rendered by means of the inflected genitive. Cf. the following quotation from *The Times* of 14 December 1979 (p. 7):

Conservative and Labour politicians from the United Kingdom voted in a block today to support the European Parliament in rejecting the EEC Council of Ministers' draft budget for 1980.

In the case under discussion, the Council of Ministers may be referred to simply as *the Council*. This usage is perfectly normal in English:

The Council could let the Parliament stew in its own juice by refusing to rush into a revised budget (...). (*The Times*, 14. 12. 1979, p. 7.)

4. ungeachtet: This preposition of concession is normally rendered in English as *in spite of*, *despite*, *regardless of* or *irrespective of*. *In spite of* is a general-purpose idiom; *despite* is a shade more formal in style; *regardless of* and *irrespective of* have a somewhat literary flavour.

For all and *with all* would be inappropriate here since they are both rather colloquial. Cf. R. Quirk et al., *GCE*, § 6.47.

Notwithstanding is a rather ponderous word which is generally restricted to formal and legalistic style. Cf. R. Flesch, *The ABC of Style*, s.v. notwithstanding; R. Quirk et al, *GCE*, § 6.47.

Unmindful of, which is generally postpositive, is a somewhat bookish expression. Cf. the German word *uneingedenk* (+ genitive), which has a decidedly quaint, old-fashioned flavour.

Despite of should be given a wide berth, although it has been listed as an equivalent of *ungeachtet* in W/H. Hornby describes this locution as 'obsolescent', and F. T. Wood condemns it out of hand as a solecism. Cf. F. T. Wood, *English Prepositional Idioms*, s.v. despite; F. T. Wood, *Current English Usage*, s.v. despite.

The expression *in despite of* should also be eschewed, although it has been recorded without any comment in G. N. Garmonsway's *Penguin English Dictionary*. Hornby describes the locution *in despite of* as 'obsolescent'; the editors of *Collins English Dictionary* classify it as 'rare'; and F. T. Wood expresses a similar opinion in *English Prepositional Idioms*, s.v. despite. Wood says that *in despite of* is seldom used, even in literary style. *The Shorter Oxford English Dictionary* enumerates four different senses in which the expression in question may be used: (a) in contempt of; (b) in open defiance of; (c) notwithstanding the opposition of; (d) notwithstanding. Senses (a) and (b) are labelled as obsolete, yet they are the only senses mentioned as 'current' in F. T. Wood's *English Prepositional Idioms*. This contradiction is somewhat puzzling. Personally, I am inclined to class *in despite of* as virtually obsolete. Even nineteenth-century authors such as Wilkie Collins (1824–1889) and Robert Louis Stevenson (1850–1894) use the modern idiom *in spite of* rather than *in despite of*. Cf. the following examples from *The Woman in White* (first issued in volume form in 1860) and *Dr. Jekyll and Mr. Hyde* (1886):

(...) Madame Fosco, in spite of her well-assumed external civility, had not forgiven her niece for innocently standing between her and the legacy of ten thousand pounds (...). (Wilkie Collins, *The Woman in White*, p. 326.)
By ten o'clock, when the shops were closed, the by-street was very solitary and, in spite of the low growl of London from all round, very silent. (Robert Louis Stevenson, *Dr. Jekyll and Mr. Hyde*, p. 26.)

In the case under consideration, special difficulties arise because the sentence has been entirely recast. In the German text, the prepositional phrase introduced by *ungeachtet* modifies the semantic unit constituted by the words *Zugunsten des Ratsentwurfs hatten ... votiert*. In the model translation, however, the corresponding prepositional phrase merely modifies the verb *had acted*. The specific verb *vote* has been replaced by the more general verb *act* in order to avoid flatfooted repetition of the same phrase, and this substitution results in a shift of emphasis. If we say: *who had acted despite their various party-political tendencies*, the focus of attention seems to be on the contrast between action and inaction rather than on the contrast between voting *for* rejection and voting *against* rejection. Comma separation, which is particularly common before such locutions as *regardless of* and *irrespective of,* would lead to a complete misunderstanding. In order to obviate such difficulties, it is necessary to use a phrase which can be more closely linked to the verb, thus making it clear that reference is not to action in general, but to the particular form of action mentioned in the relative clause tacked on to the subject nucleus. The most acceptable solutions are *without considering* and *without regard to*.

5. parteipolitischer Zugehörigkeit: *Zugehörigkeit* is a catchall term designed to cover a variety of relationships which may exist between an individual and the group or class to which he belongs. Since English has no general term for *Zugehörigkeit*, the nature of the relationship must always be specified in an English translation.
Membership would be an appropriate term here, especially since *party membership* is a standard collocation. Unlike *Zugehörigkeit*, however, *membership* is not used in the plural. For *party membership,* cf. Richard Rose, *The Problem of Party Government*, p. xxiv:

Linking the payment of additional subsidies to party membership would serve a treble purpose.

Affiliation is generally employed with reference to trade unions, though other uses are possible:

The party ... that affiliates with the Republicans (1860) (*SOED,* s.v. affiliate.)
He affiliated himself with the Union. (*CED,* s.v. affiliate.)
Is the Mineworkers' Union affiliated with the TUC? (*OALDCE,* s.v. affiliate.)
(...) middle-class unions receive little notice, for such groups prefer to present themselves as professional groups, and usually do not affiliate to the Labour Party. (R. Rose, *The Problem of Party Government*, p. 34.)
Many of these people have suffered, economically speaking, because of their political affiliations (R. Quirk/S. Greenbaum, *UGE*, § 211).

The term *affiliation fee* is also in current use:

Trade unions provide a guaranteed source of income, and affiliation fees have been steadily rising from 7½ p to 21 p per member from 1971 to 1976. (R. Rose, *The Problem of Party Government*, p. xxiii.)

Like *membership*, however, *affiliation* is not normally used in the plural.
Allegiance has a fairly wide collocational range. It may denote loyalty to a party, a ruler or a government:

Historically, class differences have not been the sole or even the chief difference in party allegiance. (R. Rose, *The Problem of Party Government*, p. 29.)
It does not follow from this, however, that class differences are automatically translated into differences in political allegiance. (*ibid.*, p. 30.)
Religious and cultural allegiance to Britain or to the Free State was however only the nominal distinction between the two communities. (Carol M. Claxton, *Background to the "Troubles"*, p. 5.)

Alignment does not mean quite the same as *allegiance*, although there are considerable overlaps in collocational range. *Allegiance* often implies a sense of duty (cf. the expression *oath of allegiance*), while *alignment* denotes an alliance or union motivated by individual preference, idealism or self-interest:

(. . .) he stands slightly outside the main alignments of British parties as a border-state Truman democrat. (R. Rose, *The Problem of Party Government*, p. xiii.)
Political involvement is likely to affect party alignment (. . .). (*ibid.*, p. 41.)

Loyalty is a more general term than *allegiance* or *alignment*. *Party loyalty* is a standard collocation. Unlike the German noun *Treue*, *loyalty* is frequently used in the plural:

Class differences have a greater influence upon party loyalties than do regional differences (. . .). (R. Rose, *The Problem of Party Government*, p. 16.)

Bias is a fairly general term which may be used to denote a predisposition, a mental tendency or inclination. *Bias* can collocate with adjectives such as *party political*. It is not used in the plural:

(. . .) an inquisitive reader might wish to know something about the author's own political party bias (. . .). (R. Rose, *The Problem of Party Government*, p. xiii.)

Note that *political party* has here been used in the sense of the German adjective *parteipolitisch*. This equivalent has not yet been recorded in the dictionaries.
Plurality may be expressed by terms such as *tendency* or *leaning*. Indeed, *leaning* is used more often in the plural than in the singular, Cf. *LEW*, s.v. Zugehörigkeit.
In the case under discussion, it is advisable to eke out the sense of the German phrase by using an adjective such as *various* or *sundry*, or a noun such as *difference*. Thus we may say *without regard to their various party political tendencies* or *without regard to differences in political allegiance*. The latter phrase has been borrowed from R. Rose, *op. cit.*, p. 30 (vide supra).

6. im wesentlichen: In this particular instance, it is impossible to render *im wesentlichen* by *essentially*. *Essentially* normally modifies an adjective and means 'in essence', 'basically', 'fundamentally'. Cf. the following quotation from Iris Murdoch, *A Severed Head*, p. 16:

(. . .) a slight drooping and discomposing of essentially fine features.

When *im wesentlichen* means 'almost all' or 'almost entirely', it should be rendered by *mostly, chiefly, mainly,* or some other word or phrase of similar meaning. Cf. the following examples:

The Normans were mostly Norsemen who had completely shed their Scandinavian speech. (S. Potter, *Our Language*, pp. 33–34.)
The study of these extracts, drawn chiefly from nineteenth- and twentieth-century writings, will bring the student into contact with a wide vocabulary and an interesting range of subjects and styles. (W. F. H. Whitmarsh/C. D. Jukes, *Advanced French Course*, p.v.)
It is chiefly used to avoid repetition of a previous remark or question. (A. J. Thomson/A. V. Martinet, *A Practical English Grammar*, p. 29.)

Property and land were still mainly in Protestant hands. (C. M. Claxton, *Background to the "Troubles"*, p. 3.)
Those opposing the Army consist mainly, though not exclusively, of the Provisional IRA. (*ibid.*, p. 7.)
This group of ruthless militants came into existence in 1970 after a split with the main IRA movement which, in the years preceding the latest Troubles, had followed a mainly political policy. (*ibid.*, p. 7.)

b) **Alternatives**

Those who had voted	*for*		the Council's draft were	*mostly*
		in favour of		*mainly*
				chiefly
				for the most part
				in most cases
French MPs – Gaullists and Communists, who had acted			*without*	*regard to*
			„	*considering*

differences in	*party political allegiance.*
„ „	*political allegiance.*
„ „	*party allegiance.*
„ „	*party political bias.*
„ „	*political party bias.*
„ „	*party political alignment.*
„ „	*political alignment.*
„ „	*party alignment.*
their various	*party loyalties.*
„ *sundry*	*party political loyalties.*
„ *different*	*party political tendencies.*
„ *divergent* „ „	*leanings.*

(8) Der Abstimmung waren am Dienstag eine sechsstündige Debatte des Parlaments sowie in der Nacht zum Donnerstag ein fünfzehn Stunden währender Einigungsversuch zwischen einer Parlamentarierdelegation und dem Rat der Finanzminister vorausgegangen.

a) **Annotations**

1. Der Abstimmung ... vorausgegangen: If we render *vorausgehen* as *precede*, we shall have to use a passive construction and repeat the preposition *by*: *The vote had been preceded by (...) and by (...).* An existential sentence would be more in keeping with the genius of the English language: *Before the vote there had been (...) and (...).*

2. sechsstündige: When used in compound adjectives, terms such as *hour* take no *s*: *a ten-ton lorry* (A. J. Thomson/A. V. Martinet, *A Practical English Grammar*, § 305), *a nine-week strike* (H. G. Hoffmann, *Aufbaukurs Wirtschaft*, p. 10), *fifteen-year-old boys* (W. Thesiger, *Arabian Sands*, p. 104).

In all likelihood, this idiom is of American origin; yet it is now part and parcel of standard British English. Older British usage is reflected in E. M. Forster's *Maurice* (p. 41), which was written in 1913−14, but not published until 1971: *a twenty-four hours' rest.* In *La langue des Américains* (p. 201), Professor Guy Jean Forgue treats the idiom in question as an Americanism and goes the length of asserting that in standard American English such usage is restricted to *year, foot, acre* and *mile* (*a three year stretch, a ten foot pole,* etc.). He adds that in other cases (nouns denoting time or distance) the use of the unmarked plural is substandard. In point of fact, however, the usage under discussion in now so widespread, even in the written language, that even the most fatuous purists would hardly dare to take exception to it:

At the conclusion of the contentious 45-minute session, Kissinger complained to network executives (. . .). (*Time*, 22. 10. 1979, p. 58.)
The 15-member Nobel Selection Committee had sifted through nominees (. . .). (*ibid.*, p. 56.)

3. Debatte des Parlaments: A literal translation would sound a trifle awkward. The modifying noun (*Parlaments*) may be converted into an adjective (*Parliamentary*). *Parliamentary debate* is a standard collocation. Cf. the following quotation from R. Sieper, *The Student's Companion to Britain*, p. 206:

Both voiced the general demand for the publication of Parliamentary debates.

4. in der Nacht zum Donnerstag: The "attempt at appeasement" began on Wednesday 12th December and finally broke down at 5 a.m. on the following day. Cf. *The Times* of 14 December 1979. *In der Nacht zum Donnerstag* may be rendered as *on the night of Wednesday to Thursday.* For the preposition *on,* cf. Hornby, *OALDCE* (s.v. night): *on the night of Friday, the 13 th of June.* For the prepositions *of* and *to,* cf. the following quotation from Iris Murdoch, *The Red and the Green*, p. 237:

Pat had decided to spend the night of Sunday to Monday at Blessington Street.

On Wednesday night would be somewhat ambiguous since *night* may denote both the period between sunset and retiring to bed and the time between bedtime and morning. Cf. *CED*, s.v. night.

5. ein fünfzehn Stunden währender: Any attempt to render the present participle as such (*lasting*) will inevitably result in a complete dislocation of the second half of the sentence.

6. Einigungsversuch: The translation equivalent given in *LEW* is *attempt at (re-)conciliation. Attempt at appeasement* is also possible. Cf. *The Times* of 14 December 1979, p. 1:

A tired and bitter Mr Lenihan, who had spent all night with the Parliament's budget committee in a hopeless attempt at appeasement (. . .).

Some translators might wish to expand the term in the interests of clarity (see the alternatives listed below), but such expansion is not mandatory. Indeed, expansion may become a vice if certain limits are transgressed. Cf. Jiří Levý, *Die literarische Übersetzung,* pp. 118−122.

7. Parlamentarier-Delegation: The equivalent given in Zahn's *Wörterbuch zur Politik und Wirtschaftspolitik* is *delegation of parliamentarians,* but this is by no means the only possible translation. We can also say *a delegation from the Parliament* or *a Parliamentary delegation.* Cf. the following quotation from the *International Herald Tribune* of 15−16 December 1979 (p. 6):

First they met alone, then all 18 of them, plus six commissioners, sat all night with a delegation of 12 from the Parliament, about 40 at a table with no dinner inside them and not enough interpreters. Then at dawn, the Parliamentary delegation reported to the Parliament's Budget Committee.

If we wish to keep closer to the translation proposed by Zahn, we may replace the noun *parliamentarians* by some term such as *European MPs, Euro-MPs* or *Parliament members*. Cf. the following quotations from the press reports on the rejection of the draft budget:

(. . .) European MPs rose to their feet in jubilation. (*The Times,* 14. 12. 1979, p. 1.)
Amid jeering from Euro-MPs, Mr Lenihan, who had badly misread the mood of the assembly, said that he foresaw months of wrangling ahead if the budget was rejected. (*ibid.*)
Mr Jenkins and other EEC officials had tried to head off the unfavorable vote in a long negotiating session with Parliament members last night. (*IHT,* 14. 12. 1979, p. 1.)

8. Finanzminister: The EEC Finance Ministers are occasionally referred to as *budget ministers*. Cf. the following quotation from *The Times* of 6 December 1979 (p. 8):

The Parliament is incensed by the treatment meted out to its proposals last month by EEC budget ministers.

However, the term *Finance Minister* is more common. In journalistic usage it is gradually ousting the longer term *Minister of Finance:*

French Finance Minister René Monory noted that in contrast to the relative optimism at last year's annual meetings in Washington, "We meet in dejection (. . .)." (*IHT,* 6–7. 10. 1979, p. 9.)
West German Finance Minister Hans Matthoefer told today's opening session that he expects the recent unrest on exchange markets to be temporary. (*IHT,* 3. 10. 1979, p. 9.)

Journalists generally prefer short words to longer words because short words can easily be strung together in new compounds, especially in headlines. Besides, short words are likely to make a deeper impact on the reader's mind. Hence, *meeting* is often replaced by *meet, prohibition* by *ban,* and *inquiry* by *probe*; and in American newspapers the noun *influence* is even replaced by the slang word *clout,* which has long hovered on the outskirts of respectability and now seems about to gain admittance to the standard U.S. vocabulary:

And although the consumer groups insist that they represent 260 million people living in the nine-nation area, farm groups have far more clout. (*IHT,* 18. 10. 1979, p. 1.)

For further examples of the influence exerted by the language of headlines, see Simeon Potter, *Our Language,* pp. 174–175.

In the case under discussion, *Finance Minister* is clearly preferable to *Minister of Finance* since the use of the latter term would result in the repetition of the preposition *of* (*the Council of the Ministers of Finance*). The ear should always be satisfied.

b) Alternatives

Before the vote there had been a six-hour Parliamentary debate on		
Tuesday as well as a fifteen-hour *attempt*	*at*	*conciliation*
	„	„ *reconciliation*
	„	„ *appeasement*
	„	*to reach an agreement*
	„	„ *reach an understanding*
	„	„ *come to an agreement*
	„	„ *bring about an agreement*
	„	„ *break the deadlock*
between a *Parliamentary delegation*		*and the Council of the*
delegation from the Parliament		
delegation of parliamentarians		
„	„	*European MPs*
„	„	*Euro-MPs*
„	„	*Parliament members*
Finance Ministers on the night of Wednesday to Thursday.		
budget ministers		

⑨ Die vom Rat unterbreiteten Vorschläge im Rahmen dieses sogenannten Konzertierungsverfahrens zur Überwindung der Meinungsverschiedenheiten waren am Donnerstagvormittag von den meisten Rednern der Fraktionen als unzureichend bezeichnet worden.

a) Annotations

1. Die ... worden: If we attempt to preserve the surface organization of the German original, the verb will be overshadowed by the subject, for there will be a long string of words between the subject nucleus (*proposals*) and the auxiliary verb *had*. The grammatical balance of the sentence can be improved by a change to the active construction. This conversion makes it possible to manoeuvre the longest word-group into end-position.

2. unterbreiten: The list of collocates given in *LEW* is quite good. The verb *put*, however, has been overlooked. Cf. the following snippet from John Ardagh, *The New France*, p. 635:

And de Gaulle himself withdrew increasingly into isolation, blocking most of the proposals put to him by his Ministers (. . .).

It should be noted that *put a proposal (*or *proposals)* is always followed by an indirect object. In the case under discussion, the verb *unterbreiten* must therefore be rendered by some word such as *make* or *submit*.

3. im Rahmen: *Rahmen* is a vogue word like the French *cadre* and the English *parameter*. Cf. E. Agricola, *Wörter und Wendungen*; M. Kinne/B. Strube-Edelmann, *Kleines Wörterbuch des DDR-Wortschatzes,* s.v. Rahmenkollektivvertrag; K. C.

Horton, *German Economic Extracts*, p. 64; P. Gilbert, *Dictionnaire des mots nouveaux*, s.v. cadre; E. Gowers, *The Complete Plain Words*, pp. 116, 278, 285.

Parameter should be used with caution. It is a mathematical term that has been twisted to so many new uses that the average native speaker is no longer quite sure what it means. The definitions given by various contemporary lexicographers include 'limit', 'condition', 'boundary', 'framework' (Gowers), 'any constant or limiting factor' (*CED*), 'a fixed limit or guideline' (*F/W*), 'any of a set of physical properties whose values determine the characteristics or behaviour of something' (*WNCD*), 'a characteristic element' (*ibid.*), 'a distinguishing or defining characteristic or feature, esp. one that may be measured or quantified' (*SOED*).

This seductive and showy hand-me-down metaphor can be avoided in various ways. A useful list of alternatives is given in *G/C*, s.v. Rahmen. As a rule, *framework* is used with reference to relatively stable structures, while *in the course of* combines with nouns denoting processes:

'Liberal in the economic sense, and avowedly capitalist, it [*sc.* the Pompidou régime] seems to be pushing France further towards an American style of prosperity, within the framework of an EEC that is scarcely less capitalist in colouring (. . .). (J. Ardagh, *The New France*, p. 644.)
im Rahmen des Marktgeschehens: in the course of the market process. (*G/C*, s.v. Rahmen.)

In the course of would be quite appropriate in the case under discussion.

4. Konzertierungsverfahrens: The first element of this compound is a neologism which has not yet been recorded in the dictionaries. *Konzertierung* is obviously a loan word adopted from contemporary French. The French noun *concertation* has a particularly interesting history. In Old French, *concertation* denoted a disputation, a contest in eloquence or a tournament. The English word *concertation* was used in much the same way. In the *SOED*, *concertation* is defined as 'contention' and 'disputation'. The French term lost currency in the sixteenth century, while its English equivalent remained in common use until the seventeenth century. It is now practically obsolete, although it has not been marked as such by the *SOED*. The French noun was revived in a most spectacular fashion during the uprising of May 1968, but it underwent an abrupt semantic shift when the would-be revolutionaries began to use it to designate various forms of group discussion between professors and students, government officials and private citizens, management and labour, etc. By the end of 1968, the word *concertation* and the forms of activity it implied had become the latest fad, and the phenomenally popular new term was included in two dictionaries of neologisms published in 1971: P. Gilbert, *Dictionnaire des mots nouveaux*, and J. Giraud, P. Pamart, J. Riverain, *Les mots "dans le vent"*. Unfortunately, the English term *concertation* has not yet been resuscitated, so that English journalists have to make do with a number of periphrastic expressions such as *group discussion*, *direct discussion*, *direct bargaining*, or *free debate*. Sometimes *consultation* is used in a similar sense. Cf. the following snippets from J. Ardagh, *The New France*:

But the strike was also the explosion of years of frustration – an outburst against employers' aloofness and secretiveness, against the boring repetitiveness of much modern factory work, against the rigid and bureaucratic chains of command, the fear of delegating authority and the lack of group discussion, which have characterized French industry at all levels, on the shop floor as well as between *cadres* and managers. (p. 58.)
As compared with the fluctuating, troublesome, but very human situation in Britain, in most French firms there is an absence of direct discussion between employers and workers. (p. 346.)
Both unions and employers have become more aware of the need for direct bargaining within firms, and are making efforts in this direction. (p. 347.)

In June I met many serious students in Paris who at first were delighted by the seizure of the Sorbonne and the outburst of free debate, but later felt the whole thing had turned sour. (p. 479.)
But the Ministry, in typical Gaullist manner, tended to decree new measures high-handedly without consultation, in order to avoid argument and obstruction. (p. 451.)

In the case under discussion, the term *collective bargaining* would be inappropriate. *Collective bargaining* (Kollektivverhandlungen, Tarifverhandlungen) is normally used exclusively in reference to industrial relations. Cf. Paul A. Samuelson, *Economics*, pp. 133–137, 546–553.

5. zur Überwindung: *Zur* followed by an abstract noun in *-ung* may be translated in various ways: *for* + *-ing* form, *calculated to* + infinitive, *intended to* + infinitive, *designed to* + infinitive, *the purpose* (or *object*) *of which is* (*was*, etc.) *to* + infinitive, etc. Here are some examples:

a Fund for the initial financing of the common agricultural policy of the European Economic Community. (A. Gilpin, *Dictionary of Economic Terms*, s.v. European Agricultural Guidance and Guarantee Fund.)
A type of index for measuring changes, e.g. in prices. (*ibid.*, s.v. Paasche Index.)
The Cordell Hull reciprocal-trade program for reducing American and other tariffs has now been with us for almost half a century. (Paul A. Samuelson, *Economics*, p. 668.)
Such a program is all the more needed now that we have a social security program calculated to relieve families from doing as much saving for their old age as would be otherwise prudent. (*ibid.*, p. 342.)
The Centre was created by the Convention on the Settlement of Investment Disputes between States and Nationals of Other States, a Convention intended to encourage the growth of private foreign investment for economic development. (A. Gilpin, *Dictionary of Economic Terms*, s.v. International Centre for the Settlement of Investment Disputes.)
Will not an active fiscal policy designed to wipe out such deflationary gaps then result in running a deficit *most of the time*, leading inevitably to chronic growth in the public debt? (Paul A. Samuelson, *Economics*, p. 338.)
An international organisation the purpose of which is to provide the parties to certain international investment arrangements with a forum to which they may turn for the settlement of any disputes. (A. Gilpin, *Dictionary of Economic Terms*, s.v. International Centre for the Settlement of Investment Disputes.)

Note that the *for-* construction may be expanded in formal style: *for the purpose of* + *-ing* form:

An organisation established in 1961 by a number of central banks to operate in the London market for the purpose of stabilising the price of gold. (A. Gilpin, *Dictionary of Economic Terms*, s.v. International Gold Pool.)

6. Meinungsverschiedenheiten: The equivalents listed in the bilingual dictionaries are not always interchangeable. It should be noted that *dissent, dissidence* and *diversity* are not used in the plural.

7. Rednern: *Platformer* is a somewhat rare word. *Orator* normally implies a value judgement.

8. Fraktionen: *Wing* would be inappropriate here since it must normally be followed by a periphrastic genitive such as *of the party*. *Caucus* must also be rejected. It could be used to translate *Fraktion* in an American context, but it would sound rather out of place in an article on the European Parliament. Note that in British English the noun *caucus* usually denotes a party organization, particularly on a local level. Cf. H. W. Horwill, *Modern American Usage*, s.v. caucus; *CED*, s.v. caucus; G. J. Forgue, *Les mots américains*, p. 30. In the case under consideration, the most appropriate equivalent of *Fraktion* is *political group*. Cf. the following quotations from the press reports on the rejection of the draft budget:

(. . .) leaders of the main political groups rose one after another to assert the Parliament's democratic right to control the budget. (*The Times*, 14. 12. 1979, p. 1.)

(. . .) then the Budget Committee members reported to their respective Political Groups. (*IHT*, 15–16. 12. 1979, p. 6.)

Possible alternatives are *parliamentary groups* (or *parties*) or *factions*. It should, however, be borne in mind that these terms cannot always be used interchangeably. *Group* may be employed either as a synonym or as a hyponym of *party*, and *faction* is a hyponym of both *group* and *party*. *Faction* often denotes a dissentious minority within a political party.

b) Alternatives

On Thursday morning most of the	*speakers*		of the	*political*	
	platform speakers			*parliamentary*	
	speech-makers			"	
				factions	
groups had described as	*insufficient*	the	*proposals*	*submitted*	by
"	*inadequate*		*propositions*	*made*	
parties				*presented*	
the Council in the course of this so-called			*group discussion*	procedure	
			direct discussion	"	
			direct bargaining	"	
			free debate	"	
			consultation	"	
designed	*to overcome*	the	*dissensions.*		
intended	" *surmount*		*controversies.*		
calculated	" "		*disagreements.*		
for	*overcoming*		*misunderstandings.*		
"	*surmounting*		*differences of opinion.*		
			divergences of opinion.		

 Vor der Entscheidung in Straßburg hatte der designierte irische Außenminister Lenihan als amtierender Präsident des Ministerrats das Parlament eindringlich davor gewarnt, den Haushalt abzulehnen.

a) Annotations

1. der designierte . . . Lenihan: The minister's surname should be preceded by *Mr* and followed by the appositive denoting his rank. Cf. the following quotation from *The Times* of 14 December 1979 (p. 1):

The Parliament's legal action came despite an appeal from Mr Brian Lenihan, the Irish Foreign Minister, and chairman of the EEC Council of Ministers, not to "go down the road of confrontation" with member states.

For a full discussion of the problem of word-order, see subsection (6) 3 above.

2. Außenminister: The Irish use two terms: *Foreign Minister* and *Minister for Foreign Affairs*. For the former term, cp. the snippet from *The Times* quoted in the previous section ((10) 1), and for the latter term, cp. section (6) 3 (b), example (viii). The current British and American equivalents of *Außenminister* (*Foreign Secretary*, etc.) have already been listed and labelled in the best bilingual dictionaries. In the case under discussion, *Foreign Minister* is preferable to *Minister for Foreign Affairs* since *Foreign Minister* combines more readily with the postpositive adjective *designate*.

3. Präsident: *President* cannot always be used interchangeably with *chairman*. In this particular instance, the correct term is *chairman*. Cf. the sentence from *The Times* quoted in subsection (10) 1.

4. eindringlich ... gewarnt: The literal translation of *eindringlich warnen* (*warn urgently*) sounds a trifle awkward. *Urge* (*O-HSG-ED*, s.v. eindringlich), *appeal* and *plead* seem much more natural in this context. All these verbs have basically the same meaning: 'to make an earnest request'. For the syntactical patterns in which the verbs occur, see Hornby, *OALDCE*. Note that the terms *appeal* and *plea* were used in the article published in *The Times* of 14 December 1979.

b) Alternatives

| Before the decision in Strasbourg, Mr Lenihan, the Irish Foreign |
| Minister designate, *in his capacity as* acting chairman of the Council |
| *as* |
| of Ministers, had *urged* the Parliament not to reject the budget. |
| *appealed to* |
| *pleaded with* |

⑪ Dies wäre eine „ernste Angelegenheit", durch die „ein tiefgreifender Konflikt in der Gemeinschaft" offenbar würde.

a) Annotations

1. wäre: This is a good example of free indirect speech. In German *erlebte Rede*, as in Latin *oratio obliqua*, the introductory verb of speech is dispensed with, and the subjunctive mode is substituted for the indicative. In English, a distancing effect is obtained by back-shifting the verbs wherever possible. Cf. the following quotation from the *International Herald Tribune* of 15–16 December 1979 (p. 6):

He appealed to the parliamentarians to reflect; it was important; it was a serious situation; let there be no confrontation.

2. eine „ernste Angelegenheit": In *LEW*, *das ist eine ernste Angelegenheit* has been rendered as *that is no laughing matter*. This translation equivalent is quite out of the question here. *That is no laughing matter* can never be expanded by means of a relative clause tacked on to the noun *matter*. The only way to expand this type of expression is to use anticipatory *it* as the sentence subject and add a gerundial construction:

It's no laughing matter working for that boss. (Bei dem Chef hat man nichts zu lachen.) (*O-HSG-ED*, s.v. lachen.)

3. ein tiefgreifender Konflikt: The most appropriate translation equivalents of *tiefgreifend* are *deep-rooted* and *deep-seated*. Cp. the following quotations:

One reason is that the war being waged inside the country is ultimately a reflection of the deep-rooted Sino-Soviet conflict. (*Time,* 12. 11. 1979, p. 23.)
The deep-seated conflict within Faust's personality imparts itself to his intellectual activities. (J. W. Goethe, *Faust I,* edd. R.-M. S. Heffner et al., p. 72.)

These collocations have not yet been recorded in the dictionaries. It is worth noting that the adjective *deep-seated* also collocates with nouns such as *prejudice, instinct* or *hunger* (in the figurative sense). Cf. the following quotation from *Reader's Digest* (June 1980, p. 201):

There is a deep-seated hunger within us that no amount of food can satisfy.

Deep-seated and *deep-rooted* both mean 'firmly established'. In the case under consideration, *fundamental* (= of great importance) might also be employed as an equivalent of *tiefgreifend*.

4. offenbar würde: Various lexicographers have rendered *offenbar werden* as *to be revealed* or *to become apparent*. However, if we adopt this type of solution, we shall have to render *durch die* literally as *through which*. In order to avoid this somewhat clumsy kind of translation, we may use a simple active construction such as *which would reveal (. . .)*.

The tense also calls for a few remarks. When Mr Lenihan made his speech to the Parliament, he considered the rejection of the budget draft as an ominous possibility rather than as a *fait accompli*. It is therefore highly likely that he used the conditional. If this is true, then the verb forms *wäre* and *würde* must be interpreted as genuine conditional forms rather than as substitutes for present tense forms (*sei* and *werde*). It is thus advisable to render both *würde* and *wäre* as conditionals. Conditionals cannot be back-shifted in indirect discourse.

b) Alternatives

That	would be a "serious	*matter"*	which would reveal "a	*deep-rooted*
Rejection		*affair"*		*deep-seated*
		business"		*fundamental*
conflict within the Community".				

⑫ Lenihan kündigte die Möglichkeit eines juristischen Konflikts vor dem Europäischen Gerichtshof im Zusammenhang mit den Auslegungen der Haushaltsbefugnisse des Parlaments an.

a) Annotations

Lenihan: Cf. note (6) 3 (c) above.

b) Alternatives

Mr Lenihan *intimated* the possibility	*of a legal conflict*	before the
hinted at	*of litigation*	
	of legal proceedings	
	of a legal dispute	

| European Court in *connection* with the interpretations of the |
| *connexion* |

Parliament's budgetary powers.

In seiner Auseinandersetzung mit dem EG-Rat war von den Straßburger Abgeordneten immer wieder darauf hingewiesen worden, daß dem Europa-Parlament mit der Direktwahl eine neue Souveränität zugewachsen sei.

a) Annotations

1. EG-Rat: This compound, which has not been recorded in the dictionaries, is simply a contracted form of *EG-Ministerrat* (= EEC Council of Ministers).

2. immer wieder: Some of the equivalents given in *W/H* are highly questionable. *Ever and anon* means '(every) now and then'. It is not synonymous with *again and again*. *Ever and again* also means 'now and then' and is marked as obsolete by the *S.O.E.D.* *Time without number*, which has been labelled as an Americanism in *W/H*, is firmly established in British English and is often replaced by *times without number* and *times out of number*. Both these expressions have been recorded in the *S.O.E.D.*, but they have not been indicated in the bilingual dictionaries.

3. war ... darauf hingewiesen worden: 'Actorless clauses' are quite common in German, but they are impossible in English. In English, the subject must be expressed. Cf. Herbert L. Kufner, *The Grammatical Structures of English and German*, pp. 12–13; W. Friederich, *Technik des Übersetzens*, pp. 97–99. In the case under consideration, the most appropriate solution is anticipatory *it*. Cf. the following example cited by W. Friederich (*op. cit.*, p. 97):

In verantwortlichen Kreisen in Paris wird darauf hingewiesen, daß ... .: It is pointed out in responsible quarters in Paris that ...

4. zugewachsen sei: The verb *accrue* is generally used of profits, interest, etc., but in legal terminology it may also be used of rights and the like. Cf. John Burke, *Osborn's Concise Law Dictionary*, s.v. accrual.

b) Alternatives

In the	*dispute* *quarrel* *altercation* *controversy* *confrontation*	between the	*Parliament* *Assembly*	and the	*EEC Council* *EEC Council of* *[Ministers*
it had been pointed out	*time and time again* *time without number* *times without number* *times out of number* *time after time* *again and again* *over and over again* *time and again* *repeatedly* *constantly*	by the MPs in Strasbourg			
that with direct election a new	*sovereignty* *independence*	had accrued to the			
European Assembly. *European Parliament.*					

 Wer, wie der Europäische Rat, Vorschläge des Parlaments einfach „abschmettere" oder allenfalls zu zaghaften Zugeständnissen bereit sei, mißachte den Willen von Millionen europäischer Wähler.

a) Annotations

1. Wer: *He who* and *he that* should be eschewed in this type of context since as a rule they are used only in gnomic utterances or solemn exhortations. Both *he who* and *he that* have a suggestion of the poetical. *He that* occurs frequently in the King James Bible (1611):

He that hath ears to hear, let him hear. (*Matt.* 11:15.)

Any person who is normally employed in officialese. *Anyone who* or *people who* are much more appropriate in a context which is neither poetical nor strictly administrative.

2. wie: It is advisable to resort to augmentation in order to produce a rhythmical pattern which is more congenial to the spirit of the English language. A verb such as *act* or *behave* may be used to expand the word-group *wie der Europäische Rat*; then *abschmettere* and *bereit sei* can be rendered as participles. This type of construction is particularly common in modern English. Cf. the following example from G. M. Trevelyan, *British History in the Nineteenth Century and After: 1782–1919* (p. 36):

(. . .) many of them, like Coke of Norfolk, became 'improving landlords', breeding sheep, sowing turnips, enclosing fields, moving among their farmers with patriarchal familiarity (. . .).

In this example, the main idea is expressed at the beginning by means of a word-group centred on a finite verb form: *many of them (. . .) became 'improving landlords'*, and the subsidiary ideas are expressed by means of word-groups centred on present participles: *breeding, sowing, enclosing, moving*. *Breeding sheep, sowing turnips*, etc. are hyponyms of the superordinate concept *to become an 'improving landlord'*.

3. „abschmettere": This verb, which has not yet been recorded in the dictionaries, may be rendered as *massacre, refuse categorically* or *condemn outright*. In the *International Herald Tribune* of 15–16 December 1979 (p. 6), Lord Kennet makes the following statement:

Indeed, the Council's massacre of Parliament's amendments has been rather greater this year than in recent years before the Parliament was directly elected.

Massacre may be used as a verb or as a noun. For *refuse categorically* and *condemn outright*, cf. the following quotations from contemporary publications:

The Queen herself has always refused categorically to be subjected to the kind of close protection people like Reagan or Brezhnev are obliged to have (. . .). (*World and Press*, 1st July issue 1981, p. 2.)

These phrasal verbs were commonly used in Middle and Tudor English, but they were later scorned by the classicists and condemned outright by Dr Johnson. (S. Potter, *Our Language*, p. 33.)

4. allenfalls: The locution *at the outside* (*LEW*, s.v. allenfalls) would be inappropriate here since it is generally restricted to informal style. A typical example (*two days at the outside*) is given in *CED*. *At best* is marked as an Americanism by *LEW*, but it is now firmly established in British English. The same goes for a large number of other words and phrases customarily marked *Chiefly U.S. Graft* (= corruption) is a case in point. This term gained currency in the U.S.A. about 1900 (cf. G. J. Forgue, *Les mots américains*, p. 33) and was labelled *Chiefly U.S.* as late as 1979 (*C.E.D.*, s.v. graft), yet the famous British historian G. M. Trevelyan adopted the word *graft* – albeit in inverted commas – as early as 1922 in *British History in the Nineteenth Century and After: 1782–1919* (p. 42 in the Penguin edition reprinted in 1979).

5. zu . . . bereit sei: English lacks any relevant idiom, and is obliged to be more specific here. *Consent to concessions* is preferable to *be prepared to make concessions* because *consent*, being a verb of action, enables the translator to enhance the symmetry of the sentence by establishing a parallel to *massacring the Parliament's proposals*.

6. mißachte: The verb must be back-shifted. Cf. note (11) 1 above.

7. Willen: The German singular ought to be rendered by an English plural such as *wishes*. This type of intra-system shift is frequent in German-English translation. Cf. *Schere (scissors), Gedankenwelt (thoughts), Verwandtschaft (relations)*. For further examples see W. Friederich, *Technik des Übersetzens*, pp. 41–44.

We may also attempt to eke out the sense of *Wille* by means of a rendering such as *wishes and aspirations*. This is an instance of hendiadys, a rhetorical device by which a single idea is expressed by two words normally connected by a conjunction. Sometimes one concept is more important than the other, as in the phrase *law and heraldry* (= *heraldic law*) (*S.O.E.D.*, s.v. hendiadys); yet in many cases the two words are of equal importance. They may even be virtually synonymous. A good example of this is provided by the expression *assemble and meet together* (*Common Prayer Book*, 1536). In *Chemins de la Traduction* (p. 257), Professor L. Bonnerot and his colleagues point out that a word of Latin origin is often coupled with a word of Anglo-Saxon origin, especially in works intended for two classes of readers — an educated élite proficient in Latin and French, and the ignorant or half-educated masses whose vocabulary is predominantly Germanic. This accounts for a good many instances of hendiadys in English, yet there are innumerable cases in which other factors come into play:

(i) the terms and conditions of the said Table. (from an endowment assurance policy quoted *in extenso* in D. Crystal/D. Davy, *Investigating English Style*, pp. 195–197.)
(ii) a person's goods and chattels. (Hornby, *OALDCE*, s.v. chattel.)
(iii) (. . .) creativity requires sensitivity — a female trait — as well as autonomy and independence — traits usually associated with males. (*RD*, December 1979, p. 216.)
(iv) Early Christian Latin poetry is for the most part the work of writers who were trained in the schools of grammar and rhetoric, schools whose tradition was continued with changes and modifications throughout the Middle Ages. (F. J. E. Raby, *The Oxford Book of Medieval Latin Verse*, p. x.)
(v) Had it not been for the example which the latter has given in studying anew, and with entire independence of tradition, the actual facts of French as he found them, I should hardly have dared to compose this little grammar, which, though written with prudence and caution, may appear to many as iconoclastic and heretical. (J. E. Mansion, *A Grammar of Present-Day French*, p. 7.)
(vi) (. . .) the distracting torment of endless, fruitless, barren attention. (Charles Lamb, *A Chapter on Ears, Essays of Elia*.)

In example (i), both of the nouns (*terms* and *conditions*) are of Latin origin. They are virtually synonymous. In the *S.O.E.D.*, *terms* (pl.) is defined as 'conditions or stipulations limiting what is proposed to be granted or done'. English legal terminology is highly complex and frequently archaic, so that legal draftsmen are often in doubt whether certain closely allied words really mean the same thing. To 'make assurance double sure', they therefore coordinate overlapping terms, relying on inclusiveness as a compensation for lack of precision. Cf. D. Crystal/D. Davy, *Investigating English Style*, p. 208.

Example (ii) illustrates the same underlying propensity. In this case, however, the native English word *goods* is complemented by a near-synonym of Romance origin. *Chattel* comes from the Old French noun *chatel* (= personal property).

Examples (iii), (iv), (v) and (vi) show how near-synonyms are coupled for euphony or emphasis: *autonomy and independence, changes and modifications, prudence and caution, fruitless, barren attention*.

For further information on hendiadys, see J. D. Gallagher, *Cours de traduction allemand-français*, pp. 96–97; W. Friederich, *Technik des Übersetzens*, pp. 46–50; A. F. Scott, *Current Literary Terms*, s.v. hendiadys; H. Lausberg, *Elemente der literarischen Rhetorik*, § 305.

8. Wähler: In this context *elector* is more appropriate than *voter* since the underlying idea is election rather than voting, and since the stress is on the relationship between the European MPs and the people who elected them rather than on the power of the individual to express his choice or opinion by casting his vote. For the use of the word *elector* in a similar context, cf. the following snippet from the *International Herald Tribune* of 15–16 December 1979 (p. 6):

In these two points it [*scil.* the European Parliament] expressed (how could it not?) the obvious interest of the great majority of its electors.

In this example sentence it would be impossible to substitute *voter* for *elector*. On the difference between *voter* and *elector*, see R. Meldau/R. B. Whitling, *Schulsynonymik der englischen Sprache*, s.v. wählen.

b) Alternatives

People who *acted* Anyone *behaved*	like the European Council,	*simply massacring* *refusing categorically* *condemning outright*	the
Parliament's proposals or *at best* *Assembly's*	*at most* *at the most*	consenting to	*cautious concessions,* *timid compromises,* *timorous*
showed no regard for the wishes and aspirations of millions of European *showed contempt for " wishes* electors.			

⑮ Der Brüsseler Rat hatte in dem von der Versammlung im letzten November aufgestockten Vierzig-Milliarden-Etat für das kommende Jahr die Mittel für die Sozial-, die Regional- und die Energiepolitik erheblich gekürzt und die geforderten „ersten Schritte zur Eindämmung der Agrarausgaben" abgelehnt.

a) Annotations

1. der Brüsseler Rat hatte . . . gekürzt: This section illustrates one of the major vices of modern German prose usage, namely the tendency to cram all kinds of information into one sentence until it bursts at the seams. In this case, there are far too many words between the auxiliary *hatte* and the past participle *gekürzt* because *Vierzig-Milliarden-Etat* is preceded by an attributive participial phrase (*von der Versammlung . . . aufgestockten*). This type of construction should not be imitated in translation since the excessive use of participial phrases (pycnometochia) inevitably generates patterns which are quite incompatible with the genius of contemporary English. In the case under discussion, the best solution is to chop the sentence into two parts, excising the attributive participial phrase and converting it into an independent clause which can then be linked up with the rest of the sentence by means of the disjunctive *but*. For a detailed discussion of pycnometochia, see H. F. Eggeling, *A Dictionary of Modern German Prose Usage,* s.v. participle (past).

2. Der Brüsseler Rat: Cp. note (3) 6.

3. Milliarden: The German noun *Milliarde* (= 1000 Millionen) may be rendered as *milliard* (British English), *billion* (American English) or *a thousand million(s)* (international English). The use of the word *billion* frequently leads to misunderstandings since a British billion is 1,000 times as much as an American billion: in British English, *billion* means a million millions, while in American English the same word means only a thousand millions, i.e. a milliard. For further details see H. W. Horwill, *A Dictionary of Modern American Usage,* s.v. billion; Norman Moss, *What's the Difference?*, pp. 29, 134.

4. Mittel für: In this case it is possible to eke out the sense of the preposition by adding *set aside*. For a similar use of the verb *set aside* cp. the following quotation from the *International Herald Tribune* of 15–16 December 1979 (p. 6):

That 2 percent [*sc.* two percent of the public expenditure of EEC members] has been set aside to be levied and spent in an agreed Community manner (. . .).

5. Sozialpolitik: In *Cassell's German & English Dictionary* this term has been rendered as *social betterment* and *social legislation*. In this particular instance, however, it is advisable to use a term which is wider in application than these locutions, especially since it is necessary to establish a parallel between the English equivalents of *Sozialpolitik, Regionalpolitik* and *Energiepolitik*. For the difference between *politics* and *policy* see H. W. Klein/W. Friederich, *Englische Synonymik*, s.v. Politik; R. Meldau/R. B. Whitling, *Schulsynonymik der englischen Sprache*, s.v. Politik.

6. erheblich gekürzt: The most appropriate translation equivalent is *slash* (= to reduce drastically). Cf. the following example sentence from *Reader's Digest* (August 1979, p. 98):

If revenues fell short, Congress would have to slash spending or impose a surtax.

Make considerable cuts in would also be an acceptable translation in the case under discussion.

7. und... abgelehnt: *As well as* + *-ing* form may be used here as a means of syntactic compression. Cf. the following example sentence from R. W. Zandvoort's *Handbook of English Grammar* (§ 67, note 3):

The author describes four different styles of standard English pronunciation, as well as including a text with a dialogue in Cockney.

8. geforderten: German attributive participles are often rendered in English by means of relative clauses or postpositive participial phrases. Hence, a word-group such as *die nach ihm benannte Philipskurve* (*Kleiner Wirtschaftsspiegel*, 12/1977) may be translated as *the Philips curve named after him*. In the case under discussion, however, the head word (*Schritte*) is followed by a lengthy postqualifier (*zur Eindämmung der Agrarausgaben*), so that it is virtually impossible to tack the past participle *demanded* on to the noun *steps*. The translator must therefore convert the past participle *demanded* into the noun *demands* (+ *for*).

9. zur Eindämmung: *Step* is normally followed by the preposition *towards:*

We have made a long step towards success. (Hornby, *OALDCE*, s.v. step.)

Eindämmung may be rendered as a gerund. In the bilingual dictionaries, *eindämmen* is often rendered as *check, control, restrain, curb, contain, bring under control,* etc. In this particular instance, however, the most appropriate equivalents are *to limit, to set a limit to* and *to put a limit on*. Examples:

We must limit the expense to what we can afford. (Hornby, *OALDCE*, s.v. limit.[2])
We must set a limit to the expense of the trip. (*ibid.*, s.v. limit[1].)
Last night's prolonged negotiations between the Council and the budget committee broke down mainly on the Parliament's demand that a budgetary limit should be put on agricultural spending in advance of the annual spring farm price settlement. (*The Times*, 14. 12. 1979, p. 1.)

10. Agrarausgaben: This compound, which has not yet been recorded in the dictionaries, may be rendered as *agricultural spending*. Cf. the snippet from *The Times* at the end of the preceding note.

b) Alternatives

Last November the Assembly had	*raised* *increased*	the budget for the	
coming year to forty	*milliards,* *billions,* *thousand million,* „ *millions,*	but the Council in Brussels	
had *slashed* *made considerable cuts in*		the *funds* *fund money for* *resources*	*set aside for* the
social, *social welfare,* *social security,*	regional and energy policies, as well as rejecting		
demands for the	*initial* *first*	steps towards	*putting a budgetary limit on* *putting a limit on* *setting a limit to* *limiting*
agricultural spending.			

Bibliography

Dictionaries, Glossaries and Encyclopedias

Agricola, A., *Wörter und Wendungen* (VEB Bibliographisches Institut, Leipzig, 1981)
Bannock, G., R. E. Baxter, R. Rees, *The Penguin Dictionary of Economics* (Penguin, Harmondsworth, 1972)
Barnhart, C. L., S. Steinmetz, R. K. Barnhart, *A Dictionary of New English 1963–1972* (Barnhart/Langenscheidt, Bronxville, N. Y., Berlin, Munich, Zurich, 1973)
Becker, U., *Mehrwertsteuer-Glossarium* (F. Knapp Verlag, Frankfurt am Main, 1968)
Becker, U., *Rechtswörterbuch für die gewerbliche Wirtschaft* (F. Knapp Verlag, Frankfurt am Main, 2nd ed. 1980)
Betteridge, H. T., *Cassell's German & English Dictionary* (Cassell, London, 2nd ed. 1958)
Buchanan-Brown, J., J. Cang, J. Crawley, B. Galushka, G. Parsons, K. Williams, *Le Mot Juste* (Vintage Books, New York, 1981)
Burke J., *Osborn's Concise Law Dictionary* (Sweet & Maxwell, London, 6th ed 1976)
Bülow, F., H. Langen, *Wörterbuch der Wirtschaft* (A. Kröner Verlag, Stuttgart, 6th ed. 1970)
Cohen, J. M., M. J. Cohen, *The Penguin Dictionary of Quotations* (Penguin, Harmondsworth, 1980)
Cowie, A. P., R. Mackin, *Oxford Dictionary of Current Idiomatic English*, Vol. 1 (Cornelsen & Oxford University Press, Berlin, 2nd ed. 1978)
Davau, M., M. Cohen, M. Lallemand, *Dictionnaire du français vivant* (E. Klett Verlag, Stuttgart, 1972)
Der neue Brockhaus, 5 vols. (F. A. Brockhaus, Wiesbaden, 5th ed. 1975)
Deutsch 2000, Vol. 1. *Glossar Deutsch-Englisch* (M. Hueber Verlag, Munich, 3rd ed. 1981)
Deutsch 2000, Vol. 2. *Glossar Deutsch-Englisch* (M. Hueber Verlag, Munich, 1974)
Deutsch 2000, Vol. 3. *Glossar Deutsch-Englisch* (M. Hueber Verlag, Munich, 1974)
Drosdowski, G., *Duden Stilwörterbuch der deutschen Sprache* (Dudenverlag, Mannheim, Vienna, Zurich, 1970)
Eichborn, R. von, *Der kleine Eichborn: Wirtschaft und Wirtschaftsrecht. Englisch-Deutsch* (Siebenpunkt Verlag, Burscheid, 3rd ed. 1980)
Eichborn, R. von, *Der kleine Eichborn: Wirtschaft und Wirtschaftsrecht. Deutsch-Englisch* (Siebenpunkt Verlag, Burscheid, 3rd ed. 1981)
Engeroff, K., C. Lovelace-Käufer, *An English-German Dictionary of Idioms* (M. Hueber Verlag, Munich, 5th ed. 1979)
Farrell, R. B., *Dictionary of German Synonyms* (Cambridge University Press, 1955)
Freyd-Wadham, H. T., *Englisches Wirtschaftsalphabet* (Th. Grossmann, Stuttgart-Bad Cannstatt, 7th ed. 1978)
Friederich, W., J. Canavan, *Dictionary of English Words in Context* (Verlag L. Lensing, Dortmund, 1979)
Funk & Wagnalls Standard Desk Dictionary (Harper & Row, New York, 1977)
Garmonsway, G. N., J. Simpson, *The Penguin English Dictionary* (Penguin, Harmondsworth, 2nd ed. 1969)
Gilbert, P., *Dictionnaire des mots nouveaux* (Hachette-Tchou, Paris, 1971)
Gilbertson, G., *Harrap's German and English Glossary of Terms in International Law* (G. G. Harrap, London, 1980)
Gilpin, A., *Dictionary of Economic Terms* (Butterworth, London, 4th ed. 1977)
Giraud, J., P. Pamart, J. Riverain, *Les mots "dans le vent"* (Larousse, Paris, 1971)
Greener, M., *The Penguin Dictionary of Commerce* (Penguin, Harmondsworth, 2nd ed. 1980)

Gruber C. M., *Wörterbuch der Werbung und des Marketing* (M. Hueber Verlag, Munich, 1977)
Gunston, C. A., C. M. Corner, *Deutsch-Englisches Glossarium finanzieller und wirtschaftlicher Fachausdrücke* (F. Knapp Verlag, Frankfurt am Main, 7th ed. 1977)
Haensch, G., *Wörterbuch der internationalen Beziehungen und der Politik* (M. Hueber Verlag, Munich 2nd ed. 1975)
Haensch, G., G. Haberkamp, *Wörterbuch der Landwirtschaft* (BLV Verlagsgesellschaft, Munich, 2nd ed. 1975)
Hanks, P. ed., *Collins Dictionary of the English Language* (Collins, London & Glasgow, 1979)
Hayakawa, S. I., P. J. Fletcher, *Cassell's Modern Guide to Synonyms & Related Words* (Cassell, London, 1971)
Hill, R. H., *Jarrolds' Dictionary of Difficult Words* (Jarrolds, London, 2nd ed. s. d.)
Hornby, A. S., A. P. Cowie, *Oxford Advanced Learner's Dictionary of Current English* (Cornelsen & Oxford University Press, Berlin, 1980)
Horwill, H. W., *A Dictionary of Modern American Usage* (Oxford University Press, 2nd ed. 1944)
Jones, T. ed., *Harrap's Standard German and English Dictionary,* Part One, German-English A–E (G. G. Harrap, London, 1963)
Jones, T. ed., *The Oxford-Harrap Standard German-English Dictionary,* Vol. II F–K (Oxford University Press, 1977)
Jones, T. ed., *Harrap's Standard German and English Dictionary,* Part One, German-English L–R (G. G. Harrap, London, 1974)
Kase, F. J., *Dictionary of Industrial Property* (Sijthoff & Noordhoff, Alphen aan den Rijn, The Netherlands, 1980)
Keppler, K., *Langenscheidts Konversationsbuch Englisch-Deutsch* (Langenscheidt, Berlin, Munich, Vienna, Zurich, 10th ed. 1980)
Kinne, M., B. Strube-Edelmann, *Kleines Wörterbuch des DDR-Wortschatzes* (Pädagogischer Verlag Schwann, Düsseldorf, 1980)
Kißling, H., *Lexikon der englischen Unterrichtssprache* (Quelle & Meyer, Heidelberg, 2nd ed. 1981)
Klein, H. W., W. Friederich, *Englische Synonymik* (M. Hueber Verlag, Munich, 4th ed. 1975)
Lewandowski, T., *Linguistisches Wörterbuch,* Vol. 1 (Quelle & Meyer, Heidelberg, 3rd ed. 1979)
Lewandowski, T., *Linguistisches Wörterbuch,* Vol. 2 (Quelle & Meyer, Heidelberg, 3rd ed. 1979)
Lewandowski, T., *Linguistisches Wörterbuch,* Vol. 3 (Quelle & Meyer, Heidelberg, 3rd ed. 1980)
Mansion, J. E., ed., *Harrap's Standard French and English Dictionary,* Part One, French-English (G. G. Harrap, London, 1961)
Mansion, J. E., R. P. L. Ledésert, M. Ledésert, edd., *Harrap's New Standard French and English Dictionary,* Part One, French-English, 2 vols. (G. G. Harrap, London, 1979)
Marcheteau, M., J. Tardieu, *Business and Economics,* Vol. 2 (A. Colin, Paris, 1970)
Meldau, R., R. B. Whitling, *Schulsynonymik der englischen Sprache* (Hirschgraben-Verlag, Frankfurt am Main, 3rd ed. 1975)
Messinger, H., *Langenscheidts Großes Schulwörterbuch,* Deutsch-English (Langenscheidt, Berlin, Munich, Vienna, Zurich, 1977)
Messinger, H., W. Rüdenberg, *Langenscheidts Großes Schulwörterbuch,* Englisch-Deutsch (Langenscheidt, Berlin, Munich, Vienna, Zurich, 1977)
Moore, L., *Dictionary of Foreign Dining Terms* (W. H. Allen, London, 1958)
Moss, N., *What's the Difference?* (Arrow Books, London, 1980)
Multilingual Vocabulary of Educational Radio and Television Terms (TR Verlagsunion/M. Hueber Verlag, Munich, 1971)
Onions, C. T., ed., *The Shorter Oxford English Dictionary,* 2 vols. (Oxford University Press, 1978)
Partridge, E., *Smaller Slang Dictionary* (Routledge & Kegan Paul, London, 1980)
Pearce, D. W., ed., *The Macmillan Dictionary of Modern Economics* (Macmillan, London & Basingstoke, 1981)
Pei, M., *Glossary of Linguistic Terminology* (Columbia University Press, New York, 1966)
Quinault, R. J., *1000 idiomatische Redensarten Englisch* (Langenscheidt, Berlin & Munich, 2nd ed. 1980)

Renner, R., R. Sachs, *Wirtschaftssprache. Deutsch/Englisch · Englisch/Deutsch* (M. Hueber Verlag, Munich, 3rd ed. 1975)
Renty, I. de, *Lexique quadrilingue des affaires* (Hachette, Paris, 1977)
Robert, P., *Le Petit Robert* (Sté. du Nouveau Littré, Paris, 1978)
Roget's Thesaurus of English Words and Phrases, ed. R. A. Dutch (Penguin, Harmondsworth, 1979)
Rüdenberg, W., K. Pearl, *4000 German Idioms and Colloquialisms* (Hirschfeld, London, 1955)
Seidl, J., W. McMordie, *English Idioms and How to Use Them* (Cornelsen & Oxford University Press, Berlin, 4th ed. 1978)
Seldon, A., F. G. Pennance, *Everyman's Dictionary of Economics* (J. M. Dent & Sons, London, 2nd ed. 1976)
Sloan, H. S., A. J. Zurcher, *Dictionary of Economics* (Barnes & Noble, New York, 5th ed. 1970)
Springer, O., ed., *Langenscheidts Enzyklopädisches Wörterbuch der englischen und deutschen Sprache*, Part I, Vol. 1 A–M (Langenscheidt, Berlin, Munich, Vienna, Zurich, 4th ed. 1974)
Springer, O., ed., *Langenscheidts Enzyklopädisches Wörterbuch der englischen und deutschen Sprache*, Part I, Vol. 2 N–Z (Langenscheidt, Berlin, Munich, Vienna, Zurich, 4th ed. 1974)
Springer, O., ed., *Langenscheidts Enzyklopädisches Wörterbuch der englischen und deutschen Sprache*, Part II, Vol. 1 A–K (Langenscheidt, Berlin, Munich, Vienna, Zurich, 1st ed. 1974)
Springer, O., ed., *Langenscheidts Enzyklopädisches Wörterbuch der englischen und deutschen Sprache*, Part II, Vol. 2 L–Z (Langenscheidt, Berlin, Munich, Vienna, Zurich, 1st ed. 1975)
Taylor, R., W. Gottschalk, *A German-English Dictionary of Idioms* (M. Hueber Verlag, Munich, 4th ed. 1978)
The English Duden (G. G. Harrap, London, 1960)
The Random House Dictionary of the English Language (Random House, New York, 1973)
The Schöffler-Weis Compact German and English Dictionary, rev. Erwin Weis & Erich Weis (G. G. Harrap, London, 1962)
Webster's New Collegiate Dictionary (Merriam, Springfield, Mass., 1977)
Webster's New Dictionary of Synonyms (Merriam, Springfield, Mass., 1973)
Weis, E., E. Haberfellner, *Business Vocabulary for All: English-German* (E. Klett Verlag, Stuttgart, 1975)
Wildhagen, K., W. Héraucourt, *English-German German-English Dictionary*, Vol. 1 English-German (Brandstetter, Wiesbaden/G. Allen & Unwin, London, 1973)
Wildhagen, K., W. Héraucourt, *English-German German-English Dictionary*, Vol. 2 German-English (Brandstetter, Wiesbaden/G. Allen & Unwin, London, 2nd ed. 1972)
F. T. Wood, *English Colloquial Idioms* (Macmillan, London & Basingstoke, 1976)
F. T. Wood, *English Prepositional Idioms* (Macmillan, London & Basingstoke, 1978)
F. T. Wood, *English Verbal Idioms* (Lensing, Dortmund/Macmillan, London & Basingstoke, 1970)
Wörterbuch Englisch (M. Pawlack, Herrsching, 1981)
Zahn, H. E., *Englisch-Deutsches Glossarium finanzieller und wirtschaftlicher Fachausdrücke* (F. Knapp Verlag, Frankfurt am Main, 1977)
Zahn, H. E., *Euro-Wirtschaftswörterbuch* (F. Knapp Verlag, Frankfurt am Main, 1973)
Zahn, H. E., *Wörterbuch zur Politik und Wirtschaftspolitik*, Vol. 1 (F. Knapp Verlag, Frankfurt am Main, 1975)

Works on English and German Grammar

Beilhardt, K., F. W. Sutton, *Learning English: Englische Schulgrammatik* (E. Klett Verlag, Stuttgart, 3rd ed. 1967)
Clément, D., W. Thümmel, *Syntaxe de l'allemand standard* (Larousse, Paris, 1976)
Close, R. A., *A reference grammar for students of English* (Longman, London, 1975)
Curme, G. O., *English Grammar* (Barnes & Noble, New York, 1947)
Dubois-Charlier, F., *Éléments de linguistique anglaise: la phrase complexe et les nominalisations* (Larousse, Paris, 1971)

Dubois-Charlier, F., *Éléments de linguistique anglaise: syntaxe* (Larousse, Paris, 1970)
Erben, J., *Abriß der deutschen Grammatik* (M. Hueber Verlag, Munich, 1966)
Friederich, W., *Englische Morphologie* (M. Hueber Verlag, Munich, 1976)
Friederich, W., *Probleme der Semantik und Syntax des englischen Gerundiums* (M. Hueber Verlag, Munich, 1973)
Grebe, P., ed., *Duden Grammatik der deutschen Gegenwartssprache* (Dudenverlag, Mannheim, 1959)
Greenfield, E. V., *German Grammar* (Barnes & Noble, New York, 3rd ed. 1968)
Hoffmann, H. G., F. Schmidt, *English Grammar Exercises* (M. Hueber Verlag, Munich, 3rd ed. 1976)
Jespersen, O., *Essentials of English Grammar* (G. Allen & Unwin, London, 1979)
Kałuża, Henryk, *The Use of Articles in Contemporary English* (J. Groos Verlag, Heidelberg, 1981)
Kufner, H. L., *The Grammatical Structures of English and German* (University of Chicago Press, Chicago & London, 1962)
Lamprecht, A., *Grammatik der englischen Sprache* (Cornelsen-Velhagen & Klasing, Berlin, 5th ed. 1977)
Philipp, M., *Grammaire de l'allemand* (P.U.F., Paris, 2nd ed. 1980)
Quirk, R., S. Greenbaum, G. Leech, J. Svartvik, *A Grammar of Contemporary English* (Longman, London, 8th impression (corrected) 1979)
Quirk, R., S. Greenbaum, *A University Grammar of English* (Longman, London, 9th impression (corrected) 1979)
Russ, C. V. J., *Contrastive Aspects of English and German* (J. Groos Verlag, Heidelberg, 1981)
Russon, L. J., *Complete German Course for First Examinations* (Longmans, Green & Co., London, New York, Toronto, 3rd impression 1951)
Schibsbye, K., *A Modern English Grammar* (Oxford University Press, 4th impression 1979)
Sutton, F. W., K. Beilhardt, *Grundzüge der englischen Grammatik* (E. Klett Verlag, Stuttgart, 1970)
Tellier, A. R., *Cours de grammaire anglaise* (S.E.D.E.S., Paris, 1967)
Tellier, A. R., *Grammaire de l'anglais* (P.U.F., Paris, 3rd ed. 1979)
Thomson, A. J., A. V. Martinet, *A Practical English Grammar* (Cornelsen & Oxford University Press, Berlin, 1969)
Zandvoort, R. W., *A Handbook of English Grammar* (Longman, London, 7th ed. 1975)

Works and Style and Stylistics

Crystal, D., D. Davy, *Investigating English Style* (Longman, London, 6th impression 1979)
Eggeling, H. F., *A Dictionary of Modern German Prose Usage* (Oxford University Press, 1974)
Flesch, R., *How to Write Plain English* (Harper & Row, New York, 1979)
Flesch, R., *The ABC of Style* (Harper & Row, New York, 1980)
Fontanier, P., *Les figures du discours* (Flammarion, Paris, 1968)
Fowler, H. W., *A Dictionary of Modern English Usage*, rev. Sir Ernest Gowers (Oxford University Press, 1980)
Gordon, I. A., *The Movement of English Prose* (Longman, London, 1980)
Gowers, E., *The Complete Plain Words* (Penguin, Harmondsworth, 1980)
Hough, G., *Style and Stylistics* (Routledge & Kegan, London, 1969)
Lausberg, H., *Elemente der literarischen Rhetorik* (M. Hueber Verlag, Munich, 2nd ed. 1963)
Malblanc, A., *Stylistique comparée du français et de l'allemand* (Didier, Paris, 1968)
Murry, J. M., *The Problem of Style* (Oxford University Press, 7th impression 1976)
Partridge, E., *Usage and Abusage* (Penguin, Harmondsworth, 1970)
Quirk, R., *The Use of English* (Longman, London, 1978)
Quirk, R., A. H. Smith, edd., *The Teaching of English* (Oxford University Press, 1975)
Reiners, L., *Stilkunst* (Verlag C. H. Beck, Munich, 1967)
Strunk, W., E. B. White, *The Elements of Style* (Macmillan, New York/Collier Macmillan, London, 3rd ed. 1979)

Turner, G. W., *Stylistics* (Penguin, Harmondsworth, 1979)
Ullmann, S., *Meaning and Style* (B. Blackwell, Oxford, 1973)
Vinay, J. P., J. Darbelnet, *Stylistique comparée du français et de l'anglais* (Didier, Paris, 1958)
Wood, F. T., *Current English Usage* (Macmillan, London & Basingstoke, 1962)

Miscellaneous Aspects of the English Language

Bacquet, P., *Le vocabulaire anglais* (P.U.F., Paris, 1974)
Forgue, G. J., *Les mots américains* (P.U.F., Paris, 1976)
Forgue, G. J., R. I. McDavid, Jr., *La langue des américains* (Aubier Montaigne, Paris, 1972)
Foster, B., *The Changing English Language* (Penguin, Harmondsworth, 1971)
Friederich, W., *Die Interpunktion im Englischen* (M. Hueber Verlag, Munich, 1977)
Jespersen, O., *Growth and Structure of the English Language* (B. Blackwell, Oxford, 1978)
Leisi, E., *Der Wortinhalt* (Quelle & Meyer, Heidelberg, 5th ed. 1975)
Palmer, F., *Grammar* (Penguin, Harmondsworth, 1971)
Potter, S., *Our Language* (Penguin, Harmondsworth, 1979)
Pyles, T., *The Origins and Development of the English Language* (Harcourt Brace Jovanovich, New York, Chicago, San Francisco, Atlanta, 2nd ed. 1971)
Rudolph, J., *Langenscheidts Handbuch der englischen Wirtschaftssprache* (Langenscheidt, Berlin, Munich, Vienna, Zurich, 2nd ed. 1976)
Schuhmacher, K. E., ed., *English – A World Language* (E. Klett Verlag, Stuttgart, 1978)
Strevens, P., *British and American English* (Cassell, London, 1978)
Wächtler, K., *Geographie und Stratifikation der englischen Sprache* (A. Bagel Verlag Düsseldorf/ Francke Verlag Bern & Munich, 1977)
Wrenn, C. L., *The English Language* (Methuen, London, 1977)

The Theory and Practice of Translation

Albrecht, J., *Linguistik und Übersetzung* (M. Niemeyer Verlag, Tübingen, 1973)
Bacquet, P., D. Keen, *Initiation au thème anglais* (A. Colin, Paris, 1975)
Bonnerot, L., *Chemins de la traduction: domaine anglais* (Didier, Paris, 1963)
Braem, H. M., ed., *Übersetzer-Werkstatt* (Deutscher Taschenbuch Verlag, Munich, 1979)
Broich, U., J. Martin, *Deutsche Übersetzungstexte für englische Übungen* (Vandenhoeck & Ruprecht, Göttingen, 3rd ed. 1968)
Buck, T., *German into English*, Vol. 1 (Vandenhoeck & Ruprecht, Göttingen, 4th ed., 1979)
Buck, T., *German into English*, Vol. 2 (Vandenhoeck & Ruprecht, Göttingen, 1971)
Catford, J. C., *A Linguistic Theory of Translation* (Oxford University Press, 1978)
Collier, G., B. Shields, *Guided German-English Translation* (Quelle & Meyer, Heidelberg, 1977)
Dinter, S., P. Ilgenfritz, *Deutsche Reden und die Technik ihrer Übersetzung* (M. Hueber Verlag, Munich, 1974)
Dinter, S. K., J. Ripken, *Deutsche Reden und die Technik ihrer Übersetzung: English Translation Supplement* (M. Hueber Verlag, Munich, 1975)
Eslava, R., *Advanced Translation Practice: German-English* (Manz Verlag, Munich, 1980)
Friederich, W., *Technik des Übersetzens: Englisch und Deutsch* (M. Hueber Verlag, Munich, 1969)
Güttinger, F., *Zielsprache* (Manesse Verlag, Zurich, 1963)
Hamblock, D., D. Wessels, *Englisch in Wirtschaft und Handel: Übersetzungstexte* (Verlag W. Girardet, Essen, 1979)
Hamblock, D., D. Wessels, *Englisch in Wirtschaft und Handel: Übersetzungstexte – Lösungen* (Verlag W. Girardet, Essen, 1980)
Herms, D., *Englisch-deutsche Übersetzung* (M. Hueber Verlag, Munich, 2nd ed., 1979)
Kapp, V., ed., *Übersetzer und Dolmetscher* (Quelle & Meyer, Heidelberg, 1974)
Kelly, L., *The True Interpreter* (B. Blackwell, Oxford, 1979)
Kloepfer, R., *Die Theorie der literarischen Übersetzung* (W. Fink Verlag, Munich, 1967)

Koller, W., *Einführung in die Übersetzungswissenschaft* (Quelle & Meyer, Heidelberg, 1979)
Kühlwein, W., G. Thome, W. Wilss, edd., *Kontrastive Linguistik und Übersetzungswissenschaft* (W. Fink Verlag, Munich, 1981)
Levý, J., *Die literarische Übersetzung,* tr. W. Schamschula (Athenäum Verlag, Frankfurt am Main/Bonn, 1969)
Malblanc, A., *Stylistique comparée du français et de l'allemand* (Didier, Paris, 1968)
Mounin, G., *Les problèmes théoriques de la traduction* (Gallimard, Paris, 1963)
Pilch, H., *Empirical Linguistics* (Francke Verlag, Munich, 1976)
Schick, P., *Deutsch-englische Übersetzungsübungen,* Vol. 2 (M. Hueber Verlag, Munich, 2nd ed. 1966)
Snell, M., *German-English Prose Translation* (M. Hueber Verlag, Munich, 2nd ed. 1978)
Snell, M., *German Thought in English Idiom* (M. Hueber Verlag, Munich, 3rd ed. 1977)
Stein, D., *Theoretische Grundlagen der Übersetzungswissenschaft* (G. Narr Verlag, Tübingen, 1980)
Vinay, J. P., J. Darbelnet, *Stylistique comparée du français et de l'anglais* (Didier, Paris, 1958)
Wilss, W., ed., *Semiotik und Übersetzen* (G. Narr Verlag, Tübingen, 1980)

Newspapers and Periodicals

Daily Express
Der Spiegel
Die Zeit
EFL bulletin
Financial Times
Frankfurter Allgemeine Zeitung
Handelsblatt
International Herald Tribune
Kleiner Wirtschaftsspiegel
Lebende Sprachen
Manager-Magazin
Newsweek
Plus
Reader's Digest
Saturday Review
Süddeutsche Zeitung
The Chronicle Herald
The Economist
The Guardian
The Journal of Political Economy
The Observer
The Times
Time
Universitas
Welt am Sonntag
Westfälische Nachrichten
Wirkendes Wort
Word
World and Press

Miscellaneous Publications (novels, essays, textbooks, etc.)

Abrams, M. H., *A Glossary of Literary Terms* (Holt, Rinehart & Winston, New York, 3rd ed. 1971)
Alexander, L. G., *New Concept English,* Vol. V (Langenscheidt-Longman, Munich, 1972)

Altenbernd, L., L. L. Lewis, *A Handbook for the Study of Fiction* (Macmillan, London, 1966)
Ambros, A. A., *Einführung in die moderne arabische Schriftsprache* (M. Hueber Verlag, Munich, 2nd ed. 1975)
Andersch, A., *Sansibar oder der letzte Grund,* ed. W. G. Hesse (G. G. Harrap, London, 1964)
Ardagh, J., *The New France* (Penguin, Harmondsworth, 2nd ed. 1973)
Arvill, R., *Man and Environment* (Penguin, Harmondsworth, 1978)
Atkins, J. W. H., *English Literary Criticism: 17th & 18th Centuries* (Methuen, London, 1968)
Auerbach, E., *Mimesis* (Francke Verlag, Bern & Munich, 3rd ed. 1964)
Bach, A., *Geschichte der deutschen Sprache* (Quelle & Meyer, Heidelberg, 7th ed., 1961)
Bain, A. D., *The Control of the Money Supply* (Penguin, Harmondsworth, 3rd ed. 1980)
Bain, A. W., ed., *German Poetry for Students* (Macmillan, London, 1946)
Baldick, R., *The Life of J.-K. Huysmans* (Oxford University Press, 1955)
Bally, C., *Linguistique générale et linguistique française* (Francke Verlag, Bern, 1945)
Barraclough, G., *An Introduction to Contemporary History* (Penguin, Harmondsworth, 1967)
Beckson, K., A. Ganz, *A Reader's Guide to Literary Terms* (Thames & Hudson, London, 1970)
Bellow, S., *Henderson the Rain King* (Penguin, Harmondsworth, 1966)
Benn, G., *Doppelleben* (Deutscher Taschenbuch Verlag, Munich, 1967)
Bernstein, H., ed., *Underdevelopment and Development* (Penguin, Harmondsworth, 1978)
Bianchi, M., W. Bliemel, A. Fitzpatrick, J. Quetz, *Englisch für Erwachsene,* Vol. 3 (Cornelsen & Oxford University Press, Berlin, 1978)
Biethahn, J., *Einführung in die EDV für Wirtschaftswissenschaftler* (R. Oldenbourg Verlag, Munich, Vienna, 1980)
Bingham, R. C., *Economic Concepts* (McGraw-Hill, New York, 4th ed. 1975)
Bithell, J., *Modern German Literature: 1880–1950* (Methuen, London, 3rd ed. 1959)
Bliemel, W., A. Fitzpatrick, J. Quetz, *Englisch für Erwachsene,* Vol. 1 (Cornelsen & Oxford University Press, Berlin, 1976)
Bliemel, W., A. Fitzpatrick, J. Quetz, *Englisch für Erwachsene,* Vol. 2 (Cornelsen & Oxford University Press, Berlin, 1977)
Booth, W. C., *The Rhetoric of Fiction* (University of Chicago Press, Chicago & London, 1969)
Bornemann, E., *Lateinisches Unterrichtswerk,* Neue Ausgabe B (Hirschgraben Verlag, Frankfurt am Main, 1975)
Boulton, M., *The Anatomy of Poetry* (Routledge & Kegan Paul, London, 6th impression 1970)
Böll, H., *Erzählungen, Hörspiele, Aufsätze* (Kiepenheuer & Witsch, Cologne & Berlin, 1961)
Böll, H., *Wanderer, kommst du nach Spa . . .* (Deutscher Taschenbuch Verlag, Munich, 22nd ed. 1980)
Bradbury, M., D. Palmer, edd., *Contemporary Criticism* (E. Arnold, London, 1970)
Brittain, F., ed., *The Penguin Book of Latin Verse* (Penguin, Harmondsworth, 1962)
Brooks, C., *The Well Wrought Urn* (Methuen, London, 1968)
Bryant, J. H., *The Open Decision* (Collier-Macmillan, London, 1970)
Butterworth, E., D. Weir, edd., *The Sociology of Modern Britain* (Fontana/Collins, Glasgow, 3rd impression 1977)
Byrne, L. S. R., E. L. Churchill, *A Comprehensive French Grammar* (B. Blackwell, Oxford, 1980)
Carstensen, B., *SPIEGEL-Wörter, SPIEGEL-Worte; Zur Sprache eines deutschen Nachrichtenmagazins* (M. Hueber Verlag, Munich, 1971)
Chomsky, N., *Aspects of the Theory of Syntax* (M.I.T. Press, Cambridge, Mass., 11th printing 1976)
Church, R., *The Growth of the English Novel* (Methuen, London, 1968)
Cicero, *Staatsreden,* ed. H. Kasten (Akademie-Verlag, Berlin, 1977)
Claxton, C. M., *Background to the "Troubles"* (Verlag Eilers & Schünemann, Bremen, 1981)
Clifford, P. M., *Inversion of the Subject in French Narrative Prose from 1500 to the Present Day* (B. Blackwell, Oxford, 1973)
Cohen, L., *Beautiful Losers* (J. Cape, London, 1970)
Cohn, E. J., *Manual of German Law,* Vol. I (The British Institute of International and Comparative Law, London, 2nd ed., 1968)

Cohn, E. J., *Manual of German Law,* Vol. II (The British Institute of International and Comparative Law, London, 2nd ed. 1971)
Colette, *Chéri/The Last of Chéri,* ed. R. Mortimer (Penguin, Harmondsworth, 1973)
Collins, W., *The Woman in White* (Penguin, Harmondsworth, 1974)
Conrad, J., *Nostromo* (Penguin, Harmondsworth, 1972)
Conrad, J., *Youth/Jugend* (Deutscher Taschenbuch Verlag, Munich, 1978)
Consumer Credit (Crowther-Report), Vol. I (Her Majesty's Stationery Service, Cmnd. 4596, London)
Conway, T., ed., *Ireland and its Problems* (E. Klett Verlag, Stuttgart, 1978)
Corder, S. P., *Introducing Applied Linguistics* (Penguin, Harmondsworth, 1973)
Crystal, D., *Linguistics* (Penguin, Harmondsworth, 1971)

Daily Mail Income Tax Guide 1968–1969, ed. P. F. Hughes (Associated Newspapers Ltd., London, 1968)
Dalton, G., *Economic Systems and Society* (Penguin, Harmondsworth, 1974)
Dauten, C. A., L. M. Valentine, *Business Cycles and Forecasting* (South-Western Publishing Co., Cincinnati, 1978)
Davidson, P., J. Norman, *Russian Phrase Book* (Penguin, Harmondsworth, 1980)
Davis, R. M., ed., *The Novel: Modern Essays in Criticism* (Prentice-Hall, Englewood Cliffs, New Jersey, 1969)
De Witt Miller, *Impossible – Yet it Happened!* (Ace Books, New York, 1947)
C. Dickens, *Our Mutual Friend,* ed. S. Gill (Penguin, Harmondsworth, 1971)
Dickinson, L. T., *A Guide to Literary Study* (Holt, Rinehart & Winston, New York, 1959)
Dixon, P., *Rhetoric* (Methuen, London, 1971)
Donaldson, P., *Guide to the British Economy* (Penguin, Harmondsworth, 4th ed. 1976)
Döblin, A., *Hamlet* (Verlag Ullstein, Frankfurt/M. & Berlin, 1961)
Döblin, A., *Wallenstein* (Walter-Verlag, Olten & Freiburg im Breisgau, 1965)
Duron, J., *Langue française langue humaine* (Larousse, Paris, 1963)
Dürrenmatt, F., A. Andersch, H. von Doderer, H. Broch, *Erzählungen/Stories* (M. Hueber Verlag, Munich, 2nd ed. 1970)
Dyson, A. E., ed., *C. Dickens: Bleak House* (Macmillan, London, 1969)

Eckersley. C. E., W. Kaufmann, *A Commercial Course for Foreign Students,* Vol. 1 (Longman, London, 1977)
Eliot, T. S., *Collected Poems 1909–1935* (Harcourt, Brace, New York, 1936)
Eliot, T. S., *The Use of Poetry and the Use of Criticism* (Faber & Faber, London, 1980)
Essen, E., *Methodik des Deutschunterrichts* (Quelle & Meyer, Heidelberg, 8th ed. 1969)
Evans, I., *A Short History of English Literature* (Penguin, Harmondsworth, 3rd ed. 1970)

Fairlie, A., *Baudelaire: Les Fleurs du Mal* (E. Arnold, London, 1960)
Fairlie, A., *Flaubert: Madame Bovary* (E. Arnold, London, 1962)
Fitzgerald, F. S., *The Great Gatsby* (Penguin, Harmondsworth, 1950)
Fontane, T., *Die Poggenpuhls,* ed. D. Barlow (B. Blackwell, Oxford, 1962)
Fontane, T., *Grete Minde,* ed. A. R. Robinson (Methuen, London, 1960)
Ford, B., ed., *The Pelican Guide to English Literature,* Vol. 7 (Penguin, Harmondsworth, 1970)
Forster, L., ed., *The Penguin Book of German Verse* (Penguin, Harmondsworth, 1961)
Foster, E. M., *Aspects of the Novel* (E. Arnold, London, 1960)
Foster, E. M., *Maurice* (Penguin, Harmondsworth, 1972)
Fowler, R., ed., *Style and Structure in Literature* (B. Blackwell, Oxford, 1975)
Fowler, W. S., *Proficiency English,* Book 1 (Nelson, Sunbury-on-Thames, 1976)
Fowler, W. S., *Proficiency English,* Book 2 (Nelson, Sunbury-on-Thames, 1977)
Fowler, W. S., *Proficiency English,* Teacher's Book 1 (Nelson, Sunbury-on-Thames, 1976)
Frisch, M., *Homo faber* (Suhrkamp Verlag, Frankfurt/M., 1962)
Frisch, M., *Stiller* (Suhrkamp Taschenbuch Verlag, Frankfurt/M., 1980)
Furst, L. R., *Romanticism* (Methuen, London, 2nd ed. 1976)
Furst, L. R., P. N. Skrine, *Naturalism* (Methuen, London, 1971)
Galbraith, J. K., *The Affluent Society* (Penguin, Harmondsworth, 2nd ed. 1970)

Gallagher, J. D., *Cours de traduction allemand-français: textes politiques et économiques* (R. Oldenbourg Verlag, Munich & Vienna, 1981)
Gaskell, P., *A New Introduction to Bibliography* (Oxford University Press, 1974)
Gesetz zum Schutz vor Mißbrauch personenbezogener Daten bei der Datenverarbeitung (F. Knapp Verlag, Frankfurt/M., 1977)
Giorgetti, P., J. Norman, *Italian Phrase Book* (Penguin, Harmondsworth, 2nd ed. 1979)
Glover, C. M., *A Concise Latin Grammar* (Meiklejohn & Son, London, 1948)
Goethe, J. W. von, *Egmont,* ed. J. T. Hatfield (G. G. Harrap, London, 1955)
Goethe, J. W. von, *Faust,* Part I, edd. R.-M. S. Heffner, H. Rehder, W. F. Twaddell (D. C. Heath & Co., Boston, 1954)
Goethe, J. W. von, *Torquato Tasso,* ed., E. L. Stahl (B. Blackwell, Oxford, 1962)
Gough, L., ed., *The Harrap Book of Modern Essays* (G. G. Harrap, London, 1952)
Green, G., *A Gun for Sale* (Penguin, Harmondsworth, 1979)
Grubel, H. G., *The International Monetary System* (Penguin, Harmondsworth, 3rd ed. 1977)
Haggar, A. J., *Inflation: Theory and Policy* (Macmillan, London & Basingstoke, 1977)
Halliday, F., *Iran: Dictatorship and Development* (Penguin, Harmondsworth, 2nd ed., 1979)
Hamblock, D., D. Wessels, *Englisch in Wirtschaft und Handel,* Vol. 1 (Verlag W. Girardet, Essen, 1977)
Harrison, P., *Inside the Third World,* (Penguin, Harmondsworth, 1979)
Hartley, A., ed., *The Penguin Book of French Verse,* 3: *The Nineteenth Century* (Penguin, Harmondsworth, 1958)
Hatto, A. T., *The Niebelungenlied* (Penguin, Harmondsworth, 1965)
Haugen, E., M. Bloomfield, edd., *Language as a Human Problem* (Lutterworth Press, Guildford & London, 1975)
Hawkins, K., *Unemployment* (Penguin, Harmondsworth, 1979)
Henrichsmeyer, W., O. Gans, I. Evers, *Einführung in die Volkswirtschaftslehre* (Verlag Eugen Ullmer, Stuttgart, 1979)
Hitchin, U., J. Norman, *German Phrase Book* (Penguin, Harmondsworth, 2nd ed. 1978)
Hoffmann, H. G., *Aufbaukurs Wirtschaft* (M. Hueber Verlag, Munich, 1972)
Hoffmann, H. G., *Aufbaukurs Wirtschaft: Lehrerhandbuch* (M. Hueber Verlag, Munich, 2nd ed. 1975)
Hoffmann, H. G., *Lebendiges Englisch,* 1 (M. Hueber Verlag, Munich, 1976)
Holister, G., A. Porteous, *The Environment* (Arrow Books, London, 1976)
Horton, K. C., *German Economic Extracts* (European Schoolbooks, London, 1970)
Hutber, P., ed., *What's Wrong With Britain?* (Sphere Books, London, 1978)
Hyman, S. E., *The Armed Vision* (Vintage Books, New York, 1955)
Ingerman, P. Z., *A Syntax-Oriented Translator* (Academic Press, New York & London, 1966)
Jaffé, C. H., *Englisch für alle Fälle* (Langenscheidt-Longman, Munich, 2nd ed. 1975)
Johnson, V., J. A. Brooks, E. Francke, *Advanced German Comprehension* (E. Arnold, London, 1975)
Kartalas, Panajotis, *Langenscheidts Sprachführer Neugriechisch* (Langenscheidt, Berlin, Munich, Zurich, 3rd ed. 1971)
Kästner, E., *Die verschwundene Miniatur,* ed. O. P. Schinnerer (G. G. Harrap, London, 1958)
Kästner, E., *Drei Männer im Schnee,* ed. C. H. Bell (G. G. Harrap, London, 1954)
Kästner, E., *Georg und die Zwischenfälle,* ed. H. J. B. Wanstall (G. G. Harrap, London, 1941)
Kayser, W., *Das sprachliche Kunstwerk* (Francke Verlag, Bern & Munich, 9th ed. 1963)
Kershaw, F., S. Russon, *German for Business Studies* (Longman, London, 3rd impression 1980)
Knight, M., D. Whitling, P. Jonason, *All Right* 1 (E. Klett Verlag, Stuttgart, 1981)
Kostuch, G., *Problems and Opinions* (Verlag Moritz Diesterweg, Frankfurt/M., Berlin, Munich, 6th ed. 1973)
Lajta, H., *Korsika* (Polyglott-Verlag, Munich, 6th ed. 1979/80)
Lamb, C., *Elia* (The Scholar Press Ltd., Menston, 1969)
Lane, A., R. Catrice, *Internationales Formularbuch* (M. Hueber Verlag, Munich, 1969)
La nouvelle économie anglaise (Ed. Economica, Paris, 1980)
Lawrence, D. H., *Sea and Sardinia* (Penguin, Harmondsworth, 1971)

Lechler, H. J., F. Ungerer, edd. *Modern Life* (E. Klett Verlag, Stuttgart, 1971)
Linnenkugel, A., P. Friling, *Lateinische Grammatik* (F. Schöning, Paderborn, 1970)
London, J., *Love of Life/Liebe zum Leben* (Deutscher Taschenbuch Verlag, Munich, 1977)
Löw, K., *Warum fasziniert der Kommunismus?* (Deutscher Instituts-Verlag, Cologne, 3rd ed. 1981)
Maney, A. S., R. L. Smallwood, edd., *MHRA Style Book* (Modern Humanities Research Association, London, 3rd ed. 1981)
Mann, T., *Buddenbrooks* (G. B. Fischer, Berlin & Frankfurt/M., 1963)
Mann, T., *Der Zauberberg* (G. B. Fischer, Berlin & Frankfurt/M., 1964)
Mann, T., *Doktor Faustus* (S. Fischer Verlag, Frankfurt/M., 1965)
Mann, T., *Sämtliche Erzählungen* (S. Fischer Verlag, Frankfurt/M., 1972)
Manekeller, W., *So schreibt man Geschäftsbriefe!* (Humboldt-Taschenbuchverlag, Munich, 1977)
Mansion, J. E., *A Grammar of Present-Day French* (G. G. Harrap, London, 1960)
Mansion, J. E., ed., *Contes choisis de Guy de Maupassant* (G. G. Harrap, London, 1980)
Marcheteau, M., J. Tardieu, *Business and Economics,* Vol. 1 (A. Colin, Paris, 1970)
Marlowe, S., *Translation* (Sphere Books Ltd., London, 1978)
Meyer-Landrut, J., F. G. Miller, G. F. Thoma, edd., *Umsatzsteuergesetz 1980* (F. Knapp Verlag, Frankfurt/M., 1980)
Milton, J., *Comus, Nativity Ode, L'Allegro, Il Penseroso, Lycidas, Sonnets, etc.,* ed. W. Bell (Macmillan, London, 1930)
Monetary Aggregates and Monetary Policy, Paper of the Federal Reserve Bank of New York (New York, 1974)
Moore, G., *Confessions of a Young Man* (W. Heinemann, London, 1952)
Moroney, M. J., *Facts from Figures* (Penguin, Harmondsworth, 1970)
Mueller, R., B. W. Meister, M. H. Heidenhain, *The German GmbH-Law* (F. Knapp Verlag, Frankfurt/M., 4th ed. 1981)
Mundschau, H., *Übersetzungskurs Französisch-Deutsch* (Manz Verlag, Munich, 1978)
Murdoch, I., *A Fairly Honourable Defeat* (Penguin, Harmondsworth, 1972)
Murdoch, I., *An Accidental Man* (Penguin, Harmondsworth, 1973)
Murdoch, I., *A Severed Head* (Penguin, Harmondsworth, 1974)
Murdoch, I., *A Word Child* (Penguin, Harmondsworth, 1976)
Murdoch, I., *The Bell* (Penguin, Harmondsworth, 1974)
Murdoch, I., *The Flight from the Enchanter* (Penguin, Harmondsworth, 1972)
Murdoch, I., *The Red and the Green* (Penguin, Harmondsworth, 1974)
Murdoch, I., *The Unicorn* (Penguin, Harmondsworth, 1972)
Newnham, R., *German Short Stories* 1 (Penguin, Harmondsworth, 1978)
Newton, E., *European Painting and Sculpture* (Penguin, Harmondsworth, 1968)
Nyszkiewicz, H. H., K. H. Rühe, edd., *Economic Texts* (E. Klett Verlag, Stuttgart, 1973)
Page, J. F., ed., *Penguin German Reader* (Penguin, Harmondsworth, 1978)
Palmer, F. R., *Semantics* (Cambridge University Press, 1979)
Pelling, H., *A History of British Trade Unionism* (Penguin, Harmondsworth, 3rd ed. 1976)
Pilz, K. D., *Phraseologie* (Metzler, Stuttgart, 1981)
Pope, A., *Poems,* ed. J. Butt (Methuen, London, 1968)
Raban, J., *The Technique of Modern Fiction* (E. Arnold, London, 1968)
Raby, F. J. E., *The Oxford Book of Medieval Latin Verse* (Oxford University Press, 1961)
Raddatz, F. J., ed., *Die ZEIT-Bibliothek der 100 Bücher* (Suhrkamp Taschenbuch Verlag, Frankfurt/M., 1980)
Rasch, W., ‚Zur Frage des epischen Präteritums', *Wirkendes Wort,* 3. Sonderheft (August 1961), pp. 68–81
Richey, M. F., *Studies of Wolfram von Eschenbach* (Oliver & Boyd, Edinburgh & London, 1957)
Ridout, R., *English Today* (Ginn & Co. Ltd., London, 2nd impression 1949)
Rippier, J. S., *Some Postwar English Novelists* (Verlag M. Diesterweg, Frankfurt/M., Berlin, Bonn, 1965)
Robertson, J. G., *A History of German Literature* (W. Blackwood & Sons, Edinburgh & London, 3rd ed. 1959)

Robertson, P., *Latin Prose Composition* (Macmillan, London, 1955)
Robinson, J., *Further Contributions to Modern Economics* (B. Blackwell, Oxford, 1980)
Rodenstock, R. et al., *Freiheitsräume in der Industriegesellschaft* (Deutscher Instituts-Verlag, Cologne, 1976)
Rose, R., *The Problem of Party Government* (Penguin, Harmondsworth, 1976)
Sachs, R., *Commercial Correspondence* (M. Hueber Verlag, Munich, 4th ed. 1975)
Samuelson, P. A., *Economics* (McGraw-Hill Kogakusha Ltd., Tokyo, 11th ed. 1980)
Saussure, F. de, *Cours de linguistique générale*, ed. T. de Mauro (Payot, Paris, 1980)
Schillemeit, J., ed., *Interpretationen 4: Deutsche Erzählungen von Wieland bis Kafka* (Fischer Bücherei, Frankfurt/M. & Hamburg, 1966)
Schmitz, A., E. Schmitz, *Kontakte Englisch* (M. Hueber Verlag, Munich, 1981)
Schneider, H., H. J. Hellwig, D. J. Kingsman, *Das Bankwesen in Deutschland* (F. Knapp Verlag, Frankfurt/M., 1978)
Schumacher, T., ed., *English Short Stories 2/Englische Kurzgeschichten 2* (Deutscher Taschenbuch Verlag, Munich, 1981)
Scott, A. F., *Current Literary Terms* (Macmillan, London & St Martin's Press, New York, 1967)
Shakespeare, W., *Hamlet*, ed. A. W. Verity (Cambridge University Press, 1950)
Shakespeare, W., *King Lear*, ed. A. W. Verity (Cambridge University Press, 1957)
Shakespeare, W., *Macbeth*, ed. A. W. Verity (Cambridge University Press, 1954)
Short Stories (Langenscheidts fremdsprachliche Lektüre, Vol. 42, Langenscheidt, Berlin, Munich, Zurich, 2nd ed. 1967)
Sieper, R., *The Student's Companion to Britain* (M. Hueber Verlag, Munich, 3rd ed. 1979)
Sieper, R., *The Student's Companion to the U.S.A.* (M. Hueber Verlag, Munich, 2nd ed. 1978)
Sillitoe, A., *Saturday Night and Sunday Morning* (W. H. Allen & Co., London, 1980)
Smith, N., D. Wilson, *Modern Linguistics* (Penguin, Harmondsworth, 1979)
Snow, C. P., *Last Things* (Penguin, Harmondsworth, 1972)
Spencer, S., *Space, Time and Structure in the Modern Novel* (New York University, Press, 1971)
Stafford, J., *Bad Characters* (Farrar, Straus & Giroux Inc., 1964)
Sternheim, T., *Sackgassen* (Limes Verlag, Wiesbaden, 1952)
Stevenson, R. L., *Dr. Jekyll and Mr. Hyde* (Airmont Publishing Company, New York, 1964)
A. T. Q. Stewart, *The Ulster Crisis* (Faber & Faber, London & Boston, 1979)
Stewart, M., *Keynes and After* (Penguin, Harmondsworth, 1977)
Storm, T., *Immensee*, ed. W. Bernhardt (G. G. Harrap, London, 1959)
Studies in Linguistic Analysis (B. Blackwell, Oxford, 4th impression 1974)
Swann, D., *Competition and Consumer Protection* (Penguin, Harmondsworth, 1979)
Swann, D., *The Economics of the Common Market* (Penguin, Harmondsworth, 2nd ed. 1972)
Thackeray, W. M., *Vanity Fair* (T. Nelson & Sons, London, s. d.)
The English Bible in Five Volumes, ed. W. A. Wright (Cambridge, 1909)
Thesiger, W., *Arabian Sands* (Penguin, Harmondsworth, 1974)
Thomas, R. H., ed., *Der Schriftsteller Dieter Wellershoff* (Kiepenheuer & Witsch, Cologne, 1975)
Thorlby, A., ed., *The Penguin Companion to Literature 2: European Literature* (Penguin, Harmondsworth, 1969)
Townsend, H., ed., *Price Theory* (Penguin, Harmondsworth, 2nd ed. 1980)
Trevelyan, G. M., *A Shortened History of England* (Penguin, Harmondsworth, 1979)
Trevelyan, G. M., *British History in the Nineteenth Century and After: 1782–1919* (Penguin, Harmondsworth, 1979)
Trevelyan, G. M., *English Social History* (Penguin, Harmondsworth, 1980)
Trevithick, J. A., *Inflation* (Penguin, Harmondsworth, 1979)
Trevithick, J. A., C. Mulvey, *The Economics of Inflation* (M. Robertson, London, 1979)
Trezise, P. H., ed., *The European Monetary System: Its Promise and Prospects* (The Brookings Institution, Washington, 1979)
Trollope, A., *The Warden* (T. Nelson & Sons, London, s. d.)
Veyrenc, C. J., *Grammaire du russe* (P.U.F., Paris, 2nd ed. 1973)
Volcker, P. A., *The Rediscovery of the Business Cycle* (The Free Press, New York & Collier Macmillan, London, 1978)

Weinrich, H., *Tempus* (Verlag W. Kohlhammer, Stuttgart, 3rd ed. 1977)
Weir, D., ed., *Men and Work in Modern Britain* (Fontana/Collins, Glasgow, 3rd impression 1978)
Wellershoff, D., *Die Bittgänger/Die Schatten* (P. Reclam Jun., Stuttgart, 1968)
Wellershoff, D., *Die Sirene* (Kiepenheuer & Witsch, Cologne, 1980)
Wetherill, P. M., *The Literary Text: An Examination of Critical Methods* (B. Blackwell, Oxford, 1974)
Whitehead, A. N., *An Introduction to Mathematics* (Oxford University Press, 1948)
Whitmarsh, W. F. H., C. D. Jukes, *Advanced French Course* (Longmans, Green & Co., London, 16th impression 1959)
Wilpert, G. v., *Sachwörterbuch der Literatur* (A. Kröner Verlag, Stuttgart, 5th ed. 1969)
Wilson, A., *Anglo-Saxon Attitudes* (Penguin, Harmondsworth, 1972)
Wimsatt, W. K., *The Verbal Icon* (Methuen, London, 1970)
Woodcock, G., *Anarchism* (Penguin, Harmondsworth, 1977)
Woolf, V., *The Voyage Out* (Penguin, Harmondsworth, 1974)
Woolf, V., *The Years,* (Penguin, Harmondsworth, 1971)
Woolf, V., *To the Lighthouse* (Penguin, Harmondsworth, 1969)
Wordsworth & Coleridge, *Lyrical Ballads,* edd. R. L. Brett & A. R. Jones (Methuen, London, 1968)
Wright, J., *A Middle High German Primer* (Oxford University Press, 5th ed. 1955)
Zuckmayer, C., *Der Hauptmann von Köpenick,* ed. H. F. Garten (Methuen, London, 1961)

Abbreviations

CED	Hanks, P., ed. *Collins Dictionary of the English Language*
DEWC	Friederich, W., J. Canavan, *Dictionary of English Words in Context*
D/R	Dinter, S. K., J. Ripken, *Deutsche Reden und die Technik ihrer Übersetzung: English Translation Supplement*
E	Eichborn, R. von, *Der kleine Eichborn: Wirtschaft und Wirtschaftsrecht* (2 vols.)
EG	Curme, G. O., *English Grammar*
FAZ	*Frankfurter Allgemeine Zeitung*
FMEU	Fowler, H. W., *A Dictionary of Modern English Usage*
FT	*Financial Times*
F/W	*Funk & Wagnalls Standard Desk Dictionary*
G/C	Gunston, C. A., C. M. Corner, *Deutsch-Englisches Glossarium finanzieller und wirtschaftlicher Fachausdrücke*
GCE	Quirk, R. et al., *A Grammar of Contemporary English*
GEG	Sutton, F. W., K. Beilhardt, *Grundzüge der englischen Grammatik*
GES	Lamprecht, A., *Grammatik der englischen Sprache*
GPB	Hitchin, U., J. Norman, *German Phrase Book*
HB	*Handelsblatt*
HEG	Zandvoort, R. W., *A Handbook of English Grammar*
HG	Gilbertson, G., *Harrap's German and English Glossary of Terms in International Law*
HNSFED	Mansion, J. E., R.P.L. Ledésert, M. Ledésert, edd., *Harrap's New Standard French and English Dictionary*
HSFED	Mansion, J. E., ed., *Harrap's Standard French and English Dictionary*
IHT	*International Herald Tribune*
LEW	Springer, O., ed., *Langenscheidts Enzyklopädisches Wörterbuch der englischen und deutschen Sprache*
LGS	Messinger, H., *Langenscheidts Großes Schulwörterbuch*
MEG	Schibsbye, K., *A Modern English Grammar*
OALDCE	Hornby, A. S., A. P. Cowie, *Oxford Advanced Learner's Dictionary of Current English*
OED	*The Oxford English Dictionary*
O-HSG-ED	Jones, T., ed., *The Oxford-Harrap Standard German-English Dictionary*
PDE	Bannock, G., R. E. Baxter, R. Rees, *The Penguin Dictionary of Economics*
PED	Garmonsway, G. N., J. Simpson, *The Penguin English Dictionary*
RD	*Reader's Digest*
RGSE	Close, R. A., *A reference grammar for students of English*
RHD	*The Random House Dictionary of the English Language*
R/S	Renner, R., R. Sachs, *Wirtschaftssprache*
SOED	Onions, C. T., ed., *The Shorter Oxford English Dictionary*
UGE	Quirk, R., S. Greenbaum, *A University Grammar of English*
W/H	Wildhagen, K., W. Héraucourt, *English-German German-English Dictionary*
WN	*Westfälische Nachrichten*
WNCD	*Webster's New Collegiate Dictionary*
WNDS	*Webster's New Dictionary of Synonyms*

Note: The first volume of *Der große Eichborn* (English-German) has just been published (Siebenpunkt Verlag, 1981). The second volume (German-English) is to be published in 1982.

Glossary of Technical Terms

actorless clause A clause in which the subject is not directly expressed: e. g. *In den Nachkriegsjahren wurde in München viel gebaut.* Synonym: **plain-predicate clause.**
adjunct An adverbial which is integrated to some extent into the structure of the clause: e. g. *quickly* in the sentence *Quickly they left for home.*
agentive *(Of a speech element)* Indicating agency, i. e. action, power or operation.
anaphora 1. *(Rhetoric)* The repetition of a word or phrase at the beginning of successive clauses. **2.** *(Grammar)* The use of a word such as a pronoun to avoid repetition of a word or words, e. g. the use of *her* in the sentence *We invited Mrs Smith because we liked her.*
animism The attribution of a living soul to inanimate objects and natural phenomena.
aposiopesis A figure in which the speaker suddenly stops, as if unable or unwilling to proceed.
appositive A unit in apposition, e. g. the word-groups *Paul Jones* and *the distinguished art critic* in the sentence *Paul Jones, the distinguished art critic, died in his sleep last night.*
aspect A verb, noun or adjective category indicating the manner in which a state or action is conceived. In this book no distinction is made between *aspect (Aspekt)* and *manner of action (Aktionsart).*
asyndeton The omission of conjunctions between the parts of a sentence, e. g. *I came, I saw, I conquered.*
attributive *(Of an adjective or adjectival phrase)* Preceding the noun modified: e. g. *drastic* in the phrase *a drastic remedy.*
back-shift Changes in tense necessitated by the shift from direct speech to reported speech: e. g. *'I'm tired', she said* → *She said that she was tired.*
balance inversion A form of inversion designed to ensure the balance of a sentence. Balance inversion is necessary whenever the verb is quite overshadowed by the subject. Cf. *FMEU*, s. v. inversion.
bathos A sudden ludicrous descent from the exalted to the ordinary in speech or writing.
bound morpheme A recurrent minimal speech element which has distinct meaning only when it is attached (prefixed or suffixed) to a word, e. g. *-s* in *bytes.*
category In J. C. Catford's theory of translation this term denotes a wide range of grammatical classes such as clause-structure patterns, parts of speech *(q. v.),* ranks *(q. v),* systems of aspects, articles and number, etc.
chiasmus A figure by which the order of words is reversed in the second of two parallel phrases.
classifying genitive A genitive indicating the class to which the head noun belongs: e. g. *a busman's holiday* (a holiday spent doing the same kind of thing as one does at work). Synonym: **descriptive genitive.**
collocation A combination of particular lexical items: e. g. *able* collocates with *worker* in the (idiomatic) collocation *an able worker.*

combining form A linguistic element that occurs only as part of a compound word, such as *anthropo-* in *anthropology* or *bio-* in *biochemistry*.

comment A part of a sentence in which something is asserted or denied of a 'topic' or subject. For example, in the sentence *He is an acute observer, he* is the topic and *is an acute observer* is the comment; and in the phrase *a good book, book* is the topic and *good* the comment. Synonym: **rheme.**

commutation The process by which one word is substituted for another within a particular construction. *Pencil* and *pen* are commutable in a construction such as *I write with a___.*

conjoin The verb *conjoin* is synonymous with *coordinate*. The noun *conjoin* denotes a coordinated clause.

conjunct An adverbial which has a connective function and which is peripheral to clause structure: e. g. *therefore* is a conjunct in the sentence *They heard the warning on the radio and therefore took another route.*

connecter A word that serves to establish a link between the constituents *(q. v.)* of a sentence: e. g. *and, but, or, so* or *because*. Synonym: **connective.**

constituent A word, phrase or clause forming a part of a larger construction.

contact clause A relative clause joined to the main clause without a relative pronoun: e. g. *we've got* in the sentence *These are the best shoes we've got.*

co-occurrence restrictions Constraints on the combination of lexical items, designed to obviate the construction of anomalous sentences: e. g. the verb *shout* must have an animate subject. Hence the sentence *The man shouted to attract attention* is acceptable, while the sentence *The bucket shouted to attract attention* is anomalous. Synonym: **selection restrictions.**

coordinator A coordinating conjunction, e. g. *and, or, both . . . and.*

copula A verb, such as *be, become, seem* or *taste*, that is used to identify or link the subject with the complement of a sentence. Synonyms: **copulative verb, link verb.**

count noun A noun which can be used in the plural without change of meaning and which is readily modified by a numeral, an indefinite article, or a word such as *many* or *few*. Examples: *cup, chair, apple*. Antonym: **mass noun** *(q. v.).*

declarative clause A clause having the nature of an explicit statement. A declarative clause may be a main clause (e. g. *He was wrong*) or a sub clause (e. g. the *that*-clause in the sentence *I told him that he was wrong.)*

deep structure *(Generative grammar)* A representation of the presumed structure of a sentence at a level where logical and grammatical relations are made explicit, before transformational rules have been applied. Antonym: **surface structure** *(q. v.).*

deictic A word such as *here* or *I*, whose reference is determined by the situation of utterance.

démarche *(French linguistics)* The special character of a language, revealed by a habitual preference for certain structural patterns.

descriptive genitive See **classifying genitive.**

determiner A word, such as a number, an article, or an indefinite adjective, that determines the referent or referents of a noun phrase.

disjunct An adverbial which is peripheral to clause structure, which has no connective function, and which can serve as a response to a *yes-no* question: e. g. *probably* in *He will probably be in Berlin on Monday.*

disjunctive A word, especially a conjunction, that serves to express opposition or contrast: e. g. *sondern* in the sentence *Er kommt nicht heute, sondern morgen.*

dummy operator A meaningless element which has syntactic but no semantic function: e. g. the form word *it* in *It riled him that no one would believe his story.*

durative aspect 1. *(English grammar)* An aspect *(q.v.)* that expresses activity considered as prolonged or continuous as opposed to activity considered as momentary or habitual, e.g. *is reading* in *He is reading a newspaper.* **2.** *(Russian grammar)* The imperfective aspect, which may express either continuous action or habitual action (e.g. as opposed to). Partial synonym: **progressive aspect.**

dynamic equivalence *(Translation theory)* 'The closest natural equivalent to the source-language message' (Nida). Antonym: **formal equivalence** *(q.v.).*

embedding The insertion of a subordinate clause into a sentence.

encoding Converting non-linguistic intentions, impulses and emotions into a system of communication.

existential sentence A sentence affirming or denying the existence of something: e.g. *There's no plug in my washbasin.*

factive noun A general abstract noun which can be used to categorize a wide range of facts, e.g. *fact, matter, thing, allegation.*

faded image A metaphor which has become so common that it is no longer recognized as such: e.g. the expression *the arm of a chair,* or the abstract noun *scruple,* which comes from a Latin word meaning a small sharp or pointed stone. Synonym: **dead metaphor.**

finite clause A clause built up around a finite verb form: e.g. *He works for a firm of adjusters.*

focus of negation The part of a negative clause in which the contrast of meaning implicit in the negation can be located: e.g. the stressed subject *we* in the sentence *WE didn't say that all wages should be paid by cheque.*

formal equivalence Correspondence between linguistic units independent of any idea of content. Antonym: **dynamic equivalence** *(q.v.).*

formative *(Generative grammar)* Any of the minimum units of a sentence that have syntactic function.

free indirect speech Any form of discourse which is half-way between direct and indirect speech. The reporting clause *(q.v.)* is generally omitted, but the potentialities of direct speech sentence structure are retained. In German this form of discourse is known as *erlebte Rede.*

frequentative aspect An aspect *(q.v.)* used to express repeated or habitual action.

functional shift The transfer of a word from one part of speech *(q.v.)* to another. Example: *to be in the swim* (verb > noun). Synonyms: **functional change, conversion** (German: *Wortartwechsel*).

generative grammar Description of a language in terms of explicit rules that ideally generate all and only the grammatical sentences of the language.

generic Applicable or referring to a whole class or group.

head The word in a phrase that determines how the phrase operates syntactically: e.g. the head of the phrase *frictional unemployment* is *unemployment,* and the head of the phrase *employers' requirements* is *requirements.* Synonyms: **head noun, head noun-phrase** (German: *Gliedkern*).

head clause The clause on which a subordinate clause depends. *Head clause* is not synonymous with *main clause* since it may be either a main clause or another subordinate clause.

hyperbolical Relating to a deliberate exaggeration used for effect.

hyponym A more specific term subsumed under a more general term: e.g. *iron* and *copper* are hyponyms of *metal.* Antonym: **superordinate.**

hypotaxis Subordination

imperfective aspect See **durative aspect** (2).

inchoative Expressing the beginning of an action. Synonym: **ingressive**.
indefinite relative clause A relative clause introduced by an indefinite relative pronoun such as *whoever*.
inflected genitive The *-s* genitive: e.g. *the director's books*.
ingressive See **inchoative**.
instrument adjunct An adverbial indicating the instrument used in performing an action. In English, instrument adjuncts are normally prepositional phrases such as *with that knife*: e.g. *You can cut the bread with that knife*.
inter-clausal Pertaining to the relationship between clauses.
intermediate string *(Transformational grammar)* A sequence of words situated between the initial string and the terminal string *(q.v.)* in a derivation (German: *Zwischenkette*).
internesting *(Generative grammar)* One of the main types of inclusion relationship between constituents *(q.v.)*. Phrase A is said to be internested in phrase B if A falls totally within B: e.g. the clause *if you agree* is internested in the clause *We shall leave . . . tonight* in the sentence *We shall leave, if you agree, tonight,* Synonyms: **medial subordination, medial branching** *(q.v.)*, **nesting** *(q.v.)*.
intra-clausal Pertaining to relationships within a clause.
Johnsonese An elaborate style of writing that abounds in Latin-derived words, in the manner of Samuel Johnson (1709–1784).
level In J. C. Catford's theory of translation this term denotes linguistic strata such as phonology, graphology, grammar and lexis *(q.v.)*.
lexical item A minimal 'fully meaningful' element, e.g. *bimetallism, bill of lading, development district*. Lexical items are often referred to loosely as 'words'.
lexicalized syntagma A syntactic unit operating as one lexical item *(q.v.)* rather than as a phrase consisting of a number of distinct lexical items: e.g. *grey area* (an area, situation, etc. lacking clearly defined characteristics) or *blue book* (a British government publication bound in a stiff blue paper cover).
lexical unit See **lexical item**.
lexical verb A verb that expresses an action or state (e.g. *see*) as opposed to an auxiliary or semi-auxiliary verb (e.g. *will, to be,* or *happen* + infinitive).
lexis The totality of vocabulary items in a language.
mass noun A noun that denotes an extended substance rather than each of a set of isolable objects, e.g. *water* as opposed to *pool*. Antonym: **count noun**.
matrix sentence A sentence in which another sentence has been embedded. Consider the sentence *He thinks that the claim that trading stamps are an irrelevance is justifiable. He thinks that the claim . . . is justifiable* is a matrix sentence into which the sentence *trading stamps are an irrelevance* has been embedded.
means adjunct An adverbial indicating the means by which an action is performed. In English, means adjuncts are usually prepositional phrases such as *by car*: e.g. *He goes to work by car*.
medial branching See **internesting**.
meiosis Understatement for rhetorical effect, especially when achieved by using negation with a term instead of using an antonym of that term. Synonym: **litotes**.
mixed metaphor A combination of incongruous metaphors: e.g. *The flame of freedom flowed freely onward*.
modifier A word or phrase that precedes a head word *(q.v.)* and qualifies its sense: e.g. the adjective *educational* is a modifier of *system* in *educational system*.
morpheme A speech element having a meaning or grammatical function that cannot be subdivided into further such elements.

nesting See **internesting**.
nomen actionis An abstract noun denoting an action normally expressed by a verb. Hence, the nomen actionis *Schlaf* corresponds to the verb *schlafen*.
nominal clause A clause having a function approximating to that of a noun phrase: e.g. *whether we need it* in the sentence *Whether we need it is a different matter*.
nonce word A word coined for a single occasion.
non-finite clause A clause based on a non-finite verb form such as a participle or an infinitive: e.g. *sitting here in the sun* in the sentence *Sitting here in the sun, we can see snow-covered hills*.
non restrictive relative clause A relative clause which does not restrict reference: e.g. *which we read yesterday* in the sentence *His explanation, which we read yesterday, is unsatisfactory*. It would be possible to omit this relative clause without impairing the sense of the main clause. Synonym: **non-defining relative clause.**
noun clause See **nominal clause.**
oligosemy The use of a word with a particularly restricted range of meaning.
operator One of the verbal forms, prepositions, articles, etc. in Basic English, Basic German, etc.
parasynthetic Pertaining to the formation of derivatives involving both prefixes and suffixes: e.g. the derivation of *encampment* from *camp*.
particularizer An adjunct *(q.v.)* which restricts the application of the communication particularly or mainly to the part focused: e.g. *mainly, particularly, at least*.
part of speech *(Traditional grammar)* A class of words sharing important syntactic or semantic features: e.g. nouns, verbs, adjectives. (German: *Wortart, Redeteil*).
perfect of experience A tense which expresses what has happened within the speaker's or writer's experience: e.g. *When I have asked a London policeman the way, I have invariably received a polite answer*.
periphrastic genitive The *of*-genitive: e.g. *the price of a commodity*.
plain-predicate clause See **actorless clause.**
polysemy The use of the same word in two or more distinct meanings.
post-modified A head *(q.v.)* is said to be post-modified when its sense is qualified by the word or phrase that follows it.
postpose *(Of an adjective)* To place after the word modified.
postpositive *(Of an adjective)* Placed after the word modified.
postqualifier A word or phrase which follows the head *(q.v.)* and qualifies its sense.
predicative *(Of an adjective)* Occurring within the predicate of a sentence: e.g. *new* in the sentence *The book is new*.
pre-modified A head *(q.v.)* is said to be pre-modified when it is preceded by a modifier *(q.v.)*.
pre-modifier See **modifier.**
prepose *(Of an adjective)* To place before the word modified.
pro-form A word having grammatical function but assuming the meaning of a word or phrase for which it substitutes: e.g. the word *there* is a pro-form for *London* in *Mary is in London and John is there too*.
progressive aspect An aspect *(q.v.)* used to express prolonged or continuous activity as opposed to momentary or habitual activity: e.g. a progressive aspect of the verb *to work* is *working*.
'push-down' clause A clause embedded within a sub clause: e.g. *we feared* in the sentence *The man whom we feared we had injured proved to be unharmed*.
rank The standing of words in their mutual relations as qualified and qualifying terms.
rank-bound translation An extreme form of translation in which translation equiva-

lences are set up between grammatical units that always belong to the same rank: e. g. the equivalence may be sentence-to-sentence, group-to-group, or word-to-word. Word-rank-bound translations may be used for pedagogical purposes, but they cannot be used for the transmission of information in everyday life.

reporting clause A clause which introduces reported matter: e.g. *he said* in the sentence *He said that Juglar's analytical technique had been adapted by Joseph Schumpeter.*

restrictive relative clause A relative clause which restricts the reference of a statement: e. g. *I bought this morning* in *Where is the book I bought this morning?* The information in this relative clause is essential to full understanding of the main clause. Synonym: **defining relative clause.**

result conjunct A connective adverbial which serves to introduce a sentence expressing the consequence of what was said before: e. g. *so* in the sentence *The shops were closed so I couldn't buy anything.*

rewriting rule *(Generative grammar)* A rule of the form A → X where A is a syntactic category label such as *noun phrase* or *clause,* and X is a sequence of such labels and/or morphemes *(q. v.).*

rheme Cf. the Greek ῥῆμα. See **comment.**

right-branching The final placement of subordinate word-groups: e. g. the placement of the sub clause *if you agree* in the sentence *We shall leave tonight, if you agree.* Synonym: **right-tending structure.**

scope of negation The range of application of a negative operator *(q. v.).*

selectional restrictions See **co-occurrence restrictions.**

semi-idiom An expression which cannot be identified conclusively as an idiom or a non-idiom: e. g. *put up,* as used in the sentence *Increased transport costs will put up the prices.*

sentential relative clause A relative clause which refers back to a whole clause or sentence, or even to a whole series of sentences: e. g. *which surprised me* in the sentence *After that things improved, which surprised me.*

simplex word A free form without affixes or other components: e.g. *tall, sell, door.*

SL Abbreviation for **source language** *(q. v.).*

source language The language being translated into another language. Antonym: **target language** *(q. v.).*

speech tag A verbal appendage which serves to identify the speaker: e. g. *he said* in *"We cannot become a factory", he said.*

stratificational grammar A theory of grammar analysing language in terms of several structural strata or layers with different syntactic rules.

style disjunct An adverbial which conveys the speaker's comment on the form of what he is saying, defining under what conditions he is speaking: e. g. *briefly* in *Briefly, there is nothing more I can do about it.*

subjective genitive A genitive which corresponds to the subject of the underlying sentence: e. g. *his parents' consent* corresponds to *His parents consented.*

subordinator A subordinating conjunction.

superordinate A more general term under which more specific terms are subsumed: e. g. *metal* is the superordinate of *iron* and *copper.* Antonym: **hyponym** *(q. v.).*

surface structure A representation of a string of elements as they occur in a sentence, together with labels and brackets representing its syntactic structure. Antonym: **deep structure** *(q. v.).*

syndetic coordination A form of grammatical construction in which words and word-groups of equal rank are connected by conjunctions.

syntagma A word or phrase forming a syntactic unit.
target language The language into which a text is translated.
terminal string *(Transformational grammar)* A sequence of words representing the final stage of a derivation. Cf. **intermediate string.** (German: *Endkette*).
terminate aspect An aspect *(q.v.)* which represents an act as a whole, as a fact, as habitual, customary, characteristic, or as a general truth. In English, this aspect is expressed by the common form of the verb: e.g. *Water runs downhill.*
ternary enumeration The arrangement of words in groups of three.
theme A part of a sentence containing a subject. Synonym: **topic** *(q.v.)*. Antonyms: **rheme** *(q.v.)*, **comment** *(q.v.)*.
TL Abbreviation for **target language** *(q.v.)*.
tonal particle A function word used to shade, emphasize and qualify meaning: e.g. *mal* in *Überleg's dir mal.* (German: *Abtönungspartikel, Würzwort*).
topic See **theme.**
topic sentence The sentence which contains the main point of a paragraph. Synonym: **key sentence.**
transferred negation The transfer of the negative from a subordinate *that*-clause to the main clause: e.g. *I don't suppose (that) he cares.*
transform The result of a linguistic transformation.
verb of complete predication A verb that has full lexical meaning as opposed to a copula *(q.v.)*.
viewpoint adjunct An adverbial which indicates the point of view from which something is considered: e.g. *visually* in *Visually, it was a powerful play.*
wh-question A question including a *wh*-word (*who, what, which,* etc.): e.g. *What did you see?*
zero *that*-clause A *that*-clause from which the conjunction *that* has been omitted: e.g. *he was wrong* in *I knew he was wrong.*

German Word Index

Roman numerals refer to texts. Arabic numerals preceded by Roman numerals refer to sections and sub-sections of commentaries. Arabic numerals not preceded by Roman numerals are page references to the introductory chapter.

aber II 10, 11, IV 4, 7
Abfertigungsgebäude II 13, 10
abgelaufen VIII 5, 10
ablehnen VIII 1, 2
abschmettern VIII 14, 3
abschöpfungspflichtig 23
Abschreibungsmodus: ~ für Investitionen VI 7, 9
Abstimmungsergebnis VIII 6, 4
Abzahlungskauf III 4, 9
Agrarausgaben VIII 15, 10
allenfalls VIII 14, 4
also II 9, 5
Amtsantritt I 1, 1
Angebotsüberschuß V 3, 4
Angelegenheit: eine ernste ~ VIII 11, 2
Angestellte(r) I 5, 1
ankommen 18
anregen 21
antizyklisch VI 1, 1
Antrittsrede I 2, 1
Arbeiter I 5, 1, I 5, 4
Arbeitslosenquote VII 3, 3
auch II 1, 4, II 3, 2, II 3, 10
auf II 13, 10, V 1, 2, V 3, 2
Aufschwung IV 4, 3
Aufsehen: ~ machen II 9, 3; ~ erregen II 11, 2
aufstauen I 4, 5
auftreten IV 9, 3
aus IV 6, 3
Ausgabenplan VI 5, 7
ausgehen VI 2, 5
ausgeprägt VII 2, 2
Auslastungsgrad VII 2, 8
auslösen IV 9, 7, V 3, 6, VI 4, 1
Außenminister VIII 10, 2
außerdem V 2, 1
Austauschverhältnis V 1, 13

Bandbreite V 3, 8
Bär: jdm einen ~ en aufbinden 33

bedenklich 30
bei III 6, 1, V 3, 5, V 3, 7, VI 8, 4, VIII 6, 7
Beifall: lang anhaltender ~ VIII 6, 10
Belebungseffekt IV 9, 4
Bemessungsgrundlage VI 7, 7
Bereich: etwas in den ~ des Möglichen bringen IV 9, 5
bereit: zu etwas ~ sein VIII 14, 5
berüchtigt III 5, 3
Berührung: mit jdm. in ~ kommen II 6, 2
Beschäftigung VII 1
Beschäftigungsgrad VII 2, 6
bestellen 18
beteiligt V 1, 6
betroffen V 3, 11
BGB 27
Bild: jdn. ins ~ setzen 29
bis VIII 5, 4
bleiben III 8, 2
Boden II 13, 6
BRD VII 5, 5
Brüsseler VIII 3, 6
BSP V 5, 3
Budget-Entwurf VIII 3, 3
Bummelstreik II 3, 3; einen ~ machen II 3, 4
Bundesbank VI 8, 4
Bundesrepublik Deutschland V 2, 5
Büroangestellte(r) I 5, 1

Chip 28

da II 4, 1
dafür III 8, 1, IV 3, 1
damit II 3, 9
Dämchen 32
Darlehen: ~ für den Wohnungsbau III 5, 1
darüber: und ~ hinaus II 12, 4
demnach VI 3, 1
Devisenmarkt V 3, 3
d. h. VII 2, 7
Dienst: ~ nach Vorschrift II 3, 3
dieser IV 8, 7

Dummheit II 2, 3
durchschnittlich: ~ bei __ liegen VII 8, 1
durchsetzen II 3, 11

EG-Haushalt VIII 1, 3, VIII 2, 3
EG-Rat VIII 13, 1
Ei: sie gleichen sich wie ein ~ dem anderen 33
Eiferstreik II 3, 6
eigentlich II 4, 2
Eigentum: ~ an der Ware III 4, 9
eindämmen VIII 15, 9
Eindämmung VIII 15, 9
eindringlich: ~ warnen VIII 10, 4
einführen V 2, 7
einhergehen VII 5, 7
Einigungsversuch VIII 8, 6
Einkommensteuer VI 7, 6
einmal II 3, 2
encadrement III 5, 3
Energiebereich IV 9, 5
entscheidend (+ für) IV 4, 5
entsprechen I 4, 1, VII 2, 5
enttäuschen I 7, 5
entweder . . . oder VI 4, 3
entwesen 32
Erfassung: statistische ~ VII 10, 7
erfordern V 4, 1
erfüllen: Forderungen ~ I 5, 2
erhalten VI 8, 3
ernst: eine ~e Angelegenheit VIII 11, 2
Ersatz II 4, 6
ertasten 32
erzwungen VI 4, 4
etwas III 3, 4
Europa-Parlament VIII 1, 1
Europäische Gemeinschaft VIII 2, 1

Fabrikarbeiter I, 5, 1
festsetzen V 1, 14
Finanzinstitut III 7, 5
Finanzlage VIII 4, 3
Finanzminister VIII 8, 8
Finanzmisere VIII, 4, 3
Finanzplanung VIII 4, 3
Finanzregelung VIII 4, 3
Flughafen II 13, 10
Flughafenabfertigungsgebäude II 13, 10
Fluglotse II 1, 2
Flugzeug: ein ~ benutzen II 7, 2
Forderung II 3, 8
Fraktion VIII 9, 8
Freiheit I 7, 11, V 2, 6
Freizügigkeit V 2, 6
für VIII 15, 4

Gattungsware 30
gegen VIII 6, 6
gegenüber V 1, 6
gemeinhin II 6, 1
Gemüse 12
gesamtwirtschaftlich VI 4, 6
gewähren I 7, 12
Gewinnzone: einen Konzern wieder in die ~ bringen IV 9, 5
gleichen IV 2
Gold-Devisen-Standard V 1, 15
groß IV 4, 8, VIII 3, 2
Größe VI 5, 5

Halbjahr III 3, 7
Haltbarkeit 33
Hand: sich die Steuerung einer Sache aus der ~ nehmen lassen I 7, 14
Haus VIII 6, 3
Haushaltsausschuß VIII 6, 8
Haushaltsentwurf VIII 5, 7
Haushaltspolitik VI 1, 2
heißen 18
hergehen 18
hierbei IV 6, 1
Hindernis (+ für) IV 4, 8
hören 32
hungrig II 13, 5

immerhin III 4, 6
immer wieder II 4, 8, VIII 13, 2
in IV 5, 5, VI 5, 6, VII 4, 4
Industrieroboter 30
Inflationsbekämpfung VI 2, 4
insbesondere IV 4, 1

jahrelang I 7, 2
jetzt III 3, 2
jeweilig VII 5, 4
jeweils IV 3, 3
Jumbo-Rat 28−9

Kahlschlag 28
Kartoffel 12
kauern II 13, 7
Kaufen auf Stottern III 4, 9
Kauf unter Eigentumsvorbehalt III 4, 9
Killersatellit 28−9
Koeffizient III 3, 5
Konjunkturaussichten IV 1
konjunkturbedingt VII 6, 2
Konjunkturerfahrungen IV 7, 1
Konjunkturforschungsinstitut IV 5, 3
Konjunkturprognose IV 1

Konkurs: seinen ~ erklären I 6, 3; seinen ~ anmelden I 6, 3
Konkursanmeldung I 6, 3
Konkurserklärung I 6, 3
können VI 6, 3, VI 7, 3
Konzertierungsverfahren VIII 9, 4
Kredit: ~ zur Förderung des Exportgeschäfts III 8, 3
Kreditkauf III 4, 9
Kreditspielraum III 3, 9
Kreditvergabe III 3, 6
Kriegsnachwirkungen VII 6, 6
künftig (adv.) III 7, 7
kürzen: erheblich ~ VIII 15, 6
Kürzung VI 5, 7

Land I 6, 2
Leine: jdn. an der kurzen ~ halten III 1
Leitwährung V 1, 9
liegen VII 10, 3
Liquidität VI 8, 6
Lohnsteuer VI 7, 6

man II 13, 2
Maschinenbereich IV 9, 5
mehr I 7, 10
Meinungsverschiedenheit VIII 9, 6
Mietkauf III 4, 9
Milliarde VIII 15, 3
mit VI 5, 2, VII 4, 3
mitklettern 30
mittler III 4, 4
Moment: der richtige ~ II, 5, 2
müde II 13, 4
mühen: sich ~ IV 5, 2

Nachfragesoginflationsmodell VI 2, 6
Nachfrageüberhang VI 3, 2
Nachkriegszeit VII 7, 4
Nacht: in der ~ zum Donnerstag VIII 8, 4
nackt II 13, 6
nennen II 3, 13
nicht II 2, 4
noch III 3, 3
nunmehr I 7,5, VIII 4, 2
nur VII 8, 2

offenbar: ~ werden VIII 11, 4
Öffnungs-Prozeß I 7, 13
oft I 7, 4

Parlament: das europäische ~ VIII 2, 2
Parlamentarier-Delegation VIII 8, 7
parteipolitisch VIII 7, 5
passiv: ~er Außenhandel III 8, 4

Pflichterfüllung II 4, 5
Postangestellte(r) I 5, 1
Präsident VIII 10, 3
Produktionskapazität VII 2, 9
Produktionsmöglichkeiten VI 4, 5
Prokurist 28

Rahmen VIII 9, 3
Rate I 6, 4
raten 18
Ratenkauf III 4, 9
Ratsentwurf VIII 7, 3
real VII 5, 3
Redner VIII 9, 7
rein II 13, 9
Rezession VII 5, 8
Rheinsalzvertrag 32
Rüstungskontrollverhandlungen 28−9

Saisonschwankungen IV 9, 4
schließlich III 8, 6
schon VII 5, 8
Schulgebäude VI 5, 3
schützen II 2, 2
Schwingung IV 3, 2
sehen II 13, 1
so III 4, 1, IV 8, 1, VI 8, 2
sogar VII 9, 4, VII 10, 4
Sozi 27
Sozialpolitik VIII 15, 5
Sozialproduktwachstum VII 2, 4
Spektrum I 1, 7
Staatsausgaben VI 2, 2
Staatseinnahmen VI 2, 3
Staatsoberhaupt I 1, 4
Stand: höchster ~ VII 4, 1
steigen VII 9, 2
stillegen VI 8, 5
Straßenbauten VI 5, 3
streiken II 4, 3
Strich: keinen ~ tun II 3, 12, II 3, 14
strukturbedingt VII 10, 2
strukturell: ~e Arbeitslosigkeit VII 6, 4
Substitutionskonto 28−9

tanzen 18
Teigwaren 13
Teilindikator VII 3, 1
Teilzahlungskauf III 4, 9
tiefgreifend VIII 11, 3
trotzdem IV 5, 1
tun II 3, 12

über: ~ oder unter V 3,9
überlagern IV 8, 6, VII 6, 3

überschreiten V 3, 7
ungeachtet VIII 7, 4
Ungleichgewicht V 3, 1
Unmut I 4, 6
unterbreiten VIII 9, 2
Unternehmung II 5, 1

Ventil I 4, 7
Verabschiedung VIII 5, 6
Veränderungsrate IV 5, 5
Verbraucherkredit III 4, 8
Vergleich (+ mit) VII 5, 1
verkleinern VI 8, 7
verkürzen III 3, 4
verlocken 21
verpflichten III 8, 5
verringern VI 6, 7
Verspätung: ~en im Flugdienst II 12, 3
versprechen 32, IV 9, 6
Verstetigung VII 7, 3
volkswirtschaftlich VII 2, 9
von V 1, 3, VIII 6, 5
vorausgehen VIII 8, 1
Vorjahr III 4, 3
Vorlage VIII 5, 5
vorsehen V 1, 5

Wachstumsrate VII 5, 2
Wähler VIII 14, 8
wahrscheinlich II 1, 3
wandern 31
Waren- und Dienstleistungsverkehr V 2, 6
warnen: eindringlich ~ VIII 10, 4

Wartungskräfte I 5, 1
Wechselkurs V 1, 7
Wechsellage IV 6, 4
weiterhin III 2, 3
Weltwirtschaftskrise VII 4, 5
wenig II 9, 4
wer II 7, 1, VIII 14, 1
wesentlich: im ~en VIII, 7, 6
wie . . . so II 3, 1
Wille VIII 14, 7
Wirtschaftskurs 33
wissen 29, 31
wobei VII 10, 5
wollen I 1, 3, I 7, 15, II 10, 4
wünschen 32

zähneknirschend I 7, 9
z. B. IV 8, 2
zeigen: sich ~ VII 7, 1
Zeit: in normalen ~en II 9, 2
Zeitpunkt: den ~ des Wechsels von einer zur anderen Lage voraussagen IV 5, 6
Zeitung: ~ lesen 30
Zentralbank V 3, 12
zerblättern 32
zugehen 18
Zugehörigkeit VIII 7, 5
zugunsten VIII 7, 2
zur (+ abstract noun in -*ung*) VIII 9, 5, VIII 15, 9
zurückweisen VIII 3, 4
zuwachsen VIII 13, 4
zwingen 21

English Word Index

about IV 4, 8
above all IV 4, 1
absent V 1, 6
accompany VII 5, 7
accord I 7, 12
accordingly II 9, 5
accrue VIII 13, 4
accumulate I 4, 5
action II 5, 1
addition: in ~ V 2, 1
adherence II 4, 5
adopt VIII 5, 6
adoption VIII 5, 6
aerodrome II 13, 10
aeroplane: go by ~ II 7, 2; travel by ~ II 7, 2
affected V 3, 11

affiliation VIII 7, 5
affiliation fee VIII 7, 5
after all III 4, 6, III 8, 6, IV 5, 1
again: ~ and ~ II 4, 8, VIII 13, 2
against V 1, 8
agree: ~ to demands I 5, 2
agricultural spending VIII 15, 10
air: go by ~ II 7, 2; travel by ~ II 7, 2; ~ service delay II 12, 3
air controller II 1, 2
airfield II 13, 10
airport II 13, 10
air station II 13, 10
air terminal II 13, 10
air traffic controller II 1, 2
alignment VIII 7, 5

all: ~ things considered III 8, 6
allegiance VIII 7, 5
already in VII 5, 8
answer: ~ claims I 5, 2
anti-satellite 29
anyone: ~ who II 7, 1, VIII 14, 1; if ~ II 7, 1; ~ + -ing form II 7, 1
appeal VIII 10, 4
appear: it ~s that VII 7, 1; there ~s to be VII 7, 1
applause VIII 6, 10
apt II 1, 3
argue I 4, 1
arms control negotiations 29
around V 3, 9
as II 4, 1; ~ early ~ VII 5, 8; ~ far back ~ VII 5, 8; ~ high ~ VII 9, 4; ~ long ago ~ VII 5, 8; ~ many ~ VII 9, 4, VII 10, 4; ~ much ~ VII 9, 4; as . . . so II 3, 1; ~ to IV 4, 8; ~ well ~ + -ing form VIII 15, 7
asininity II 2, 3
Assembly VIII 2, 2
at II 13, 10, IV 4, 8, V 1, 2, V 1, 3, V 3, 5, VI 8, 4, VIII 3, 5; ~ best VIII 14, 4
attempt: ~ at appeasement VIII 8, 6; ~ at (re)conciliation VIII 8, 6
attract: ~ notice II 9, 3; ~ wide attention II 11, 2
authority: the ~ies V 3, 12
average VII 8, 1
avgolemono 13

back in VII 5, 8
back up: ~ a claim/demand II 3, 11
bad temper I 4, 6
ballot result VIII 6, 4
ban VIII 8, 8
band V 3, 8
bankrupt: declare o. s. ~ I 6, 3
bankruptcy: file a ~ petition I 6, 3; file for ~ I 6, 3
bar (sb.) IV 4, 8
bare II 13, 6
bargain: into the ~ V 2, 1
barrier IV 4, 8
basis of assessment VI 7, 7
battle (vb.): ~ inflation VI 2, 4
because II 4, 1; this is ~ IV 1
begin: ~ a go-slow strike II 3, 4, II 3, 12
between VIII 3, 5
bias VIII 7, 5
bid fair to IV 9, 5
big IV 4, 8, VIII 3, 2
billion VIII 15, 3
bit: a ~ III 3, 4; just a little ~ III 3, 4

black: put a company in the ~ IV 9, 5
black-coated worker I 5, 1
blue-collar worker I 5, 1
bottled-up I 4, 5
bring IV 9, 5
Bronx cheer VIII 6, 10
Brussels Commission VIII 3, 6
Brussels Treaty Organization VIII 3, 6
budget committee VIII 6, 8
budget draft VIII 3, 3, VIII 5, 5, VIII 5, 6
budget estimates VIII 3, 3
budget minister VIII 8, 8
budgetary draft VIII 3, 3
burst of expansion IV 4, 3
business outlook IV 1
but II 10, 1, IV 4, 7
buyers over VI 3, 2
by V 3, 10

ca'canny (sb.) II 3, 3
ca'canny (vb.) II 3, 4
calculated to + inf. VIII 9, 5
can (vb.) VI 6, 3, VI 7, 3
caucus VIII 9, 8
central bank V 3, 12
chairman VIII 10, 3
chance: the ~s are that II 1, 3
check: hold s. o. in ~ III 1
cheering VIII 6, 10
chiefly VIII 7, 6
chip 28
claim II 3, 8
clapping VIII 6, 10
clean sweep policy 28
clench: through ~ed teeth I 7, 9
clout VIII 8, 8
coefficient III 3, 5
coerce VI 4, 4
collective bargaining VIII 9, 4
combat (vb.): ~ inflation VI 2, 4
commonly II 6, 1
comparison VII 5, 1
compel VI 4, 4
compulsory VI 4, 4
conceal VII 6, 3
concede I 7, 12
concerned V 1, 6, V 3, 11
concertation VIII 9, 4
concomitant: be the ~(s) of VII 5, 7
condemn: ~ outright VIII 14, 3
conditional sale agreement III 4, 9
Conjuncture Institute IV 5, 3
consequence: as a ~ III 4, 1
consequently II 3, 9, II 9, 5, III 4, 1
console desk II 12, 3

265

consultation VIII 9, 4
consumer credit III 4, 8
consumer loan III 4, 8
consumption loan III 4, 8
continue III 2, 3
contrary: on the ~ III 8, 1
controller II 1, 2
correlate VII 2, 5
correlation VII 2, 5
Council of Ministers VIII 7, 3
country I 6, 2
couple (vb.) VII 7, 2
course: in the ~ of VIII 9, 3
cower II 13, 7
craftsman I 5, 1
create: ~ excitement II 9, 3
credit: allowing/extension/granting of ~ III 3, 6
credit sale agreement III 4, 9
crouch II 13, 7
currency market V 3, 3
current VIII 5, 10
currently II 6, 1
cut (sb.) VI 5, 7
cycle induced VII 6, 2
cyclical VII 6, 2
cyclically conditioned VII 6, 2
cyclically induced VII 6, 2

dash: cut a ~ II 9, 3
decided VII 2, 2
decisive IV 4, 5
deep-rooted VIII 11, 3
deep-seated VIII 11, 3
defined VII 2, 2
delivery delay II 12, 3
demand II 3, 8
demand inflation VI 2, 6
demand-inflation model VI 2, 6
demand-pull inflation VI 2, 6
demand-pull model (of inflation) VI 2, 6
denseness II 2, 3
depression VII 5, 8
Depression years VII 4, 5
describe II 3, 13
designed to + inf. VIII 9, 5
despite IV 5, 1, VIII 7, 4; ~ of VIII 7, 4; in ~ of VIII 7, 4
determinant IV 4, 2
different IV 3, 4
difficulty IV 4, 8
diminish VI 6, 7
direct bargaining VIII 9, 4
direct discussion VIII 9, 4
discontent I 4, 6

disequilibrium V 3, 1
displeasure I 4, 6
disreputable III 5, 3
dissatisfaction I 4, 6
dissent VIII 9, 6
dissidence VIII 9, 6
distinct VII 2, 2
distinctive VII 2, 2
divergence indicator V 3, 8
diversity VIII 9, 6
dollar-gold exchange standard V 1, 15
doubt: no ~ II 1, 3
down (vb.): ~ tools II 4, 3
draft budget VIII 3, 3, VIII 5, 7
drowsy II 13, 4
due to VI 5, 2
dullness II 2, 3
dumbness II 2, 3
during VII 4, 4

earth II 13, 6
economic VII 6, 2
economics IV 8, 3
economist IV 8, 3
edge up VII 9, 2
EEC Parliament VIII 1, 2
effort: make an/some ~ IV 5, 2
elector VIII 14, 8
embark: ~ on a go-slow strike II 3, 4, II 3, 12
employment VII 1; level of ~ VII 2, 6; rate of ~ VII 2, 6
encounter IV 9, 3
encourage: ~ job-hopping 21; ~ speculation 21
endeavour IV 5, 2
energetic IV 9, 5
energy IV 9, 5
enforce II 3, 11
engage: ~ in a work-to-rule II 3, 4, II 3, 12
ersatz II 4, 6
especial: in ~ IV 4, 1
especially IV 4, 1; ~ as II 4, 1; ~ since II 4, 1; more ~ IV 4, 1
essence: lose ~ 32
essentially VIII 7, 6
establish V 2, 7
establishment V 2, 7
Euro-MP VIII 7, 7
European Assembly VIII 1, 1
European Community VIII 2, 1 VII 5, 2
European Economic Community VIII 2, 1, VIII 5, 2
European MP VIII 7, 7
European Parliament VIII 1, 1
European Parliamentary Assembly VIII 1, 1

even III 3, 3; VII 9, 4; ~ so IV 5, 1
ever and again VIII 13, 2
ever and anon VIII 13, 2
evidence: there is ~ that VII 7, 1
example: by way of ~ IV 8, 2; for ~ IV 8, 2
exceed V 3, 7
excess of supply V 3, 4
exchange market V 3, 3
exert: ~ o. s. IV 5, 2
exhausted II 13, 4
expect: to be ~ed + inf. II 1, 3
expenditure plan VI 5, 7
experience: ~ a change I 4, 2
extreme II 4, 5

facilities VI 4, 5
famished II 13, 5
farinaceous products 13
fatigued II 13, 4
favour: in ~ of VIII 7, 2
Federal Republic V 2, 5
Federal Republic of Germany V 2, 5
Federal Reserve Bank VI 8, 4
fight (sb.): ~ against inflation VI 2, 4
fight (vb.): ~ inflation VI 2, 4
finally III 8, 6
finance house III 7, 5
Finance Minister VIII 8, 8
financial: ~ arrangement VIII 4, 3; ~ difficulties VIII 4, 3; ~ planning VIII 4, 3; ~ position VIII 4, 3; ~ settlement VIII 4, 3
find IV 9, 3
finger: not to lift/raise/stir a ~ II 3, 14
fix (vb.) III 3, 5
flagitious III 5, 3
floor II 13, 6
fluctuation VII 2, 3
fluctuation margin V 3, 8
fly (vb.) II 7, 2
fog over VII 6, 3
follow: ~ sth. upwards 30
folly II 2, 3
foolishness II 2, 3
for VIII 7, 2; ~ + -*ing* form VIII 9, 5; ~ all VIII 7, 4; ~ all that IV 5, 1
forecast IV 1, IV 4, 8
foreign exchange market V 3, 3
Foreign Minister VIII 10, 2
Foreign Secretary VIII 10, 2
former: the ~ IV 8, 7
framework VIII 9, 3
free debate VIII 9, 4
freedom I 7, 11
FRG VII 5, 5
frequently I 7, 4

fulfil: ~ demands I 5, 2
fulfilment: ~ of one's duty II 4, 5
fundamental VIII 11, 3
furore: create/make a ~ II 9, 3
future: in ~ III 7, 7; in the ~ III 2, 3, III 7, 7

general: in ~ II 6, 1
generally II 6, 1; ~ speaking II 6, 1
generics 30
German Federal Republic V 2, 5
Germany V 2, 5
gnash: ~ o's teeth I 7, 9
GNP VII 5, 3
go along with VII 5, 7
go beyond V 3, 7
gold exchange standard V 1, 15
go-slow movement II 3, 3
go-slow strike II 3, 3, II 3, 6
government expenditure VI 2, 2
government receipts VI 2, 3
graft (sb.) VIII 14, 4
grant I 7, 12
gray-collar worker I 5, 1
great IV 4, 8
Great Contraction VII 4, 5
Great Depression VII 4, 5
grope: ~ towards 32
ground II 13, 6
group discussion VIII 9, 4
growth: ~ rate VII 5, 2; rate of ~ VII 5, 2
guard II 2, 2

half of the year III 3, 6
half-year III 3, 6
hand: keep a tight ~ on s. o. III 1; not to lift a ~ II 3, 14; on the other ~ III 8, 1
have an impact II 9, 3
he: ~ that II 7, 1 VIII 14, 1; ~ who II 7, 1, VIII 14, 1
head of state I 1, 4
hence II 3, 9, II 9, 5, III 4, 1, VI 6, 6
henceforth III 7, 7
henceforward III 7, 7
hereafter III 7, 7
hindrance IV 4, 8
hire-purchase III 4, 9
hire-purchase agreement III 4, 9
hire-purchase finance house III 4, 9
hoax: be a victim of a ~ 33
hobnob II 6, 2
hold 33
hoop: go through the ~s I 6, 3
hope (sb.): hold out ~s of sth. IV 9, 5
House VIII 6, 3
however II 10, 1, III 4, 6, IV 4, 7

huddle II 13, 7
hungry II 13, 5

ill-famed III 5, 3
ill humour I 4, 6
ill-reputed III 5, 3
imbalance V 3, 1
immobilize VI 8, 5
impediment IV 4, 8
important IV 4, 5, IV 4, 8
imprudence II 2, 3
in III 6, 1, IV 5, 5, V 1, 3, VII 2, 3, VII 2, 4, VII 4, 4, VII 10, 6
inaugural address I 2, 1
income tax VI 7, 6
index VII 3, 1
indicator VII 3, 1
induce: ~ investment IV 9, 7
industrial robot 30
infamous III 5, 3
inflation model VI 2, 6
instal(l)ment: by ~s I 6, 4; in ~s I 6, 4; ~ business III 4, 9; ~ buying III 4, 9; ~ contract III 4, 9; ~ plan III 4, 9; ~ purchase III 4, 9; ~ selling III 4, 9
instance: for ~ IV 8, 2
insubstantial: become ~ 32
intend I, 3; ~ ed to + inf. VIII 9, 5
intention I 1, 3
intervention margin V 3, 8
investment allowance VI 7, 9
involved V 1, 6
irrespective of VIII 9, 5

jaded II 13, 4
job action II 3, 3
jobless rate VII 3, 3
jumbo council 28–9
jump VII 9, 2
just as: ~ . . . in the same manner II 3, 1; ~ . . . likewise II 3, 1; ~ . . . so II 3, 1; ~ . . . so also II 3, 1; ~ . . . so too II 3, 1

keel: put sth. back on an even ~ IV 9, 5
keep on + -ing form II 4, 8
key currency V 1, 9
killer satellite 29
know: I wouldn't ~ 29

labour (sb.) I 5, 1, I 5, 4
labour (vb.) IV 5, 2
labourer I 5, 1
land I 6, 2
large VIII 3, 2

latter: the ~ IV 8, 7
laugh: that is no ~ing matter VIII, 11, 2
launch: ~ a go-slow strike II 3, 4, II 3, 12
leading-strings: hold/keep s. o. in ~ III 1, III 2, 1
leaning VIII 7, 5
leash: have/hold s. o. in ~ III 1, III 2, 1; keep a tight ~ on s. o. III 1
lending capacity III 3, 9
let down I 7, 5
liberalization process I 7, 13
liberty I 7, 11
lid: put a ~ on spending VI 5, 7
lie VII 10, 3
light: in the ~ of IV 6, 3
like as II 3, 1
likely II 1, 3
liking: to the ~ of VIII 5, 8
limit (sb.): put a ~ on VIII 15, 9; set a ~ to VIII 15, 9
link (vb.) VII 7, 2
liquidate V 4, 2
liquidity VI 8, 6
liquid resources VI 8, 6
little II 9, 4; a ~ III 3, 4
logically II 9, 5
loyalty VIII 7, 5

maiden speech I 2, 1
mainly VIII 7, 6
maintain V 1, 7
make: ~ an impact II 9, 3; ~ a proposal VIII 9, 2
manufacturing capacity VII 2, 9
margin: ~ available for lending III 3, 9; ~ for (further) lending III 3, 9; ~ of exchange rate fluctuation V 3, 8; ~ of fluctuation (for a currency) V 3, 8; ~ of permitted fluctuations V 3, 8
marked VII 2, 2; strongly ~ VII 2, 2
market: in the ~ V 3, 2; on the ~ V 3, 2
massacre (vb.) VIII 14, 3
maximum II 4, 5
may VI 6, 3
mean I 4, 1; V 4, 1
meaning VII 2, 7
measure I 7, 6
mechanic I 5, 1
medium-sized III 4, 5
meet (sb.) VIII 8, 8
meet (vb.): ~ demands I 5, 2
membership VIII 7, 5
mere VII 8, 2
middle-sized III 4, 5
milliard VIII 15, 3

Minister for Foreign Affairs VIII 10, 2
Minister of Finance VIII 8, 8
model of inflation VI 2, 6
more I 7, 10
mostly II 6, 1; VIII 7, 6
mount: ~ a work-to-rule strike II 3, 4; II 3, 12
movement of goods and services V 2, 6
much: not ~ II 9, 4; not ~ of a II 9, 4

naked II 13, 6
national revenue VI 2, 3
neutralize VI 8, 5
never-never: buying on the ~ III 4, 9
nevertheless III 4, 6, IV 5, 1
newly-drafted budget VIII 5, 7
newspaper: read ~s 30
night VIII 8, 4
no less than VII 10, 4
nonetheless IV 5, 1
notorious III 5, 3
notwithstanding IV 5, 1, VIII 7, 4
now III 3, 2, VIII 4, 2; by ~ I 7, 7

oblige III 8, 5
observance II 4, 5
observe V 1, 7
obstacle IV 4, 8
obstruction IV 4, 8
obtain VI 8, 3
obtuseness II 2, 3
occupation VII 1
odds: the ~ are that II 1, 3
of IV 4, 8, IV 5, 5, VII 10, 6
often I 7, 4
on VIII 8, 4
once II 3, 2
one II 13, 2
operation II 5, 1
opportunity: an ~ arises/occurs/offers/presents itself II 10, 2
orator VIII 9, 7
ordinarily II 6, 1
organize: ~ a slow-down strike II 3, 4, II 3, 12
oscillation IV 3, 2
outlet I 4, 7
outlook for the economy IV 1
output capacity VII 2, 9
outside: at the ~ VIII 14, 4
overall II 6, 1
overlap IV 8, 6
overlay IV 8, 6
over-punctilious II 4, 5

overshoot V 3, 7
owing to VI 5, 2

package I 6, 4
paella 13
pain: be at ~s to IV 5, 2; take ~s to IV 5, 2
parameter VIII 9, 3
pare down VI 6, 7
Parliament VIII 2, 2; ~ member VIII 8, 7
parliamentary: ~ debate VIII 8, 3; ~ delegation VIII 8, 7; ~ faction VIII 9, 8; ~ group VIII 9, 8; ~ party VIII 9, 8
part: on the ~ of V 3, 10
particular: in ~ IV 4, 1
particularly IV 4, 1; more ~ IV 4, 1
party loyalty VIII 7, 5
party membership VIII 7, 5
party political VIII 7, 5
pasta products 13
pea: they are as like as two ~s 33
peak VII 4, 3; hit a ~ VII 4, 3; reach/rise to a ~ VII 4, 3
peg (vb.) V 1, 14
pending VIII 5, 4
pent-up I 4, 5
people: ~ who II 7, 1; VIII 14, 1
peformance: ~ of a duty II 4, 5
permitted fluctuation limit V 3, 8
person: any ~ who II 7, 1, VIII 14, 1
petulance I 4, 6
picture: put s. o. in the ~ 29
plane: go by ~ II 7, 2; take a ~ II 7, 2; travel by ~ II 7, 2
platformer VIII 9, 7
plaudits VIII 6, 10
plead VIII 10, 4
political: ~ economist IV 8, 3; ~ economy IV 8, 3; ~ group VIII 9, 8; ~ party (adj.) VIII 7, 5
poll VIII 6, 4
possible: make sth. ~ IV 9, 5
post-office worker I 5, 1
post Second World War period VII 7, 4
post-war years VII 7, 4
potato 12
practical VII 6, 2
precalculation IV 4, 8
prediction IV 4, 8
prepare II 10, 5
present (sb.): at ~ III 3, 2
present (adj.) V 1, 6; at the ~ time III 3, 2
preserve II 2, 2
president VIII 10, 3
press: ~ a claim/demand II 3, 8, II 3, 11
previous VIII 5, 10

principally IV 4, 1
probably II 1, 3
probe (sb.) VIII 8, 8
production: ~ capacity VII 2, 9; ~ facilities VI 4, 5
productive capacity VII 2, 9
programme I 6, 4
Prokurist 28
prominent VII 2, 2
promise (vb.) IV 9, 5
pronounced VII 2, 2
property: ~ in the goods III 4, 9
proposed budget VIII 5, 7
protect II 2, 2
public: ~ economist IV 8, 3; ~ revenue VI 2, 3; ~ spending VI 2, 2
purchase: ~ of goods on the deferred payment system III 4, 9; ~ on deferred terms III 4, 9
purpose: for the ~ of + -ing form VIII 9, 5; the ~ of which is to + inf. VIII 9, 5
push II 3, 11
put: ~ a proposal to s. o. VIII 9, 2

quantity VI 5, 5

range (vb.) VII 10, 3
range (sb.): ~ of fluctuations V 3, 8; ~ of permitted fluctuations; ~ of variation V 3, 8
rate of change IV 5, 5
rather III 3, 4
ravenous II 13, 5
ready: get ~ + inf. II 10, 5
real VII 5, 3; in ~ terms VII 5, 3; in terms of ~ value VII 5, 3
realize II 3, 11
reason: for that ~ III 4, 1; the ~ for this is that IV 3
receive VI 8, 3
recession VII 5, 8
reduce VI 6, 7, VI 8, 7
referendum vote VIII 6, 4
refuse II 3, 14; ~ categorically VIII 14, 3
regardless of VIII 7, 4
reject VIII 1, 2
relation: in ~ to V 1, 8
relative to V 1, 8
remain III 8, 2
repeatedly I 7, 4
repute: of bad/evil/ill ~ III 5, 3; in bad ~ III 5, 3
require V 4, 1
reserve currency V 1, 9
respond: ~ to demands I 5, 2

restraint: hold s. o. in ~ III 1
result: ~ of the poll VIII 6, 4; ~ of the vote VIII 6, 4; ~ of the voting VIII 6, 4
resultant VI 3, 1
revenue VI 2, 3
Rhine pollution treaty 32
rise VII 9, 2
roads VI 5, 3
rub: ~ shoulders with s. o. II 6, 2
rule: as a ~ II 6, 1; ~s and regulations II 4, 5
run (vb.) VII 10, 3

safeguard II 2, 2
safety valve I 4, 7
same: all the ~ IV 5, 1; just the ~ IV 5, 1
satisfy: ~ claims I 5, 2
scenario IV 1
schools VI 5, 3
sector IV 9, 5
see II 13, 1; we ~ that VII 7, 1
seeing that II 4, 1
sensation: create a ~ II 9, 3
series I 6, 4
set aside VIII 15, 4
settle: ~ a claim II 3, 11
shade: a ~ III 3, 4
shoot up VII 9, 2
short: make ~er III 3, 4
shorten III 3, 4
showdown VIII 3, 7
sign: there are ~s that VII 7, 1
silliness II 2, 3
since II 4, 1
slash VIII 15, 6
sleepful II 13, 4
sleepy II 13, 4
slightly III 3, 4
smidgen III 3, 4
snag IV 4, 8
so II 3, 9, II 9, 5, III 4, 1, VI 8, 2
social: ~ betterment VIII 15, 5; ~ legislation VIII 15, 5
soil II 13, 6
somewhat III 3, 4
specially IV 4, 1
spectrum I 1, 7
spending: ~ plan VI 5, 7; ~ project VI 5, 7
spent II 13, 4
spite: in ~ of VIII 7, 4; in ~ of that III 4, 6, IV 5, 1
splash: make a ~ II 9, 3
spread V 3, 8
squat II 13, 7
stage: ~ a go-slow strike II 3, 4, II 3, 12
stand VII 10, 3

starving II 13, 5
state revenue VI 2, 3
statistical survey: make a ~~ VII 10, 7
stay III 8, 2
step (sb.) VIII 15, 9
sterilize VI 8, 5
still III 3, 3, III 4, 6, IV 5, 1; ~ and all IV 5, 1
stimulate: ~ discussion 21
strictly speaking II 4, 2
strike (sb.): be (out) on ~ II 4, 3; come out on ~ II 4, 3; go on ~ II 3, 4
strike (vb.) II 4, 3; ~ work II 4, 3
string: have/keep s. o. in/on a ~ III 1; lead s. o. in a ~ III 1
strip: ~ of leaves 32
strive IV 5, 2
stroke: not to do a ~ of work II 3, 14
structural unemployment VII 6, 4
struggle (vb.) IV 5, 2
stumbling-block IV 4, 8
stupidity II 2, 3
subject: ~ to entry levies 23
submission VIII 5, 5
submit VIII 5, 5, VIII 9, 2
submittal VIII 5, 5
substitute II 4, 6
substitution account 28–9
superimpose IV 8, 6
superpose IV 8, 6
surrender: ~ control I 7, 13

take strike action II 3, 4
tall VIII 3, 2
tax: ~ burden VI 6, 4; ~ load VI 6, 4
taxation VI 6, 4, VI 7, 5
technological IV 9, 5; ~ unemployment VII 6, 4
technology IV 9, 5
tendency VIII 7, 5
term (vb.) II 3, 13
term (sb.) in ~s of V 1, 8; ~s of trade V 1, 13
then III 4, 1
thereby II 3, 9, VI 6, 6
therefore II 3, 9, II 9, 5, III 4, 1
those who II 7, 1
though IV 4, 7, IV 5, 1, VII 10, 5
thought: a ~ III 3, 4
throw: be ~n into the waste-paper basket 31
throw out VIII 1, 2
thrust: the general ~ of economic policy 33
thus II 3, 9, II 9, 5, III 4, 1, IV 8, 1, VI 6, 6, VI 8, 2
tick III 4, 9

tighten up VI 8, 7
time: at ordinary ~s II 9, 2; at the same ~ IV 5, 1; by this ~ I 7,7; from this ~ forward III 7,7; from this ~ on III 7,7; in normal ~s II 9, 2; many a ~ I 7, 4; many ~s I 7, 4; ~ and again II 4, 8; ~ and ~ again I 7, 4, II 4, 8; ~s out of number VIII 13, 2; ~(s) without number VIII 13, 2
timing II 5, 2
tired II 13, 4
tired-out II 13, 4
to VIII 6, 6
toil (vb.) IV 5, 2; ~ and moil IV 5, 2
tooth: through clenched teeth I 7, 9; gnash one's teeth I 7, 9
tortellini 13
touch: get in ~ with s. o. II 6, 2
tradesman I 5, 1
trial of strength VIII 3, 7
trifle: a ~ III 3, 4
trigger (vb.) V 3, 6
trouble (sb.): take much ~ IV 5, 2
trouble (vb.): ~ o. s. IV 5, 2
try: ~ and ~ IV 5, 2; ~ o's level best IV 5, 2
tuckered out II 13, 4
turn-up IV 4, 3
under V 3, 5
undertake: ~ a go-slow strike II 3, 4, II 3, 12
unemployment VII 3, 3; ~ figure VII 3, 3; ~ rate VII 3, 3; ~ ratio VII 3, 3; level of ~ VIII 3, 3

unintelligence II 2, 3
unmindful of VIII 7, 4
unrest I 4, 6
upswing IV 4, 3
upturn IV 4, 3
upward II 12, 4
urge VIII 10, 4
usually II 6, 1
utilization VII 2, 8
utmost II 4, 5

variation VII 2, 3
vast VIII 3, 2
vegetable 12
vent I 4, 7
vis-à-vis V 1, 8
voter VIII 14, 8
voting result VIII 6, 4
vulgarly II 6, 1

wage-earning community I 5, 1, I 5, 4
way back in VII 5, 8
we II 13, 2

weary II 13, 4
West Germany V 2, 5
white-collar worker I 5, 1
whittle down VI 6, 7
who II 7, 1
whoever II 7, 1
whosoever II 7, 1
why: that is ~ III 4, 1
widely II 6, 1
win: ~ a claim II 3, 8, II 3, 11
wing VIII 9, 8
with IV 4, 8, V 3, 10, VI 5, 2, VI 8, 4, VII 4, 3, VII 10, 5, VIII 6, 7; ~ all VIII 7, 4
without considering VIII 7, 4
without regard to VIII 7, 4
witness (vb.) II 13, 1

worker I 5, 1, I 5, 4
working: ~ man I 5, 1; ~ regulations II 4, 5; ~ rules II 4, 5
work-slowdown II 3, 3
work-to-rule II 3, 6
work-to-rules action II 3, 3
world economic crisis VII 4, 5
world-wide economic crisis VII 4, 5
worn-out II 13, 4
worry: be a source of ~ to s. o. 30

year: for ~s on end I 7, 2; last ~ III 4, 3; the ~ before III 4, 3; the preceding/previous ~ III 4, 3
yet III 3, 3, III 4, 6, IV 5, 1
you II 13, 2

Subject Index

abstraction 26–7, I 4, 2, IV 8, 9, VI 2, 1, VIII 6, 2
acronyms 27, VII 5, 5, VIII 1, 2, VIII 5, 2
adaptation 33
adjective order 23–4
adverb order V 1, 4
ambiguity VIII 1, 2, VIII 15, 3
amplificatory noun phrase tags II 1, 1
amplificatory tag statements II 1, 1
anaphora II 13, 1, II 13, 8, VIII 3, 7
anaphoric *to* II 7, 4
animism V 1, 5, V 4, 1
anticipatory *es* 14, 18
anticipatory *it* 14, 21, V 2, 2, VIII 11, 2, VIII 13, 3
anticipatory *was* II 4, 7
aposiopesis VI 5, 3
apposition IV 8, 3, VIII 6, 3, VIII 10, 1
appositive clauses VI 2, 1
articles I 1, 4, I 2, 2, I 2, 3, II 1, 1, II 2, 1, II 8, 1, II 10, 2, II 13, 6, III 2, 2, III 5, 3, IV 9, 2, V 2, 3, VII 2, 1, VII 5, 3, VIII 2, 2, VIII 6, 3, VIII 6, 5
asyndeton 19, VI 5, 3, VI 5, 4
attributive constructions (German) 17–8, III 3, 8, IV 9, 2, V 1, 1, V 1, 10, VIII 3, 1, VIII 15, 1, VIII 15, 8
augmentation 21, I 4, 2, I 7, 3, I 7, 9, II 5, 2, II 11, 1, III 5, 3, V 3, 11, VI 2, 1, VI 3, 1, VI 5, 6, VI 6, 1,VI 7, 2, VI 8, 5, VII 9, 3, VII 10, 2, VIII 7, 5

balance inversion II 3, 1
borrowings 12–13, 28, II 3, 6, II 4, 6, III 5, 3, V 1, 8, VI 8, 4
bridge constructions 31
but in front-position II 10, 1

calquing 28–9, II 3, 6, VIII 9, 4
catachresis I 6, 4
category shifts 30
causal clauses II 4, 1, IV 3, 1
chassé-croisé 30
chiasmus VI 7, 1
class-shifts 30, IV 3, 3, IV 3, 4, IV 6, 2, IV 8, 9, IV 9, 1, IV 9, 6, V 2, 2, VI 2, 1, VII 2, 9, VII 5, 4, VII 5, 6, VII 8, 1, VII 8, 2, VIII 8, 2, VIII 15, 8
clauses of circumstance II 4, 1
clause-structure shifts 31, I 4, 3, I 7, 9, II 13, 3, IV 3, 4, IV 6, 2, IV 6, 4, IV 8, 9, IV 9, 1, IV 9, 2, V 1, 5, V 5, 1, VI 2, 1, VI 4, 2, VII 2, 5, VII 6, 5, VII 7, 1, VII 7, 2, VIII 3, 1, VIII 5, 1, VIII 7, 1, VIII 9, 1
clipped words 27
colons II 3, 7, II 13, 8
commas I 6, 1, II 1, 1, II 4, 1, IV 4, 4
comparative clauses II 3, 1
compounds 23, 27, 28, II 12, 3, IV 9, 2, VI 1, 4, VI 1, 6, VII 2, 4, VII 3, 1, VII 6, 2, VII 10, 2, VIII 4, 3, VIII 8, 3
condensation 26–7
conditional clauses II 7, 1

connecters IV 4, 4, IV 8, 5, VI 6, 6
continuative *when* II 10, 4
contracted forms II 8, 2
convoluted syntax 27

dashes I 6, 1, IV 4, 4
daß-clauses 14
demonstrative adjectives II 1, 1, III 5, 3
durative aspect I 1, 3, II 4, 3, III 2, 3

ellipsis 21–2, II 3, 1, II 3, 12, II 4, 9, III 4, 4, III 4, 7, IV 8, 5, VII 10, 7
embedding 24, II 4, 7, II 4, 9, VI 2, 1, VI 5, 1
equivalence 33
equivalence relationship VIII 6, 5
existential sentences 14–7, IV 3, 4, VIII 8, 1

free indirect speech I 1, 5, IV 8, 8, VIII 11, 1, VIII 11, 4, VIII 14, 6
frequentative aspect V 3, 7
functional shift I 1, 2
future tense I 4, 8, III 2, 1, III 4, 2, VIII 5, 3

genitive 19, I 1, 2, I 1, 4, I 4, 2, I 5, 4, III 3, 9, IV 4, 6, V 3, 10, VII 2, 3, VIII 2, 3, VIII 3, 5, VIII 5, 2, VIII 6, 9
geographical names as adjectives I 1, 2
Germanic words I 7, 4

hendiadys VIII 6, 10, VIII 14, 7
historic present VII 4, 2, VII 6, 1

if-clauses 14, 17
imagery I 1, 7, I 4, 7, I 6, 4, I 7, 9, III 1, III 3, 1, IV 9, 5, V 3, 7, VI 5, 5, VI 5, 7, VI 6, 4, VI 6, 7, VI 8, 7, VII 9, 2, VII 10, 3, VIII 9, 3
impersonal constructions 18
inchoative aspect *see* ingressive aspect
indefinite relative pronouns II 7, 1, VIII 14, 1
infinitive constructions I 1, 3, III 2, 3, IV 4, 8, V 5, 1, VII 10, 1
-*ing* form I 1, 3, I 1, 6, II 13, 3, III 2, 3, IV 4, 5, IV 9, 7, VI 5, 6, VI 5, 7, VI 6, 6, VI 7, 5, VI 7, 8, VII 9, 3, VII 10, 4, VIII 14, 2, VIII 15, 7
ingressive aspect II 3, 3, II 4, 3, II 10, 5, VII 7, 3
inter-rank shifts 32
intra-system shifts 30–1, VIII 14, 7
inversion 32

Johnsonese II 10, 3

level shifts 32, VII 10, 7
levels of formality 25–6
lexical encoding systems 12–3
literal translation 29
litotes II 2, 4
loan translations *see* calquing

medial branching IV 9, 2
modulated transposition 33
modulation 18, 20–1, 32–3, I 4, 1, IV 6, 2, IV 9, 5
must and *have to* I 4, 8

negation 18–21, 32, II 2, 4, II 3, 14
nominal relative clauses II 4, 7
nonce words VII 2, 4, VII 7, 3

oligosemy VI 7, 6
one and *you* II 13, 2
parallelism I 4, 2, I 7, 6, I 7, 7, II 3, 1, II 3, 5, III 4, 7
past perfect (English) I 1, 5, III 5, 2, VII 3, 2
past perfect (German) VII 3, 2
past tense *see* preterite
perfect of experience III 5, 2
perfect tense (German) II 3, 5
plain predicate clauses 21, VIII 13, 3
pluperfect *see* past perfect
polysemy VI 7, 6
position of adjectives V 1, 6, V 3, 11
position of adverbs II 6, 1, III 4, 1, III 4, 6, IV 4, 1, IV 5, 1, VI 8, 2, VIII 4, 2, VIII 5, 9
present participle constructions II 3, 14
present perfect tense (English) II 12, 1, II 13, 1, III 5, 2, VII 3, 2, VII 10, 3
present tense I 4, 8, III 2, 1, VIII 4, 1
preterite (English) I 1, 5, VII 3, 2, VII 10, 3
preterite (German) 31, II 3, 5, II 12, 1, II 13, 1
progressive aspect I 5, 3, II 3, 12, IV 5, 2, VII 10, 3, VIII 6, 10
purpose clauses V 5, 1
'push-down' clauses 24–5, II 4, 7, II 4, 9
pycnometochia VIII 15, 1

relative clauses I 3, 1, II 4, 7, II 13, 3, IV 4, 4, IV 8, 5, V 1, 11 VIII 3, 7
reported speech I 1, 3, I 4, 8, IV 8, 6
right-branching structures IV 9, 2
Romance words I 7, 4

scalar adjectives VIII 3, 2
semantic gaps 12–3, 28
semantic implication II 4, 1

sentence movement 22–5
sentential relative clauses IV 4, 4
so + inversion II 3, 1
speech tags I 1, 5, II 7, 5, IV 8, 8
standards 27–8
structure-shifts 31
stylistic systems 22–7, VI 4, 3, VI 5, 1, VII 3, 7, VIII 6, 1, VIII 8, 8
subjunctive (German) I 1, 3, I 1, 5
substantivized adjectives of quality II 8, 1
successive aspect IV 5, 2
syllepsis II 3, 12
syndeton 19, 20
syntactical systems 13–22

tense sequences (recent tendencies) IV 9, 6, VII 10, 3
terminate aspect I 1, 3, III 2, 3, IV 5, 2, VIII 6, 10
ternary enumeration I 7, 1
theme and rheme *see* topic and comment
titles VIII 6, 3
topic and comment 22, 26, IV 4, 8, IV 9, 1, VI 7, 1

transposition 21, 30–2 *see also* class shifts, intra-system shifts, structure-shifts, inter-rank shifts, level-shifts

vectorial adjectives VIII 3, 2
verbosity IV 4, 8
voice VII 10, 1, VII 10, 5, VIII 9, 1

wenn-clauses 14, I 1, 5
werden + infinitive II 7, 3
what-sentences II 3, 13, II 4, 7
who and *whom* II 4, 7
wh-questions with embedded sub clauses II 4, 7
wie-clauses II 4, 7
will + infinitive II 7, 3
with + *-ing* form II 13, 3, VI 5, 2, VII 10, 5
word-for-word translation *see* literal translation

zero *that*-clauses I 1, 3, IV 8, 4, IV 9, 1
zeugma II 3, 12

Buchanzeige

Gallagher

Cours de Traduction allemand-français
Textes politiques et économiques

Deutsch-französische Übersetzungsübungen
Lehrbuch mit Texten über Politik und Wirtschaft

Von John D. Gallagher, Lehrbeauftragter für Wirtschaftsfranzösisch an der Universität Münster/Westf.

Für alle Wahlfachstudenten in Wirtschaftsfranzösisch und für alle Französisch-Übersetzer und -Dolmetscher mit Schwerpunkt für Wirtschaft und Politik liegt hier ein systematisches Übersetzungslehrbuch vor mit Musterübersetzungen (auch von Prüfungstexten), „Explications" und zahlreichen „Variantes".

R. Oldenbourg Verlag München Wien